ABOUT THE AUTHORS

Mark Gately has been a journalist since 1984, and
Mirror's cricket writer since 1990. In 1994, he received the NSW Cricket Association media award for the best story in connection with the NSW Sheffield Shield team. Before joining the *Telegraph Mirror*, he worked as a finance writer with *The Sydney Morning Herald*, and then as a general writer and the sports editor on the *Northern Herald*. In 1992, he wrote the bestselling biography of Steve and Mark Waugh, *Waugh Declared*.

Geoff Armstrong is one of Australia's leading sports researchers and author of *A Century of Summers*, the critically acclaimed story of the first 100 years of the Sheffield Shield. He has worked as the editor and researcher for a number of recently published cricket books, including Steve Waugh's diaries on the 1993 Ashes tour and the 1994 Australia tour of South Africa, and Mike Whitney's autobiography, *Quick Whit*.

During Sydney summers, Gately and Armstrong are rivals in the NSWCA's Municipal and Shires competition – Gately with the Warringah Cricket Club and Armstrong with the Burwood Briars.

THE PEOPLE'S GAME

Australia in International One-Day Cricket

**Geoff Armstrong
and Mark Gately**

IRONBARK

AUTHORS' THANKS

We are indebted to the many noted and approachable cricket figures who agreed to be interviewed for the book. For many of them, the development of one-day international cricket has meant that their time is very precious, but they still managed to give some of that time to us. Similarly, many of the great names of the '70s and '80s were generous in offering their views on the modern game. The support of these people was crucial in creating the final product.

Special thanks to Bob Hawke for providing the foreword. Having an Australian and a cricket lover of Mr Hawke's stature contribute in this way adds a great deal to the book, and we are appreciative of his generous support.

Special thanks also to the Managing Editor of *Inside Edge* magazine, Norman Tasker, for his painstaking efforts as editor of the book and his support of the entire project. Thanks also to Ian Russell, who provided the statistics and made time to check the accuracy of the manuscript; to Ian Heads, for his assistance and support; to Pan Macmillan for providing the opportunity to write the book; to the people at *Inside Edge* magazine, to Clifford White, Patrick and Annabel Eagar, Mark Ray and John Mikulcic for their help with the photos; and to Kylie and Rebekah at Brevier Design, who are more patient than they should be.

First published 1994 in Ironbark by Pan Macmillan Australia Pty Limited
St Martins Tower, 31 Market Street, Sydney

Reprinted 1994

Copyright © Geoff Armstrong and Mark Gately 1994

National Library of Australia
cataloguing-in-publication data:

Armstrong, Geoff
The people's game

ISBN 0 330 35590 2

1. Cricket – Tournaments – Australia – History. 2. Cricket players – Australia –
Interviews. I. Gately, Mark. II. Title.

796.358650994

Typeset and design by Brevier Design
Printed in Australia by McPherson's Printing Group

Front cover design: Jayem Productions
Front cover photograph: Australian Picture Library (David Cannon – All Sport)
Back cover photograph: Australian Picture Library (Chris Cole – All Sport)

CONTENTS

FOREWORD

by Bob Hawke

For better or worse we have been destined to live in the most rapidly and dramatically changing era of all human history. The world I live in today is unrecognisably different to the one into which I was born.

Many people have been perplexed and frightened by the way these changes have impinged on the comfortable familiarity of their daily lives and they sought reassurance in the fact that some things they cherished were unchangeable.

Cricket was in this category. Men in creams would continue to engage in this fascinating contest, as they had for generations, hoping for a victory but accepting as part of its mystery that five days of ritualised clash of bat and ball could end with no decision. They did not show the cynicism of the English aristocrat who observed that 'Cricket is a game which the English, not being a spiritual people, invented to give themselves some concept of eternity'.

Cricket was different; the joy was in the game itself. To see the majesty of a cover drive, the audacity of a hook off the eyebrows from a life-threatening bouncer, the artistry of the hardest shot of all – the drive to the boundary between mid-on and mid-wicket – the perfect delivery swinging late to take the off bail or induce a diving catch in the slips, the leg-side stumping to the well-pitched wrong-un, the bullet-like throw stranding the batsman out of the crease – all these were rewards enough. In a world dominated by harsh competition which demanded a victor in all contests between individuals and between groups, the possibility of an honourable draw had its own attractions. Like a symphony concert featuring Beethoven and Mahler there was no need for a decision on relative merit – the joy is in the music itself and its interpretation.

But nothing is sacred. In the 1970s the demands for results and instant gratification prevailed and one-day international cricket was born. The traditionalists were horrified as professionalism was made paramount and cricket under lights gave a garish hue to the multi-coloured uniforms which supplemented the customary creams of the cricket they had known and loved. The great game was riven as officials and players split into rival camps and engaged in expensive litigation.

But as is so often the case in human affairs, what was seen initially as tragedy has turned to triumph. The circle of those who have come to love this greatest of all sports has been enlarged by hundreds of thousands who previously had been lost by the esoterics of the game.

For our migrants of non-English-speaking background the very language of cricket was among the greatest mysteries. To them a 'fine leg slip' may well have been an exotic garment, 'a square leg' some poor misshapen creature, 'extra cover' some additional insurance and what were they to make of someone 'sitting on the bat at silly point'?

With the televising of one-day cricket all these enigmas were resolved by easily understood diagrams and explanations. I have lost count of the number of migrants who told me they were converted to the game in this way and who now flash their enjoyment of it as part of their proud commitment to the Australian way of life.

One-day cricket has created some problems for players but, overall, it has been a force for good in this game we love. Geoff Armstrong and Mark Gately have told the story of its development well and with verve.

I congratulate them and commend this book to all who, like me, are devotees of this great national, and international, sport that does so much to bring so many people together in Australia and around the world.

— **Bob Hawke,**
August 1994

JUDGEMENT NIGHT

Tuesday, November 28, 1978 ... the day of WSC's first night cricket match in Sydney. Two months before, in a competition that featured 12 Melbourne-based teams, Hawthorn had won their fourth Victorian Football League flag after a rugged battle with North Melbourne. Four weeks earlier Arwon, ridden by Harry White, had won the Melbourne Cup. Ten days before, in the chilly north of England, the Australian Rugby League team had won a tight Test series over Great Britain. Tracey Wickham was our best achiever in world sport. Kieren Perkins was five years old. These were the days of Malcolm Fraser. Until recently they had been the days of Gough Whitlam and Sir John Kerr as well. In England, Margaret Thatcher was not yet prime minister. In the USA, Ronald Reagan was a presidential hopeful, Bill Clinton not yet Governor of Arkansas. Bob Hawke was the head of the Australian trade union movement, Paul Keating a member of the shadow ministry, Alexander Downer a diplomat's son. The music was disco, The Eagles and *Eagle Rock*. Colour television in Australia was four years old, Don Lane its most popular star, while multi-cultural TV was still to reach its first birthday. And cricket was about Test cricket, the Shield, tradition, the ABC and days in the sun.

Or it had been ... until WSC.

WSC stood for World Series Cricket. Many said it stood for Packer ... Kerry Packer – the second son of the late media magnate Sir Frank Packer and now the head of the Nine television network. In the winter of 1977, Kerry Packer had been the focus of an audacious and some thought sacrilegious hijack of world cricket. With one flourish of his mighty chequebook, he had signed most of the world's best players, including the heart of the Australian team, to play for his own organisation and be covered by his television station. This was a cricket concept far removed from what had gone before. Packer was about high-class entertainment superbly televised ... and international one-day cricket, under lights, with a white ball and wearing coloured clothing was a big part of that. He was about sudden change in a world where change was slow to come. In his first summer, 1977-78, the crowds stayed away as he and the 'official' cricket authorities staged an ugly war for respect, credibility and the attentions of the sporting public. The Australian Cricket Board was confident of holding their traditional audience. Packer needed more ...

On the morning of November 28, 1978, the early editions of the Sydney afternoon daily the *Sun* hit the streets. From the front page roared the message: 'PACKER: SYDNEY DECIDES TONIGHT'.

'By midnight tonight,' began the lead story, 'Kerry Packer will know whether

World Series Cricket is a white elephant or whether he has struck batting oil in his multi-million dollar cricket gamble ...'

Packer's money had constructed six floodlight towers around the Sydney Cricket Ground, so his players could play night cricket on the famous ground. And now was the test, for the occasion of his first encounter under those lights had arrived. This was the first significant clash of WSC's second season. Australia, starring Dennis Lillee, Rod Marsh, and Greg and Ian Chappell, were to play the feared West Indies – Viv Richards, Clive Lloyd, Michael Holding, Andy Roberts and all – in a limited-overs match. Such matches, far removed from the five-day Test match, had been the closest thing to a breadwinner WSC had staged in its first year. Before the emergence of Packer, they had hardly been heard of at international level in Australia.

WSC officials predicted a crowd of 15,000 to 20,000, if only to see the novelty of cricket in the moonlight. 'If we get 20,000 or more we're cooking with gas,' a spokesman told the *Sun*. In the event they got fifty ... 50,000 rock'n'rolling fans who came to see the stars and the lights and the cricket. The entertainment was exquisite, performed by the best in the world, and better still ... Australia won. Every single nerve that tingles during a major sporting event was jabbed during that extraordinary night and every patriotic and jingoistic nerve was struck as well. *C'mon Aussie, C'mon*, WSC's advertising jingle that had raced to the top of the charts, filled the air, both from the public address system and from hordes of kids, young and old, in the outer. The masses laughed at the golf buggies that delivered the drinks to the players, and danced with the rock band who played throughout the dinner break. The great Bill O'Reilly, writing in the *Sydney Morning Herald*, said the ground took on 'the appearance of a football final afternoon'. Even with the many instances of appalling behaviour by the mob on the Hill, and the amazing amount of alcohol consumed, it was a magic night.

'It was a tremendous thrill out there,' Lillee told reporters. 'The atmosphere was at least the equal to any Test match in which I've played.'

The ground, bar for some empty seats in the members' area, had been packed by the dinner break. But there had still been thousands outside. Packer had decided to let them in, free of charge, lest they miss the moment. So into the hallowed members' area they poured – eskies, shorts and all – as symbolic a gesture as any on the night. Ladies were seen in the hallowed Members' Pavilion. The crowd was logged at 44,377, but was at least 5000 more than that. And to top it all, the fans who had ventured to the ground in the early afternoon now believed Australia was the best team in the world. All in one day. Such a concept, unfamiliar in international cricket but inevitable in most popular sports, had proved its great appeal.

When the Aussie batsman Ian Davis hit the winning run, the crowd charged onto the field. Fireworks lit the night sky, as if the floodlights weren't doing their job. But then the lights dimmed, and the post-mortems began. Was the huge crowd no more than a one-night wonder? Perhaps the drunken louts would keep the real people away. Was this just a game for yobbos and football fans? 'The Board will now watch future attendances at night matches to see whether the interest is maintained,' commented Australian Cricket Board chairman Mr Bob Parish.

Others suggested the Board move more rapidly. 'There is a bandwagon rolling,' wrote the Sydney *Daily Mirror*'s correspondent Frank Crook, 'and the ACB has just enough time to get on board before it gathers much more speed.'

Crook's thoughts were echoed by the *Sun*'s Norman Tasker. 'Establishment cricket is no longer dealing purely with a pirate organisation which hijacked its top players,' Tasker wrote. 'It is now dealing with a whole new concept – a floodlit extravaganza which has hauled cricket into the modern era. Night cricket offers an alternative which fits snugly into the leisure patterns of today. People don't have to give up a weekend to sit through a drawn-out game. The message to the Australian Cricket Board is to gear itself accordingly. Now is the time to accommodate the two sides to the game.'

With the first hurdle so emphatically left behind, WSC conducted the vast majority of their limited-overs matches under the floodlights of the SCG and VFL Park, their base in Melbourne. Consequently, throughout the summer, the one-day matches were telecast on the Nine

Dennis Lillee, Australia's premier bowler through the 1970s and early '80s, and man of the match on November 28, 1978 – the night when the lights of the Sydney Cricket Ground shone upon limited-overs international cricket for the first time and showed there was a sizeable market for this style of cricket in Australia.

network during the evening, when most TV sets were on. A whole new audience was introduced and attracted to the thrills and action of one-day cricket. They realised, through the quality of the television coverage, that the cricket was fair dinkum and much more than the circus the so-called 'experts' had tagged it. One-day cricket had previously been seen as an occasional light-hearted romp between Test matches, not a serious, significant entity in its own right. Gradually these new fans left their lounge rooms and ventured to the grounds, bringing their sun screens, their jumpers, their involvement and their friends. And gradually many of the traditional cricket connoisseurs were lured as well. This revolution continued long after WSC had ceased to be an item. By the 1990s, limited-overs international cricket was clearly the most popular and most lucrative form of the game, not just in Australia, but throughout the cricket world.

The moment this process began was Tuesday night, November 28, 1978. In the eyes of the Australian sporting public, that was when limited-overs international cricket got serious. In the dressing room after that famous fixture had been won, the man of the match, Dennis Lillee, looked up at the scrum of reporters around him and smiled: 'When Mr Packer started WSC, the Australian Cricket Board said: "We'll let the people be the judges."

'It looks like they have.'

KEEPING PACE WITH SOCIETY

Limited-overs cricket played by first-class cricketers has its origins in the conclusions reached by an MCC committee back in the 1950s. The committee had been established in 1956 in England to examine the decline in attendance figures at the County Championship matches in the preceding years. That committee, chaired by the veteran cricket historian and administrator H.S. Altham proposed a one-day knockout competition be introduced, to lure new and disillusioned cricket followers through the gate, and to fund what had become a desperately unprofitable county competition.

That solution did not appeal to the traditionalists at Lord's, but dire circumstances forced the issue. In 1962 a pilot series, featuring Leicestershire, Derbyshire, Northants and Nottinghamshire, was organised, with innings of 65 six-ball overs, and each bowler limited to no more than 15. The next year a knockout competition, sponsored by the Gillette razor company and involving all the counties, was introduced, with its sole charter being to support the finances of the County Championship.

Opposition to this revolution was considerable, with many protesting at the meddling with the rules, and the use of corporate sponsors. The revered cricket writer Neville Cardus suggested the limited-overs game be called 'snicket' or 'slogget' – but not cricket. However, by season's end many had been converted, especially after a stirring Lord's final, before a full house, was won by Sussex. In the *Daily Express*, their renowned sporting columnist Peter Wilson wrote: 'If there has ever been a triumphant sporting experiment, the knockout cricket cup for the Gillette Cup was that experiment. A year ago, anyone suggesting that on a cold, damp September Saturday afternoon, Lord's, the temple of tradition, could be transformed into a reasonable replica of Wembley on Cup Final day, would have been sent post haste to the nearest psychiatrist's couch.'

In 1964 matches were reduced to 60 overs per side, with bowlers limited first to 13, and later 12 overs each. The cricket was colourful and often exciting. Television expanded the audience, and the September final quickly became a major event on the British sporting calendar. Such success made a further step in the evolutionary process inevitable, and in 1969 a second limited-overs competition was introduced.

Exhibition matches, involving past and present cricketers, played over four hours, and sponsored by the tobacco company Rothmans, had been extremely popular on British Sunday television since the mid-1960s. With the public's response to these matches firmly in mind, the counties opted for a Sunday competition of their own, won support from one of Rothmans' chief competitors, John Player and Sons, and created the John Player League. This competition was designed with the television cameras firmly in mind. Innings were limited to 40 overs, bowlers' run-ups were curtailed (the contest had to be completed in the hours after the Sunday roast), and the match-of-the-day was televised on BBC2.

Later that year, a limited-overs competition involving first-class cricketers was introduced in Australia. The Australian Cricket Board of Control saw in a sponsored limited-overs competition a means of making some additional income, a fact especially relevant in 1969-70 as the Australian Test team was away touring India and South Africa. The Board, through the financial backing of the Vehicle and General Insurance Group, created the V&G Australasian Knockout competition, which involved all the Sheffield Shield sides, Tasmania (who were not then involved in the Shield) and the New Zealand Test team, who to that point had played just one Test match against Australia (in 1946). V&G's trophy was won in its inaugural year by the Kiwis, who defeated Victoria in a one-sided final before more than 14,000 people at the MCG on New Year's Day, 1970.

The promotion work for that competition was handled by a public relations firm headed by Richie Benaud. In an article written for *Australian Cricket* magazine's 1970 Yearbook, he labelled the competition 'a great success', and continued: 'An interesting point I found in all the organising was the amount of discussion that took place before, during and after the series on the concept of what is virtually instant cricket. In one year the one-day knockout match has been accepted by the public, though, it is true, not by all cricket administrators.

'One of the strangest reactions I found was that of relief from many people that they were able to watch or read about a cricket match concluded in one day between two major teams. Not all the tactics employed met with widespread approval, nor were they expected to, for in the inaugural year here, as in England, there was an emphasis on defence from the fielding side, this sometimes going as far as the non-employment of slip fieldsmen to slow and medium pace bowlers.'

Before the V&G series, cricket other than in its traditional form had rarely been played in Australia. Single, double and even triple-wicket matches were often played among the country's finest cricketers in the 19th century. Occasionally at district level matches were played over a single day, such as in Sydney during the Second World War, when the great spin bowler Bill O'Reilly took an extraordinary number of wickets for his club, St George.

In the late 1960s, two former Test batsmen developed competitions of a different kind. Jim Burke had introduced a limited-overs series among Sydney grade clubs in 1967-68, and soon after Bob Simpson conducted a number of double-wicket contests involving some of the world's finest players, including Gary Sobers, Graeme Pollock, Wes Hall and Colin Milburn. But these promotions were seen as a sideshow, far removed from the main event, which, of course, was the traditional

Test match, with the charm and excellence of the Sheffield Shield in support. The Australian public was not yet aware that a revolution was on the horizon.

The first limited-overs international came about by accident, or perhaps more accurately, by an act of God. For many years the major profit-earner for the Australian Cricket Board of Control had been the Christmas-time Test match at the Melbourne Cricket Ground. But in 1970-71, an Ashes season, the Test was completely destroyed by the weather, forcing Australian cricket officials to seek an alternative means of making money during the remnants of the festive season. The England side that was touring that summer, under the captaincy of the Yorkshire-born off-spinner Ray Illingworth, was a tough, professional outfit that reflected the defensive but successful approach to cricket of its skipper. The side was built around the prolific but careful run-scoring of Geoffrey Boycott (with John Edrich and Brian Luckhurst in support), the all-round opportunism of the South African Basil D'Oliveira, and the moody but superb fast bowling of the imposing John Snow. The Australians appeared well equipped with a batting line-up that included the captain Bill Lawry, Ian and Greg Chappell, Doug Walters, Ian Redpath and Keith Stackpole, but in the early exchanges they were hindered by impotent bowling resources as limited as anything the country had put on the paddock since the 1920s.

The first two Tests of the summer, in Brisbane and then Perth, were contested at a snail's pace – the batting frustratingly watchful, the bowling unpenetrating, the umpiring ultra-conservative (through the six-Test series only seven batsmen were given out lbw – all of them Englishmen). Even so, interest was high for the third Test, Melbourne's only scheduled international of the summer.

The Test was intended to begin on Thursday, December 31, but by then the elements had taken control. The morning dawned dull and overcast, after a night of consistent rain. The day's cricket was abandoned, as was day two. When Saturday was also washed out, and an earlier decision not to play on the scheduled Sunday rest day affirmed, the match was abandoned, only the third time in Test history and the first time in Australia that a Test had been lost completely to the weather. The loss in revenue caused by the abandonment of the Test was estimated at $80,000. Jack Ledward, the secretary of the Victorian Cricket Association, suggested the wash-out would lead to a significant reduction in the cash hand-out to his district clubs at the conclusion of the season. To soften this financial burden, plans were made for a substitute Test to be played before the end of January. At the same time, the chairman of the Australian Cricket Board of Control, Sir Donald Bradman, announced that, if the clouds cleared, a limited-overs match, sponsored by Rothmans, would be played between the two countries on the Tuesday, January 5, with $2400 being on offer for the winners, $1200 for the defeated, and $200 for the man of the match (to be judged by the visiting English Test umpire, Charlie Elliott). Significantly, both captains backed the multinational company's support of the one-off match.

'I feel sponsorship of cricket will be a most important aspect of the game in years to come,' Lawry told the Melbourne *Age*. 'This gesture by Rothmans is a most important lead in international cricket.' Illingworth remarked: 'Purely from a

The Age

Ian Chappell, Australia's top-scorer in the first-ever one-day international, against England at the MCG on January 5, 1971, lofts the English captain, Ray Illingworth, to the extra-cover boundary during his innings. The keeper is Alan Knott.

DAY ONE: INTO THE GREAT UNKNOWN

The repercussions of the hastily arranged 40-over fixture between Australia and England at the MCG are now all too obvious, but at the time the participants had no more idea of the impact of their trail-blazing than Christopher Columbus did when he laid claim to the 'New World' in 1492.

Two days after the first limited-overs international, Graeme Kelly of the *Australian* quoted Aussie skipper Bill Lawry in his 'Talking Sport' column as saying: 'It is good cricket and the crowd enjoy watching the game but we will have to be careful that one-day matches are not killed by being overdone.

'I feel there is enough scope for a one-day competition between the states conducted by V and G and also for a match or two against touring sides,' said Lawry. 'I also think the matches should always involve top players. If these principles are followed one-day cricket should continue to draw big crowds. But if the matches are of a low standard or too frequent I think spectator appeal might begin to dwindle.'

More than two decades later the above pronouncements look a little naive, but they illustrate the innocent beginnings of a game that has come to dominate the lives of our professional players and to threaten the very existence of institutions like English county cricket, the Sheffield Shield and even Test cricket itself.

Newspapers of the day reported that the crowd-drawing potential of one-day cricket was 'rammed home' by the enthusiastic patronage of that first international limited-over contest.

The crowd of 46,006 (who paid $33,894.60 to watch the game) surpassed the five-day attendance aggregate of 42,376 for the first Test of the series, played in Brisbane. Gate receipts for the 'Gabba Test exceeded the takings at the MCG by just $2717.50. The second Test in Perth likewise suffered by comparison, although not to the same extent – a total attendance of 84,142 paid $106,748 to see that five-day contest.

Lawry admits today that memories of the game have become dim, principally because the game was such an aberration. 'It's not like the Ashes, where something sticks in your mind – it was an exhibition game. We just played it and won, and went on with the rest of the Test series,' he said. 'We wanted to win – you wanted to win every game you played – but we couldn't take it seriously because it wasn't normal.'

Lawry's successor as Australian captain, Ian Chappell, remembers that the decision to rearrange the tour itinerary caused a deal of consternation, especially with the Englishmen.

'Sir Donald Bradman made the announcement of the whole thing – the cancellation of the Test match, the fact that there was going to be a rescheduled Test match, the fact that we were going to get paid for the washed-out Test and also a one-day fee.' Chappell recalled. 'We weren't used to changes like that. If a game was messed about by rain it usually just petered out. It was unusual for administrators to think along those lines. I think the ACB had to do a lot of fast talking, a lot of wheeling and dealing, because the Englishmen weren't happy about the deal. The one-day match was neither here nor there to them – they were mainly pissed off that they would have to play an extra Test match. I know Illy (Ray Illingworth) went really crook. The general feeling in the Australian side was a one-day match was better than going through the motions in what was left of the Test.'

Of the Australians' attitude to the game, Chappell said: 'While we were playing England – and you never liked losing to England – as I recall we adopted a very casual approach to the game. As much as you could have a casual approach under Bill. We tried hard but it was just an exhibition game to us. I think we just went out to play, did our best and entertained the crowd. I wouldn't say we treated it as a practice match. We were just mainly pleased to be out in the middle playing, because you got sick of sitting around playing cards and wasting time. We'd played next to nothing in the way of one-day cricket, and the team that played was just the Test side. There was no specific selection for that type of game. And our strategy as far as I was concerned was to bowl the opposition out rather than contain them.'

Lawry had sent the Englishmen in on a wicket that was still recovering from the poor weather of the previous days. By the afternoon the pitch had improved, and the Australians fancied their chances.

'It was such a middle-of-the-road total that I figured all we had to do was play as we always had,' remembers Chappell. 'We just went out and batted normally – we didn't really know what we were doing.' Chappell said two things that stick in his mind from the very first limited-overs international were a catch he dropped off the bowling of 'Froggy' Thomson and a six he struck off

Illingworth. The catch came from the eventual man of the match, John Edrich, and was described by Chappell as probably the easiest he dropped in a lifetime of cricket. He had to take only a step or two to complete the catch after the ball had ballooned off the handle of Edrich's bat. But he made a mess of it.

When the $200 man-of-the-match cheque was being awarded to Edrich, Doug Walters sidled up to Chappell and quipped: 'You're very unlucky you didn't get that Chappelli. They should have given it to you for dropping Edrich and prolonging the game.'

The six came when Chappell decided to hit out with the match well and truly in Australia's keeping. Chappell remembers Norm O'Neill, the former champion Australian batsman who was commentating on radio, complimenting him on the shot, and that he had given the spectators something to enjoy rather than coasting to victory.

Chappell recalls one dilemma: 'When the game finished, it was just business as usual – you sat down and had a beer. The most difficult decision was which dressing room to drink in, because traditionally you drank in the rooms of the team that fielded on the first day and alternated each day after that.'

And of the discussions that went on after the match had been won: 'There was a bit of talk about the game, but I can't remember anything specific – which basically means that Walters didn't make any smart comments and Marshy was probably too new to the team to come out with anything silly.'

The Age

Rod Marsh, in his first season as Australia's Test wicketkeeper, hooks England's Peter Lever to the square-leg boundary to seal his side's victory, by five wickets, in the inaugural one-day international.

financial aspect, no English cricketer is so well off that he can ignore sponsorship of the game, or fail to realise the benefits of it.'

Each team's innings would be limited to a maximum of 40 eight-ball overs, with each bowler restricted to a maximum of eight overs. Television audiences in NSW and Queensland could watch the match live all day on the ABC, while Melbourne viewers would have to make do with the final stages, telecast by both the ABC and GTV Channel 9. Under normal circumstances, January 5, 1971, would have been the fifth and final day of the Test – traditionally the last day is played out in front of the match's smallest audience. However, a one-day international was something different, and few were really sure what the Melbourne sporting community would make of it. From early morning, the traffic queues showed they were arriving in their thousands. The attendance was much greater than most had anticipated, a boisterous, vibrant crowd – 46,006 in all – and more than one critic noted that there appeared to be more women and children than had been seen in the past. Many were intrigued by a bounty of $2000 that the Melbourne Cricket Club had promised to the first batsman to break the clock on the top deck of the Members' Pavilion. Such a feat had never been achieved, not even by the mighty heroes of long ago.

R.S. Whitington, in his book of the 1970-71 MCC tour *Captains Outrageous*, a book that went to great lengths to denounce the negative attitudes of the two Test teams, wrote of the game's opening exchanges: 'Lawry won the toss and sent England into bat, the accepted move in one-day, limited number of overs knockout games ... Boycott and Edrich began to run what in the Tests had been 'impossible' runs, to play what had become 'impossible' strokes. It was all one of those impossible dreams come true. Before long the impossible became the ordinary, and miracles took a moment or two longer. Almost all the balls outside the off stump were stroked ...'

The match had the crowd involved from the jump, and especially in the afternoon as Ian Chappell and Doug Walters took control. The English innings had been dominated by Edrich, who scored 82 in a racy manner few Test spectators in Brisbane or Perth would have thought possible. The tough left-hander lacked support, but was particularly severe on the Victorian medium-pacer Alan Connolly, who went for 62 runs in eight wicketless overs.

Of the other Englishmen, only first wicket Keith Fletcher, and the No. 8, keeper Alan Knott, scored more than 20, as the innings ended at 190, with four balls still available. Australia's two spinners, the off-breaker Ashley Mallett and the part-time top-spinner Keith Stackpole, took three wickets each, while the veteran paceman Graham McKenzie, and the frenetic, bouncer-happy Alan Thomson, each had their moments on a sometimes unreliable pitch.

An English run-rate of nearly five runs per over had set the mood, and when Australia batted, the Victorian crowd slow-handclapped Lawry as early as the second over. At 19, Stackpole hit a return catch to Ken Shuttleworth, after which Lawry, mainly through quick singles, and a scratchy Ian Chappell took Australia to 51 at tea, after 11 overs. Immediately after the resumption, the local captain edged his opposite number behind, to bring in Walters to play just about the most positive innings by an Australian batsman all summer. Walters had been severely tested by the speed of Snow in the Test series, but now, with the great paceman limited to just eight overs, he was confronted by Illingworth's off-spin and stole the show. 'Dancing to the ball, he struck four after four, and looked a glorious batsman,' wrote Whitington. He blasted six boundaries while striding from 4 to 29, and by the time he was dismissed, for 41 from a dynamic 41 balls, the tempo of the Australian innings had been established.

Walters' brilliance inspired Chappell, who gradually regained some of the form of 1968-69, when he had dominated the West Indies. After 27 overs Australia was 3-138 (England at the same stage had been 3-140), but in the next few minutes the victory was confirmed, as Chappell went past his fifty during a single D'Oliveira over that cost 17 runs. He was eventually stumped, charging at Illingworth, for 60, to leave Rod Marsh and Greg Chappell the job of coasting to victory – to the persistent roars of the crowd, all of whom stayed to the finish.

Reaction to the game was positive, though many cautioned against a sudden explosion of one-day matches on the cricket itinerary. Whitington, clearly excited by what he had seen (and, it must be stressed, deeply disturbed by the soulless sport he had witnessed in the Tests), suggested that the future of international cricket lay in instituting rules that 'limited the number of overs bowled in the first innings of both teams and then letting them fight it out to a finish on uncovered wickets in the knowledge that one or the other must win, in the equal knowledge that one or the other must lose'.

In *Australian Cricket*, the editor, Eric Beecher, took a different, more cautious line. He liked cricket the way it was (though he believed it needed to be sold in the market-place more aggressively), and felt it was not for cricket to 'keep pace with society'. 'Cricket today needs to be alert to the many movements of our society without actually being influenced by all of them,' Beecher wrote. 'For one of cricket's greatest attractions in this age of high speed and excitement is its leisureliness. The moment the game tries to keep up with, rather than provide a rather enjoyable supplement to, this speeding up, it will change dramatically and for the worse.'

It must be remembered that the limited-overs international had been staged to make up for funds lost because of Melbourne's tardy new year's weather, not as a test of the one-day game's public appeal. Australian cricket in 1971 did not have an uneconomical county championship to support, or full-time cricketers with salary requirements beyond the reach of the system then in place. The fixture list as it then stood was paying its way, and though the exuberant grins of the fans, who in a solitary day had seen both the first ball and the aggressive Australian victory, urged a review, the cricket hierarchy were happy with the game as it had always been.

The days of significant international limited-overs cricket in Australia were still a number of Test series away.

2

THE TIMES ARE A-CHANGIN'

t is easy, more than two decades after the first limited-overs international, to sit back and be critical of cricket officialdom for not scheduling many more of these matches in the seasons immediately after that first game. With the benefit of 20 years hindsight, there is no reason to believe that the extraordinary crowd-drawing ability of limited-overs international cricket in the 1980s and '90s would not have existed throughout the 1970s. But to put such criticism would be to some extent unfair, because by all but ignoring the potential profits of limited-overs cricket, the Australian Cricket Board of Control was doing no more than reflecting the thoughts of most people in Australian cricket at that time.

There *were* many people at that time who pushed the fact that it was the Board's duty (and the players' role) to provide attractive cricket. Board officials publicly acknowledged this responsibility. However, limited-overs cricket, despite the positive public reaction to the 1971 international, was, with a few notable exceptions, not seen as the way to meet the public's demands.

Most observers at this time were happy with Test cricket, which, it was argued, had been an integral part of Australian life for decades. Australians doing battle on the field, both at home and abroad, in matches that sometimes stretched for many absorbing days, was a tradition that had stood the test of time. The bravado of champions such as Trumper and Bradman, Miller, O'Reilly and Benaud had become folklore. The future, if left untouched, promised more adventures. This was a view put in the SCG members' bar, by the patrons in the outer at the Adelaide Oval, and by schoolboys all over the country, who devoured the memories of their coaches, fathers and grandfathers.

Those against the 'new' game argued that limited-overs cricket reduced standards, and if standards dropped the future of the sport was in jeopardy. 'The one-day gimmick must so lower the standard in genuine cricket that even the Tests will lose their appeal,' warned one English critic. While most condemned or ridiculed limited-overs cricket, one or two celebrated voices were heard in support. Sir Donald Bradman, in an interview in 1971, commented: 'One-day matches appeal to a section of the public and seem destined to play a larger part in our future programs. It is a question of hastening slowly and making the best of the merits of each type of game. 'A few months later, Richie Benaud, in an article in *Australian Cricket*, wrote: 'The traditionalists shudder at the thought of one-day beer matches. But, like it or not, knockout cricket and sponsorship are here to stay; a fact for which we should give three hearty cheers. Both are tied in with finance and providing the varied entertainment desired by the public. Look at the crowd of 45,000 present at the sponsored one-day knockout match last year in Melbourne. The game provided wonderful entertainment and was the forerunner of other matches of this type between international teams.'

Bradman and Benaud, despite their experience and status, were, at this time, two voices running against the tide. For most, the MCG crowd figure for the one-day international of 1971 was quickly dismissed as an example of the sports-mad Melbourne public's propensity to watch anything even remotely connected to sport. Those crazy Melburnians had, after all, been robbed by the weather of their Christmas Test match. They probably would have gone to watch a game of baseball. And many who had attended that one-day match had never gone to the cricket in the past. In all likelihood, it was suggested, they would not go again.

This view was put by the cricket establishment and supported, almost to a man, by the cricket media. Many followers sneered at the abbreviated game, which was labelled, as it had been in England, as 'not being cricket'. And, significantly, the players did not care for it, treating it as little more than a harmless diversion.

South Africa, then the most powerful country in world cricket, were scheduled to tour Australia in 1971-72. But after the controversial and often ugly battles between police and anti-apartheid demonstrators that had ruined the 1971 South African rugby tour of Australia, there was never any chance of the cricket tour going ahead. On September 8, 1971, Sir Donald Bradman announced that the Board of Control had accepted the advice of police and politicians, and abandoned the tour. In its place would be a tour by a sponsored Rest of the World side, who would play five five-day 'Tests' against the Australians, and two limited-overs matches, one in Sydney and one in Melbourne, on consecutive days in mid-January.

Although the abandonment of the South African tour met with a universal, if resigned, acceptance, its replacement with a 'non-Test' series, albeit against a side that included such names as Sobers, Pollock, Kanhai, Zaheer, Gavaskar, Lloyd, Greig and Bedi, met with some disapproval. The sponsored tour was dismissed by many commentators as a cynical, money-grabbing exercise, and a shabby replacement for a tour that had promised to be one of the best of all time.

The early performances of the World team were little more than terrible, pleasing no-one but the sceptics. But gradually the tourists (who had been dragged together at what amounted to the last moment) found form and eventually edged out the Australians 2-1 in the 'Test' series. It was a summer of some real highlights, chief among them the fantastic second-innings 254 by the World XI captain, Gary Sobers, in the third match, at the MCG, and the remarkable, explosive fast bowling of Western Australia's Dennis Lillee, who in the second international, at the WACA Ground in Perth, reduced the visitors' first innings to just 59, finishing with 8-29 from 57 frightening deliveries.

The Australians, on the back of Lillee's speed and a first-day century by Doug

The Age

England all-rounder Tony Greig welcomes a keen supporter onto the MCG during the only one-day international of the 1974-75 Australian season, which England won narrowly by three wickets. The fans in the outer enjoyed the occasion, but umpire Robin Bailhache was less amused.

Walters, had that match in Perth all but won by stumps on the second day. But a surprisingly large crowd still attended the game's last rites on the third morning (a Saturday). Rather than send these enthusiasts home, the two sides agreed to an impromptu 25-overs-a-side exhibition, which the World side won by 14 runs, 8-244 to 7-230. Even the cynical were entertained, and the scorers exhausted, by the tidal wave of runs that flowed from the 50 (eight-ball) overs. On the following Monday, a further 40-overs-per-side match was arranged, and won by the World XI. It featured some fine batting from the Indian keeper/opening batsman Farokh Engineer, Pakistan's Zaheer Abbas, and the Australian Keith Stackpole, as well as some crafty left-arm finger spin from Norman Gifford of England.

The scheduled limited-overs match in Sydney on January 15 was ruined by the weather, which prevented a ball being bowled. In Melbourne, the clouds stayed away, but the World XI were bowled out for just 75, in 25.5 overs, a target the Australian openers, Stackpole and John Inverarity of Western Australia, reached in little more than an hour. This ridiculously easy victory won the Australians $2000 in prizemoney. Walters, who took 4-28 from eight overs, and Zaheer, who top-scored for the World XI with 20, received $250 man-of-the-match awards. A further

15-overs slog was then staged, in which Ian Chappell kept wicket because Marsh had sustained a minor injury earlier in the day. The Australians won this hit as well, by six runs (9-150 to 6-144). The brief summary of the day in Melbourne by *Australian Cricket* was intriguing, and summed up the then wary, often cynical approach of the cricket media to limited-overs cricket. The magazine devoted just five arid paragraphs to the match and in one of them suggested there had been a 'certain amount of disinterest' (apparently by the players) that made the cricket 'worth forgetting'. 'The only consoling factor,' it continued, 'was the 42,121 crowd which added $35,072 to cricket's coffers.'

Australian Cricket was the only monthly cricket magazine published in Australia at that time. Its editorials throughout that summer reflected an unease in the cricket community over the changes that were becoming evident in the cricket world, including the rise of limited-overs cricket. The reason one-day matches were being staged was to raise money, but it was becoming evident that the people who were paying that money through the gate had not been regular members of the cricket fraternity, a fact the magazine viewed with concern. In its October 1971 issue, the magazine wrote: 'The sweeping trend towards professionalism and, in turn, sponsorship, the rise out of all proportions of one-day games, the vast changes in the concept of cricket touring. All are important aspects in the changing cricket spectrum, and nearly all have developed rapidly and unexpectedly over the past decade or less. Many traditionalists are still recovering, or trying to prepare themselves for the next shock. They view this trend with growing hostility: but more, they regard it as a very real threat to the future of cricket as it has become accepted for so many years.'

The magazine's view, it appeared, was mirrored at the highest administrative levels. The 1971-72 interstate limited-overs knock-out (sponsored by Coca-Cola) was given scant status by the Board of Control, who scheduled matches to coincide with the Australia-World XI five-day internationals (but played in different cities), and put the only match to be played at the MCG on a working-day Friday. However, it appeared the Board's stance on limited-overs cricket had been softened slightly when the itinerary for the 1972 Australian tour of England was released. It included five Test matches, and *three* one-day matches to be played within five days in August. Originally the two countries had decided on a six-Test series, but later reduced the number of Tests to five, to make room for the potentially lucrative one-day series, in which the 'Prudential Trophy', put up by the Prudential Assurance company, would be at stake. The motivation for this change was strictly financial (and pushed most strongly by the English authorities) and the matches were scheduled so that the final two would be played on the Bank Holiday long weekend, when high crowd figures were most likely. Played over 55 overs per side, they would be the second, third and fourth limited-overs internationals ever played.

By 1972 the English authorities were playing the one-day matches at county level for all they were worth. A third competition, the Benson and Hedges League Cup, was introduced, to be played during May and June. In his book of the Australians' tour, *The Ashes 1972*, the veteran author and commentator John Arlott wrote that limited-overs cricket 'had saved the three-day (county championship) game. It is as if international contract bridge were subsidised by the televising of nap schools'. Arlott went on to suggest that the atmosphere at Lancashire's home ground of Old Trafford for John Player League fixtures was 'more like that of a Manchester United match' than a cricket contest. If the English Test and County Cricket Board welcomed these new, rowdier fans, they also welcomed their money. For 1972, admission prices for all Gillette Cup matches were doubled, a move the English cricket writer John Thicknesse suggested 'freshly illustrated the hard-headed business sense implicit (in cricket administration) in the past decade'. For nine straight seasons the Cup final had attracted a sell-out 25,000 crowd to Lord's. Now, with one stroke of an accountant's pen, the annual takings from the final had been doubled, to £50,000.

The 1972 Test series was one of the most vibrant on record, and eventually ended locked at two Tests all, with England retaining the Ashes. It was a summer of many highlights – the West Australian swing bowler Bob Massie's extraordinary 16-wicket debut at Lord's, the match-winning spin of England's left-arm Derek Underwood at Headingley, the batting of the Chappells and Stackpole, the pace bowling of Snow and Lillee, the exuberance of England's South African-born all-rounder Tony Greig. It was a series that did much for the appeal of Ashes cricket, which had lacked excitement and verve during the 1960s and into the '70s.

The one-day internationals that followed were, in a cricket sense, something of an anti-climax, although they did feature the first century scored in this type of match (by the English opener Dennis Amiss) and a fine performance by the Australians in the second match, at Lord's, which they won by five wickets. The crowds were substantial, though not sell-outs, and the prevailing opinion after the three matches had been concluded was that the series would have been better off had it been scheduled before, rather than following, the Test series.

The Australian attitude to the limited-overs series was described by captain Ian Chappell in his book of the tour, *Tigers Among the Lions*. Of his team's approach after the final Test, he wrote: 'There were still the three one-day "Tests" to play and these would be very interesting, although much more relaxed than the official series.' Later he called the one-day matches against England 'light-hearted', and said: 'One-day cricket is an unusual type of game. I quite enjoy a little of it, but would not like to play it regularly. The amount we play in Australia is, I feel, just about right. If played too often the limited-overs game tends to foster defensive attitudes which are not good for cricket.'

England took the limited-overs series by two matches to one. They won the first match by six wickets, after Australia had finished at 8-222. Ross Edwards, with 57 (run out off the innings' last ball), top-scored for the Australians. Lillee bowled off a short run at the Englishmen, and with Boycott, Amiss and Fletcher handling him and Massie comfortably, the English victory came off the first ball of the 50th over. At Lord's, the home side (with Lillee off his full run) were restricted to 9-236, a target reached in the 52nd over. The third game at Edgbaston was the closest of the series. Australia's batting effort (9-179) seemed totally inadequate, but the English-men took 51.3 overs, and needed eight wickets and a late flurry from Greig to scrape home. Keith Stackpole, who square cut the first ball of the one-day series, from

KEITH STACKPOLE: OPENING UP

In his prime Keith Stackpole was an opener who could brutalise a bowling attack with punishing strokeplay, and seemed a perfect fit for the embryonic one-day cricket. But he admits he was as much handicapped by the casual attitude to one-day cricket which prevailed as any of his fellow players.

'When the first one-day international came along it just took the place of a Test match. It was just a nice simple one-day match, there didn't seem to be much in it,' said Stackpole. 'The attitude then was "oh, go out and get off to a quick start". It didn't matter if you lost wickets, you'd never get bowled out in 40 overs. But then it evolved that you did, that you got into trouble, and of course the more risks you took the bigger the penalty.'

That early naivety was compounded for batsmen by the fact they were not forced into a different mindset by the fielding side's approach. 'The major difference was that the fielding captain and bowlers genuinely tried to get you out,' Stackpole said. 'They'd open up with three slips, and perhaps not a third man, hoping to get a couple of snicks and a couple of early wickets. They played it in a similar format to a Test match, trying to get early wickets with not a great emphasis on stopping runs.

'It was over in England that they started pacing themselves. Everyone began to realise there was more to this game than met the eye. Suddenly people became conscious of run-rates and that's when people started to get serious about it,' Stackpole recalled.

The three-match limited-overs series that followed the eventful 1972 Ashes tour of England was the first time one-day cricket had been given a formal place in the international cricket calendar. But the format did not get off to a spectacular start. 'It was unfortunate that it was staged at the conclusion of the tour,' Stackpole recalled. 'For the first match in Manchester the approach was a bit flippant because it was the end of the series and most people just wanted it over and out. After losing the first one suddenly we realised we had to get serious about it. It was one-all when we got to Edgbaston. That was a fairly serious game and we were outplayed.'

Stackpole admitted having problems adjusting to limited-overs cricket despite the game being apparently perfect for his robust approach to batting. Just as he had to tone down his game to succeed in Test cricket, so also he had to put a clamp on the adrenalin to score consistently in the slather-and-whack arena.

'I had to alter the way I played,' he said. 'I was an aggressive player but

Snow, for four and went on to score 37, 52 and 61 in the three matches, was named Australia's 'Man of the Series'. A rugged, burly opening batsman, Stackpole was at the peak of his form. Today, he is most remembered for his powerful, almost habitual hook shot, a stroke that remained effective against even the fastest bouncers. But he could also drive and cut, and in the slips he was safe and surprisingly agile. He possessed an array of strokes that made him perhaps as well suited to the

early on I used to go out even crazier because I thought I had to get runs quickly. Bang, slap and you got out for 15 or something and suddenly you realised that you had to get your head down and get some big scores. So I had to change my attitude.'

Stackpole enjoyed having the opportunity to play limited-overs cricket but admits he didn't really take advantage of the possibilities open to him batting at the top of the order.

'I enjoyed it but I didn't realise at the time the important role that openers and first-wicket-down batsmen would play in the evolution of one-day cricket. Now one-day cricket is tailor-made for the top four batsmen. 'I feel sorry for the Steve Waughs and the guys at five and six these days because it's a tough position to play in one-day cricket. You've got very little chance to build an innings. At the most you might end up getting a 20 or 30. Or you come to the wicket when the side's in real trouble and when they're in trouble it's usually because there's something in the wicket and you have to counter that, too.'

Not surprisingly, having only dabbled in one-day cricket when both the game and its players were blind to its potential, a part of Stackpole still regrets missing out on the chance to play the game as it is played now. 'I am disappointed that I missed the one-day cricket boom. I was in the twilight of my career

and only had a couple of years to go so it didn't have any affect on my career.'

That's not to say he thinks he would be an instant success if he was granted his wish. 'I would have had to become a more agile fielder – there's no doubt about that. I was a close-to-the-wicket catcher but I would have had to become more versatile and perhaps get a bit fitter. Being able to send a few overs down and bowl tightly I would have been in the game a lot and that would have been terrific.'

Two men he thinks would have taken to modern limited-overs cricket like ducks to water – and without having to change a thing – are old mates Bob Simpson and Bill Lawry. 'I shudder to think what Bob and Bill would do if they were still around,' he said. 'They'd run fielding sides off their legs. They'd just bat through the 50 overs. I'd hate to think what their opening record would be because it would suit them with all the gaps that are there.'

And then there's the vibrant showcase that is day/night cricket. 'I think any player who never played day/night cricket would love to have played under lights. Sometimes when you're at the MCG or SCG and you've got a full house you think "God, I wish I'd played that. It must be fantastic out there". That's one thing we old guys will never experience.'

demands of limited-overs cricket as any Australian opener to play the game.

There were other Australian highlights, such as wicketkeeper Rod Marsh's stunning catch, diving way to his right, of Boycott off Graeme Watson in the first match, Greg Chappell's stylish 48 at Lord's, which won him the man-of-the-match award, and Lillee's stirring 11 overs in the match at Edgbaston, when he took three wickets for 25, and almost won a match presumed lost. The matches had been absorbing, entertaining, and profitable for the organisers. But Australia would not play another limited-overs international until March, 1974, in Dunedin on the South Island of New Zealand. In the meantime they played home Test series for the first time against Pakistan (1972-73) and New Zealand (1973-74), and toured the West Indies in early 1973. The Australian tour to New Zealand in early '74 included two limited-overs (35 eight-ball overs per side) internationals, which were played on the final two days of the tour. The Australians won both comfortably, the first by seven wickets, thanks to half centuries by Stackpole and Ian Chappell, and the second by 31 runs, in which the South Australian opener, Ashley Woodcock (playing his only international), and Ian and Greg Chappell dominated a scoreline that reached 5-265, the first time Australia went past 250 in these matches. In both games, awards were given for the best batsman, bowler and fieldsman on either side. The Australian winners were Ian Chappell (batting), Gary Gilmour (bowling) and Walters (fielding) in the first game, and Woodcock, Ashley Mallett and Ian Redpath in the second.

During the New Zealand tour, the itinerary for the 1974-75 Ashes series in Australia was announced. It included a single limited-overs international, to be played in Melbourne on New Year's Day, the day after the scheduled final day of the third Test. Three days later was scheduled the first day of the fourth Test, in Sydney. Such a program could not possibly have been designed with the players' performance standards in mind. The match appeared little more than a quick grab for cash, scheduled for a public holiday when a big crowd could be expected, even if high-quality cricket could not. In the four years since the inaugural one-day international, attitudes to such matches had changed little if at all.

The match began less than 17 hours after the end of the third Test. It was eventually won by the Englishmen, a result that stunned all Australian cricket fans, who, after seeing their team totally dominate the Test series to that point, had thought of them as little short of unbeatable. But the defeat, and the ordinary Australian display, was quickly put down to the local team's relative inexperience at the limited-overs game, and to the absurd scheduling of the match. Australia had batted first and been dismissed for 190, with 5.3 overs left wasted. Ian (42) and Greg Chappell (44) were the team's top-scorers. The Englishmen's reply was led by the openers, Amiss and David Lloyd, who added 70 for the first wicket (Australia had lost their first two wickets for 11). After that start the result was in little doubt, even with Greg Chappell's controversial run out of the English No. 3, Brian Luckhurst, who was first warned and then dismissed for backing up too far at the bowler's end. The visitors' victory came with 23 balls to spare, and added $1200 to their tour kitty. The Australian opening bat, Wally Edwards, bowled the game's final ball, which ran for a sundry. This was Edwards' only one-day international. His limited-overs international career bowling figures remain at 0.1 overs; 0 maidens; 0 wickets; 0 runs. The Australians were given $600, and Ian Chappell and Amiss won $100 bonuses for being judged their side's men of the match. However, both teams donated half their winnings to an appeal fund that had been established for victims of the devastation caused by Cyclone Tracy in Darwin a week earlier.

The game had attracted 18,977 people, a disappointing turn-out when compared

The Age

The controversial run out of England's Brian Luckhurst by Greg Chappell during the match at the MCG on New Year's Day, 1975. Five balls earlier, Chappell had warned the Englishman about backing up too far. When Luckhurst left his crease early once again, Chappell went through his bowling motion without delivering the ball and then turned, and with a gentle back-handed throw broke the stumps.

to four years before, and especially to the extraordinary crowds (over 77,000 on Boxing Day, and more than 250,000 in all) that had watched the Melbourne Test. This was seen by most as a vindication of the approach taken by Australian officialdom to such cricket. The limited-overs international, coming so soon after the massively supported Test, was clearly poorly programmed, but even so the Australian team's popularity was so high that many more spectators had been expected. Australian officials argued that the summer's timetable was already full to overflowing and that the fans were already getting all they could consume. There was not room for Tests, the Sheffield Shield, an interstate one-day series, grade cricket *and* one-day internationals. And the Test players were already having difficulties gaining the necessary leave from their employers. In the mid-1970s, all Australian cricketers needed a 'day' job to supplement their cricket incomes. Test cricketers since the 1920s had had problems finding bosses who were prepared to put up with the demands of international and interstate cricket.

But the times were-a-changin'. Advertising on the boundary fences of the major Australian cricket grounds had only recently been permitted. The Chairman of the Australian Cricket Board, Mr Tim Caldwell, during an interview in which he expressed concern at the ever-increasing cost of running the game at all levels, admitted that he could see the day coming when the Australian team would be sponsored, and the players would wear the name of that sponsor on their cricket shirts. As record gate followed record gate during the 1974-75 Ashes Test series, the players began to publicly question their meagre financial returns from the sport. Why, they asked, were so few of the dollars being handed over at the turnstiles being passed on to them?

And in 1974 came a technological development that would have an enormous impact on Australian cricket. On October 7, trials began for the coverage of 'outside' events by *colour* television. Both the Caulfield and Melbourne Cups were beamed into Australian households in living colour, followed just weeks later by the sight of the Australian cricket team terrorising the Englishmen. The cricket made wonderful television. The sight of a powerful, exciting Australian team in living colour was the most successful advertisement for the game in this country since the days of Bradman. As the Chappells, Walters, Marsh, Lillee and a new fast bowler – a fiery, belligerent 'ocker' called Jeff Thomson – won Test after Test in a macho and cavalier style, they attracted many new fans to international cricket, and in doing so broadened the sociological make-up of the cricket community. Such was the appeal of Ian Chappell's Test team, Australian cricket was attracting a 'new' fan, the same fan who had been lured by the one-day game in England. Forward thinkers, however, realised the Australian Test side might not always have the colour and excitement of the greats of 1974-75. Ways had to be found to keep these new fans at the grounds. If the rising costs of running Australian cricket were to be met, it would be these fans, as it had been in England, who would pay the bill.

3

AGAINST THE WORLD

At a reception held in the famous Long Room at Lord's in early June, 1975, the Australian captain Ian Chappell was asked how seriously his team would be playing for the Prudential Cup. His reply was succinct. 'The Australians will be fighting all the way.'

'But our emotions,' he admitted, 'will be pinned more firmly on the retention of the Ashes later in the season.'

The Prudential Cup was known to most commentators, players and cricket followers as 'The World Cup'. The trophy had been put forward by the Prudential Assurance company as the prize for the winner of a two-week tournament that would feature eight teams – Australia, East Africa, England, India, New Zealand, Pakistan, Sri Lanka and the West Indies. The countries were split into two groups of four, and after a round-robin series in each group the top two teams would qualify for the semi-finals. All matches would be played on a 60 six-ball overs per side basis, with each bowler limited to 12 overs.

After the Cup, the Australians would remain in Britain for a shorter-than-normal Ashes tour that would include four Tests. This, as Ian Chappell had indicated, was the primary focus for the players. The Australian selectors chose 16 players for the tour of whom two, the Victorian leg-spinner Jim Higgs and his state keeper, Richie Robinson, were omitted from the Prudential Cup squad. The Cup squad was: Ian Chappell (capt), Greg Chappell (vice-capt), Ross Edwards, Gary Gilmour, Alan Hurst, Bruce Laird, Dennis Lillee, Rick McCosker, Rod Marsh, Ashley Mallett, Jeff Thomson, Alan Turner, Max Walker and Doug Walters.

The selection of the side met with some criticism, especially from the South Australian leg-spinner Terry Jenner who had been in the Test XII all season but was now by-passed, and from Queensland, where the omissions of the State keeper John Maclean and the left-arm fast-medium bowler Geoff Dymock were deplored. Dymock, who had played in the sixth Test against the Englishmen just weeks before, lost out to Gilmour, whose performances with the ball in the 1974-75 season had been disappointing, but who was a better, more exciting batsman. The decision to go with Gilmour appeared to have been made with the Prudential Cup in mind, where, it was thought, his all-round qualities might be handy. This would prove an inspired choice. The Gilmour/Dymock debate aside, the selectors had paid scant attention to the requirements of the limited-overs competition. But, in reality, there was little need to. The Test XI looked, on paper, to be a well-balanced 'one-day' side. The batting line-up was naturally aggressive. In Walters and Greg Chappell, the squad had two quality batsmen with a proven ability to take Test wickets, and in Marsh a wicketkeeper who would score runs aggressively and regularly from No. 7. Lillee and Thomson were a fearful prospect in any type of cricket, while Walker's medium-pace guile and control were renowned. And if the spin-bowler had a place in one-day cricket (a subject of some debate at this time), then Mallett, arguably the best off-spinner to play for Australia since World War I, was surely the man for the job. Before the limited-overs internationals began, the Australians were no better than 4-1 fourth favourites for the Cup, a seemingly extravagant price after the Ashes series of the previous English winter. The bookmakers were paying more attention to the Australians' lack of one-day experience than to the power and suitability of their line-up. The West Indies, at 9-4, were the popular picks, with England, the same England that had been so thoroughly vanquished in Australia, at 11-4. Pakistan were 7-2, the rest 12-1 or longer. While many were counting their pounds and pence at the betting shops, most pre-tournament discussion centred on the International Cricket Conference's decision (following a submission from Pakistan) to ban bouncers from the Cup. The umpires would be calling any ball that reared over the head of a batsman standing in his normal position a wide.

Australia were drawn in clearly the more difficult quartet, Group B, alongside the West Indies, Pakistan and Sri Lanka. With only two teams to go through, their opening match against the Pakistanis at a sold-out Headingley assumed vital importance. Neither side wanted to require a victory over the much-vaunted West Indians. The Cup was awaited with great interest in Britain, something that, as John Woodcock of the *Times* pointed out, would have been 'unthinkable' just 20 years earlier. This fervour was not as evident in Australia, where the ABC, who were sending their famous commentator Alan McGilvray over for the Test series, chose not to provide a ball-by-ball coverage of the competition.

Times would change. Prior to the Cup, there had been just 18 limited-overs internationals played worldwide – two in Australia, 11 in England, and five in New Zealand. In 1975, all the cricket nations were concerned with getting the appropriate balance between limited-overs and more traditional cricket, between 'the Bay City Rollers and the London Symphony Orchestra' as Woodcock put it. The Prudential Cup represented the first time one-day cricket would be played as more than just a sidekick to a Test series. It therefore had the opportunity to give limited-overs cricket international credibility and significance.

The crucial Australia-Pakistan match on June 7, before a sell-out Headingley crowd (the gates were closed 40 minutes after the start) was won by the Australians, chiefly because of an impressive bowling performance spearheaded by Lillee, who finished with 5-34. Pakistan (who had reached 4-181) were bowled out in the 53rd over for 205. Lillee's final six overs yielded 10 runs and four wickets. Earlier, Ian Chappell had won the toss, batted, and watched Ross Edwards (80 not out) steer his side to 7-278. At 6-195, the Australians were in some trouble, but Walker and

Patrick Eagar

The tiny West Indian Alvin Kallicharran hooks Dennis Lillee during his explosive innings in the Group B World Cup match at The Oval in 1975. In one sequence of 10 predominantly short-pitched deliveries from Lillee, Kallicharran smashed 35 runs, to lead his side to a conclusive victory. However, as Australia had won their first two qualifying matches they moved on with the West Indies to the semi-finals. Kallicharran finished this match with 78, Lillee with figures of 1-66 from 10 overs.

ALAN TURNER: THE FIRST CENTURION

Opener Alan Turner holds the distinction of being the first Australian to score a century in a limited-overs match. Like so many incidents and accidents in one-day cricket Turner's century against Sri Lanka in the 1975 World Cup tournament came out of the blue, a product of the situation on the day. Turner was by no means the highest-profile player in the star-studded Australian line-up.

In fact, Turner's prospects at the start of the tour did not bode well as far as record-breaking feats were concerned. 'I went to England with everyone expecting me to be the Matt Hayden, No. 3 opener, hanging around serving the drinks and playing in the up-country games,' he recalled. Rick McCosker had just established himself as a Test opener and with Keith Stackpole retired and Ian Redpath unable to tour, Turner was competing with West Australian opener Bruce Laird for the chance to partner McCosker. 'I wasn't in the higher-profile lead-up games but I did pretty well in matches we played amongst ourselves,' said Turner. 'I got the nod, I guess, for the World Cup because I was perhaps a little more aggressive than Bruce.'

When the match against Sri Lanka rolled around things simply fell into place for the likeable left-hander. 'I got caught up in the spirit of the one-day game,' said Turner. 'We wanted to post as many runs as we could because if the Sri Lankans could do anything it was bat. Their bowling wasn't world class, I think you'd have to admit that, but they'd been making some pretty reasonable scores and just not bowling the opposition out. So there was always a need to score a substantial amount of runs to protect yourself against them.

'Things just sort of developed,' he recalled. 'We got off to a pretty good start. The bowling wasn't very frightening and once we got into it we really got into it and the runs just seemed to flow. The Oval was a very good wicket and it was a very big ground but very fast. Things just started to happen for me and I started to smash them around. At the end of it I was actually enjoying it. I was hitting the ball very well, I don't think I've hit the ball better, and you certainly didn't have to worry about life and limb with those guys. There's nothing like a perfect English batting wicket; there's not much devil about it. It was one of those games and one of those days.'

There was one disruption the Australian openers had to overcome and it wasn't a hostile spell of bowling. 'About 20 Sri Lankans put on a demonstration for about 10 minutes,' said Turner. 'They sat on the wicket and had to be removed by the police. I think I was trying to maintain

Thomson supported their West Australian colleague, and 79 runs were added in the final 10 overs.

When Pakistan batted, Thomson's first over included four no-balls and a wide (he would end the innings with 12 no-balls), and when it finally ended he responded to the large, howling Pakistani contingent beyond the boundary with a derisive 'V'

concentration as much as anything. I didn't know much about the political scene in Sri Lanka and I didn't know how rabid these people were. At the outset, when they invaded the ground, I didn't know if they were out there to do us any harm so I was keen to keep an eye on them. But they were pretty passive and didn't try to bother me or Rick. They just made a general nuisance of themselves and one by one were carried off.'

Wisden still records Turner's 101 as the only World Cup century scored before lunch, but unfortunately Turner's momentous century was overshadowed by a spectacular exhibition of pace bowling by fast bowler Jeff Thomson – then in his absolute prime having just devastated England during their Ashes tour of Australia. Again there was no warning of what was to come as the aggressive Sri Lankans set about chasing the Australians' imposing total with gusto.

'They weren't overawed by Lillee or Thommo or anyone else, or the amount of runs we got,' said Turner. 'They got stuck into it. They were very good at the hook and cut and I seem to recall Lillee and Thommo gave them every opportunity to hook and cut. The runs came thick and fast.'

Things took an ominous turn for the worst when Thomson, sick of the upstart Sri Lankans treating his bowling with such disrespect, began to wreak havoc. His first victim was Duleep Mendis. 'That guy must have the hardest head I've ever

seen because all I heard at fine leg was a sort of dull clunk like someone hitting a hammer on a bit of hard wood,' said Turner. 'Mendis hit the deck. He wasn't with us. It was a tremendously quick bouncer from Thommo and admittedly Mendis wasn't the sort of bloke who had an ideal hooking technique. He didn't get inside the line, he tended to pull it from around his head.

'The other balls that got those fellows on the sandshoes were fantastic deliveries. They weren't there to intimidate, they were there to knock middle and leg stump out of the ground and those blokes got their feet in the road. Jeff was in his prime. He would have bowled as quick that day as he'd ever bowled because that's the only way Jeff knew how to bowl. He wasn't the sort of guy who'd back off, he'd just run in and let it rip. I don't think he was any different from the day he started to the day he finished.'

When the wreckage had cleared Australia had collected the win and continued on their way towards an eventual appointment with the West Indies in the final. Turner said the mood in the dressing room afterwards certainly had things in perspective. 'At the end of the day we as an Australian team looked back and thought "gee, we were pretty lucky to get away with that". That was the feeling that I had. I think we might have felt a little bit of relief.'

sign. His response at the bowling crease was more telling – eight overs for 25 runs and one wicket, the key dismissal of Zaheer, caught mishooking for 8. Chappell's strategy was surprising and innovative, using Mallett and then Walters as his first two changes after just four overs each from Lillee and Thomson. Walker, the Test first-change, was kept for the later overs. Chappell later explained that he had brought the spinner on early because Pakistan's opening bat Majid Khan had been sorely troubled by the South Australian's bowling in Australia in 1972-73. Mallett and Walters were expensive, Walters especially so, but Walker was a superb foil to Lillee, conceding just two-and-a-half runs an over as the Pakistanis folded late in the day.

The British press reaction after the game centred on Thomson's troubles with the popping crease, and the spectators. Terry Brindle, in the *Yorkshire Post,* described the fast bowler as a 'profound disappointment', while Alex Bannister in the *Daily Mail*, wrote that 'Thomson's technical problems may be easier to overcome than his temperament.' The *Guardian*'s Eric Todd thought the now infamous gesture to the crowd was 'not the thing of cricket'.

The top two places in Group B were decided four days later. Pakistan fought out an extraordinary match with the West Indies, which was won by Murray and Roberts, the West Indians' last pair, who added 64 often frantic runs to win the match with two balls to spare, while Australia played out a somewhat bizarre match with the Sri Lankans at The Oval, succeeding eventually by 52 runs (5-328 to 4-276). The match at The Oval featured the first century by an Australian in limited-overs internationals – 101 by the NSW left-handed opener Alan Turner, and a first-wicket stand of 182 by Turner and McCosker, who scored 73. Turner had first played for the NSW Sheffield Shield team in 1968, but this was his first tour with a full Australian team. His backlift was more than straight, often disappearing behind his pads, and he struck many of his runs on the leg side. Something of a surprise choice for the tour, he established a place for himself in the top XI, and during the Cup was one of Australia's best batsmen. His controversial run out in the final would prove one of the key moments in that match. He retired from first-class cricket in the season after his omission from the Test side in 1977, having played for Australia in just six limited-overs internationals, five in the 1975 Prudential Cup, and one in 1975-76 in Australia.

Turner's first 50 against Sri Lanka came in the 21st over, his 100 before lunch, and he set the scene for later cameos by Greg Chappell (50) and Walters (59), who added 117 in 19 overs. The Sri Lankans had been humbled in the debut match (beaten 86 to 1-87 by the West Indies), and not even the parochial Sri Lankan demonstrators who invaded the pitch before the start of play expected the Australians to have any difficulties. But the pitch was placid, and there were long stages when the Australians, as their skipper later put it, 'couldn't get a wicket'. Lillee, who started with four slips and a gully, was strangely ineffective, and not long after tea, the total had reached 2-150, off 31 overs, with the two batsmen, Duleep Mendis and Sunil Wettimuny, well set.

Thomson then came back to bowl a frightening spell, which brought no wickets, but forced the two Sri Lankan batsmen from the field, retired hurt. First Mendis was struck a heavy blow to the chest, and then, in the same over, took a fast riser on his forehead. He was taken to hospital, where he was detained overnight, suffering from concussion. Later Mendis had this to say on facing Thomson: 'It was certainly an experience, although I don't remember too much about it. The ball came down very fast and I couldn't get out of the way. The next thing I knew I was being carried off.'

No sooner had Mendis left the field, when Wettimuny, who had been hit a number of times on the legs and body, was struck a painful blow on the right foot. After discussions with his captain Anura Tennekoon (the new batsman) he opted, perhaps reluctantly, to continue with a runner. Thomson bowled the yorker, Wettimuny again put his foot in the way, and stumbled away in total agony. Thomson won few friends by then throwing down the wicket as the batsman danced in pain. 'I'm going, boss, I'm going,' the batsman was reputed to have said, when asked by his captain as to how he was feeling. Wettimuny limped most of the way to the pavilion, but had to be carried for the final few metres by team-mates. X-rays later showed that the instep was not broken, but severely bruised.

Afterwards, there was much criticism made of Thomson's bowling and attitude, but the Australian manager, Mr Fred Bennett, put the debate right when he commented: 'What was he supposed to do – bowl underarm?'

The Sri Lankan run chase petered out in the final overs, but the Australians still had wounds to hide. Mallett had gone for 72 runs from his 12 wicketless overs, Walters 33 from six, Greg Chappell 25 from four. The captain, with 2-14 from four overs, had the best of the bowling figures, though a number of press reports were critical of his tactics, especially his field placements, and what they perceived as a disinterested approach by the Australian fieldsmen. The victory had Chappell's side safely in the semi-finals, although before that they faced the West Indies at The Oval. This, the first of so many limited-overs meetings between the two cricket nations, had been eagerly awaited, especially as it gave pundits the chance to compare the two teams' fast bowlers, Lillee and Thomson versus Andy Roberts and Keith Boyce. The game was sold out more than a week before, and authorities suggested that perhaps as many as 150,000 tickets could have been sold. The fact that both sides were already semi-final-bound diminished little of the public's anticipation, and tickets were being sold on the morning of the match for ten times their original value. As events turned out, the match itself was for much of the day one-sided, and ended as a comprehensive seven-wicket triumph for the West Indians, who blasted out their rivals for 192 (Edwards 58, Marsh 52), and then raced to victory in just 46 overs.

At the 24th over, Australia had been 5-61. Walters had been run out by Gordon Greenidge, who made a risky single suicidal by running from near the square-leg umpire to mid-wicket, to shatter the bowler's-end stumps with a shy of explosive accuracy. Turner, so dominant against the Sri Lankans, had been constantly beaten for pace by Roberts, and was struck an angry blow on the knee by the ball that had him leg before. The Chappell brothers were both caught behind off Boyce. The partnership between Edwards and Marsh took Australia to 160, but from there the innings folded, Roberts being much too quick for the tail.

Greenidge was out early when the West Indies batted, but from there the match was a carnival, as the two diminutive left-handers, Roy Fredericks and Alvin Kallicharran, thrashed the Australian bowling, and especially Lillee, who finished with 1-66 from 10 overs. In his eighth and ninth overs, Lillee went for 35 runs from just 10 deliveries (seven fours, one six, one single, one scoreless), most of them off bouncers, and all to Kallicharran. Off the 11th ball, Kallicharran was caught, skying

GARY GILMOUR: 'THINGS JUST CLICKED'

The inaugural World Cup gave birth not only to cricket's first genuine world crown but also gave impetus to the dazzling all-round talents of Gary Gilmour. The Australian squad was at the height of its powers in 1975 so at the beginning of the tour the prospects did not look particularly bright for the prodigiously talented Novocastrian. 'When you looked at the team that's how I went away – as a back-up,' said Gilmour. 'I had to do really well to get a berth, it was up to me to make them pick me.'

He did that, after being made 12th man early in the tournament, and by the semi-final against England his moment of truth had arrived. 'I'd done fairly well in the lead-up games, so I was pretty confident and when I saw the conditions – the weather and the wicket – on the day of the match I felt even better.'

Gilmour said that at the beginning of the tour the fast bowlers had been forced to toil away on wickets which were dry and dusty because of a lack of rain. But by the time the semi-final rolled around the sky was overcast and the wicket nice and green. Australian captain Ian Chappell then made the picture perfect for Gilmour by asking him to open the bowling.

'I didn't even expect to get the new ball,' he said. 'It was just one of those days. Things just clicked. Once the ball left my hand it started to swing around heaps and once that happens you get your tail up and nothing can go wrong. Wherever I put the ball, whatever I wanted it to do, it just happened. Everything landed on the spot.'

From Alan Turner's viewpoint, Gilmour, also his team-mate with NSW, never played better. 'He probably exhibited every ounce of talent he had in him that day,' said Turner. 'I stood back in awe.' Gilmour destroyed the Englishmen, leaving the Australians a paltry total to chase, but soon his team-mates were succumbing to the conditions that had assisted him earlier in the day. Before he knew it the young allrounder was padded up and heading towards the wicket where a laconic Doug Walters was waiting for him. Normally he would have been entitled to be nervous but his success with the ball had erased any doubts from his mind.

'I was probably in the right frame of mind to go out and bat,' he said. 'I was 23 and I'd bowled well, so I was confident.

a hook shot, but by then the damage was more than done, and in the final overs, as Rohan Kanhai and Viv Richards cruised to victory, the many West Indians in the crowd taunted the Australians, asking Chappell 'to bring on his fast bowlers'.

Ian Chappell was quoted after the tournament as suggesting that the Australians had not played as hard in this match as they might have. Even so, most critics considered the win, or more accurately, the ease and brutality of the win as a huge psychological blow. Chappell's captaincy was again criticised – Murray Hedgcock, the *Australian*'s London sporting correspondent, called it 'amateurish'. But Chappell and his team had little time for the critics, and even less for psychology. The loss

I always assumed if I went out and hit the ball nothing could go wrong, so I just went out and played my natural game. I had nothing to lose really. I don't know how long it took to get those runs – it went so quickly because Doug was up the other end getting his share of fours. In a situation like that it's always good to have an experienced guy there. What he told me I wouldn't have a clue – it would have been something bloody stupid but I always had confidence when I was batting with him.'

The sense of having been reprieved hung heavily in the dressing room afterwards according to Gilmour. 'I think we were all relieved to scrape home. Where we should have walked it in we struggled.' Gilmour said even though his own performance was very satisfying the knowledge that he had helped create history was more of a buzz. 'It was the first World Cup so knowing that I'd helped us get a trip to Lord's for the final was more satisfying than my own performance because we were going to be involved in a part of history.' Gilmour rated the final as 'probably one of the greatest games of one-day cricket ever played'. But that's another story.

England's newspapers, as well as those from home, seized on the new star of Australian cricket with relish but

Gilmour, as down-to-earth and pleasant a man as you'll ever meet, did not let the sudden rush of attention go to his head. 'I treated it as a bit of a joke,' he said. 'I played cricket mostly for the enjoyment. I found being tagged Gary Glitter quite funny.' Newspapers reported that Gilmour was besieged by English counties offering him contracts and, in fact, he almost signed with Sussex. But the lure of playing for Australia and an awareness of the huge workload he would be asked to shoulder at Sussex persuaded him to turn his back on the offer. 'I knew the way I'd performed I'd be in with a chance to play the West Indies and I wasn't going to sit out the series because I'd stolen a bit of a march on Max (Walker). If I'd played there I would have been bowling 30 overs a day and carrying Sussex on my back because John Snow was on the verge of retiring. At 23 I didn't see any enjoyment in it. If Snow had kept going it might have been different.'

Surprisingly Gilmour has only one souvenir of his stellar performance that day in 1975 – a video. And it took him some years to track that down. On the day of the semi-final he could secure neither a stump nor the ball with which he created so much havoc.

sent Australia back to Headingley, to face the top team from Group A – England, who had won their three matches easily, and with some style. Keith Fletcher and Dennis Amiss, humiliated by Lillee and Thomson in Australia, had both scored heavily, and the team's lowest score in three matches had been the 6-266 that had been much too good for New Zealand.

The English press and public saw the semi-final as a means of avenging the loss of the Ashes. John Arlott, in the *Guardian*, suggested the match might be 'the most abrasive, if not the most spectacular' of the competition. He doubted the Australians would not bowl short at the Englishmen, despite the assault of Fredericks and

Kallicharran at The Oval. 'Last week's mistake could be today's masterstroke,' he wrote. The Australians reluctantly jettisoned the off-spin of Mallett for the left-arm fast medium of Gilmour. That tactic was mirrored by England, who left out their spinner, Underwood. This thinking reflected the weather, and suspicions about the quality of the Headingley wicket. On an overcast day, and on the same pitch that had been used for the Australia-Pakistan match 10 days before, Gilmour and Lillee bowled the match's opening overs... and Gilmour proceeded to wreck the English innings. Chappell bowled him out, by which time England had been reduced to as little as 7-37, and the left-hander's bowling figures were remarkable: 12 overs; six maidens; 14 runs; six wickets.

Chappell had won the toss, which proved crucial, as the ball swung prodigiously from the opening ball. Lillee bowled a maiden, two runs crept from the next two overs, and then Amiss, shuffling across, was trapped by a late in-swinger. Barry Wood was bowled off his pads by the first ball of Gilmour's fourth over. Three Gilmour overs later Greig half-drove, half-lunged at a wide out-swinger, and was caught in dramatic fashion by Marsh, diving somewhere between slip and gully. Frank Hayes drove a unique loose ball bravely through mid-on, but then offered no more than a pad at a prodigious in-dipper which would have bowled him. Fletcher had laboured more than an hour for eight before he was lbw as well, going back to a good-length inswinger, and then Knott too was trapped by the swing, the final wicket of Gilmour's deadly spell. Walker joined in, having Chris Old caught at second slip, and then, at 51, Snow was caught by Marsh down the leg-side off Lillee. The English captain, Mike Denness, mounted something of a rearguard, and number 10, Geoff Arnold, found 18 streaky runs before the end, which came in the 37th over, with the total at 93.

All the memories of the Test series of '74-75 had come flooding back, though ironically the chief executioner was not Lillee, Thomson or even Walker. But the game was not over. John Snow had not been in Australia, and now he, with Old, reduced Australia, amid increasing joy, to 6-39. Turner and both Chappells were lbw, and McCosker, Edwards and Marsh bowled as Australia lost six wickets for 22, the final four for seven. But the local crowd's excitement tempered, and then sank, as Walters and Gilmour, with a mixture of skill, aggression and good fortune, saw Australia into the final. The next morning Gilmour's face dominated the British papers' back pages, and was even on the front page of the *Times*. In that paper's sports page, John Woodcock wrote: 'In all their history England and Australia can have played few more dramatic games of cricket than yesterday's semi-final.' Of Gilmour, Woodcock enthused: 'As Davidson used to do so devastatingly, and Sobers has done in his time, Gilmour left his victims with little idea which way the ball was going'. Ian Chappell told reporters: 'Beating England at their own game of one-day cricket after being told we couldn't play that game was a real thrill.'

The Australians had become used to being told they could not play the one-day game. Even the veteran cricket writer and former Australian Test batsman Jack Fingleton had commented, in the aftermath of the Australian loss to the West Indies at The Oval: 'The Australians may not think much of the one-day game, but if they are to earn the cash rewards they should pay it the compliment of learning how to play it properly.' As if responding to Fingleton, the Australian captain, after the semi-final win, remarked: 'I'm pretty sure we can take the West Indies. We learned a lot when they beat us last week.' The Australians had not liked or agreed with much of what had been written of them. Now they were just one victory from winning a competition (and a first prize of £4000) that few had thought they could win. Lord's had been sold out for the final since before the semi-finals. Expectations were high and the West Indies installed as 6-4 favourites, while authorities prayed for a continuation of the fabulous weather that had prevailed throughout the Cup. The final was to be played on June 21, the longest day on the northern hemisphere calendar. As things would turn out, the authorities would need every ray of sunlight to sustain the greatest limited-overs match ever played.

4

THE LONGEST NIGHT

Interest in the Prudential Cup grew quickly in Australia. Although the traditional broadcaster, ABC Radio, chose not to provide anything more than news reports, 40-minute highlights packages were shown on ABC-TV (of action from rounds one and then three) on consecutive Sunday nights. Gilmour's semi-final extravaganza was also the subject of a 40-minute highlights show. In the West Indies enthusiasts had made do with regular radio broadcasts. In the days before the final, countless thousands in the Caribbean made preparations to listen to a live broadcast, and on the Thursday before the final, it was announced that Australian listeners would have the same opportunity, as commercial radio indicated they would pick up the BBC's ball-by-ball coverage. Soon after the ABC announced it would televise the final live – by satellite and in colour. The highly popular Saturday-night current affairs show, *Four Corners*, was pushed back from its regular 8.30pm timeslot to 10pm, the lunch-break in the cricket, and for a brief period later in the evening, because the ABC could not book the satellite for the entire night, an alternative program was scheduled to fill the gap. But for most of the night of June 21-22, scores of Australian families, traditionalists and otherwise, would stay up to see if their cricket team could confirm they were indeed the champions of the world.

In London, Cup final day dawned bright and sunny. With all tickets sold, authorities anticipated a crowd upwards of 27,000, nearly three times the number of spectators who had attended the previous five-day Australia-West Indies Test match, at Port of Spain, Trinidad, in 1973. Many would come from the large West Indian community in London and beyond. Both sides announced unchanged line-ups, which almost certainly meant that all the overs would be delivered by bowlers paced between fast and medium. That being the case, some critics pondered whether even the longest day of the year would be enough to see the final through.

Ian Chappell won the toss and, as he had done at Headingley for the semi-final and the West Indies had done at The Oval, sent the opposition in. As play began, Lord's was a crazy mix of traditional serenity and boisterous colour, MCC members and the music of drums, whistles and bugles. In the opening over, Lillee was on line, and the West Indian openers, Fredericks and Greenidge, appropriately watch-

Patrick Eagar

West Indies captain Clive Lloyd hammers another boundary during his fantastic century in the 1975 World Cup final at Lord's. The keeper is Rod Marsh, the fieldsman at cover Alan Turner.

ful. But, at the other end, six runs came from a Gilmour over that included three no-balls, and the match was on its way. By the final ball of the third over the score had reached 12. Lillee tried a bouncer, and Fredericks was on it in a flash, swatting it high into the crowd at fine-leg, who reacted, for the first of countless times during the day, like soccer fans at Wembley. But they were celebrating a goal disallowed. Fredericks had slipped as he completed the shot, and kicked down his wicket. One of the bogeymen from The Oval was gone. The final could hardly have had a more dramatic start. Kallicharran started as he had finished the week before, cover-driving, then hooking Gilmour for four. Greenidge, at the other end, was circumspect, worth no more than the occasional single. Why, asked the whispers in the stands, was Greenidge so slow? In the 10th over, the West Indies were 27, of which Greenidge had but five, when Kallicharran, to great enthusiasm from the Australians, uncharacteristically jabbed at Gilmour and was caught behind. Rohan Kanhai had been drafted into the West Indian squad when Sir Garfield Sobers dropped out, injured, in the week before the tournament. At 39, after one of the truly great cricket careers, Kanhai was finished with Test matches; in fact this would be the last time he would play for the West Indies at any level. Appropriately, he came in to play a crucial innings. In the years ahead, when this famous game is discussed time and again, most discussion centres on Clive Lloyd's extraordinary performance. Kanhai, in at 2-27 with Fredericks and Kallicharran gone, would bat beyond Lloyd, to a point when a hefty innings total was all but assured.

By the time of Kallicharran's fall, Greenidge's innings was struggling beyond the point of repair. Lillee gave way to Thomson, who set about restoring his somewhat tarnished reputation. His first over cost a single, his second only two (including a no-ball), and, while Kanhai drove him away to the cover boundary in the third, his fourth was a maiden to Greenidge. After 18 overs, the total was only 50, of which Greenidge had just 13, from 80 minutes of intense torment. Then Thomson bowled a beauty, very quick, on line, perhaps moving away. Greenidge was half-back, then half-forward as the ball took the outside edge and barely carried to Marsh behind the stumps. Before the match, many observers had questioned the Caribbean temperament, suggesting that the biggest threat to a West Indies victory was the players themselves. 'An approach to the game which is almost always a delight can just occasionally be a disaster,' wrote one critic. Now Clive Lloyd, the West Indian captain, set about righting this misconception, in the most destructive of ways. A tall left-hander, renowned for his batting power and fantastic fielding, Lloyd had been his side's leader since 1974, when they had won a difficult series in India and drawn two Tests with Pakistan. Ian Chappell was quick to recognise that the opposition's innings was on the verge of crisis. He brought back his biggest trump, Lillee, replacing the rejuvenated Thomson (6-1-8-1), and Lloyd took 11 from the champion's first over, including a six into the crowd beyond square leg. While cans clattered and bugles sang out around the ground, in the pavilion the members, in their traditional, sober way, quietly wondered if the game's balance was about to change.

From the other end, Max Walker was his industrious self, bowling medium-pace cutters and in-dippers on a consistent line. Kanhai had dropped anchor, as Lloyd began to change the mood, while Lillee, despite Lloyd's affrontery, charged in, with two slips and a gully to encourage him. A crucial sequence came just before lunch. A half-hearted appeal from Lillee for a catch behind was turned down, and then the paceman went past Lloyd's outside edge with a slower ball. The next ball was short, and Lloyd aimed a mighty heave towards the grandstands, only for the ball to hit high up on the splice, and loop in a cruel parabola to short mid-wicket. Stationed there was Ross Edwards, recognised with Walters as the surest Australian out-fielder. But Lloyd's hefty swing had him on the back foot, and his desperate lunge forward and to his left was too hurried. The chance went down.

Four Corners went to air with the West Indies 3-91, after 28 overs. In the overs up to lunch Lloyd had been outscoring Kanhai five to one, and after the break that trend continued, as the veteran did no more than keep the bowlers out. For nearly 12 overs either side of lunch Kanhai's score remained unchanged, until the return of Walker, at the 35-over mark with the score 3-118. Before the Cup many had suggested that Walker would become the success story of the tour. 'He could be another Alec Bedser in English conditions,' was the judgement of the former Surrey batting champion, Ken Barrington. Now Lloyd took Walker's bowling apart, in a devastating, ruthless slaughter. Walker's seven overs in the morning had cost just 22 runs. Now his last five went for 49 as Lloyd raced to his century and the total neared 200. Of all the brutal blows perhaps one stood out, a savage pull off the front foot that sent a good-length ball into the screaming masses at square leg. Walker could do no more than bowl again and wonder. The crowd was playing out a calypso carnival, celebrating fours, sixes and even easy singles with fervent delight. The clattering of cans echoed around the ground, while back in Australia, another nervous beer was sought from the fridge, or perhaps a strong coffee to fight the night away. Chappell's field settings seemed irrelevant as Lloyd smashed away, though Kanhai was dropped twice, at 20 and 34, first by poor Edwards, dashing in from deep cover point, and then by Lillee diving forward from deep fine leg.

Lloyd's hundred came 10 overs after his 50. But soon after he was out, caught, amid some confusion, by the keeper, scooping up a faint edge down the leg side. Lloyd's demise had seemed so unlikely. The umpires conferred, as Marsh held the ball aloft, before sending the bemused captain on his way. In blasting 102 he had faced just 82 balls, and left the crease with the score on 199 in the 45th over. The trumpeters and flag bearers rose with the members as he strode to the pavilion. His innings had provided what seemed an impenetrable platform for a mountainous score. However, his dismissal set off a mini-collapse, as Kanhai drove around Gilmour, and Viv Richards was bowled by the left-armer as well. Gilmour's eventual five wickets (which would cost him 48 runs) would leave him the top wicket-taker for the tournament – in just two matches. But the Australians' respite was temporary, and Boyce, Bernard Julien and the little wicketkeeper, Deryck Murray, with a mixture of slogs, clean hits (including a hooked six by Murray off Lillee) and aberrations in the field, took the total to 291. That score looked, to all but the most pessimistic in the crowd and the most optimistic still awake in Australia, to be a winning one.

While Turner and McCosker were walking back onto Lord's to begin the Australian reply, clocks on the east coast of Australia were well past midnight. The early overs of the Australian innings did little to change expectations, as the batsmen struggled against Roberts' pace, which appeared to match the quickest of Thomson. At the other end, the left-handed Julien seemed almost pedestrian, and soon Boyce replaced him, and had McCosker caught, low down, by Kallicharran in the slip cordon. This brought in the Australian captain.

Ian Chappell had been out of form during the World Cup, but now he bustled in, all nervous energy, to lead from the front. In Turner he found a willing ally, and with Roberts seen off the pair fought Lloyd's policy of containment and forged a reply. Julien came back to be hooked and off-driven for boundaries by Chappell, and then Turner, after inside-edging Boyce past the off-stump and keeper for four, stepped into an off-drive that raced to the foot of the pavilion. After 20 overs the run-rate had reached four an over. Lloyd, the fifth West Indian bowler (and a very occasional and reluctant Test medium pacer), came to the crease. Chappell played his first ball quietly to forward short leg, and called for a run. Turner started, propped, and then sprinted, while Richards was on the single in a flash, and without breaking stride broke the keeper's-end stumps with a side-arm throw. Chappell later contended that Turner was safe, and video of the run out suggests it was a very near thing. But the umpire went with the West Indians. It was 2-81. Greg Chappell played out the rest of the over for no return, but from the next four overs the brothers reaped 26 runs. The younger Chappell looked in imperious form, and at tea (6pm Lord's time, 3am in Sydney, Melbourne and Brisbane, 1am in Perth), Australia were 2-107 from 25 overs. Much would depend on Roberts' second spell, and the Australians' ability to get at Lloyd. With Walters, Edwards, Marsh and Gilmour to come, the run-rate required (less than six per over) was demanding but very possible.

Many exhausted Australian schoolboys failed to survive the tea interval, and their fathers were carrying them to bed as the final session began. Lloyd had Roberts back for the resumption, and Ian Chappell flicked him fine for four, and then two. In less than seven overs, the partnership had yielded 32 runs. Both batsmen took singles from Lloyd, and then Greg Chappell was run out, again by Richards, in quite amazing fashion.

Ian Chappell had pushed Roberts square on the off-side, where neither Greenidge, running in from backward point, nor Richards, the cover-point, could quite reach the ball. As the ball trickled past Richards (who had been put off by Greenidge's charge at the ball), the batsmen, after some uncertainty, set off for the run. Richards, meanwhile, had recovered in a flash, pivoted, and thrown the keeper's stumps down, with Greg Chappell many metres from home. It was an astonishing piece of athleticism by the fieldsman. To criticise the batsmen for taking the single would be to suggest that such a fielding effort was even remotely possible.

Doug Walters came in at No. 5, as he had throughout the Cup. In the Tests that followed he would bat after Edwards, at No. 6. Walters' batting efforts on his previous trips to England had been mediocre (in 1968) and dismal (1972), but during this tournament, in both the semi-final and final, he went some way to restoring his reputation. Facing Roberts first-up, he forced him away for two, then four. Chappell joined in, forcing the dangerman straight for three. But at the other end, Lloyd was calmness personified, and his first seven overs cost just 15 runs, before Chappell finally drove him, twice in an over, for four.

Walters was the most popular cricketer in Australia, and those half-asleep in their bedrooms were revived as he mounted an assault on the fast-medium Vanburn Holder. Twice Holder was thrashed through the off-side field, and a vicious pull was painfully deflected by umpire Spencer at square leg, but still went for four. The umpire would spend the rest of the match with blood seeping from a leg wound. In all Walters took 23 brilliant runs from four Holder overs. After 38 overs, Australia stood at 3-162, Chappell 62, Walters 29. For the first time since not long after Lloyd's arrival in the middle all those hours ago, the match was evenly poised.

At 7.07pm, Lord's time, Lloyd began his 10th over, to Chappell. The first ball was clipped to almost vacant territory at wide mid-on, and Chappell, after some hesitation, set off for the run. Patrolling the mid-on/mid-wicket region was, inevitably, Richards. Walters, sensing the peril, was reluctant to go. But his partner was committed. Richards, instead of throwing to the keeper, where a run out was assured, threw to the bowler's end. The throw was precise, Lloyd had the bails off in a flash, and the Australian captain was gone by a metre. How a game can change. The next 11 balls brought eight runs, six of them to Walters, including a superb cover drive for four off Lloyd. But with Ian Chappell gone the West Indian drums

Patrick Eagar

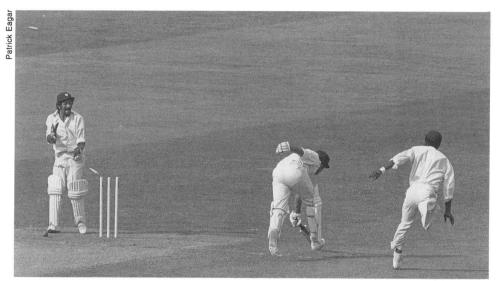

The crucial run out of Alan Turner in cricket's first World Cup final. Australia had reached 1-80 in reply to the West Indies 8-291 when Ian Chappell called Turner for a sharp single. The NSW opening batsman, who earlier in the tournament had scored Australia's first-ever century in one-day internationals (101 against Sri Lanka at The Oval), hesitated before dashing for the run, but was narrowly beaten by a rapid pick-up and throw by Viv Richards (right). The keeper is Deryck Murray.

beat louder, while the sun aimed for the horizon – in two hemispheres. Marsh, in ahead of Edwards, looked strangely out of touch. Then Walters, aiming for a much-needed attack of Lloyd's last two overs, missed an attempted swing to mid-wicket and was bowled, amid scenes of great jubilation, on and off the field.

Marsh and Edwards combined to add 25, of which the keeper scored only nine, before he was bowled, swinging at Boyce. The asking rate was now more than seven an over. Gilmour hit over the top, and then again, before skying a catch to Kanhai running in at square leg. Each wicket was wildly celebrated as the West Indian victory became more and more assured. In fact the police were struggling to keep the masses behind the boundary ropes. In the 53rd over, Edwards lobbed a weak catch to the covers, and four balls later Walker was run out, after setting off for an illogical run to short fine leg. Thomson's refusal to run from the bowler's end gave Walker just enough time to turn and see Holder shatter the stumps with an emphatic throw. Forty-nine balls remained, Australia 9-233, the crowd on the boundary edge ready for the final surge to their heroes. If the end was near nobody told the last Australian pair. Roberts had been kept for the final overs, and now he charged in at Thomson, who, as simple as you like, straight-drove him for four. The next ball was pushed to short cover, thoughts were of a single, but Roberts raced down the pitch, and turned and threw the bowler's-end stumps down. 'They're real eagle eyes today,' Richie Benaud told his TV audience around the world. 'I think if

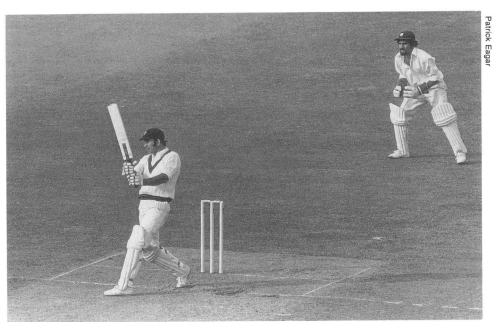

Patrick Eagar

Doug Walters slams a cover-drive during his innings of 35 in the World Cup final.

they threw left-handed, some of the right-handers, they'd still hit the stumps.'

Roberts charged in again, and Thomson drove the ball to the throng at square-leg – another four. Holder to Lillee, who drove with a flourish over the top to the vacant wide mid-on boundary. Then came a single, two more, then another single. In three overs the two fast bowlers added 20. The absurd had quickly become unlikely, perhaps even improbable. With four overs left the requirement was 36. The ball was edged towards fine leg, and Thomson, like an Olympic sprinter in pads', dived back for the second run, with the crowd edging towards the wicket, anticipating a run out. Holder bowled a no-ball, the last thing Lloyd needed, the batsmen turned one into two once more, and then Thomson was caught by Fredericks at cover, as jubilant fans invaded the field.

But something was wrong. People were all over the ground, but the batsmen had set off for a single. Fredericks shied at the bowler's end. Then came the realisation, ever gradual, that umpire Spencer had again called no-ball. The throw flew past the stumps, and was lost in the crowd, as Lillee and Thomson turned for the overthrow. The batsmen ran a second, then a third. The game became a parody. Lillee, it was later revealed, was urging his partner to keep running, until the game was won. Thomson was uncertain. 'One of the so-and-sos,' he exclaimed, 'might have the ball in his pocket!' Lillee was insistent, but the umpires called a halt, and signalled to the scorers that three runs had been scored. Or was it two? The crowd was reluctantly pushed back behind the rope, like a horse refusing to go into the barrier. Holder finally completed the over, and the scoreboard settled on 9-268. Twenty-four still needed, in 18 balls.

At 24 minutes to nine, Roberts bowled again. This was the over that all but sealed the game. The batsmen's assignment was dreadfully taxing, as Lloyd had eight on the fence, with little Fredericks a lonely figure at conventional cover. Twice the ball beat the desperate edge, and just three singles came, as Roberts produced six balls of stirring accuracy. Holder bowled the first ball of the 59th over to Lillee, who found a single wide of mid-on, then a leg-bye, then another single. But much more than a run a ball was required now. As if sensing this, Thomson swung, missed, and set off for a ridiculous bye to the keeper. Lillee sent him back, but Murray had already underarmed the ball back at the stumps. Thomson's late dive through a cloud of dust left him short – the fifth run out of the innings.

What followed was an amazing, very un-Lord's-like scene, as cricketers, with no time to celebrate victory or bemoan defeat, dashed for the pavilion, sidestepping supporters like halfbacks through the forwards. Thomson emerged without his bat, gloves and jumper. 'As a seasoned surfer,' wrote John Woodcock on the following Monday, 'this was the worst dumping he can have had.' The end had come at 8.42pm, in light that had just begun to fade. The longest day had done its job. Soon after the Prudential Cup and man-of-the-match award were presented to Lloyd, amid scenes of exuberant joy from the West Indian crowd. Their drums and music would play long into the night.

Meanwhile, on the east coast of Australia, as many weary sports fans finally went to bed, the time was fast approaching 6am.

5

FINDING THE RIGHT MIX

The critics' reaction to the World Cup final was laced with exuberance and passionate applause. Jack Fingleton called it 'a game never to be forgotten, in line with the Brisbane Tied Test', and described Lloyd's batting as 'one of the greatest innings in all cricket history'. The London *Daily Telegraph*'s editorial asked if there had ever been a more exciting cricket match. Sir Leonard Hutton, the legendary former England batsman and scorer of a 13-hour 364 in a timeless Test match in 1938, wondered 'if even the Ashes series will be something of an anti-climax'.

The theme was picked up in Australia. The Sydney *Daily Telegraph* thought 'there had never been a more thrilling, red-blooded game of cricket'. Eric Beecher, from 1973 to 1977 the editor of *Cricketer* magazine in Australia, called the match 'as fitting a finale as the most ambitious script-writer could have created'.

Why was the match *this* good? Lloyd's showpiece was a classic, but cricket had produced many such celebrated innings. The fast bowling had been sustained but not frightening. The winning margin – 17 runs – was tight, but not nail-biting; in fact for at least the last 15 overs a West Indies victory was at least extremely likely. Many a Test had brought a closer finish. Not an over of spin had been bowled, catches had been dropped, wickets thrown away. But the tension and the sense of occasion had been there throughout, and the many fabulous things that had been achieved all had been packaged between the first and last ball of a single day's play.

And the people, the colourful crazy crowd, the radio listeners in the Caribbean and millions in Britain and Australia watching on colour television, had been part of it all – as they had rarely been in the entire history of international cricket. Those who had paid their pounds or sacrificed their sleep had been given an awesome display of cricket – and a result! And as the winners carried the tag 'champions of the world', then the result, and the sport that preceded it, became something memorable and wonderfully special. This was how the viewers saw it. However, Ian Chappell, interviewed later, admitted his side didn't enjoy losing, but also that 'there wasn't quite the same feeling when we lost as there is in a Test match'. Nonetheless, he called the tournament an 'outstanding success', praising the 'great comradeship among the players, great cricket and the great financial benefits to cricketers and cricket authorities'. All agreed, and there was much debate as to where and when the next World Cup would be staged – whether another World Cup would be held was no longer an issue. Various observers pushed the claims of England, the West Indies, India and Pakistan, Australia and Australasia. Most thought England the choice venue, though some believed that the West Indies, as holders, had the right to defend the Cup at home. Clive Lloyd did not agree. He thought a Cup in the Caribbean would involve too much travelling, and added, 'I don't think we would make as much money as can be made here (in England) or in Australia'. Meanwhile in Australia, negotiations were stepped up for a financial bonanza – a West Indies tour of Australia in 1975-76. Originally an Australian team had been scheduled to travel to South Africa, but, for the same political considerations that had stopped the 1971-72 South African tour of Australia, that trip was no longer on the agenda.

For the last word on the first World Cup we turn to the former English captain Tony Lewis. In his book of the 1975 English cricket season, *A Summer of Cricket*, Lewis wrote: 'Before this season, in the minds of those who had to play it, international one-day cricket was always the necessary evil which followed the Test matches. Players always welcome the extra money and set out to see that justice is done on the field for the sponsor's sake. There are other motivations too. Old rivalries die hard. Dennis Lillee, for example, is not going to take a pounding from Tony Greig if he can help it, at any sport, Prudential or ping-pong. Large crowds help to build up the atmosphere. People enjoy the prospect of the best cricketers rushing at each other's throats in a duel to the instant death, and so in a way, full theatres draw more out of the protagonists themselves. Yet the actual contests before this competition have meant little more than that. There have been no tears, curses or recriminations in the losing dressing room. No-one has sat, head in hands, limp with disbelief as he would if a Test match had been lost. Prudential cricket results (before the World Cup) have mattered little. This one had to be different, if only because it was the very reason why eight countries found themselves in conflict at the same time. It was unique. It also came before the Tests; no side-show this time ... '

By the time the Australian players arrived back home in September, after retaining the Ashes one-nil, a six-Test tour of Australia by the West Indians in 1975-76 had been confirmed, and strong rumours were circulating that at least six of the senior players on the World Cup/Ashes tour had threatened the Australian Cricket Board with strike action if player payments were not substantially increased. The Board denied they had been intimidated by the players' stance (or even that the threat of a strike existed), but then decided to give their Test players almost double in 1975-76 what they had received the previous season. Announcing the decision, the new Chairman of the Board, Mr Bob Parish (who had succeeded Tim Caldwell in September, 1975), stated that: 'The Board has a resolution that it will pay the players the maximum that it can, after taking into account its responsibilities to the game ... '

The 'game' that Parish was referring to was all the grades of cricket that came under the Board's administrative wing, from the highly profitable Tests and the

DOUG WALTERS: ADAPTING TO CHANGE

Doug Walters is a modern-day legend in Australian cricket. Not only was he an extravagantly gifted batsman but he remained committed to a crowd-pleasing philosophy of attack that resulted in much suffering for the bowling fraternity. The Australian cricketing public drew him to their bosom and clasped him tightly there – not only during his playing career, but long into retirement. The fans loved him not just because of his remarkable talent with a cricket bat but because behind the flashing blade and keen eye was a bloke just like them – a man who smoked, enjoyed his beer and gambled. That devotion was expressed in the unofficial Doug Walters Stand on the SCG Hill – a tribute the SCG Trust made official when they built a stand on that corner of the Hill in front of the old scoreboard and named it after Walters.

Given Walters' flair it would be natural to assume that he embraced one-day cricket as the perfect arena for his talents. In fact the reverse is true. He admits that he approached the game with the same off-hand attitude that many of his team-mates exhibited but, more importantly, he said he was on a hiding to nothing batting in the middle order. 'I never particularly liked the game,' said Walters. 'I don't see how anyone can like the game batting No. 6. You've only got a couple of overs normally by the time you get there to do anything. It's either the fact that you've got to score 20 off the last two overs or 20 to win the game. I don't think I was ever overly successful in one-day cricket. I attacked it basically the same way as if it had been a Test match or any other game. I guess you're a victim of circumstances to a degree when you're batting in the middle order and if I had my time over again I think in one-day cricket I'd much prefer to open. They're the only ones who can really play their natural game.

'I did open in one game during World

unprofitable Sheffield Shield matches, right through to junior and schools cricket. Whenever it was suggested that the players were deserving a much greater percentage of the takings from the substantial Test match crowds, Board officials would point out that cricket at every level needed funding, and that Test matches were very much the primary source of those funds. Even with these parameters, the West Indies series proved a goldmine for the Board, and a brilliant success for the Australian team, who won the series five Tests to one. The first day of the third Test, at the MCG, drew more than 85,000 people, the highest of the many substantial crowds the Tests drew during the year. The Test series was heavily promoted, and covered live on both the Seven Network and the ABC. Less heavily pushed, but still covered by both networks, was the only limited-overs international scheduled for the summer, a match played at the Adelaide Oval on Saturday, December 20, and won comfortably by the home team, by five wickets with more than eight overs to spare.

The game took place a week after the caretaker Liberal Prime Minister, Malcolm

Series Cricket but unfortunately that wasn't overly successful. Andy Roberts knocked me over pretty early in the piece.'

The one part of limited-overs cricket that Walters confessed to having enjoyed was the fielding. The pressure of staying on the ball while coping with one-day cricket's helter-skelter pace in the field was a challenge he enjoyed. 'Fielding I quite enjoyed because there's always something happening in one-day cricket. The fielding side of it played a pretty important role. Every run you saved was one less that you had to get.'

Although Walters' game blossomed in the '60s he was still around when limited-overs cricket was in full swing during the Packer years, and for a short time after the reconciliation. He therefore had much greater exposure to the game than many of his contemporaries but still did not quite grasp the innovation as those who followed later like Dean Jones.

'It may have come a little late for me,' Walters said. 'One-day cricket should have suited my style of play but the general attitude we had to one-dayers probably reflected a bit on that ...'

Walters is another who believes the take-it-or-leave-it attitude of Australia's international one-day pioneers militated against their getting the most out of the new form of the game. It's obviously a bit hard to take things seriously if the rest of your team is not 100 per cent switched on.

'I think everyone took it as a bit of a joke in those days,' said Walters. 'It was a bit of hit and giggle. No-one took it that seriously. Under Ian Chappell in World Series Cricket we took it reasonably seriously but when Ian was captain he had an attitude that it wasn't the real game of cricket and he set normal fields and wasn't prepared to go ultra-defensive.'

A large part of Walters' summer is spent commentating on limited-overs matches for radio. He said that while he considered one-day cricket was never that much fun to play, he found it exciting to watch as he described the action on radio in recent times.

Fraser, had trounced Gough Whitlam, until November 11, 1975, the Labor PM, in the most controversial and bitter of all Australian federal elections – a result that began more than seven successive years of conservative government. The second Test, played in Perth, had been concluded four days earlier, the third was scheduled to begin on Boxing Day. No trophy was at stake for the one-day match, and although it was previewed in some papers as a 'grudge' match, or as a 'chance for revenge' after the Australians' loss at Lord's, it attracted no more than 14,168 people. *Cricketer* called the match a 'real anti-climax', and suggested the West Indians looked 'lethargic'.

Highlights of the match, which was played over 40 eight-ball overs, were Viv Richards' innings of 74, half-centuries by the Chappell brothers, and a clever bowling display by Max Walker, who took 4-19 from 6.6 overs. After having been so devastated by the West Indian captain at Lord's, Walker might have gained some satisfaction from his dismissal of Lloyd in Adelaide – caught Marsh for one – but, judging by the mood in which the game was played, it seemed he would much rather have wreaked his revenge during a Test match.

Following the Test series, the Board announced it was awarding the Australian players a bonus of $400 per Test for their performances during the West Indies tour. This was double the bonus handed out the previous season. This meant that a cricketer who played in all six Tests would receive about $9000 for his season's efforts. While the Australian players reacted favourably to this announcement, from the Caribbean came news of dissent from the West Indian players, who stated that they were 'not entirely satisfied' with the financial returns from the tour. The player payments problems faced by the Australian Board were rapidly spreading around the world.

Before the season ended came the most exciting one-day match played by first-class cricketers in Australia to that point. The Gillette Cup final, between Queensland and Western Australia at the 'Gabba (and televised live throughout Australia), went down to the final ball, bowled by Queensland's Jeff Thomson. The match attracted more than than 11,000 fans, who stayed to the very end to see WA No. 11, Mick Malone, caught by Greg Chappell at mid-off with four runs still needed for a tie. This was the first major cricket trophy Queensland had ever won. In scenes reminiscent of the Prudential Cup final, people lined the boundary edge during Thomson's last over, and more than once dashed onto the field, anticipating the final wicket. Police were needed to keep the local supporters in line.

It was a match of many highlights, perhaps the most memorable being a Thomson over late in the day in which the WA all-rounder Ian Brayshaw struck two huge sixes – one a hook to fine leg, the other a swing to the greyhound track beyond long-on – and then had to dive for cover to avoid a fast beamer. The game was a tense and serious battle, as was shown when, with the last WA pair at the wicket, Chappell (the bowler) tried to run out Wayne Clark, the non-striker, for leaving the crease too early. Chappell broke the stumps, but Clark was safe.

At the season's end, Greg Chappell suggested that the formation of a players' trade union was imminent. The London *Sunday Times* reported that Bob Hawke, the president of the Australian Council of Trade Unions and federal president of the Australian Labor Party, was privy to the cricketers' lobbying. Around the same time, the Victorian and South Australian Cricket associations announced record bonuses for their Shield cricketers. And it was announced in Pakistan that negotiations were at an advanced stage for that country to make a three-Test tour of Australia in 1976-77.

A potentially difficult situation was looming. There was no chance of Pakistan drawing the crowds and funds that the England and West Indies tours had accumulated. But the players were pushing for even more money than they had won from the 1975-76 season. The Australian Cricket Board was quickly finding itself in a financial dilemma not unlike that which the English officials had tried to resist years before, if inspired by different causes. In the 1960s it was the English county championship that needed supporting. In Australia in the mid-1970s it was cricket across the board, exacerbated by the growing demands of their star players. In England the answer had been limited-overs cricket, but Australian officials did not value the game and, supported by the traditionalists that shaped much of their thinking, resisted the temptation to program more one-day matches.

The players, too, did not see one-day cricket as the answer. In his 1976 autobiography, *Chappelli*, Ian Chappell wrote at some length on the future of Australian cricket. He argued that if the Board continued to program annual Test series and regular overseas tours then it was essential that the players become full-timers. 'The existing half-in, half-out situation is unsatisfactory if players continue to be required for so much international cricket,' he wrote. Two pages earlier, Chappell had written of one-day cricket: 'I think every first-class cricketer realises that one-day cricket is here to stay. It has become a vital part of the structure of cricket, and I am annoyed when I hear people suggesting that Australian cricketers don't approach one-day matches seriously ... ' Chappell went on to list what he thought were the game's good and bad points. It was popular among spectators, encouraged shot-making, and demanded high fielding standards. But it pushed the spin bowler out of the game, and discouraged all but the very top-order batsmen. Because of this, he concluded, Australian administrators needed to be 'cautious' in deciding how much one-day cricket was played. Chappell saw corporate sponsorship, not limited-overs cricket, as the way to fund the evolution towards full-time professionalism.

But what of the people, the men, women and children who paid their money at the gate, and who were, after all, the consumers whom the sponsors would be hoping to attract? What of those who had witnessed on television the 1975 World Cup final? And the 11,000 at the ground, and thousands on TV, who were thrilled by the finish of the 1975-76 Gillette Cup? These matches, rather than the solitary 1975-76 one-day international, were the barometer which should have been used to measure the popularity of limited-overs cricket. The trouble with that match in Adelaide, which had attracted so few people, was that there was nothing at stake. No trophy, no world title – the match was an exhibition, and dismissed by the public, cricket purists and otherwise, as no more than that.

The public's response to the World Cup and Gillette Cup finals indicated that there was a genuine public demand for limited-overs cricket in Australia, so long as the matches had meaning in their own right. But the cricket officials of 1976 seemed ignorant or dismissive of this fact.

What was needed, as Sir Donald Bradman had intimated back in 1971, was a balance between the two games. In 1971, Sir Donald had suggested this was so because of the section of the public who liked the one-day game. Five years on, this was still so. But by 1976, because of the pressing funding requirements the game faced, the need for that balance had suddenly become much more crucial. The future of the game depended on it.

ASHLEY MALLETT: COME BACK, SPINNER!

It has been difficult for spinners to break into the Australian one-day side. Until the success in 1993-94 of the leg-spinner Shane Warne and, to a lesser extent, Tim May (an off-spinner), the off-breaker Peter Taylor was perhaps the only genuine Australian spinner to have made a name for himself in one-day cricket. His handy batting and excellent fielding would have been factors in his selection. Too often the preference was for mediocre medium-pacers.

Even worldwide things had become progressively tougher for the slow bowling fraternity, although Pakistani leg-spinners Abdul Qadir and Mushtaq Ahmed carried the torch in sometimes spectacular fashion. Ashley Mallett is arguably the best off-spinner Australia has produced this century – certainly the best of the modern era. Because he cracked the Australian side before the advent of international limited-overs cricket Mallett is in the unique position of having experienced both the heady times when two spinners were a must and the dark times when the wicked medium-pacers ruled the planet.

'I've seen both sides of the coin really because when I started most sides usually played a couple of spinners,' said Mallett. 'Until about 1974 Australian attacks used a balance of pace and spin. Then Dennis Lillee and Jeff Thomson came along and they

were so successful spin was virtually shoved into a corner and forgotten. From that point on for me to survive in the Test side it was a matter of keeping it tight, resting the quicks, taking a few catches in gully and perhaps getting a few runs at the tail of the innings.

'I changed my whole attitude to bowling. To survive I just couldn't bowl the way I had before because I knew I wouldn't get enough overs. I became negative over a period, and I probably didn't realise it at the time.'

Neither did he realise that things could only get worse. Mallett must have sensed it, though, because he did not welcome the advent of international limited-over cricket with open arms.

'I played in the first one-day international and it was considered a bit of a joke,' he said. 'We played it as an ordinary sort of game, it was just that it was limited to 40 overs. We didn't play horses for courses. We just played normal cricket and had normal field placements.' While Mallett did not immediately appreciate the significance of one-day cricket he quickly became aware of the essential nature of the contest. 'Bowlers were limited and batsmen weren't,' he said. 'A bloke couldn't come out and kick the batsmen off the ground after he'd faced 60 balls but we were limited to bowling a limited number of legitimate deliveries. It was just another way of saying the batsman is king.'

Mallett had built his reputation as an

off-spinner, never the most highly regarded or glamorous of the bowling trades, because he was devoted to the notion that it was his job to get batsmen out – not just hold them at bay while the fast bowlers were resting. He said he tried to stay true to that philosophy in the embryonic stages of limited-overs cricket.

'In the early '70s I just bowled the same way as I would in any first-class game, trying to get people out and not worrying so much about bowling maiden overs. Obviously not trying to give runs away but bowling aggressively and tightly at the same time.' He now regrets that he made any attempt to conform. 'I did alter the way I bowled with one-day cricket in mind but in retrospect I probably shouldn't have,' he said. 'I used to be annoyed when the captain insisted we had to have men deep at mid-off and mid-on. That was always an easy single even if you bowled a good line and length. I'd rather a bloke hit me for four than singles because you're bowling to a different batsman every second ball. I felt I was more in control if I had the same blokes up the other end.

'With the field spread it was pretty difficult for me, to keep the runs down and get people out. I'd rather have the field up saving the single and having the batsmen take the chance of trying to go over the top rather than the defensive mode of having blokes on the fence. And I didn't like bowling without a slip – I thought that was diabolical. I hated it.'

That attitude eventually cost Mallett his place as far as one-day cricket was concerned – not that he was too worried about it. He was not prepared to alter his principles completely for the sake of pragmatism.

'For part of the 1979-80 season I was in the one-day squad but I wasn't picked for the first one-dayer,' said Mallett. 'Our captain Greg Chappell was bowling off breaks, little darts, pitching them outside leg stump and going down the leg side. I think he bowled a couple of maidens. I thought, "I'm glad I'm not playing. If I was asked to bowl that way I probably wouldn't so it's probably best that someone else can bowl that negative stuff". I just wouldn't have found it much fun. I certainly wouldn't have bowled that way if I was asked. Maybe Greg realised that and decided not to play me.

'I remember Tony Greig was doing that during World Series Cricket, bowling that negative stuff down the leg side. Thankfully nowadays the umpires call them wides.'

Mallett, who has been a tireless missionary for the cause of slow bowling in this country with his Spin Australia clinics, is thrilled that spinners have forced their way back into one-day cricket in the 1990s. 'I think it's great,' he said. 'A good spinner is as good as any other good bowler of any type. It's just conditioning and we're starting to break out of that now. People are starting to realise that if a bowler is good enough he can play any form of cricket.'

6

MONEY TALKS

By the start of the 1976-77 Australian season, the question of player payments was the burning issue in the game. Despite the Board's attempts to douse the fire, the country's best cricketers still believed they were, to put it bluntly, being ripped off. One comparison often used was that of the Australian wicket-keeper Rod Marsh with his brother Graham, one of the golf world's leading professionals, and the earner of US$117,774 from his sport in 1974 (not including appearance fees and endorsements). The players perceived the Board's treatment of them as arrogant and heavy-handed. Constantly in the back of their minds was a comment by the secretary of the Board, Mr Alan Barnes, in January 1975. Barnes had said: 'If they (the Australian Test players) don't like the conditions there are 500,000 other cricketers in Australia who would love to take their places.' And, the players assumed, 500,000 cricketers who would draw the million-dollar crowds they were attracting.

In late 1975, the Sydney-based entrepreneur Mr Kerry Packer had approached the Board seeking exclusive television rights to top-class cricket from after 1975-76 for his Channel Nine network. The Board took months to reply to Packer's initial approach, and then did no more than state that they were willing to negotiate. The only trouble was that the Board had, in that period, finalised a deal with the long-time TV broadcaster of cricket in Australia – the ABC. Packer was told he would be able to negotiate for no more than commercial screening rights. This, Packer assured them, was not good enough. He came back with an offer of half-a-million dollars per year for exclusive rights – a sum five times the amount which appeared on the ABC contract. But the Board, citing their considerable loyalty to the ABC, refused the offer. Packer then decided that he would have to set up his own international cricket contests, and televise them himself.

In September 1976, a Channel Nine executive wrote to the Melbourne Cricket Club asking for the use of the MCG for a series of matches in the summer of 1977-78. The Club sought more information, but none was forthcoming. Six weeks later, the ex-Australian player Bob Cowper wrote to his former team-mate Ian Chappell (who had retired from first-class cricket after the 1975-76 season), informing him of the aborted negotiations between Packer and the Board. Cowper suggested that the attitude of the Board Chairman, Mr Parish, had been 'unco-operative', and that, by ignoring Packer, the Board had rejected an opportunity to provide contracts for the leading players of 'between $20,000 and $30,000' for a 12-week period during the summer. Cowper admitted that the Board would have had to schedule its playing dates outside this 12-week period, but described the offer by Packer as 'an absolute bonanza' for the players, and commented that 'if the Board does not want to get involved with Packer at least they should match his offer'. Packer's concept involved not just 'Test' matches, but a series of limited-overs matches as well. These one-day games had, after all, proven perfect for television and would also draw the crowds through the gate – a salient point given the huge sums he was prepared to inject into the game.

At the same time as Packer was considering the rebuff from the Board, two other men were also wrestling with the idea of privately promoted cricket. In November 1976, John Cornell and Austin Robertson became involved in a debate with some NSW and West Australian Shield cricketers over the question of inadequate player payments. Cornell and Robertson were former sports journalists from the *Daily News* in Perth (Cornell had by 1976 become established as a television producer and business manager, but was best known as Paul Hogan's dopey sidekick, 'Strop', on Hogan's TV shows). They had recently begun managing the business affairs of a number of sportsmen, including Dennis Lillee, Rod Marsh, Graham Marsh and the tennis champion John Newcombe, and were astounded by what they saw as the miserable incomes of the country's best cricketers.

These two would-be promoters decided to play on the feelings of the players. But they needed a backer, and turned to Kerry Packer, whom Cornell had already met through his television dealings. Cornell, who was not fully aware of how far the aborted negotiations between Nine and the Board had gone, suggested to Packer that they organise a series of Tests and limited-overs matches 'along the lines of the Cavalier matches that had been played in England in the 1960s'. Packer took the concept a step further. He was, as Cornell later put it, 'galvanised' by the idea. 'Why not do the thing properly?' roared Packer. 'Why not get the world's best players to play the best Australians.' The Australian Test team was involved in a hectic schedule at this time. Their 1976-77 itinerary included six Tests (three against Pakistan in Australia, then two in New Zealand, and finally the 'Centenary' Test against England at the MCG) but no one-day matches save for two matches against invitational sides in New Zealand. At the end of the season was an Ashes tour, including five Tests and three limited-overs internationals. While the summer was played out, Cornell and Robertson, as principals of their company JP Sport Pty Ltd, set out to sign players for the Packer-backed series that would begin in Australia in 1977-78. First to sign in January 1977 was Dennis Lillee, for $35,000 a year.

Among the paragraphs in his contract was the following: 'The Promoter is engaged in the business of promoting organising and conducting professional sporting events and plans to promote organise and conduct a number of Series of professional Cricket Matches in Australia and elsewhere in the Seasons hereinafter defined ... A 'Season' would run from September 1 to March 30, and a 'Series' could extend up to 65 days ... devoted to six matches described as Test matches (and each being of up to five days duration) six Limited-Over Matches (each being of two-days duration) and an as yet undecided number of other matches all of which matches in a Series shall together constitute a Tour.'

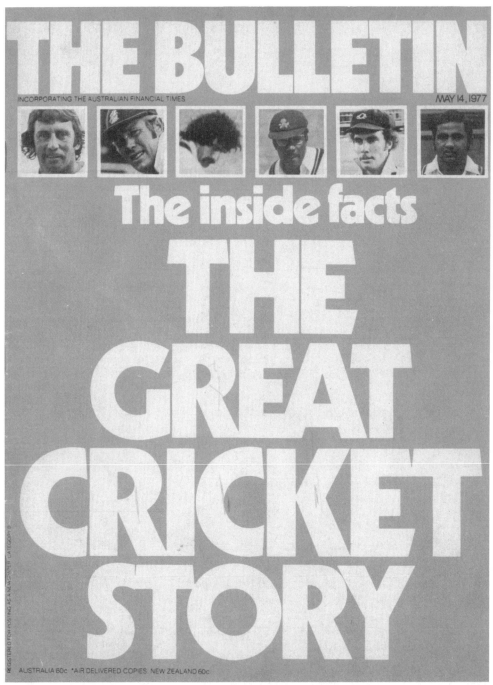

The front cover of the May 14, 1977, edition of the Bulletin, *announces the revolution that was to become World Series Cricket. The players featured on the cover are (left to right): Ian Chappell, Tony Greig, Dennis Lillee, Clive Lloyd, Greg Chappell and Mushtaq Mohammad.*

Until mid-winter 1977, plans existed for a series of matches between Australia, captained by Ian Chappell, and a World XI, captained by Tony Greig. Reflecting the depth of feeling against the Board, not one Australian player approached knocked back the opportunity to join Packer's series, or ruined the veil of secrecy that surrounded the negotiations. Packer later described the alacrity with which the players accepted his offer as 'frightening'. As contracts in Australia were being signed, the organisers found that players from overseas were also falling over each other to join. Only one player, the Englishmen Geoff Boycott, refused the offer. Largely because of the influence of the West Indian captain, Clive Lloyd, Packer eventually found he had enough West Indians to create a third team. Because of this, the amount of limited-overs 'international' matches scheduled for 1977-78 was increased to 12.

The story of cricket's great hijack broke on May 9, 1977, when reports in the *Age* and the Adelaide *Advertiser* revealed the basis of Packer's plans. Two days later, in one of Packer's own magazines, the *Bulletin*, full details were given to a stunned cricket community. Within two more days, Tony Greig had been fired as England's captain. The focus of media attention was in England, where the bulk of Packer's Australian players were in the early weeks of an Ashes tour. Negotiations and counter-negotiations continued throughout the tour, which inevitably took place in an acrimonious atmosphere, the cricket totally dominated by the war of words and eventual legal suits that resulted from Packer's coup. Weeks of argument and conjecture culminated on July 26, when the International Cricket Conference ruled that any player signed with Packer would not be able to play for their countries after October 1, 1977. A week later, in London, JP Sport (and three players, Greig, Snow and the South African Mike Procter) sought a High Court injunction against the ban. In Sydney during the same week, writs were issued against three Board officials claiming they had contravened the Trade Practices Act. In late July, Jeff Thomson had announced he would not honour his Packer contract. Rumours spread of a split in the Australian camp on tour, with non-Packer players (there were four) allegedly believing they were being discriminated against. And near the tour's welcome end, it was announced, to some sniggering from Packer's opponents, that three of the Packer one-day matches would be played under floodlights at VFL Park in Melbourne.

Amid this raging controversy, Australia, without the unavailable (because of injury) Lillee, lost the Ashes 3-0 with little more than a yelp, being totally domi-nated in the second, third and fourth Tests. Before this debacle, they lost the three-match Prudential Trophy limited-overs series as well, falling in the first two matches before gaining some solace from a fighting win at The Oval. Prior to the one-day series, the Australians decided that, since consistently dreadful weather had given them precious little match-play in the tour's opening weeks, they would use the Prudential Trophy games for match practice, and give everyone in the tour party at least one appearance. This despite the fact that the three matches had prizemoney at stake of £2000, winner-take-all. Only Greg Chappell, the captain, would play in all three matches, but his attitude to the series was revealed in an interview he gave before the first match. Explaining the omission of Thomson, who had been under an injury cloud, Chappell said: 'Thommo's injury is not serious; we just want him 100 per cent for the Test matches. And the Tests are the matches that matter.'

In the first match, at a sold-out Old Trafford, the Australians could do no better than 9-169 from their 55 overs after Chappell had won the toss. Five Australians – the young batting sensation David Hookes, fast-medium bowler Mick Malone, leg-spinner Kerry O'Keeffe, promising WA batsman Craig Serjeant and the firebrand fast man from NSW Len Pascoe – made their limited-overs international debuts in this match, as did the new English captain Mike Brearley. The game's beginnings set the mood for the tour, as the first two wickets, the NSW pair of Ian Davis and Rick McCosker, fell for just two runs. Chappell made 30, Serjeant 46 and Rod Marsh smashed 42 off just 31 balls before the end. But the total seemed inadequate, and eventually was, despite some ordinary English cricket in the afternoon.

The English top-scorer was the left-hander from Middlesex, Graham Barlow, with 42, but his run out with the total at 4-123 was inexplicable. Barlow, at the bowler's end, had been refused a second run and, his back turned, was strolling back towards his crease. The ball was returned to keeper Marsh, who, seeing Barlow far from awake, threw the stumps down. Two runs later Greig was run out as well, but Alan Knott and Chris Old saw England towards their eventual victory, by a somewhat precarious two wickets. Chappell later blamed his tactics for the loss – by using his front-line bowlers in the early exchanges he had left himself with few resources for the final overs. Marsh was named man of the match.

The second match, played two days later at Edgbaston, was an embarrassing debacle for Chappell's batsmen. But the batting disasters came only after one of the more extraordinary bowling results in one-day cricket. The Australian attack included Thomson, Walker and Malone, but they remained wicketless, while two 'part-timers', Chappell and Gary Cosier, took five wickets each, Chappell for 20 runs from 11 overs, Cosier for 18 from 8.5.

In the history of international one-day cricket to August 1994, this represents the only instance of two bowlers taking five wickets in the same innings. That it was done by Chappell, a medium-paced seamer good enough for no more than 47 wickets in 87 Test matches, and Cosier, a portly right-hander who bowled slow, usually harmless cutters from a brief, waddling approach, remains amazing. England, who at one stage had crashed to a ridiculous 7-90, were bowled out for 171, off 53.5 overs.

One dismissal stood out. In the Centenary Test in Melbourne 10 weeks before, England's Derek Randall had won the man-of-the-match award with a stirring 174 as England fought to save the game in the fourth innings. Randall was quickly perceived by many (including the Australians, who had been taken with his character in standing up to Lillee) as being not much short of the entire future of English batting, if not English cricket. In this second match he was in at 1-19, after Chappell had trapped Brearley lbw. The Australian captain, having noticed Randall's predilection for the front foot, decided to bowl a bouncer first ball, at which Randall aimed an ambitious swat, only to be caught behind. The Australians' joy was unrestrained, and from this point Randall's potential influence on the summer's cricket began to wane.

Patrick Eagar

Two shots from Greg Chappell's extraordinary hundred in the third Prudential Cup match in 1977, at the Oval, which was completed in eerie light during a driving rainstorm. The keeper (above) is Alan Knott; the other batsman (below) is Jeff Thomson.

Patrick Eagar

Australia's reply was pathetic – all out for 70 in just 25.2 overs. The batting was below strength – Walters, Hookes and McCosker did not play – but the strokes were puerile, the techniques inadequate, the surrender total. Chappell, with 19, top-scored, but the efforts of Davis (0), Serjeant (2), Cosier (3), Hughes (2) and Robinson (12) suggested the Australians would not be scoring enough runs during the summer to retain the Ashes.

At The Oval, England batted first and lost 10 wickets for 81, but only after their openers Amiss and Brearley began the day with a 161-run stand. Amiss' hundred was his fourth in limited-overs internationals. In reply McCosker fell early but Robinson, the Victorian wicketkeeper and Marsh's understudy on this tour, played his way into the Test side as an opening batsman, no less, with an innings of 70 runs and some bravado. He and Chappell added 148 for the second wicket. At the 23-over mark rain began to fall, which forced the players from the field and sent most of the crowd to the exits. But the players returned, after some prompting from officials and sponsors who wanted the game finished that evening if possible. The organisers knew that the following day was Jubilee Day, when all of London would be celebrating the 25th anniversary of Queen Elizabeth's reign, and that no TV cameras would be spared for the cricket.

So – despite poor light, and then falling rain which developed into a downpour, the umpires remained on the field as Chappell, with an unbeaten 125, saw Australia home. Afterwards, Chappell called the flooded conditions the worst he ever batted in, while the next day the cricket writers, in looking at the Australian team's prospects, were asking, to their eternal shame, 'whether the tide had turned?' However, that rain-soaked win was just about the only highlight of the tour. By season's end Chappell had announced his retirement from Test cricket, and the cricket world remained in turmoil. Nobody knew just where the split would lead the game.

The story of Packer's cricket hijack is one of the most written about in Australian sport. It is not the intention of this book to trace the story in detail, especially the lengthy and costly legal challenges, but it is important to stress the significance of Packer's cricket – which became known as 'World Series Cricket' – in terms of the development of limited-overs international cricket in Australia. Put in its most simple terms, WSC came about because of the failure of the Australian Cricket Board (and their administrative colleagues the world over) to recognise the depth of feeling in the ranks of their best players over the issue of inadequate player payments. From that feeling came a militancy that left the players totally receptive to a promoter with the dreams and money of Kerry Packer.

Packer had the funds, the circumstances, and the television facilities to bring off his giant coup. But he still had to sell his game to pay the rent. The source of much of that rent money would be limited-overs cricket.

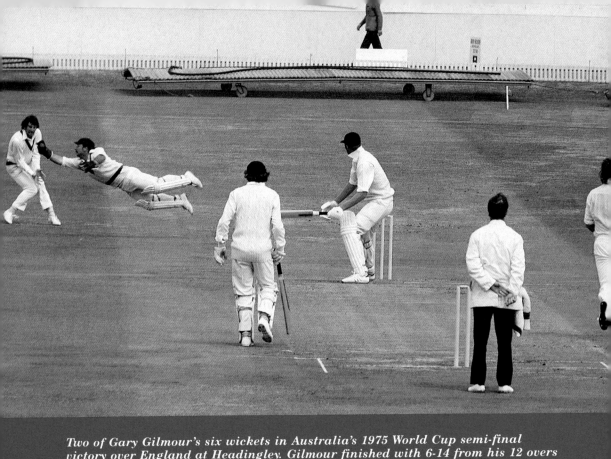

Two of Gary Gilmour's six wickets in Australia's 1975 World Cup semi-final
victory over England at Headingley. Gilmour finished with 6-14 from his 12 overs
as the home side crashed to 93 all out.
Above: Tony Greig, caught in spectacular fashion by Rod Marsh.
Below: Frank Hayes, palpably lbw.

Above: The crowd at Lord's after the exciting end to the 1975 World Cup final, won by the West Indies over Australia by 17 runs.

Below: The great Dennis Lillee, bowling against the West Indies during the first World Series Cricket match to feature coloured clothing, at the SCG in January 1979.

A spectacular sunset dominates the scene at VFL Park in Melbourne during a WSC day/night match in 1977-78.

Two shots from the World Series Cup of 1979-80, the first season in which one-day international cricket was a significant part of the official cricket calendar.
Above: Ian Chappell sweeps Viv Richards on his way to 63 not out against the West Indies at the SCG.
Below: England's Geoff Boycott attacks a Rodney Hogg short ball at the MCG.

One of Rod Marsh's three final-over sixes off the New Zealand medium-pacer Lance Cairns in the first World Series Cup match of 1980-81. Marsh took 26 runs from the over's first five balls, and was caught off the sixth.

The immensely popular Doug Walters plays a typical pull shot during his remarkable 'comeback' season in 1980-81.

World Series Cricket
The greatest international cricket event ever seen in Australia

On November 20 this year, the best of the world's professional cricketers arrive in Melbourne to join Australia's top players in a summer-long series of the most exciting professional cricket matches ever seen in Australia.

Continuous top class cricket

Almost from the moment they arrive, the cricketers will play continuous top class cricket right around Australia. As well as six five-day Super Tests, the series includes 15 one-day International Cup matches, several night matches and an additional schedule of matches played in the country areas.

Australia's team will be strengthened by the return of Lillee, Ross Edwards, Gary Gilmour, Ian Redpath and Ian Chappell (seen here).

The Super Test stars also will be involved in coaching aspiring schoolboy players in NSW.

The full details

This special four page supplement is your liftout guide to the World Series Cricket 1977-1978 summer schedule. Inside you'll find details of players, matches and advice on how to book tickets for the matches.

WORLD SERIES CRICKET

The Australian Women's Weekly, September 28, 1977.

As the first season of World Series Cricket approached, sports fans were hit with a flood of advertisements and promotions the like of which had not been previously seen in the world of cricket. The batsman wearing the baggy green cap in this promotion, the front page of a four-page lift-out in the September 28, 1977, edition of the Australian Women's Weekly, *is Ian Chappell, who had confirmed he was coming out of retirement to lead the WSC Australians.*

IAN CHAPPELL: LEADING THE WAY

It is no exaggeration to say that Ian Chappell is one of the most important figures in the development of international one-day cricket. First as a player and then as captain of the Australian team, Chappell was involved from the very beginning. He was there when the game took its first tentative step in Melbourne on January 5, 1971, and was at the heart of the explosion that was Kerry Packer's World Series Cricket.

Interestingly, Chappell admitted to harbouring the same flippant attitude to one-day cricket in its infancy as his team-mates. But it appears that he recognised the game's potential a lot more quickly than most.

'Really the whole time I played cricket under the Board it was an afterthought,' said Chappell. 'It was obviously a much more meaningful game in England. I guess after the 1975 World Cup final was when I thought to myself 'this game is here to stay' because of the fact that it was a full house and it was such a terrific game and a good atmosphere.

'Up to that point, much in the way players did in those days, we thought if they put it on we'll play in it. I hadn't thought much about whether it was here to stay. But the World Cup final was such a success, and then when I got back home so many people told me they stayed up until six o'clock in the morning watching it, and what a great game it was. Suddenly I thought "this was an occasion as well as a good cricket match".'

Chappell said his attitude towards one-day cricket changed over the years. In 1972, when the three-match one-day series was tacked on the end of the Ashes series in England, he had put so much into the Test series that he had nothing left mentally for the limited-overs fixtures. He told Dennis Lillee, who had run himself into the ground in the Oval Test, that he could bowl off a short run in the one-dayers. But the fiercely competitive Lillee quickly scotched that idea after English opener Dennis Amiss scored a hundred in game one. Chappell may not have been too concerned about the one-dayers but Lillee wasn't going to be flogged around the ground whatever the circumstances.

Before the match Chappell had called a meeting with manager Ray Steele and vice-captain Keith Stackpole and suggested that Stackpole should take over the captaincy for the one-dayers because he had exhausted himself mentally in the Test series. 'I said I didn't feel that fussed about the one-day games and suggested that it might be a good idea if we had Stacky captain the one-day games because it needed a fresh mind and I wasn't feeling that way. But Stacky piped up and said, "I don't take these things too seriously either so it might be just as well if you captained them". Certainly at that stage as far as I was concerned the one-day game was purely an afterthought.'

However casually he might have taken the game in those fledgling years Chappell was still sensitive to any criticism of Australia's approach. The sting of that criticism in the early '70s was that much sharper because much of it came from England. They had invented limited-overs cricket so many Englishmen, particularly members of the press, adopted a superior attitude towards Australian attempts to play it. It was a mistake. Chappell and his fellow Australians may not have cared one way or the other about limited-overs cricket, but they certainly didn't take kindly to being lectured by Englishmen. The Australians exacted their revenge by knocking England out of the inaugural World Cup.

'During the 1975 World Cup I got sick of the Pom journalists continually saying that we weren't very good at one-day cricket and the main reason was we didn't know how to play it because we played too aggressively,' said Chappell. 'It always gets up my nose when anyone suggests that cricket is played too aggressively, because I think that's the only way you should play it. It became more of a motivation, and certainly when we played England in the semi-final of the World Cup that was one match I really did want to win.'

Despite Chappell's greater awareness in the wake of that World Cup he still wasn't fully awake to the possibilities of one-day cricket. Neither was anyone else. As is so often the case the eye-opener for all concerned was money. 'It really wasn't until World Series Cricket came along that one-day cricket started to take on much more importance,' said Chappell. 'Obviously if you didn't win a lot of matches you didn't win a lot of prizemoney.'

World Series Cricket is generally credited with bringing the flower of one-day cricket to full bloom, but what is not widely known is that WSC's championing of limited-overs cricket came about almost by accident. Even World Series Cricket's principals needed to have their eyes opened by the public's enthusiasm.

'The first day-night game we played against the World XI (in December 1977) was not a qualifying match for the finals but from memory there was quite a good crowd,' said Chappell. 'I think it was probably about that stage that the decision was made, although judging by Kerry's attitude and probably to a lesser extent (John) Cornell's attitude they may well have had in their minds that one-day cricket would play an important part. Still, I think at first they thought that the Test matches would be well attended and when they weren't I think that obviously came as a bit of a shock to them and so they started looking at other avenues. The fact that quite a few people turned up for that first day-nighter, even though it was a bit of a trial game and then the fact that the final between Australia and the West Indies at the Showground brought in a full house ... I think it was about that stage that the powers that be decided that this was the way to go. And obviously getting back on the SCG and the success of that convinced them that this was the way to go. It was probably more so the second season of World Series Cricket that the importance of one-day cricket hit home – certainly to the Australian players.'

As captain of the Australian side and a member of the committee that formulated policy for World Series Cricket, Chappell was an integral part of the innovations that were churned out by the professional troupe in those two exciting seasons of rebellion. He

Continued over page

LEADING THE WAY

Continued from previous page

may have made his Test debut in 1964-65 and has always declared himself a traditionalist, but he welcomed WSC's ground-breaking innovations with open arms. He believes that had as much to do with his sporting background as his innate pragmatism.

'As far as I'm concerned I'm more of a traditionalist than people think but I'm also practical,' said Chappell. 'Day-night cricket to me was exciting. I enjoyed it. I couldn't see any minus marks. It made sense. I'd played night baseball in Adelaide so I was aware of the fact that for some reason playing under lights is more of a spectacle, offers the crowd a bit more.'

His baseball background also made Chappell more receptive to the 'sacrilege' of coloured clothing. That, though, was not the principal reason for Chappell's acceptance and encouragement of the push for bright new gear. 'I actually had something to do with the coloured clothing,' he said. 'Everyone jumps up and down about coloured clothing but they don't give it much thought because it was purely a logical exercise. The first game we played with a white ball I moved out of the slips and went into the backward point area. It became clear to me very quickly that it was bloody dangerous having white clothes and a white ball because someone cut the ball at me and obviously coming out of the guy's white clothing I didn't see it. I thought to myself "someone's going to get killed here – particularly a guy fielding in the gully where there's a fair chance that a cut shot is going to

continue to fly on the same line as the guy who hit it".

'The next day I said to Richie (Benaud) "we've got to do something about this or someone is going to get killed". Whether or not coloured clothing was already in the pipeline I don't know.' Chappell was also right behind any rule changes that encouraged positive play. 'I thought the circles were a great idea. In general it's fair to say that captains will tend towards the negative rather than the positive if left to their own devices. So anything which stopped them from getting into a negative gear was a good thing.'

Chappell is considered one of the best captains Australia has ever produced because of his straightforward commitment to attacking cricket and his no-nonsense approach to captaincy. That carried through to limited-overs cricket. 'I don't seem to recall that I spent any more time, probably if anything a little less time, on tactics for one-day cricket. You put in as much time as you had to. If you were playing well there wasn't too much to discuss but if you lost games and made mistakes you had to put a bit more time into working out why. In general it was about half an hour of a team meeting for a Test match and it was probably about the same for a one-day game. More so during World Series Cricket.'

He followed the same philosophy towards batting in one-day cricket. 'I tried to bat the same. I think it's much easier. In general I tried to approach it the same way... I was trying to score off every ball. So I didn't find it a great adjustment. 'One area I did struggle to come to grips with was batting in the middle order. I batted at six during World Series Cricket quite a bit because we had a lot of young players in the middle order, fellows like (David) Hookes and (Ian) Davis and (Martin) Kent. We had a tendency to get away and do quite well and then suddenly we'd lose a lot of wickets with guys trying to slog. So I figured that it was probably better to send them in earlier where they had a bit more time. Especially a guy like Hooksey who could thrash an attack and really take a game away from the opposition. Kent was the same. And then if I came in in the middle order and we were in a bit of trouble with my experience I could help the younger blokes along a little bit and try to stop them slogging.

'Even more so than the younger blokes (there was) our idiotic wicketkeeper who had a tremendous ability to score runs, but because one-day cricket was fairly new at that stage Rodney thought it was designed for him to have a slog,' said Chappell. 'He thought this was the perfect game of cricket because it meant he had an open licence to slog. So he needed a bit of nursing as well. You had to say "you don't have to hit every ball for six Rodney".'

While the move down the order may have benefited the team it was a two-edged sword for Chappell personally. 'I felt it helped us a bit in the middle order but what used to annoy me was coming in with a couple of overs to go. I remember getting out once after coming in with just a couple of overs to go and trying to slog one and hitting it straight up in the air. I remember walking off saying to myself "if I wanted to play bloody baseball I'd go and play baseball". That was the one thing I didn't ever come to grips with – giving my wicket away. I didn't like giving my wicket away any time.

You did it through stupidity in the longer game and that used to annoy the hell out of me but at least on those occasions it was my own fault. But on the occasions when I felt I was forced into it by the nature of the game (one-day cricket) then that really used to get up my nose.'

Chappell also spent some time at the top of the order – again for the sake of the team. While he didn't mind opening the innings it was not something he particularly wanted to do. 'I was a born No. 3 as far as I was concerned. That's where I wanted to bat from the time I can remember. My preference was always to bat at three but there were times I wasn't happy with our scoring rate early on. A couple of times I thought if I want to set a higher target I've got to go in and show the way I want it done. The other thing I had to consider was (brother) Greg's situation. I've always believed you need to have your best strokemakers, the guys who are most likely to make a hundred, in the top three. So my feelings were in a lot of cases that if I opened then I could bat Greg at three rather than having him at four and running into a situation where he was going in with only 20 or 25 overs to go. I always got the feeling that Greg would feel a bit frustrated in that situation because he liked to build up his innings at his own pace.'

Chappell said the one-day innings he considered his best came about in 1979-80 – the first season of the reconciliation. He had been upset that the selectors had overlooked him for the Test matches, feeling even at 36 that

Continued over page

LEADING THE WAY

Continued from previous page

he was a much better batsman than some that were picked, but he scored the necessary runs in Sheffield Shield cricket and was given an opportunity – in the limited-overs matches.

'I was selected in the one-day side which both surprised me and annoyed the hell out of me, because I obviously considered myself at that stage to be more of a Test match player than a one-day player. We were playing the West Indies at the SCG and we got in trouble early. It was 4-44 when I came in and Greg and I put on 50. Then Rod Marsh and I put on 66 and Dennis Lillee and I put on a few at the end. I was 63 not out and we got to 176. I felt at least what I'd done with that innings was get us to a total where we had a bit of a chance because we had Lillee, Len Pascoe, Rodney Hogg, Geoff Dymock and Greg. As it turned out we bowled them out for 169 and I caught Desmond Haynes for a duck in the first over.'

Chappell was in no doubt when asked who was the player he considered best suited and most in tune with the one-day game. 'Viv Richards. Absolutely no doubt,' he said. 'I guess Viv had a bit of an advantage because he didn't have to change his natural game too much – if at all. He was a very attacking batsman no matter what brand of cricket he played.' He was just as swift when asked to pick the best Australian. 'A guy like Greg. He didn't have to make too much of a change. He always scored quickly because he had a lot of shots and hit balls into the gaps. He was a brilliant fielder in whatever position he fielded. A lot of people tend to forget how good an outfielder Greg was but he was probably the best outfielder I've had anything to do with in an Australian team. Viv is the only bloke I would think of putting ahead of him internationally and I'm not even sure I'd do that when it came to outfielding because Greg was so good.

'One-day cricket probably gave him more of an opportunity as a bowler than Test cricket even though under certain conditions he was quite a useful medium pacer in Test matches. Near the end of his career he had the ability to be a very economical one-day bowler and he also had the ability to pick up five wickets.'

7

WORLD SERIES CRICKET

By October of 1977, the world of cricket was a world divided. The Packer camp was condemned as a body with no objective other than television ratings and the bastardisation of the game. 'Mr Packer, I feel, does not understand the chemistry of Australia's cricket lovers,' wrote one such lover in the *Sydney Morning Herald*. 'It seems that Mr Packer's advisers cannot make him understand that those who fill Australian cricket grounds comprise about 90 per cent of knowledgeable cricket watchers and about 10 per cent of the much-publicised yobbos. It is only the latter who will be interested in the Packer circuit.' World Series Cricket officials were consistently claiming they would not alter the fabric of the sport, but others were far from convinced.

'World series organisers say they will not tamper with the fundamental framework of the game,' wrote Eric Beecher in *Cricketer*. 'But the spectre of a company (JP Sport) led by two of Australia's best-known television comedians (John Cornell and Paul Hogan) is hardly comforting to those who fear cricket is about to be carelessly thrown onto the public operating table.'

By September, Packer had revealed some of the innovations that would stun the cricket world. They included a myriad of TV cameras to get every angle, cricket under lights, coloured clothing, microphones on the field, and, most unbelievable of all, pitches developed in glasshouses and then transferred to the middle of makeshift cricket stadiums. This concept, developed by the former 'Gabba curator, John Maley, came about because of Packer's inability to get access to the traditional cricket grounds, which chose to ban him in favour of their long-term clients. Packer was forced to go to other venues – VFL Park in Melbourne, the Sydney Showground, Football Park in Adelaide and Gloucester Park in Perth – which did not have a traditional cricket square. Hence the need for the 'glasshouse' pitches, which Maley would later describe as being 'as good as any wickets in Australia'.

By the time of the first official WSC match, 55 players had been signed. They were: Australia: Ian Chappell (captain), Ray Bright, Greg Chappell, Trevor Chappell, Ian Davis, Ross Edwards, Gary Gilmour, David Hookes, Martin Kent, Bruce Laird, Robbie Langer, Dennis Lillee, Ashley Mallett, Mick Malone, Rod Marsh, Rick McCosker, Graham McKenzie, Kerry O'Keeffe, Len Pascoe, Wayne Prior, Ian

Redpath, Richie Robinson, Max Walker, Doug Walters. (Two more players, Graeme Watson and Dennis Yagmich, would be signed during the season.)

Rest Of the World: Tony Greig (England, captain), Dennis Amiss (England), Asif Iqbal (Pakistan), Eddie Barlow (South Africa), Denys Hobson (South Africa), Imran Khan (Pakistan), Alan Knott (England), Majid Khan (Pakistan), Mustaq Mohammad (Pakistan), Graeme Pollock (South Africa), Mike Procter (South Africa), Barry Richards (South Africa), John Snow (England), Derek Underwood (England), Bob Woolmer (England), Zaheer Abbas (Pakistan). (Hobson and Pollock would not play in any matches.)

West Indies: Clive Lloyd (captain), Jim Allen, Wayne Daniel, Roy Fredericks, Joel Garner, Gordon Greenidge, Michael Holding, David Holford, Bernard Julien, Collis King, Deryck Murray, Albert Padmore, Viv Richards, Andy Roberts, Lawrence Rowe. (The West Indian players were also eligible for selection for the World side for their SuperTests against Australia.)

World Series Cricket had already had a major impact in England, where the Cornhill Insurance company had announced it was plunging $1.6 million into English cricket, a move that led to a massive increase in the payments being made to England's Test cricketers. Among the players who had knocked back WSC offers since that announcement were Bob Willis and Derek Randall. In Australia, the Board announced the minimum payment to its players in the five-Test home series against India in 1977-78 would be $1852 per Test, an increase of around 50 per cent on the Pakistan Tests of 1976-77. In both England and Australia, officials, to some derision, explained that these pay increases were not a response to Packer, but a sign of the times, and increasing sponsorship. Soon after the ACB produced a shock of its own, announcing that the 41-year-old Bob Simpson, who had last played Test cricket in early 1968, would be returning to captain the 'official' Australian side.

Simpson's return was a popular, and for a time, successful one, as he more than matched the Indian spin attack. The Australia-India Test series developed into a beauty, Australia winning the first two Tests, in Brisbane and Perth, by narrow margins (16 runs, then two wickets) before India fought back with resounding victories in Melbourne and Sydney. In the fifth Test, in Adelaide, Australia set the Indians 493 to win the series, a task they almost managed, finishing just 48 runs short. Simpson scored two centuries, and over 500 runs, in the series, while Thomson was always quick and a young NSW batsman, Peter Toohey, aggressively effective. The player of the series, however, was the Indians' renowned opener, Sunil Gavaskar, who scored a hundred in each of the first three Tests, while their celebrated spin attack of Bedi, Prasanna, Chandrasekhar and Venkataraghavan offered a marvellous and challenging contrast to cricket's plethora of pace attacks. While this absorbing series was being played out, World Series Cricket struggled, amid much conjecture, criticism and continued legal wrangling.

The weeks leading up to WSC's first 'Supertest' on December 2, 1977, were a mixture of the encouraging and not-so-encouraging for Mr Packer. In late October, the *Sydney Morning Herald* and Melbourne *Age* published the results of an opinion poll which claimed that 55 per cent of Australians believed the Packer series would improve cricket for the public. Twenty-nine per cent felt cricket would be damaged,

The players who made up the original WSC Australian squad. Back row (left to right): Dennis Lillee, Martin Kent, Ray Bright, David Hookes, Richie Robinson, Max Walker, Ian Redpath, Kerry O'Keeffe. Middle: Rick McCosker, Graham McKenzie, Wayne Prior, Ashley Mallett, Len Pascoe, Mick Malone, Ian Davis, Gary Gilmour. Front row: Trevor Chappell, Doug Walters, Greg Chappell, Ian Chappell, Rod Marsh, Bruce Laird, Ross Edwards. Absent: Rob Langer.

while 16 per cent did not know. Seventy-eight per cent felt the Packer players should have been eligible to play for their countries. WSC's agenda for the season showed six Supertests (three Australia v the West Indies matches, three Australia v the World), 12 one-day 'internationals' (nine round-robin matches, plus a three-match 'finals' series) for the 'International Cup', and a 'Country Cup' circuit, featuring two- and three-day matches in towns and cities such as Lismore, Geelong and Hobart. This country cavalcade would be a part of both years of WSC, featuring games between the 'Cavaliers' (a collection of players dropped from the major-cities circuit) and whichever of the three WSC teams was available. Each International Cup match offered a $1500 prize – winner take all. The only one-day match on the Indian tour of Australia was a game in Launceston, against Tasmania.

On November 6, at Kalgoorlie in country Western Australia, a WSC 'Invitation XI' defeated a local team in a 35-over match. Marsh and Lillee were the stars. Two days later, WSC authorities announced a stunning rule change for its limited-overs matches. Reviving a concept that had been used in the South African version of the Gillette Cup in the early 1970s, measures were introduced that would limit the ability of captains to be too defensive. In South Africa, it had been compulsory to have at least two fieldsmen in the slip cordon and illegal to have more than a fine leg and third man further than 30 metres from the bat for the first eight eight-ball overs of the innings. For the remaining overs no more than five fielders were allowed more than 30 metres from the bat. The breaking of these rules meant the umpire would call no-ball. No-balls and wides in South African Gillette Cup matches cost four runs. Tony Greig, who had played under these rules, put them forward and they were accepted, in modified form, for the 1977-78 WSC season.

It was decided two circles, 60 metres in diameter, would be drawn on the field,

IAN CHAPPELL: REBEL WITH A CAUSE

When World Series Cricket split Australian cricket asunder in 1977, the players who threw their lot in with the imperious Mr Packer were branded as traitors. They were quickly tagged rebels by those in the establishment camp and their captain Ian Chappell was vilified as the biggest rebel of them all. Chappell already had a track record of bucking the system so he was an obvious target. Chappell, for his part, was more than ready for a stoush yet he feels the portrait painted of him at the time was wrong. It is an image, he said, that a lot of people have had trouble shaking.

'I didn't feel like an anti-establishment rebel,' said Chappell. 'I've had people say to me "you seem like quite a reasonable person" and I say "well, what did you expect?" and they'd reply "I've just been told that you're anti-establishment and bolshie".

'A lot of times when my name is written it's the 'controversial' Ian Chappell. That's garbage. Is stating your opinion or seeing something that is wrong and trying to point it out controversial? If it is then I'm controversial but that's not the way I see it. I just see there's a problem and I want to fix it. That's the way I worked within the team as captain, that's the way I worked on my own game – if I had a problem I went and tried to fix it. And I expected the same sort of response from the administrators.'

If Chappell went about his off-field responsibilities with the passion and demeanour of a union organiser it was because he felt the same way. He demanded absolute loyalty and devo-tion to the team cause from his men and felt compelled to offer the same in return. 'I felt that if I was asking for 100 per cent from my players on the field, which I obviously was, then they had every right to expect 100 per cent support from me off the field. If there was any fight between the Board and the players they had every right to expect that I would go and fight for them.

'I didn't back away from that, and who else was going to stand up for them if there was a problem? There were a number of problems in those days. Whether or not I went about it the right way is obviously open for discussion, and I'd probably be the first to say it perhaps wasn't the smartest way to go about it, but I'm the sort of person who's pretty open. If something is bothering me I'm going to tell you it's bothering me. I'm not one for playing little games. I wanted it fixed then and there. I didn't look upon the Board very favourably. It was Bob Parish or Ray Steele who said "we've been stabbed in the back". That's rubbish. They weren't stabbed in the back because I was approached on two or three occasions about playing in a professional troupe – both in Australia and overseas. On each occasion I said to the guys who were trying to set up the operation "what you need to do is do it in conjunction with the boards because they've got the grounds and without them you're not going to get the thing off the ground". To my knowledge those people on each occasion went to the Board or boards involved and were snubbed.

'The interesting thing is I continued to have a good relationship with those Board members who I considered to have a bit of sense. They didn't necessarily always agree with me, but I had their respect and they understood that deep down I had a love of the game of cricket. I had the best interests not only of cricket but also, obviously, of my players at heart, and I think they appreciated that.'

The media by and large portrayed the confrontation as an 'us versus them' war. Depending upon the individual correspondent's point of view it was either the aggrieved players bravely seeking justice from the dictatorial Australian Cricket Board, or the ungrateful and greedy players holding the selfless guardians of the game to ransom. But the reality, certainly as far as the players were concerned, was a lot more complex.

'There was a mood of excitement,' said Chappell. 'Obviously there was the fact that you're in on something that's just starting and something that is markedly different to anything else that had happened. Obviously there were fears, not so much in my case because I'd retired and it didn't much matter to me about playing international cricket anymore, but there were certain fears among the younger blokes. I felt some worries that young blokes like Hookes and Bright might be kept out of the game for the rest of their lives. But I always felt that there would be an opportunity for them to get back into international cricket again.

'There were very much mixed emotions but there was also a satisfaction that we'd all had the guts – especially the really young players. I was delighted to hear of someone talking to Craig McDermott recently. Craig said something along the lines of "every day I play cricket I think to myself I'm better off because of those guys who played World Series Cricket". He's the first guy who didn't play WSC that I've heard express that opinion and I'm glad he thinks like that because it took a lot of guts for many of those guys to put their hands up and do it. It's nice to know that those sort of efforts are appreciated by present-day players. In among those emotions there was also a feeling that there was an opportunity to provide for financial security.'

Those broiling emotions coalesced into a fierce determination to make the venture a success when WSC became a reality. 'Once we realised that it was going to go ahead,' Chappell reflected, 'once we knew we were actually going to play and it was going to go ahead, then came the feeling that "right, we've made a decision, now let's play the best possible cricket we can".

'Anybody I've spoken to – and that includes my brother Greg, Viv Richards, Dennis Lillee, Clive Lloyd – they say it's far and away the hardest cricket they ever played,' Chappell went on. 'And one reason for that is you didn't go back to Shield cricket to get back into form. If you were out of form your next game was against Garner and Roberts and Holding.'

There was also no doubt in the WSC Australians' minds about their status. 'There may have been some people out there who didn't think we were the Australian team, but there wasn't any doubt in our minds,' Chappell said. 'We felt we were the best Australian team and we would have been quite happy to play against the actual Australian team any time, any day of the week, anywhere. There's that pride of performing and it didn't matter particularly that we weren't in the baggy green cap.'

centred on the stumps. For the first 10 eight-ball overs, seven fieldsmen, excluding the bowler and wicketkeeper, had to be inside the circle when the ball was delivered. Two of these had to be in 'catching' positions. For the final 30 overs, five men were allowed outside. The penalty for breaking this rule was one run, the umpire calling no-ball. Such an innovation was welcomed by some, and derided by others, such as the Melbourne *Herald* editor, Terry Vine, who suggested the new rule had 'all the hallmarks of professional wrestling'.

On November 16, just under 5000 people watched a WSC practice match on a Melbourne suburban park. Two days later, a ban on Packer's cricketers performing on the SCG was confirmed in Sydney's Equity court. The prospect of the WSC band playing at Sydney's finest cricket ground had been the subject of much debate and legal manoeuvring. First, on July 25, the SCG Trust had stated that the ground was not available. Two days later, the NSW Labor Government sacked the Trust, apparently because of the WSC decision (although the NSW Minister for Sport, Mr Ken Booth, had foreshadowed major changes to the Trust in late 1976, not long after his party's return to power after almost a decade in opposition). On September 30, the new Trust announced it had accepted a 'considerable financial offer' from WSC for the use of the ground on 13 days (that did not clash with ACB fixtures) in 1977-78, but that decision was challenged in the Equity Court by the NSW Cricket Association, which led to the November 18 ruling. On November 30, the conservative opposition used its majority in the NSW Upper House to adjourn debate until February on legislation that would have overturned the Equity Court ruling. This action, in many ways a pyrrhic victory for the NSWCA, meant that World Series Cricket would not be played on the SCG until November 28, 1978.

The loss of the SCG was seen as a setback but not a disaster for Packer. With the glasshouse pitch experiment shaping as a winner, the grounds he had were at least adequate, and he had the game's best players. As Phil Tresidder wrote in *Australian Cricket*: 'Jack Nicklaus versus Tom Watson would be top value on a public golf course, just as it was at Turnberry.' Earlier in the year, Nicklaus and Watson had played out one of golf's all-time classic showdowns in the British Open at Scotland's famous Turnberry course.

Three days before the politicking over the SCG concluded in the NSW Upper House, a four-day 'practice' match at VFL Park, between an Australia XI and a World side, had ended. The match attracted just over 10,000 spectators in total, a tonic for Board supporters, but dismissed as irrelevant by WSC spokesmen who pointed out the game had not been promoted or televised. However, the first Supertest, between the WSC Australians and the WSC West Indians, which began five days later, certainly was, to the point of saturation, and was almost as poorly attended, drawing just less than 14,000 to the three days play. One critic estimated the crowd when the first ball was bowled as being as little as 400 ... in a stadium that could comfortably house more than 70,000.

One player missing from that Supertest was Ian Redpath. At best an occasional bowler, he had had the experience of dismissing Clive Lloyd in a warm-up one-day match at Geelong on November 30. But his extravagant celebrations were cut painfully short when his Achilles tendon snapped, putting him out for the season.

David Hookes, batting at the Sydney Showground in 1977-78 in one of the first helmets to appear on an Australian cricket field. Earlier in the season, Hookes' jaw had been shattered by an Andy Roberts bouncer in a Supertest against the West Indies at the same ground.

The outstanding West Australian swing bowler, Mick Malone, who, unluckily, is best remembered as the bowler West Indies No. 11 Wayne Daniel slogged for six to end a thrilling one-day match under lights at VFL Park during WSC's first season.

Even so, Packer announced he would be paid in full.

The poor crowds reflected a public perception that the contests were no more than exhibitions. The competitiveness of the players was not being appreciated or recognised by the spectators. Maley's glasshouse pitches may have developed VFL Park into a cricketing Turnberry, and the players may have been the Nicklauses and Watsons of their sport, but the public believed there was no Open Championship at stake. Just healthy contracts to fulfil.

On the following weekend two limited-overs matches – Australia v the World and Australia v West Indies – were played at Football Park in Adelaide, in front of terribly sparse crowds (1690 on the Saturday, 2315 on the Sunday). The Adelaide venue quickly became a proverbial wasteland for WSC, a fact organisers blamed on the inherent conservatism of the city. Despite a better turnout for a West Indies-World encounter on December 28, the one-day finals, originally scheduled for Football Park in early February, were transferred to Sydney.

On December 14 came a momentous day for limited-overs cricket – the first night match – although few at the time appreciated its significance in the story of the one-day game. Played at VFL Park, with a white ball, fielding circles, white clothing and black sightscreens, the match drew just 6442 people. It was not televised, in fact the match was little more than an experiment, to see if playing under lights was feasible, which the cricketers quickly affirmed. Much was made of the white ball, which spectators all around the ground pronounced as much easier to sight than the traditional red one. After the match WSC officials were toying with the idea of using a white ball in all their matches (which they eventually did not do, although they were used in all the one-dayers). The match was won by the Australians, by six wickets.

Not all were impressed. In *Cricketer*, Eric Beecher wrote: 'What could possibly be attractive about Packer night cricket that is not attractive about Packer day cricket – except the novelty? For by 10 o'clock it was decidedly chilly (outside the executive bars) and you couldn't even get a sun-tan.'

The second Supertest, at the Sydney Showground, drew marginally better crowds, but was a disaster of another kind for WSC officials. David Hookes, whose dashing young profile had been heavily promoted, had his jaw smashed by an Andy Roberts bouncer and was put out for most of the season. Almost immediately, a number of players were placing orders for a style of batting helmet that had been pioneered in earlier WSC matches by Dennis Amiss. The original model looked for all the world like a motor-bike rider's, but a newer sleeker model was being worn by season's end. Before long it was not unusual to see a batsman striding to the wicket in a helmet; by the early '80s the helmet had become as much a part of the cricketer's kit as the thigh pad and the batting glove.

On December 24, the West Indies defeated the World side by 67 runs, before 3147 at VFL Park. Two crucial Melbourne dates, December 26 and 27, were washed out and then, after 7166 attended a one-dayer in Adelaide on December 28, only 15,613 watched the third Australia-West Indies Supertest at Football Park over the New Year holiday period. Adelaide's rejection of the Supertest came despite an emphatic performance by the Australians, who won by 220 runs in four days.

MARTIN KENT: CRICKET UNDER LIGHTS

Night cricket is arguably the most important and most enduring legacy of Kerry Packer's World Series Cricket revolution. A vast new army of fans was mobilised when the lights were turned on and so spectacular was the growth of one-day cricket that purists were quickly bemoaning the threat to Test cricket. There may have been little more than 6000 fans on hand when the night cricket revolution was born at VFL Park in Melbourne but there was no doubt about the crowd's response – or that of the players lucky enough to take part. Young Queenslander Martin Kent was an enthusiastic supporter of the concept right from the very start. He said that there was no resistance from the players to Packer's audacious gamble. Quite the opposite in fact.

'I thought it was a fantastic innovation and was just rapt to be part of it,' said Kent. 'We walked over coals for Kerry because he didn't leave any stone unturned. Anything and everything we wanted within reason he supplied. If he had wanted us to play in pitch black with a luminous ball we probably would have done it.'

The Australians' preparation for their date with destiny was relaxed to say the least. 'We did have only one practice under the lights and that wasn't a net, we just had hit-ups and catches on the ground,' said Kent. That easy going approach to an historic moment in cricket continued once combat began. 'We treated it as a game once we were under way. The expectation was there at the start but when the lights came on and it was our turn to use them I gave no credence to it. But now I look back and realise being part of the first night game is something to treasure.'

There had been some concern that

It was clear by this time that the public had all but rejected the Supertest concept, in favour of the Australia-India Test series. The third Test, in Melbourne, coincided with that third Supertest in Adelaide, and drew more than 82,000 people to its first four days. But at a different level, the wheel was turning. On January 7, over 13,000 people ventured to Gloucester Park for an Australia-West Indies International Cup clash. The next day nearly 9000 people watched a rain-delayed Australian victory over the World XI. The fact that people were slowly warming to WSC's limited-overs internationals was emphasised when, three weeks later, only 13,562 spectators in total bothered to watch a fabulous exhibition of batting (Barry Richards, Viv Richards, Greenidge and Greg Chappell were all magnificent) in the four-day Supertest in Perth.

On January 21 and 22, crowds of around 6000 watched two International Cup matches in Sydney. Following the second match, the carnival moved to Melbourne for the first official night match at VFL Park. This was an event described by the *Australian*'s correspondent Geoff Slattery as a 'triumph for the Packer organisation'. Played on January 23 between Australia and the World XI, it attracted a crowd of 10,272, the best yet for WSC in Melbourne. Those there, Slattery wrote,

batsmen would find it difficult to pick up the ball in flight but it turned out to be baseless. The only problems Kent encountered were minor in comparison. 'When I first went out to bat the first couple of balls probably scooted on a little bit quicker than I expected but once I'd gotten over that I was into it. Probably the thing I found difficult to adjust to was the glazing of the eyes in the night air and bright lights. I was forever blinking and I had never had any trouble with my eyes. But it was very seeable. There were no real problems seeing when you were batting. From a fielding point of view it took some adjustment if you were fielding square of the wicket.'

Even as World Series Cricket was changing the face of the game, and despite the fact that the one-day revolution was now close to a decade old, there were still many players who were hamstrung by a traditional mindset when it came to taking limited-over cricket seriously. Kent, despite his youth, was one who did not exactly welcome the innovation unreservedly. 'I didn't like the one-day game at the start but generally I enjoyed it,' he said. 'Still, I preferred Shield and Test cricket. I'd suggest that at that stage there were probably more blokes around who were less akin to one-day cricket than the longer game but we were in a changing era and were quite happy to go along with it.'

Kent admits, rather flippantly, that he was well suited to one-day cricket. 'I was always a bit of a slogger and my approach to the game didn't change much – if it was there to hit then I hit it.' Kent said he had little time for one of the most persistent criticisms of one-day cricket – that it affects a player's form in first-class cricket.

'I never thought playing the one-day game ever detracted from my form in four-day cricket,' he said. 'It was easier to maintain form ... a means of keeping form.'

'cheered every ball the Australians bowled and jeered every action of that man they love to hate – the World captain Tony Greig'. Greig, whose form had been moderate, had become established as public enemy No. 1, a role other great players, including Richard Hadlee and Javed Miandad, would fill in the Australian summers that followed. The match was played under the constant threat of rain, which added further weight to the crowd figure, and was eventually curtailed with 8.7 overs left. Australia won via their superior run-rate.

The following night came one of the best remembered conclusions to a limited-overs international match played in Australia. With the weather still threatening, and the start delayed, the match was reduced to 38 overs. Even so, the final dramatic ball was not delivered until near midnight, with most of the 21,636 crowd still standing in their seats. Australia had scored 9-212 during the afternoon (Greg Chappell 68, Edwards 30, Marsh 27), a target which seemed beyond the West Indies, as they gradually fell behind in their run-chase. A brisk 58 by the unheralded Jim Allen (which included a six off Gilmour from the first ball he faced), and a quickfire 30 by Julien kept them in with a chance, but with only 12 balls and the last West Indian partnership, Garner and Daniel, at the wicket, and 22 still needed, an

Australian victory seemed assured. However, Garner smashed 16 from the 37th over, bowled by Greg Chappell, to set up the memorable finale.

Ian Chappell gave Mick Malone the final over, and he responded magnificently. The fast medium bowler from WA gave precious little away and only two runs came from his first four balls. Daniel was left on strike, with few ideas but to charge and swing as hard as he could, which he did with devastating consequences. Malone, seeing Daniel coming at him, dropped it slightly shorter and wide of leg stump, but into the 'slot' from where the West Indian sent it far beyond the boundary rope.

The WSC organisers, Australians all, didn't know whether to laugh or cry. The result was sickening, but the crowd figure and highly dramatic television a perfect tonic. The *Australian* headlined the night as 'PACKER'S JACKPOT', and underneath ran a story by Greg Chappell headed 'IT'S A FAIR DINKUM CROWD PULLER'. In his article, Chappell began: 'Despite what anyone might tell you, there is only one reason why the attendances at World Series Cricket night matches at VFL Park have been so outstanding – the high standard of cricket being played.' Eching this theme in the following autumn, Ian Chappell claimed WSC was 'the best standard of cricket I have ever played in over a full season'.

The following night, nearly 18,000 saw the World XI defeat the West Indies by five wickets. Asif Iqbal, with a masterly, unbeaten 113, scored the first century under lights. Earlier in the season, in a match at the Sydney Showground, Asif had been involved in an incident that reflected the need for coloured clothing in matches where the white ball was in use. A brilliant fieldsman, he had lost the ball in the batsman's white clothing, and consequently had been able to do no more than flinch when the regulation catch had been hit to him in the covers. This was not the only instance where the white ball/clothing conundrum had caused concern. Slip fieldsmen had complained of catches being lost in the whites of either batsman, while the umpires had found difficulty with lbw decisions, not knowing where exactly the white ball had struck the white pad. A problem of a different kind came when the white ball became scuffed and marked. Some players found that, in the later overs, the ball was extremely difficult to sight. That problem was solved by introducing a new ball from each end. The batsmen were not totally enamoured to this solution, but it was settled on as the least-worst remedy.

The winner of the International Cup was decided through two semi-finals and a final. The top two teams after the nine Cup matches, the West Indies and the World XI, played out an exciting semi-final on February 3, before a disappointing Friday crowd of just 2500. The West Indies, spearheaded by Andy Roberts who took the first five wickets of the innings for 17, scraped through by 22 runs, despite a fighting stand between Greig and Knott. The next day, the World, as the first semi-final's losers, played the third-placed Australians, before a crowd of just over 8000. The locals, in something of a surprise, won through comfortably, by six wickets, after the World were bowled out for 128, of which Zaheer scored 57.

The final attracted over 20,000 to the Showground, on a day that had dawned wet and windy. When the Australians bowled the West Indies out for just 124, the crowd was in little short of a frenzy, but in the afternoon, the batsmen wilted against

Australia's Martin Kent hooks the West Indies' Collis King during a WSC match at VFL Park in 1977-78. The other Australian batsman is Ray Bright.

the fearsome attack, and were all out for 99. The weather, which had wrecked the pitch's preparation, was the real destroyer, though Daniel, with 5-25, had the best of the bowling figures. The West Indies, therefore, were World Series Cricket's inaugural one-day champions.

But for most in the Packer camp, and many beyond, it was the drama that led to Daniel's six under lights at VFL Park that was the high point of the season. That was cricket theatre, and TV drama, at its very best. To many television viewers, what was perhaps equally as memorable as Daniel's mighty blow was the Australians' devastated reaction to that cruel loss. Events and responses such as these led to the watching public realising that the players valued their performances, and that winning and losing *did* matter. After the first Supertest, the famed English writer, Ian Wooldridge, had written in the London *Daily Mail*: 'All the Supertest lacked was passionate partisan involvement and it is hard to see how, if ever, its players are going to surmount this hurdle.' It was the intensity, ability and fervour of the players, so clearly depicted by the outstanding TV coverage, and especially by the many close-up TV angles (a key element of Channel Nine's cricket telecasts), that eventually made this hurdle climbable.

The release of TV ratings figures showed that WSC matches, especially the limited-overs internationals, had been viewed in large numbers. Even the most vehement of Packer's critics conceded that Channel Nine's coverage, with extra cameras, the brilliant work of Richie Benaud, additional replays and action shown from behind the bowler's arm at both ends (previously the coverage had always been from the one main camera, which meant that for every second over the audience's view was blocked to some extent by the keeper, the stumps and the batsman), was superior to that of the past. That quality was reflected in the ratings.

If the battle between the Board and Mr Packer was seen as an election, then the role of Packer's TV coverage (call it 'advertising' if you like) was a pivotal fact in the chase for votes. Such was the quality of Nine's cricket and his coverage, that gradually, ever gradually, WSC brought people round. Not all certainly, but many. There were a number of 'purists' who could never be bought. And at the same time the cricket and the coverage brought the 'new' cricket fan to the game, the one who had been lurking, all but ignored, since that first limited-overs international of New Year's Day, 1971. The same fan who had been introduced to English cricket through the limited-overs matches of the 1960s.

Mr Ray Steele, the ACB treasurer, acknowledged this in an interview in 1979. 'WSC has got a lot of football followers going out there for one-day games,' Steele said. 'I think many of the attendances include people who have never been to a cricket match before.' These were the people John Arlott had identified in 1972 – the men, women and children who made Old Trafford at a one-day game reverberate much like the Old Trafford football ground did for Manchester United matches. These sports fans were blissfully ignorant of the traditions and intricacies of five-day cricket, but were sold on the glamour and pace of limited-overs matches.

A number of them had stayed up to watch the World Cup final action of 1975 when Lillee, Thomson, the Chappells, Walters and Marsh had been playing for the world in a day. Because of them, Australian cricket would never be the same.

8

THE PATH TO COMPROMISE

While World Series Cricket was gradually developing a foothold in Australia on the back of the growing popularity of limited-overs cricket, 'establishment' cricket was having to come to terms with dwindling attendances at its matches. The tour by India, despite its 'success' in drawing reasonable crowds (in comparison to expectations and the Supertests), had been far from the money-making bonanza that the 1974-75 Ashes series and the subsequent West Indies tour had been. And the Sheffield Shield, which had been reduced in stature by the absence of its stars, was now costing a fortune.

Yet the Board, in order to ensure there were no more defections, was paying its players little less than the Packer enterprise. In February 1978, the Board sent its Australian team to the West Indies for a tour that suffered from a distinct lack of interest in Australia. As Brian Osborne noted in the 1979 *Wisden*, the sporting public had by then had enough of first-class cricket, after the Ashes tour of 1977 and the twin series (ACB and WSC) of 1977-78. By the start of 1978-79, WSC, much by the marketeers' design, was perceived as a form of cricket dominated by its limited-overs matches. In the other corner, the Board was promoting its highest card – an England tour of Australia – with the theme that Test cricket was trusted and respectable.

In his preview of the 1978-79 season *Cricketer*'s new editor Ken Piesse saw a troubled time ahead for the Ashes series: 'The promise of sun-filled days watching the best cricketers in the world is no longer a simple prospect for cricket lovers,' Piesse wrote. 'It must now be measured in terms of allegiances and unsatisfactory compromise. For England v Australia in 1978-79 is NOT the best cricket. The best cricketers are those competing for money, under lights, in colours, in short snappy contests which surely bear little resemblance to those long languid peaceful days which used to be what Test cricket was all about.'

Cricket traditionalists looked towards the season with much trepidation. A comparison of their best side, now captained by the 26-year-old Victorian Graham Yallop (Simpson had retired after failing to gain assurances about his place in the Test side), with the WSC Australians drew sighs of despair. During the winter, Packer had obtained the use of the 'Gabba in Brisbane, which meant they could take their cricket north for the first time. Playing at traditional Test match venues, the 'Gabba and the SCG, gave the troupe added respectability. New players had been signed by WSC, including the South Africans Kepler Wessels (who was 'qualified' to play for Australia), Garth Le Roux and Clive Rice (who would play for the World) and Desmond Haynes, Richard Austin and Colin Croft of the West Indies.

Unfortunately Packer's biggest signing, Jeff Thomson, was kept out of the season's cricket by a legal dispute – the full High Court finally confirming, in a decision that came less than 24 hours after the first night match at the SCG, that a signed ACB contract bound the great fast bowler to establishment cricket. Thomson opted to sit out the season. WSC's 1978-79 agenda included a 16-day sojourn to New Zealand in November (in which the Kiwi fast bowler Richard Hadlee made a 'guest' appearance for the World XI), before an intensive cavalcade of cricket between November 23 and February 4 that involved a seemingly continual run of limited-overs matches and five Supertests. After that, a WSC Australian team would tour the West Indies.

Sponsors were flocking to the World Series. Companies like Goulburn Valley canners, Goodyear tyres, and McDonald's family restaurants offered prizes and giveaways, to players and fans alike. Ball-by-ball commentaries would be heard on commercial radio, but only in the host city when the cricket wasn't being televised. And, in another decision made with the television cameras firmly in mind, the number of balls in each WSC over was reduced from eight to six.

The Australian component of the WSC season began with four 'preliminary' one-day matches in Western Australia. Then came the famous night of November 28, when the lights were turned on for the first time in Sydney. Australia's final winning margin in this opening International Cup clash was five wickets, after the Windies had been bowled out for just 128 (Lillee 4-13, Greg Chappell 5-19) and Bruce Laird, Greg Chappell, Ian Chappell and Ian Davis had scored the runs with 13 overs to spare. Another international match was played the following night at the SCG, between Australia and the World, and despite a stormy evening that ended the World's reply in the 31st over (Australia winning though a superior run rate), 14,817 came through the gate.

The WSC organising committee had decided they would be playing their night cricket ace for all it was worth – so the success in Sydney was very welcome, and vindicated their decision to give Adelaide's Football Park a second, floodlit chance. Even the Supertests in Sydney and Melbourne would include night-time play. Of the International Cup matches, only those played at the 'Gabba were scheduled to finish in the sunlight. Those two 'first-up' wins for the Australians put them on top of the International Cup standings, a spot they would not relinquish throughout the preliminary matches. Along the way they produced some marvellous performances, especially by the bowlers, who were able to demoralise the West Indies – Richards, Lloyd and all – for innings totals such as 66 (Greg Chappell 4-15, Gilmour 3-9), 126 (Lillee 3-15) and 103 (Walker 5-23) during the summer.

On January 13, around 2000 people attended a Benson and Hedges-sponsored limited-overs international between Brearley's Englishmen and Yallop's Australians at the SCG. The match was eventually abandoned, due to rain, after just 7.1

Max Walker, who took more wickets in WSC's one-day internationals than any other Australian bowler.

WSC IN THE WINDIES: RUNS, RUM AND RIOTS

World Series Cricket's tour of the West Indies in 1979 was ground-breaking in that it was the first major tour in which one-day cricket played a major role – 12 of the 17 fixtures were limited-overs contests. That placed new demands on the mental and physical fitness of the Australian players.

A four-month Ashes tour was tough but when the different demands of one-day cricket were added to the peculiar problems of the West Indies – the draining travel between islands, the heat, the basic amenities – the 1979 World Series Cricket tour became a particularly taxing one. The Australians took six seamers on tour but by the one-day match in Dominica had been reduced to two fully fit pacemen – Len Pascoe and Mick Malone. Dennis Lillee had badly strained ligaments in his back and Gary Gilmour had aggravated a groin injury while Jeff Thomson and Greg Chappell also had back strains.

Batsman Martin Kent said the unusually large number of one-dayers just added to the pressures of what would have been a gruelling tour anyway. 'It was a very tense time,' he said. 'There was a lot of cricket and a fair bit of travelling between the islands, and the competition was very hot.'

It is possible for a player's commitment to wax and wane during a long tour, and when the extra pressures the WSC Australians faced on the 1979 tour are thrown into the mix any loss of enthusiasm would be perfectly understandable. But enthusiasm was maintained against a traumatic backdrop.

overs, but in most of Sydney the weather remained fine all day, and few who had considered venturing to the ground in the morning would have let a potential washout sway their thinking. Commenting on the 'crowd', the ACB chairman, Mr Parish, suggested, perhaps with one whimsical eye on the weather, that a point of saturation had been reached in terms of the amount of cricket being played in Australia.

Four days later, Parish's opinion was blown out of the water when over 45,000 fans travelled to the SCG to see a crucial International Cup match between the WSC Australians and the WSC West Indians. Australia had already qualified for the best-of-five finals of the Cup (worth $35,000); the West Indies, a point behind the World XI on the competition table (two points were awarded for a win) needed to win this encounter to join them. The contrast in crowd figures illustrated starkly the public's perception of the two cricket camps. The 'traditional' Ashes series was a throwback to the days of yesteryear, when one-day matches had not yet been imagined. Why then, it was asked, were these men of the past playing a style of cricket that had nothing to do with them?

WSC's January 17 encounter at the SCG was the first match to feature coloured clothing. From the start of the season, a green seam had been added to the white ball, in an attempt to alleviate the problems of the white ball being lost in oppo-

The tour was placed in danger by a number of riots, the most serious of which occurred when the start of the Supertest in Guyana was delayed by heavy rain. The fans were let into the ground and promised action when the prospects of play were minimal at best. A few hours mixing sun and alcohol finally sparked a riot that had all the players fearing for their safety as the crowd stormed the pavilion and destroyed the place.

'I think all of us that day felt threatened,' said Kent. 'We made no bones about it. We donned our helmets, stuck our bags in a corner, wrapped towels around our arms and got a bat in hand. We just weren't sure what to expect. When you see your security guard come in and hide as well it doesn't give you a lot of confidence as to what is about to happen. After a lengthy team discussion that evening we chose to stay on and play. At the end of the riot we realised the anger wasn't directed at us or at WSC. It was anger at the administrators and there was some unrest on the political scene which just fuelled the fire. From that point on we were very happy to see the end of Guyana. It was kiss-the-tarmac stuff when we got to the next stop.'

Apart from that traumatic day in Guyana, Kent said he loved playing in front of the West Indian crowds because of their deep appreciation of the game, their respect for good cricket and their willingness to applaud a good performance by players of either side – particularly if it was a batsman. 'It was just enjoyable to play in front of people who enjoyed cricket for what cricket was,' said Kent. 'Then there was the colour, the characters who'd dress up and play steel drums – we were just about sick of steel drums by the end of the tour.'

nents' whites. But this was always seen as a short-term gesture, with coloured clothing seen as the ultimate solution. By January, dyed leather pads and gloves were available, and the Australians took the field, to a chorus of wolf-whistles, in canary yellow (some, including the promoters, called it wattle), the West Indies in coral pink. Later, in the Supertest grand final, the World XI would wear sky blue.

The WSC publicity machine had chosen not to heavily publicise that the teams would not be in white, for fear they would be ridiculed for an outlandish gimmick. The clothing, as was constantly stressed, was no gimmick, but a response to a difficulty created by the white ball. A problem of a different kind arose when the West Indies players saw their clothing for the first time. In the Caribbean, the gay population wore pink almost as a habit, and the players did not think their new colours would boost their image at home. Consequently, the tailors made what English cricket writer Alan Lee, in his book of the summer, *A Pitch in Both Camps*, called 'some reassuring colour adjustments' before the West Indians' true colours were revealed.

In the afternoon, Australia struggled to reach 9-149. At this point, everything was fine, but during the dinner break rain began to fall, creating the scenario for a farcical evening. It was determined that a draw was enough for the West Indies to reach the finals, and, with the rain continuing to fall, this appeared the most likely outcome. At least a third of the crowd acknowledged this, and departed for home, while an unhealthy proportion of the remainder moved to the bar. Soon the less sober patrons in the outer, especially those on the Hill, were throwing their empty cans onto the field, in apparent protest at the delay in play. Then came the streakers, who had become a regular and increasingly tiresome feature at every night match.

Officials seemed determined to give the spectators some cricket and a result, despite the fact that a draw would suit them, as the West Indians would represent a better attraction than the World XI in the limited-overs finals. A ground announcer told the throng that the game could not recommence until the field was cleared of cans. Then the voice of Richie Benaud came over the public address, informing the remaining spectators that, after various compensations had been made because of the loss of playing time, the West Indies required just 49 runs from 16 overs. Not for the last time in limited-overs cricket, the calculations made necessary by rain had thrown all the advantages to the side batting second.

The West Indies reached that target in nine overs, despite the loss, to the bowling of Lillee and Pascoe and the frenzied roars from the crowd, of Greenidge, Richards and Lloyd. When the 'winning' run was scored, the masses invaded the pitch, despite pleas from the loudspeakers for them to stay behind the fence. All in the press box believed the game was over, as did the television audience, who had been informed by the Channel Nine commentators. However, the umpires, Douglas Sang Hue and Gary Duperouzal, did not. A match, they argued, was not a match until 15 overs had been bowled by both sides. So the fans were asked, encouraged, pushed and thrown back beyond the boundary, and another three overs bowled before the rain returned at 10.25pm and washed out what might have been left of the play. As the lights had to be turned off at 10.30pm because of council restrictions, it was not known how, or when, all the remaining balls would have been bowled. The ground announcer decided the West Indies had won, but down in the Australian dressing room Ian Chappell would have none of it. He knew the result had no bearing on who he would be facing the finals, but the preliminary matches were played on a winner-take-all basis and, as far as the Australians were concerned, the West Indies had not won. The result was finally confirmed late at night, to the disgust of the Australians, as a win to the West Indies. But, as Alan Lee recorded, the shemozzle was still apparent the next day. The *Sun* ran the following back-page headline: 'IT'S A DRAW – WSC ADMIT BUNGLE'. On the other side of town, the *Sun*'s afternoon rival, the *Daily Mirror*, led with 'WINDIES WIN – OFFICIAL'.

It would be announced in February that Brearley's England side would again be touring Australia in 1979-80, but only to play in a series of limited-overs internationals that would also feature India (who were scheduled to compete in that summer's official Test series). The reason for the change of policy on limited-overs internationals was, according to one ACB official, 'in keeping with the policy of the cricket establishment not to give WSC an inch of breathing space'. Yet, as early as January 17, Bob Parish had received written authorisation from officials at Lord's to negotiate with Mr Packer in order to bring about a compromise. These early negotiations were conducted amid more secrecy.

The International Cup finals that followed the coloured confusion at the SCG should have been WSC's crowning triumph, but instead they ended in fiasco. All the finals matches were played at VFL Park (the Supertest final and grand final were to be played under lights at the SCG), and after three matches, the best-of-five series stood at West Indies 2, Australia 1. Wessels had dominated Game 1 with a superb 136, before the two West Indian victories, by four and seven wickets respectively, had eventuated. Game 4 was eagerly awaited – one more Australian loss and night cricket was finished for the season in Melbourne – and more than 20,000 people came out to see the match ... until the bitter end. Those who arrived before the lights came on saw a brilliant home-town batting display, especially from Marsh and Kent who added 99 for the sixth wicket. The final Australian score of 240 (Malone was run out off the final ball of the 50th over) was their highest one-day score of the season.

Midway through the evening, as the sun disappeared beyond the skyline, and the blazing lights took over, the Australians, or more precisely Lillee, had their rivals down at 6-132. First the great fast bowler had the prolific Lawrence Rowe, who many considered the batsman of the summer, plumb lbw. Then Collis King was given out caught behind. The dismissal itself appeared clearcut – King, caught Marsh bowled Lillee, 3. In fact Lillee did not even look at the umpire as he jubilantly raced to his keeper. But umpire Col Hoy (who had given the last decision in the 1960 Brisbane Tied Test) was unmoved. Marsh fell to his knees in despair, before he and Lillee turned to the other umpire, Gary Duperouzel. That Marsh had caught the ball was not in doubt. The batsman was still there because the snick had not been seen or heard at the bowler's end. The 'out' was not the business of the man at square-leg, but Hoy was convinced by the Australians that he should talk with Duperouzel, who it appeared had heard the edge that Hoy had missed. Finally, after a long discussion, King was given out – at least a minute after the ball had been bowled. The batsman looked angrily demoralised by it all. But Clive Lloyd was still to be dismissed, and with Bernard Julien he built a fightback.

Ian Chappell, whose captaincy throughout the two years of WSC was as superb as it had been in his Test career, decided on a gambler's change. David Hookes was brought into the attack to bowl left-arm wrist spinners. General belief at this time was that spinners of any kind were out of place in the one-day game. Some were even questioning the future of wrist spinners in the Test arena. Chappell could have turned to Walker, Lillee, Malone, or even his medium-paced brother Greg. Instead Hookes, in his second over, broke the stand, Julien misjudging a slog into the outfield. It was 7-172.

Lloyd had been struggling with a torn groin muscle, and at this point called for a runner. Out came King, but the Australians objected on the grounds that King was the fastest runner in the West Indies squad. This argument was justified by the umpires, which did little for the West Indians' mood. Their opening bat, Richard Austin, filled the void. Chappell persisted with Hookes, who then had Andy Roberts caught, in spectacular (and controversial) fashion by Lillee, hands above his head, feet off the ground, on the deep mid-off boundary rope. The dismissal was not immediately disputed by the West Indians, but should have been, as Lillee had fallen back onto the boundary rope (which was laid on the ground) after snaring the

Ian Chappell makes a strong point to the umpire during the first match to feature coloured clothing, at the SCG on January 17, 1979. The match ended amid great controversy, after a series of rain interruptions had reduced the West Indies target to 49 from 16 overs. When they reached that total in nine overs, it was believed the match had ended, but the umpires argued that 15 overs had to be bowled for the result to stand. When the rain returned before the remaining overs could be completed, not even the umpires were sure if the game had been won, lost or drawn.

catch. Under the laws being used, the correct ruling was six not out. Afterwards, Brad Boxall in an *Australian Cricket* article that confirmed the catch was illegal described Lillee's heroics as 'one of the greatest outfield catches ever taken'. Roberts later called Lillee a 'f——— cheat'. The scorebook said 8-187. Eight overs to go.

Chappell persisted with Hookes for one more expensive over, as the stricken Lloyd, with Joel Garner, chased the prize. Then came the chain of events that would ruin this fantastic contest. Time was running out for the Australians to complete their 50 overs. The match had to end at 10.30pm, according to restrictions applied by the local authority, the Waverley Council. But permission was sought, and won, for the game to continue to 10.45pm. Andrew Caro, the managing director of WSC, asked Wayne Prior, the Australian 12th man, to relay this information to the players and umpires, but in the confusion, Prior told only his team-mates. Upstairs, the news of the extension was passed on to the TV commentators, while on the field Ian Chappell decided to keep Lillee for the 47th and 49th overs. However, the umpires and batsmen were still thinking in terms of the clock, and the fact that the game would be decided by a comparison of each side's run-rate at 10.30. The floodlit crowd, most of whom did not know of the council restrictions, let alone the animated discussions in the WSC boardroom, were left in the dark. With the 46th over about to begin, and Lloyd in full cry, the difference was 30. Max Walker was poised to begin his eighth over – and the fans prayed that he and Lillee would see the Australians home. But the clock showed 10.29pm, which mattered much to the men from the Caribbean, and Julien raced onto the field, to tell his captain that, according to the calculators in the dressing room, 17 runs were needed from the next six balls for the win.

The first ball was thrashed over square leg by Lloyd for six. Then a four, two singles, and another four. With each blow, the three batsmen met in mid-pitch, to discuss the equation. It was the '75 World Cup final all over again, as Walker was smashed about the ground. Another two from the last ball meant 18 from the over. As far as the Australians were concerned, the game was slipping away. Only 13 were needed now from 24 balls.

In fact the game was gone. The batsmen were racing/hobbling from the field, as their excited team-mates danced towards them. The stunned fieldsmen looked to the umpires, who were collecting the stumps and bails. The International Cup was over! The crowd stood silent, unbelieving. Rarely could a big crowd have felt so empty. It was as if the VFL grand final had been called off 10 minutes from time. Not only had the game been lost, the exciting climax that had been building all evening was gone – without warning. The bemused and belittled faces of the Australians reflected a feeling that pervaded the crowd and the TV audience at home. For the WSC administration it was an embarrassing and incompetent performance. Almost as Mr Packer was closing the door on the Australian dressing room to personally apologise to the players, Andrew Caro was drafting his letter of resignation.

The Australians then went to Sydney to lose the Supertest grand final to the World XI, before setting off to the Caribbean for a two-month cavalcade through the islands. This series, like the ACB tour of a year earlier, aroused scarce interest in

Australia. The fact that Channel Nine could not provide extensive coverage of the tour back to Australia did not help at all. For many, the chief interest of the tour centred on the performances of Jeff Thomson. The Board had relented on the Thomson contract furore (they could have prevented him playing until the start of 1979-80), and the champion fast bowler joined 16 of his colleagues for a tour that is remembered as much for the crowd disturbances that followed the action as for the cricket. The crowd trouble was never worse than in Bridgetown in Barbados, where the second Supertest had to be abandoned after a series of disturbances, which left the players marooned, terrified and wary of missiles as they crouched in their dressing rooms. Never have batting helmets been more tightly worn. The Australian squad was: Ian Chappell (captain), Ray Bright, Greg Chappell, Trevor Chappell, Gary Gilmour, David Hookes, Martin Kent, Bruce Laird, Dennis Lillee, Mick Malone, Rod Marsh, Rick McCosker, Kerry O'Keeffe, Len Pascoe, Richie Robinson (player-manager), Jeff Thomson, Max Walker. Ian Davis and Ian Redpath were unavailable, while Kepler Wessels was not considered because of his South African connections. The tour schedule originally involved five Supertests and 12 limited-overs internationals. Two of those 12 one-dayers were abandoned, and the Australians won only two of the remainder.

While the crowds were rioting in the Caribbean, critics in Australia were pondering local crowd figures which showed the degree of acceptance of WSC-style cricket. An average 9364 per day watched the 1978-79 Supertests (the Ashes series had averaged 13,419 per day), but that, for the organisers, was a bonus. Australia's International Cup matches drew more than 320,000 people in total – an average of more than 20,000 per game. On top of that, Mr Packer admitted in newspaper interviews that he was delighted with his TV ratings, in which his matches had more than held their own against the Ashes Tests, and in some cases completely blown the establishment cricket away. And it was on the TV battle-ground that Packer wanted to win his war. 'That's where it's decided,' he had once claimed. 'On that box!'

Colour TV had changed cricket. The public's perception of the game had changed, as had the way the game was highlighted and marketed. Cricketers who had in the past been heroes with the bat and ball were now sex symbols or public enemies. Whereas some schoolboys in the early '70s had wanted but could not find T-shirts with their heroes' faces on them, now a new generation had a choice of designs. And they could sing along as well. World Series Cricket had ridden to fame on the back of a simple and now famous theme song, called *C'mon Aussie, C'mon*. Throughout the summer, crowds in their thousands sang the jingle to encourage their heroes, and entertain themselves. The tune eventually went, Beatles-like, to the top of the charts, and remains today one of the greatest triumphs in the history of Australian advertising.

However, while the masses were singing they were also rebelling, and some stinging censures were made of the WSC crowds. One such example appeared in the March 1979 *Australian Cricket*. In an article headlined 'Gorillas' (Ian Chappell, after the rain-ruined SCG match of January 17, had likened the rowdier elements in the crowd to 'bloody gorillas'), Sydney sports writer Ray Chesterton wrote:

'One thing is certain: whatever stormy path WSC may still have to travel to win general acceptance with cricket's hierarchy, they have at least notched one dubious first.

'Their matches have spawned the oddest and most unlikely cricket supporters in the world.

'Sounding like an unholy alliance between a Banshee and a punk rock group, and with the volatility of gelignite, the crowds attract as much interest as the game – as long as you're watching from a distance ...

'They are impatient to a degree that is threatening. Not for them the gentle appreciation of a well-hit shot or an equally well-fielded interception.

'They want blood, and fiery head-on clashes between their star personalities, along with a touch of Hollywood.'

During the season, 'dry' areas (sections where alcohol could not be consumed) were introduced at the WSC grounds, a tacit acknowledgement from their officials that the crowds they were attracting were threatening to run out of control, and drive families and the more sensible away. The WSC marketing executives pushed the need to keep the 'new' fans, including a substantial number of ladies, entertained and involved, but cricket of any kind is not a game that can sustain fanatical interest through every over, and a succession of ugly incidents were recorded. Ground invasions occurred too often, arrests for drunkenness became a media statistic, and can-throwing was as regular as a return to the keeper.

The question of crowd misbehaviour, especially in Sydney, became an issue that would plague limited-overs international cricket in Australia for years to come. It led to the gradual destruction of the celebrated SCG Hill in the 1980s, after police argued that crowd control would be easier if the once charming stretch of grass was replaced by rows of individual plastic seats. Even into the '80s the Hill was an entertaining and worthwhile place to watch a cricket Test. But for a night match it was deadly.

Of their fans, Andrew Caro wrote, in his 1979 book on his WSC experiences, *With A Straight Bat*: 'It's all very well to admire the dignified attitudes of the past, but if there is a crowd of 30,000 most will be under 30, and a large proportion under 20. They remember little, and care less, about the good old days. Many have not seen a cricket match before and are keen to become engrossed in this new scene. If cricket is to survive and grow in competition with other forms of entertainment, other sports and pastimes, it has to appeal to people for whom Neville Cardus is unknown and Bradman is the name of a stand. As they become acquainted with the game he may be accepted as a legend by the new public, but the aim of World Series Cricket is to "first catch your fish" ...

'Personally, I would prefer to have cricket played with enthusiasm and crowd involvement, even the worst kind ... than allow it to be suffocated by genteel apathy at Lords (sic).'

That second paragraph reeked of arrogance, an indifference to the potential problems of crowd misbehaviour, and an ignorance of the great value and quality of the cricket that had been played in the previous century. But even Ray Steele, the ACB treasurer, conceded that the bringing of these new people through the turnstiles was 'probably a good thing'. This was a rare concession by the Board at that

DAVID HOOKES: MAINTAINING TRADITIONS

David Hookes and his peers stepped onto cricket's main stage just as one-day cricket was taking off. Hookes, perhaps more than any contemporary, seemed perfectly suited to the frenetic new version of the game. Hookes had a breathtaking array of strokes, a superb eye and the courage it took to utilise his natural gifts.

But, just as in Test cricket, Hookes was unable to translate his undoubted talents into consistent success in the international one-day arena. In 39 limited-overs matches for Australia the dashing left-hander scored 826 runs at an average of 24.29, with five half-centuries and a highest score of 76. While he enjoyed playing one-day cricket it would be wrong to assume that he gave the game his heart. For all his brashness and flamboyance at the crease David Hookes was, and is, more comfortable with the heritage and ethos of the traditional game.

'My generation played first class cricket in the mid-to-late '70s – Allan Border, Kim Hughes, Graeme Wood, Rick Darling,' said Hookes. 'We were still brought up under the tradition of Test cricket. There was no TV, no video replays, there was no World Series Cricket. So all our love for the game came from playing cricket, and going to the Test matches, and going to Shield games and reading cricket books by Jack Fingleton and Don Bradman and Victor Trumper.

'Although we were brought into the embryonic stages of the one-day game we really were tagging on the end of traditional cricket,' Hookes said. 'So it wasn't too hard for us to be traditionalists. We all thought one-day cricket was an important part of the game from a revenue aspect, but the players now have changed to it being an important part of the game from their own point of view.'

Hookes burst into the public eye with his memorable Centenary Test innings, which capped off a dazzling second season in Sheffield Shield cricket. He went on the troubled 1977 Ashes tour before

time – even when they were planning a program for 1979-80 that included a limited-overs international series they continued to deride WSC's concentration on one-day night cricket as being opportunistic and short-sighted. At the same time, WSC officials slammed the Board's preference for Test cricket as being old-fashioned and out-of-touch. Meanwhile, as bumper crowd figures and TV ratings strengthened WSC's hand, and the ACB auditors recorded the story of a summer of great expense and mediocre returns, those who cared for the future of the game began to despair ...

It was hoped calm heads would prevail. The entertainment that was limited-overs cricket was here to stay – public demand had seen to that. The new fan, despite his erratic behaviour, had been given his one-day fare. At the same time, Test cricket, the sport that had been so much a part of the character and quality of the Australian summer, was struggling, in desperate need of a compromise between the two factions. In the autumn of '79, that compromise came about.

he was plunged into the maelstrom of World Series Cricket. Apart from the obvious off-the-field pressures, Hookes also had to cope with the radical switch in emphasis of the games themselves – one-day cricket was quickly becoming king. And, despite being a 22-year-old with a healthy appetite for new and exciting experiences, he was not totally bowled over by the new format.

'From a selection point of view, yes, I was happy to play so much one-day cricket,' said Hookes. 'But from a philosophical point of view as somebody who loves the game and the traditions and the history and the legacy that's been left, no, I wasn't.' In fact, Hookes believes the timing of his emergence on the main stage ultimately cost him dearly. While it laid the foundation for an exciting attacking style that kept people flocking to Adelaide Oval for many years, Hookes wrote in his biography *Hookesy* that he developed a poor mental attitude that would prevent him reaching his potential on the Test scene.

'I guess probably when I batted for the first couple of years under the bonus points system in the Sheffield Shield (where points were awarded for runs scored and wickets taken in a set number of first-innings overs) I was probably playing one-day cricket anyway,' he said. 'Of the 15 or 16 times I batted in my first year there was only about four times where I could play a normal innings. My initial introduction to first-class cricket was very much in a one-day manner without my realising it and the one-day games that followed in World Series Cricket I just played the same way because that's all I learned. One-dayers in those days were still hit-and-giggle matches. That was probably a disappointing aspect of my first years in cricket.'

Many middle-order batsmen complain about the limitations and restrictions of coming in late in the innings. They complain of the pressure of having to perform straightaway. Most eye the coveted top three or four positions in the batting order because those are the ones that traditionally produce the vast majority of the runs. But not David

Continued over page

In April, after three months of talks, the ACB announced it had granted PBL Sports Pty Ltd, a promotions company owned by Mr Packer, the exclusive rights for a term of 10 years to promote the program of cricket organised by the Board and to arrange the televising and merchandising of the game. Those television rights went, inevitably, to the Nine network. What Mr Packer could not get in 1976 he had in 1979.

For the final word on World Series Cricket, we turn to Lynton Taylor, WSC's general manager, who in the 1979 *Australian Cricket Annual* commented: 'What World Series achieved over two years was to introduce new audiences to the game. Something like 50 per cent of our crowds had not been to cricket before. About 90 per cent of those crowds indicated they would be coming back. The age group has lowered dramatically ... what is obvious is that cricket must hold onto the new young audience we developed over the last two years.'

MAINTAINING TRADITIONS

Continued from previous page

Hookes. He not only rejects those criticisms but takes a diametrically opposed view. 'I always thought that mentally one-day cricket was a very easy game to play for a middle-order batsman,' he said. 'Probably the odd times I opened or batted three it was different because I think I played a bit more normally. But of course if you bat in the middle order you can't really fail. You either make runs or you get out trying to make runs. People accept the fact that you can get out playing an aggressive shot quite early in your innings if you're in the middle order.

'There's no question that there's less pressure. When you wake up on the morning of a one-day game against the West Indies you have a far different feeling inside your guts than when you wake up on the morning of a Test match. There's much more awareness of the game of cricket when you're playing a Test match. 'The thing about batting in a one-day game is that you actually know where the bowler's going to bowl. He's got to bowl it basically in the same spot six times in a row. He hasn't got much leeway.

'A good score 15 years ago was 180 to 190 and now 260 is more the norm so from the slather-and-whack game of the mid-'70s it's become more refined and probably a bit more difficult to play, from the point of view of people expecting you to play more normally. I still think that mentally, as a middle-order batsman, it's a pretty easy game to play.'

While Hookes may disagree with most other batsmen on certain aspects of one-day cricket there is one area where he is in full agreement. To him, as with other players, one limited-overs game is the same as the next – repeated ad infinitum until they blur into one long tunnel of cricket. When asked for a highlight of his nine years in international one-day cricket he could come up with just one.

'Only Viv's innings in Melbourne in 1979-80 and probably only because of the enormity of the score. If he'd made 105 off 85 balls I wouldn't have remembered it as easily as his 153,' Hookes said. He certainly had no great regard for his own achievements in the one-day arena. 'I got 76 against the Poms in Adelaide but who cares?' he said. 'There were some exciting finishes but that's my point – it's the last five overs that you remember. Mick Malone being hit by Wayne Daniel out of the park at Waverley – you remember one delivery out of the whole game! I wouldn't know who made a score in that game.'

9

TESTING TIMES

efore a WSC bowler had hurled the first ball in anger, 44 limited-overs internationals had been played across the world. Excluding the 1975 World Cup (which featured 15 matches in total and five involving Australia), Australia had played just 11 – six in England (the 1972 and 1977 Prudential Cup series), two in New Zealand (in 1973-74) and three in Australia (versus England in 1970-71 and 1974-75 and against the West Indies in 1975-76).

In 1977-78, five limited-overs internationals were played – three in England between the home country and Pakistan, and two in the West Indies, for the Guinness Trophy, between the men from the Caribbean and the touring 'ACB' Australians. The first of those two games in the West Indies, before a packed Recreation Ground at St John's, Antigua, was something of a mismatch. Coming after the first season of WSC, the Australians were without their Packer players, whereas the West Indies Cricket Board of Control decided to go with local public opinion and against the prevailing ICC viewpoint, and choose their strongest available side. This team inevitably featured many of WSC's finest, including Richards, Roberts, Daniel, Garner and Murray (Lloyd, Greenidge and Holding could not play), and proved far too powerful. Ironically the team's stars on the day were not the Packer players, but two new men – a sensational opening batsman named Desmond Haynes (who scored 148) and a fearsome fast bowler, Colin Croft (who took 3-44).

The Australian XI that was overpowered included nine cricketers new to limited-overs internationals – the captain Bob Simpson, Ian Callen, Wayne Clark, Rick Darling, Trevor Laughlin, Steve Rixon, Peter Toohey, Graeme Wood and Graham Yallop. The two 'survivors' were Jeff Thomson and Gary Cosier, who had matches of vastly different fortunes. Thomson's 10 six-ball overs cost 67 runs, and he had bitter trouble with the umpires, who persistently no-balled him. Simpson at one stage took the extraordinary step of leaving the field to find a set of rules, as his and his fast bowler's interpretation of the no-ball rule apparently differed from the umpire's. Simpson had more troubles when he bowled his leg-breaks, as Haynes attacked him unmercifully, hitting one delivery clean out of the ground. The West Indies finished their 50 overs at 9-313.

Cosier, who in his previous one-day international had taken 5-18 off 8.5 overs, this time took 0-32 off four. However, when he batted he was superb, striking a brave and belligerent 84 against the best the local bowlers could fire at him. But he

Graham Yallop, who led Australia for most of the 1978-79 Australian season.

received little support, and the Australian reply was always well behind the required run-rate. When the game was called off with the Australian reply 36 overs old (the West Indian attack, dominated by their four fast bowlers, had bowled their overs at a funereal rate), the Australian total stood at 7-181. By the time the Australians played their second and final limited-overs international of the tour, at Mindoo Phillip Park in St Lucia, a selection dispute between Lloyd and the WICBC had led to all the WSC players withdrawing from the Test series. With the Packer players available the West Indies had won the first two Tests emphatically. Consequently the local side had eight new and less-gifted players in their line-up for this second match, which, because of rain, was reduced to 35 overs per side. On a suspect batting surface the game remained in doubt until the very end. The locals, sent in, scraped and scavenged to 139 all out (off 34.4 overs), which seemed inadequate. But the Australians fared only fractionally better in the late afternoon, and the result came down to the final ball of the final over, from which the second-last Australian partnership, Thomson and Callen, found the winning run.

In 1978-79, the Australian Cricket Board's major sponsor, Benson and Hedges, put up a trophy bearing their name to be fought for in a three-match series between Australia and England. In scheduling this series, the ACB adopted a similar approach to limited-overs international cricket to that of their English counterparts, who had included three or four limited-overs internationals in each English season's program since 1972 (except 1975, the World Cup year). The first Benson and Hedges Cup match of 1978-79, scheduled for Boxing Day in Melbourne, was washed out without a ball being bowled. The second, in Sydney on January 13, suffered almost the same fate – abandoned after just 7.1 overs. Finally, at the third try, the series 'began' – with barely a whimper. Back at the MCG, the Australians batted first and very badly, and were bowled out in 33.5 eight-ball overs for 101. The English reply took 28.2 overs and cost three wickets. The crowd of more than 14,000 went home disappointed, and largely unentertained. The only feature had been the superb English fielding – David Gower's two-handed leaping mark off Australia's top-scorer, Graeme Wood, was rated on par with some of the greatest catches ever taken by a VFL footballer, while Derek Randall's electric run out of Yallop from extra cover was equally remarkable.

The teams then went to Adelaide to play the fifth Test, where, in a surprise pre-match announcement, the ACB disclosed that from 1979-80 all Australian cricket would revert to six-ball overs. This left Pakistan as the only cricket nation still bowling eight-ball overs. The decision apparently came after a meeting of the players' committee, and had been accepted unanimously by Board delegates, who believed it would create a faster over-rate and lead to brighter cricket. The six-ball over had been used in 1978-79 in the Australian Gillette Cup, after a suggestion from Bob Simpson.

The Adelaide Test ended with the fourth English Test victory of the summer. The teams then returned to Melbourne, where, on February 4, Australia experienced a welcome change of fortune in the re-scheduled Boxing Day limited-overs international. The revival was unexpected, especially as the fast bowler Rodney Hogg, who had performed so admirably in the Tests to that point (taking an Australian record 40 English wickets), was resting a minor injury. The pitch for the match was damp at the start, and, even without Hogg, Yallop's successful coin toss should have won a huge advantage. But although Brearley, Randall and Graham Gooch fell cheaply, Boycott batted cleverly on the tricky wicket, and Gower was fantastic, playing just about the innings of the season – ACB or WSC – for 101 off 100 balls.

It had been suggested that the left-handed Gower was the one English establishment batsman that Packer wanted on his books, and in this innings he showed why, with a series of immaculately placed cuts, glances, drives and pulls. The Australian team's fallibilities and the batsman's rare skill were never better exemplified than by the innings' final ball. Gower, on 97, was obliged to wait while captain Yallop and bowler Laughlin pondered which parts of the MCG fence they would protect with their fieldsmen. The two Victorians were roundly heckled by many in the crowd of more than 11,000, as it became apparent their sole strategy was to prevent the Englishman from reaching three figures. Laughlin started, stopped, moved a man here and there, started again ... and was thrashed to the extra-cover boundary. At that moment Gower was the hero of the day.

Few gave the Australians much chance of reaching the 213 needed for victory, but Hughes, who made 50, played an innings of quality, and Toohey, a bitter disappointment in the Test series (after batting with great flair against India and in the West Indies the previous season, his stocks had slumped to the point where he was dropped to 12th man for the Adelaide Test), scored an unbeaten 54. But the key innings came from Cosier, another reject from the Test team, who smashed 28 from just 14 balls, and excited the MCG faithful and those watching on ABC-TV as they had rarely been moved all season. At one stage Cosier and Toohey added 26 in just nine balls, and 40 in three overs. One colossal six from Cosier was measured at 130 metres, and the game was finally won with 10 balls to spare, at 7.25pm, with many ABC viewers around the country still waiting for their 7pm news.

The unexpected Australian win led to another match, to decide the series. Played in Melbourne three days later, it was a disappointing, soulless affair which the Australians won comfortably, by six wickets with a massive 18.3 overs to spare. A lifeless, unpredictable pitch did not help, but the English batsmen looked disinterested and dismayed. Batting first, their total was only 94.

It was a game of few adventures, though Brearley, who top-scored with 46, made something of a name for himself by running out his wicketkeeper, David Bairstow, as they vainly sought a *sixth* run. A drive wide of mid-on had pulled up centimetres

GRAHAM YALLOP: FIGHTING FOR PRIDE

The huge disparity in Test experience between the visiting Englishmen and Australia in the 1978-79 season was cruelly exposed by the final series margin of 5-1 in favour of the tourists. The young Australians, drafted to win back the Ashes that their much more lauded World Series Cricket rivals had lost in 1977, tried hard and produced some outstanding individual performances, but they could not avoid stumbling to a crushing defeat.

However, despite their even larger deficit of experience in limited-overs cricket, they not only held their own but managed to restore a modicum of pride with a 2-1 one-day series victory over the Poms in the Benson and Hedges-sponsored series.

Limited-overs cricket was by now firmly entrenched in the English domestic scene, but even the most experienced Australian players, and that's not saying a lot, had played only a handful of one-dayers. As far back as 1972 the English, and their press in particular, had been exhibiting a superior attitude when it came to limited-overs cricket so their setback at the hands of the Australians was a major blow to their honour.

Graham Yallop was given the unenviable task of leading the Australians that summer and while he put up a commendable showing, particularly with the bat, he was always fighting an uphill battle. He admits that in the one-day arena in particular he was as clueless as his team-mates. But he said the simple virtue of perseverance paid off handsomely for the home team.

'The players played very well,' said Yallop. 'They were very inexperienced with only a handful of Tests between them. It was the blind leading the blind. It was tough for the players, trying to find their feet. They were playing well at Shield level at the time they were selected but there's a huge gap between Shield and Test cricket. In those days it was very difficult no matter what form of cricket we played. We were playing it by ear every time we went out in the field or went out to bat. It was a lot of guesswork. We had the techniques of course but there's a lot of difference between having the correct technique and being able to produce at the top level. For me it was a learning curve but I felt the players started to perform exceptionally well towards the end of the season. We were delighted at the success we had.

'We were totally inexperienced with one-day cricket. I think we'd played one or two games at state level but from an international point of view none of them had played before. It was a whole new ball-game. We were beginners. We were triers and we persisted and we won the one-day series quite convincingly.'

Yallop said that apart from perseverance the Australian tactics pretty much came down to sticking to the basics. 'I was limited in the amount of one-day cricket that I had played,' he said. 'Certainly it was guesswork, but the more one-day cricket we played the better we became.

'We concentrated a lot of our time

and effort on fielding and the bowlers were instructed to bowl line and length continuously for 10 overs instead of trying to bowl the opposition out. It was a totally different ball game and we approached it from that point of view. When batting, of course, we tried to get on with the game.'

Yallop didn't deny that facing the more-experienced Englishmen at a game they regarded as their own was daunting. But, in the end, that only made the taste of victory all the more sweet.

'We knew we were the underdogs,' he remembered, 'but it was a two-horse race and we felt we had as good a chance as the English did – especially on our home soil. It was very satisfying to beat them. They were put out to say the least. I can't remember the details of it but I do remember holding up that trophy.'

Another important component of Australia's against-the-odds limited-overs win was a pragmatic evaluation of tactics in the opposition camp – not the Englishmen but the Australian, West Indian and World teams doing battle in World Series Cricket. On the surface the feud between the establishment and the World Series rebels may have appeared bitter but Yallop was not stupid. If there were lessons to be learned from the 'Packer Circus' he was going to take advantage of the opportunity.

'We certainly watched some of their matches and particularly the way the West Indies approached the one-day game,' he said. 'We took notes on how they played it because they were the kings of one-day cricket. We took a lot of notes on their attitudes, how their bowlers bowled and the amount of concentration that was necessary to play one-day cricket in the field. So we did learn considerably from undoubtedly the best one-day cricketers in the world.' Such initiative was a necessary virtue because Yallop and the players were not blessed with the extensive support system that now sustains and guides our elite cricketers. The rookie captain and his green-as-grass crew were having to fend for themselves on the field while coping with pressures that would eventually get the better of an all-time great like Greg Chappell.

'We didn't have a coach, we didn't even have a manager,' said Yallop. 'They were the days when the captain did the whole lot. There was no-one to talk to apart from the selectors so it was tough. We basically had to do it ourselves.'

An attacking left-handed batsman whose career with the Australian team did not end until 1984, Yallop was a big supporter of the new game and enjoyed considerable success at it. He certainly did not need to be convinced of its future.

'One-day cricket is a necessary part of the game,' he said. 'I found it quite exciting from a player's point of view, because it's an intense game. You're concentrating on every ball – especially in the field. I enjoyed batting in one-day cricket. You do have to change your approach, but it wasn't difficult to adjust. We started to play so much one-day cricket that you adjusted very quickly. In the late '70s it became part and parcel of the game so you had to get used to it.'

from the distant fence, and resulted in an all-run five, though the fifth run was a rushed affair, made easier by a wild return that sailed over the keeper's head. The short, squat Bairstow, many metres past the keeper's stumps, appeared exhausted, and responded to his captain's call for a sixth like a front-rower forced to chase a winger. He was eventually out by more than a metre. Of the bowlers, the Victorian paceman Alan Hurst, who had impressed all summer, took 2-7 from five overs, while the left-handed Geoff Dymock dismissed Boycott and Randall in his first two overs, which proved sufficient to win the man-of-the-match award.

A week later England were back on the job, destroying the Australians by nine wickets in a dismally attended sixth Test in Sydney. The performance of the locals was lambasted and lampooned in the media – the fleeting glory of the Benson and Hedges Cup win soon forgotten. Few who followed the fortunes of Yallop's side that fateful season would today have any memory of the limited-overs success, in much the same way that few WSC followers would recall the performances of Ian Chappell's team in the Supertest series. Such was the perceived (and marketed) importance and lack of importance of the two styles of cricket.

The ICC had decided 18 months earlier that the 1979 World Cup would be held, as it had in 1975, in England. By the time the first ball was bowled in that second Cup, World Series Cricket had come and (barely) gone. Pakistan and the West Indies, reflecting their local public opinion, quickly restored their WSC players, while Australia and England went with the best of what they knew from the past two seasons. For England that policy was far from a burden, for only Knott and perhaps Underwood would have made a full-strength squad (Greig, who was by then based in Australia, would not have been available). Australia was represented by a compilation of untried tyros and a selection of the players who had been humiliated by England in the Test series in Australia just months before. Hughes, rather than Yallop, was now the captain, while, somewhat strangely, three players who had made worthwhile contributions to the Benson and Hedges Cup win – Toohey, Wood and the Queensland all-rounder Phil Carlson – had been left out because of indifferent form in the Tests that followed the limited-overs success.

Hughes had won the leadership after first becoming the third Australian vice-captain of the season (after Cosier and the Queensland keeper John Maclean) and then captain after Yallop, because of injury, was forced out of the second Test against Pakistan (a two-Test Australia-Pakistan series had been played in Australia in March). With the new skipper in charge Australia had won an unexpected victory over the Pakistanis, and Hughes kept the job for the World Cup and the six-Test tour of India scheduled to begin in September. The full Australian World Cup squad was: Kim Hughes (captain), Andrew Hilditch (vice-captain), Allan Border, Gary Cosier, Rick Darling, Geoff Dymock, Rodney Hogg, Alan Hurst, Trevor Laughlin, Jeff Moss, Graeme Porter, Dav Whatmore, Kevin Wright, Graham Yallop.

The 1979 World Cup again featured Australia, England, India, New Zealand, Pakistan, Sri Lanka and the West Indies, but the eighth nation represented this time was Canada, who, like Sri Lanka, had forced their way into the main draw via a preliminary tournament played out by the 'associate' members of the International Cricket Conference. As in 1975, all World Cup innings were confined to 60 overs,

The cover of the official program for the 1978-79 Benson and Hedges Cup, played between Graham Yallop's Australian team and the touring Englishmen led by Mike Brearley (right). The Australians, who were thrashed 5-1 in the battle for the Ashes, stunned the visitors by winning the one-day series 2-1.

with no bowler permitted more than 12. And umpires were again instructed to be severe on wide bowling, and to no-ball bouncers that flew above the batsman's head.

Australia's performances in the Cup were grossly disappointing – heavy losses to England and Pakistan, before a hefty, but meaningless, defeat of Canada – though by the time the Canada match was reached few believed the side was capable of mixing it with the world's best. The batting was too often below standard, and the strategies used were often bewildering. Against England, the innings disintegrated after Hilditch, Darling and Border had taken the score to 1-97. Eight wickets then tumbled for 56, and, at the 60-over mark, the total stood at a sorry 9-159. Some hope was revived when Hogg and Hurst reduced England to 2-5, but Brearley and Gooch added 108 for the third wicket, to set up Gower and Botham for an unbeaten sprint to the line. Victory was achieved with almost 13 overs to spare.

Border, a short, rugged left-hander from NSW, had come into the Australian side for the third Test against Brearley's team. In his second Test, in Sydney, he had impressed against the English spinners, especially in the second innings when his team-mates fell about him. Then, against Pakistan (Imran and all) he had scored his maiden Test hundred fighting a losing cause, before a composed double of 85 and 66 not out allowed his team to square that series in Perth. He had played in the first two Benson and Hedges Cup matches against England, but lost his place to Toohey for games three and four. Back in the XI for the World Cup, he scored 34, 0 and 25 in Australia's three games. With the compromise between the ACB and WSC, Border was chosen in all but the final one of Australia's limited-overs internationals at home in 1979-80. That would be the only limited-overs match featuring Australia Border would miss until the last of a five-match series in India in October 1984, a run of 92 out of 93 possible games. Australia's next limited-overs international after that 'event' in India was Border's first as his country's captain – the beginning of an extraordinary decade-long reign. Of all the things, good and bad, to come out of the ACB's two-year battle with WSC, there is no doubt the most significant was the emergence of Allan Border.

Hogg could not play in Australia's second World Cup match against Pakistan because of bronchial trouble, but rather than bring in another bowler, the Australians played the Victorian left-hander Moss in the middle order and used the part-timers Border and Yallop as the 'fifth' bowler. The gamble proved disastrous. Yallop went for 56 from eight overs and Border 32 from four, as Pakistan smashed 7-286. Rain postponed the Australian reply until the following day, but the result was never in doubt. Only Hilditch (72) and Yallop (37) batted at any length, the run-rate was always pedestrian, and the innings finally ended a ridiculous 90 runs short in the 58th over. The Pakistan captain, Asif Iqbal, was awarded the man-of-the-match award, for his batting (he scored 61) and his captaincy. The Australians had been outmanoeuvred as well as outplayed.

Australia's match with Canada started in sensational style, the Canadian opening batsman G.R. Sealy cracking the final four balls of Hogg's opening over for fours. Hogg, like Jeff Thomson four years earlier, had been ridiculed in the British tabloids, who wondered whether his performances in Australia had been something

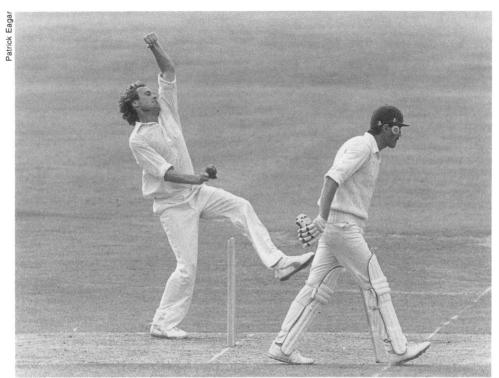

Patrick Eagar

Rodney Hogg bowling during Australia's ill-fated 1979 World Cup campaign. The batsman is England's Graham Gooch. Australia's only victory during the tournament was over the lowly Canada.

of a fluke. Mr Sealy must have thought so, but his daring assault proved a false dawn, and the Canadians, who had been thrashed by Pakistan and humiliated by England (who dismissed them for just 45, in 40.3 overs), were all out for 105 (Hurst 5-21 from 10 overs, Hogg 0-26 from 12 balls), before the Australians cruised to a seven-wicket victory in 26 overs.

The Cup eventually went, once again, to the West Indies, who, thanks to stirring performances by Richards and Garner, won the final against England by 92 runs. After the annual ICC meeting that followed the competition it was decided that the Cup would be held every four years from 1979, and that the '83 tournament would be staged once again in England. Delegates felt that England, with its large West Indian, Pakistani and Indian communities and the relatively small distances between major centres, was the most viable venue for a competition of this kind.

In September, Hughes took his team to the sub-continent, to lose a six-Test series two-nil. No limited-overs internationals were played. By this time the ACB and WSC had signed their peace pact, and WSC players were back in the fold, if not in India. In Sydney, the ACB announced a 67 per-cent rise in ticket prices for international matches during the coming season, an increase blamed on 'alarmingly rising overheads'. In Melbourne, an announcement was made that lights would be

BOB PARISH: ALL'S WELL THAT ENDS WELL

Given that the two-year battle between Australian cricket's establishment and Kerry Packer's World Series Cricket was by Bob Parish's own admission traumatic, the generous nature of the former Australian Cricket Board chairman's assessment in 1994 of the causes and effects of the whole mess is a little surprising. Parish admits to several errors and miscalculations by the Board, and says he bears no grudge against those who conceived of and staffed the rebellion. In fact, he believes World Series Cricket's championing of the one-day format was a turning point for the game of cricket.

'There was never any animosity as far as Mr Packer was concerned,' said Parish. 'I have said publicly on several occasions that I believe World Series Cricket was a catalyst towards the establishment of what is now the most popular side of cricket – the limited-overs game.' Parish said that once peace was made the WSC experience pushed the ACB into adopting innovations that it might never have got around to implementing. 'The Board was forced by that contract to get into limited-overs cricket and coloured clothing to a greater extent than it would have and in quicker time than it would have,' he said. 'Because there were still a number of people on the Board, and no doubt there still are, who were against limited-overs cricket and the effect they thought it would have on Test match cricket.'

Parish said the Board had not been entirely unaware of the implications of the 46,000-strong crowd that had patronised the first official one-day match in Melbourne. Still, he admits their enthusiasm for the new game wasn't what it might have been.

'Up to that point we hadn't played very many matches,' he said. 'The Melbourne game in 1970-71 indicated interest in limited-overs cricket and certainly from that moment on we were ready to program one-day cricket. But not to the extent we did after we entered into the peace treaty with World Series Cricket. I don't think the Board realised at the time the marketing value of limited-overs cricket. But it would have happened – there's no doubt about that. We were concerned at the fall-off in attendances at Sheffield Shield matches and concerned with the fall-off in Test matches as well.'

Parish said the ACB wasn't exactly Robinson Crusoe in missing the significance of the new game and the opportunities for growth that it presented.

'Really, I believe that the attendances at the SCG in the second year of World Series Cricket, 1978-79, were the first time that anyone realised, including Mr Packer, the real impact of one-day cricket – especially day-night cricket. But even then if it had been left to the Board at the time I don't believe the Board would have embraced it. There were a lot of traditionalists on the Board who would rather watch a Test match than a "fun-and-games" game. That's fine if you can afford to put the Test matches on because they're not cheap things. It had to be proven and it took quite a number of years, in fact it took the life of the contract, to convince some people that the future of cricket lies in one-day cricket.'

Although Ian Chappell said he believed each of the various promoters who had attempted to get a professional cricket circuit of the ground had contacted the Board, Parish said the Packer revolt came out of the blue as far as he and his colleagues were concerned.

'The thing came as a complete surprise on May 9, 1977, when we received a letter from Mr Packer advising us of the fact that he intended to start a professional cricket team. He offered co-operation with the Board but at that stage we were not in a position to do that. We simply wrote back and said that his letter would be considered at our next Board meeting. And from then on World Series Cricket started.'

Parish said the Board had no illusions about the problems it faced. 'The threat was more than a threat – it was definite. It was taken seriously there was no doubt about that.'

While he believes the Australian Cricket Board has not received the credit it should have for attempting to improve the players' lot in the mid-'70s, Parish admits that the Board must accept some of the blame for the split. 'The Board made mistakes, there's no doubt about it. People who have been on the Board would be the first to admit it. I don't think any administration of anything is perfect but the Board had taken steps prior to WSC to bring the players into the administrative side of the game through the players' sub-committee, which was established in 1976 before we knew anything about Packer. We had already passed resolutions that the Board would pay players the maximum it could afford to pay them taking into consideration its responsibilities to cricket throughout the country. The Board was very much aware of its responsibilities.

'I really believe that the whole thing that happened with World Series Cricket came because we made a mistake in that we didn't check with Channel 9 before we entered into a verbal agreement with the ABC,' Parish explained. 'We had always negotiated television rights since 1956 with the ABC and the Federation of Australian Commercial Television Stations (FACTS). FACTS was never interested in televising cricket and the ABC always was but not on an exclusive basis. We were approached by Channel 9 who expressed an interest in televising cricket. We took it to mean they were interested in the commercial side of television when in fact they should have said they wanted total exclusivity.'

That misunderstanding sparked the crisis but even if the Board had been aware of Packer's true intentions it is not certain that they would have or could have accommodated him. 'Would the Board have agreed to total exclusivity?' mused Parish. 'It did in 1979 agree to the principle of total exclusivity but it had had two years of competition. It's all hypothetical. Maybe if the amount of money suggested after we had entered into the contract with the ABC was proposed to the Board the Board might have looked at that and said we can't afford to turn it down. But there was no money suggested in the initial discussion. The only amount of money came up after we informed Kerry that we had entered into a contract with the ABC.'

Parish said the eventual reconciliation came about because both sides
Continued over page

ALL'S WELL THAT ENDS WELL

Continued from previous page

were better served making up rather than fighting on. 'We had two years of trauma until it became pretty obvious that the game needed the marketing expertise (that WSC had) and I think Kerry realised too that he probably needed the support from the grass roots of the cricket organisation.

'From an Australian point of view it was costing the state associations a hell of a lot of money. There were some people who thought we should fight on but what would have happened to international cricket? Maybe Australian cricket could have survived. NSW and Victoria could have survived but one or two of the other associations might have been in financial difficulty. And the effect throughout the world if World Series Cricket had gone into England or New Zealand in a big way would have been a bit of a mess.

'I think the biggest problem would have been the 1979 World Cup. It was scheduled to be played in England and the players' association over there had tabled a motion that their players would not play against World Series Cricket players. They hadn't voted on it, it had been deferred until April 1979. If they had taken that action and Pakistan had selected their four WSC players in their squad – the West Indies certainly would have – what would have happened to the World Cup?

'It would have had a disastrous effect on the 1979 World Cup and that World Cup was one of the ways and means that the countries who had participated in the legal action in 1977 would have recovered their costs.'

Ever sticklers for the book, the Australian Cricket Board waited for the green light from world cricket's governing body before entering into negotiations with Packer. 'The International Cricket Conference sub-committee came to Melbourne in January 1979; they interviewed Kerry and came back to us and gave us

---

constructed at the MCG, in time for the 1980-81 season (in fact, the lights would eventually not be turned on until 1985). And, in another significant change, the interstate limited-overs competition had a new sponsor, the fast-food multinational McDonald's, and was programmed as something of an Australia-wide carnival from November 10 to 25.

When the inaugural McDonald's Cup began it represented the first chance since the compromise for television viewers to see Australia's WSC and ACB cricketers on the same playing field (five Shield matches had been played but not televised). While the early Cup matches were being played, the Australians arrived home from India, in time to hear four different versions of *C'mon Aussie C'mon* being aired on television and radio, and media debates as to whether Hughes should retain the Australian captaincy, or even his place in the side. WSC batsmen such as the Chappells, Hookes, Laird, Walters, Kent, Davis and McCosker were now available, to compete with Hughes, Border, Yallop, Wood, Toohey and company. Could Kevin Wright possibly hold his wicketkeeping place over Rod Marsh in the

permission to act unilaterally,' said Parish. He then met with Packer's right-hand man, Lynton Taylor, and over a period of three months the details were hammered out.

As far as Parish was concerned there was no doubt about the ACB's principal goal in the negotiations. 'The thing we wanted to achieve was to see World Series Cricket go away. That was our main goal. We never made any huge sums of money. The point about it is that it was not a bonanza as some people thought. It was purely and simply a reasonable arrangement financially. The great point about it from our point of view and the international point of view was that World Series Cricket would cease to promote matches throughout the world.'

The peace agreement went swiftly from negotiations to sub-committee to Board vote, and by May 1979 the deal was done. 'We had a meeting in Sydney in early May 1979 and the decision was unanimous,' Parish said. 'The sub-committee that had arrived at the decision was made up of myself, Sir Donald Bradman, Tim Caldwell and Ray Steele, and the sub-committee's report was approved unanimously by the Board.'

Parish said there was no ill-will or resentment towards the players who had gone over to World Series Cricket – either during the fracas or after the reconciliation. 'None whatsoever. That was part of the agreement and Mr Packer was very, very strong on that point. That there would be no selection bias. There was no feeling whatsoever towards the players who had participated. There was some disappointment at the time and no doubt some people carried on feeling a little disappointed.'

Many figures in the establishment predicted dire consequences would result from first WSC and then the Board's deal with the devil, but Parish believes nothing but good has come from the whole affair.

'One-day cricket hasn't done any harm at all to the game,' he said.

Australian and WA sides was another poser? What of Lillee, Hogg, Thomson, Pascoe, Malone, Walker, Clark, Hurst, Gilmour and Dymock? Pub, workplace, classroom and loungeroom debates about the likely Australian team had rarely been so animated.

For Andrew Hilditch, the Australian cricket team's vice-captain in India, the harsh reality of this new world was emphasised almost as soon as the plane hit the tarmac. While his state colleagues in the touring team, Allan Border and Geoff Lawson, slipped back into the NSW XI for the state's second McDonald's Cup match, Hilditch was made 12th man. One day Australian vice-captain, the next NSW 12th man ... without even one chance to fail! As fans, officials, commentators and cricketers approached the new international season, few on either side of the fence knew exactly what to expect. Or what to hope for ...

A WHOLE NEW
BALL GAME

On May 30, 1979, the chairman of the Australian Cricket Board, Bob Parish, made one of the most significant statements in the long history of Australian cricket. It read:

I am pleased to announce that the agreement between the Australian Cricket Board and PBL Sports Pty Ltd has been signed and will be lodged with the Trades Practices Commissioner.

Under the agreement the Board has granted PBL Sports Pty Ltd the exclusive rights, for the term of 10 years, to promote the program of cricket organised by the Board and to arrange the televising and merchandising in respect of that program. For the first three years of the agreement, the Board has agreed that PBL Sports Pty Ltd may arrange a contract for the televising of the program with the Channel Nine network.

World Series Cricket Pty Ltd will cease to promote matches in Australia or elsewhere during the term of the agreement. However, under the program the World Series logo will continue to be worn in international one-day matches by Australian players.

The Australian Board will have the exclusive responsibility for the selection of Australian teams, and has agreed that no player will be excluded from selection by reason only of that player having participated prior to the commencement of the 1979-80 cricket season in any match not authorised by the Board. There will be no change in Board policy that Australian teams will be selected only from those players who participate in Sheffield Shield cricket.

It is envisaged that the program each season will comprise five or six Test matches and an international one-day series, to be known as the Benson and Hedges World Series Cup, of 15 matches plus a final which will be the best of five matches. These international matches will involve two overseas teams and the Australian team. The program will also include the Sheffield Shield competition and a one-day series of nine matches between the states.

Playing conditions for all matches will be under the control of the Board and the Board has agreed to consider favourably the introduction of the 30-yard circle in limited-overs matches, day/night matches and, on an experimental basis, the use of coloured clothing in Benson and Hedges World Series one-day limited-overs international matches.

The program for the 1979-80 season will not be finally determined for some weeks. England and India have accepted invitations to come to Australia in 1979-80. The Board has agreed to ask the Indian Board to defer their visit until next season, 1980-81, and will invite the West Indian Board to send an official team to participate in the 1979-80 program.

A basic program of matches has been prepared by the Board program committee. All matches will be played on venues as determined by the Board.

The following prizemoney will be provided: for each Test – $A10,000 comprising $A6000 to the winner, $A3000 to the loser, $A1000 to the player of the match. For each one-day match – $A5000 comprising $A3000 to the winner, $A1500 to the loser, $500 to the player of the match. For the one-day final – $A50,000 comprising $A32,000 to the winner, $A16,000 to the loser, $A2000 to the player of the match.

The Board is pleased to advise that the Benson and Hedges company will continue to be the sole and official sponsor of international cricket in Australia, of the Sheffield Shield competition and the Australian team.

Finally, although the Board's cricket sub-committee, first established in September 1976, and which comprises three Board representatives and an elected player representative of each of the states' practice squads will continue to meet regularly, the Board has agreed that the Australian captain, for the time being, and/or a players' representative elected by the states' six representatives, may attend Board meetings on request or by invitation to discuss any matters they may wish to discuss or that the Board may wish to discuss with them. The Board will also endeavour to arrange that the captain of a state team and/or the elected players' representative may similarly attend state association meetings.

The Board is unanimously of the opinion that its decision to accept the proposal from PBL is in the best interests of Australian and international cricket.'

Many in the cricket world had been aware that negotiations had been going on between the Board and WSC, and it had been expected that Mr Packer would win his long-sought television rights. But very few had expected the extent of the ACB's backdown. The public's reaction was perhaps best summed up by Gordon Ross, in the 1980 edition of *Wisden* when he wrote: 'From the outside, it appeared that from being arch-enemies with no compromise possible in any set of circumstances, the two parties had wed, and were now hand in hand ...'

A day after Mr Parish's statement, the Test and County Cricket Board, which had originally believed it was sending to Australia an England squad to play in a series of one-day matches against Australia and India, announced that for the '79-80 tour England would appear in no more than 11 one-day matches, and that no abnormal conditions would be tolerated. The TCCB also indicated the Ashes would also not be at stake for the three-Test England-Australia series the Board was proposing, a decision that was widely criticised in Australia.

English officials were bemused that the ACB had seemingly adopted the one-day game as their own, after years of scant interest. And they were disturbed that the Australian officials were so keen to adopt many of the innovations introduced by WSC – after all, the limited-overs game had been developed in Britain – and consequently refused to agree to the use of fielding circles, the white ball during strictly 'day' matches, and to changes in playing times that would have meant all 50 overs in an innings being bowled without a break. The ACB had also suggested that fines be introduced for instances where less than 50 overs were bowled in the permitted time, but this was dismissed by the West Indies.

Sadly, many of the disputes over rules and playing conditions had not been settled when the English and West Indies squads arrived in Australia, and the English captain, Mike Brearley, was obliged to support and justify many of the TCCB objections. This led to Brearley, who the previous summer had established a reputation for leadership few touring captains have matched, being ridiculed in the Australian press. Brearley arrived in Australia in the spring of '79 wearing a thick, almost 'WG-like' beard, and after his explanations for his Board's decisions were denounced as stubborn and unbending he was lampooned as a cricketing Ayatollah. 'Australia and West Indies can play with green balls and hockey sticks if they like,' he fumed at one difficult press conference. 'Our agreement was to play under existing laws if there was any disagreement.'

The various arguments for and against coloured clothing within Australian officialdom led to an absurd compromise. Instead of genuine colours, the players were handed predominantly white gear which featured tracksuit-type coloured collars and trim. The gear may have been stylish, but its introduction was unnecessary, even stupid. The coloured gear had been introduced to offset the problems caused by the white ball being lost in white cricket gear, but this new attire did not do this. After trials under lights, Brearley and his players recognised the need for coloured clothing, but handed back the stripes they had been allocated (the Australians and West Indians kept theirs). The Englishmen did, though, keep the royal blue pads they would wear to aid umpires who might have been hindered by white balls crashing into white pads near or in front of the stumps.

PBL had wanted to stage the one-day matches as an Australia-wide tournament before the season's Test matches. But the ACB had rejected such a concept, arguing that it would cheapen the Tests, which would have appeared as an afterthought. The program that was finally agreed to bore a strong resemblance to the WSC programs of the past two seasons, with a maximum 15 one-day internationals (including a best-of-three final) and six Tests, all of them intertwined so that no one series had any continuity. Greg Chappell later described the season's itinerary as 'impossible'.

The first international of the 1979-80 Australian season was a limited-overs match played in Sydney, under lights, on November 27, 1979, just four days before the start of the first Test of the summer. The game involved the new ACB-WSC Australians and the World Cup-winning West Indies, and the Australian side (chosen by a five-man selection committee that included the incumbent Australian captain Kim Hughes) featured eight former WSC men – Greg Chappell (who was named captain), Marsh, Lillee, Laird, McCosker, Hookes, Bright and Pascoe (a late replacement for Jeff Thomson) – plus Border, Hughes and Hogg. Geoff Dymock,

Australian opener Bruce Laird swings a ball to the leg-side boundary during a one-day international at the SCG in 1979-80. Note the difference in the clothing, between Laird's striped trim and coloured pads and the all white of England's Derek Underwood at mid-wicket.

the Queensland medium-pacer who had laboured with some success through the heat of India, was 12th man.

Much of the pre-match conjecture centred on the Australian pace attack, and especially the role of Hogg, who, after his dismal World Cup and a soulless tour of India, had been dismissed by more than one critic as a one-season wonder. Chappell gave the new white ball to Lillee and Pascoe, and they responded by reducing the West Indies to 2-18 within seven overs, before Hogg was given the 13th over. Almost immediately Desmond Haynes hooked at a riser, but the ball struck up near the handle and the bowler was left with a simple catch ... which he dropped, perhaps the easiest chance ever spilt on the famous ground. From there Hogg's afternoon went downhill, and he finished with 0-49 from his 10 overs, while Pascoe and surprisingly Border bowled the tourists out for 193.

The 20-minute afternoon break had come after 28 overs, at 4.10pm (four o'clock was the scheduled time for the interval, provided 28 overs had been bowled), during which time the West Indian captain, Clive Lloyd, who was not out at the time, had been interviewed on Channel Nine. During the dinner break between innings, there were problems with fans enjoying themselves on the field, perhaps dancing to the tune of *C'mon Aussie*, which was played incessantly. But then, as the sun slowly departed for the west, and the umpires, dressed in their 'day/night' outfits – black round-neck tops and trousers, with mustard coats and white hats (for all-day games they wore usual white shirts, tie and black trousers) – strode out to the middle, 'traditional' cricket finally had its chance to welcome the phenomenon of night cricket.

McCosker fell in the second over, lbw to Holding, but then Laird, the solid WSC man, and Border, the ACB's brightest prospect, steadied the ship in a 36-run stand that saw off Roberts and Holding. However, both batsmen fell to Croft, who was also unlucky not to gain a caught behind decision from the second ball the No. 4 Chappell faced. Laird's dismissal made it 3-52, but then Hughes strode out to change the game. One stroke, an arrogant flourish off the off-spin of Richards that sent the white ball high up into the moonlit football fans on the Hill, was the shot of the night. He and Chappell put on 92, and though Hookes was bowled second ball, Marsh came in to see the innings home. Chappell remained 74 not out, and was named, perhaps surprisingly after Hughes' innings, as man of the match. For an evening at least, the crowd of more than 21,000 roared and the shine was back in Australian cricket.

The following night's match between England the West Indies was a tight affair that is remembered for Brearley's final-over strategy that left all but the West Indian batsmen, the umpires and the bowler surrounding the boundary. England had reached 8-211 from their 50 overs, before a brief shower reduced the target to 199 from 47 overs. Until Derek Randall produced one of cricket's greatest catches (an extraordinary jumping, diving, one-handed grab at full pace, sprinting backwards) to dismiss Roberts at 6-177 in the 44th over, the West Indies looked safe. In the end the game came down to the final over, and then the final ball, as the West Indies' final pairing needed three. Botham was bowling to Croft, and even the wicket-keeper, David Bairstow (who removed his gloves), retreated to the fence. The bowler bowled, Croft swung, missed and lost his leg bail. In the aftermath, one of the umpires was knocked over by the invading 6120 crowd, while those who had unsuccessfully pushed for the fielding circles that would have denied Brearley his final ball tactic sat back, vindicated but disgruntled.

After Australia had drawn the first West Indies Test in Brisbane, the carnival moved to Melbourne, where a glorious 92 by Greg Chappell was not enough to prevent England winning by three wickets in the second-last over. The Australian side had three changes from the side that had played in Sydney – one new face, the Victorian opening batsman Julian Wiener, and two warhorses, Doug Walters and Jeff Thomson – while a feature of the English reply was the batting of the rejuvenated Geoff Boycott. Left out of the side for the match against the West Indies in Sydney because his batting was considered too rigid and slow for limited-overs cricket, the Yorkshireman was a revelation, scoring 68 in superb style. This innings set the pattern for Boycott's tour (he would twice win man-of-the-match awards in one-day matches), and later Greg Chappell would describe Boycott's batting in the one-dayers in 1979-80 as 'real virtuoso stuff'.

And so the season wound on. Significantly, while the Australians had little trouble winning the three Test matches against the Englishmen, they could not gain a solitary one-day victory against the 'old' enemy, losing their remaining three matches, all under lights in Sydney, by 72 runs, by four wickets (on Boxing Day) and two wickets. The final loss was the most frustrating. Openers McCosker and Wiener had added 74 in the first 23 overs, and then Lillee, Pascoe and Greg Chappell had reduced the opposition to 6-61, then 7-105 and 8-129 chasing 164. The unlikely English hero was Graham Stevenson, who had come to Australia only as a mid-tour replacement for the injured paceman Mike Hendrick. He was playing his first international match of the tour. After an untidy first spell he had come back to take four wickets and run out a fifth (four Australians made ducks), and then, after coming to the crease at the fall of the eighth wicket, had hit 28 of a partner-ship of 35 with fellow Yorkshireman David Bairstow to win the game with seven balls to spare.

Against the West Indies, the Australians had more success, though not enough to force a place in the World Series finals. In the second clash between the two sides, in Melbourne the day after the first Australia-England contest, Viv Richards smashed an unconquered 153 and Desmond Haynes 80 as the West Indies won easily by 80 runs (2-271 off 48 overs to 8-191 off 48). Richards' score was then the highest scored in a limited-overs international played outside England, and his second-wicket partnership with Haynes of 205 the first to go past 200 in any one-day international. Richards was already recognised in Australia as an outstanding talent, but it was this innings, coming after a superb Test century in Brisbane, that finally established him as a genuine champion in the eyes of the Australian public. Greg Chappell, who had tried to set fields to stem the Richards avalanche, commented that the display 'was the best I've seen anyone play for its controlled, consistent aggression'.

The crowd for this match was 39,183, almost 15,000 more than had seen the Englishmen defeat the Australians the day before. During the weekend 75 people had been arrested for drunk, disorderly or obscene behaviour, and the obligatory streaker had appeared on both days, though on the Sunday during the Australian innings he had felt the full weight of an angry Greg Chappell's flashing willow. This would not be the last time that Chappell, frustrated that an intruder had chosen to disrupt his concentration, would assail the naked offender with his bat.

In his book of the season, *Cricket Contest*, Christopher Martin-Jenkins wrote of the crowd: 'The glorification of the pop element in WSC cricket had undoubtedly encouraged the crowd's loutishness. This perhaps paled in comparison with the deeds of the football mobs in England, but it was nonetheless deplorable at cricket matches.' The SCG Trust's response to the problem had been to ban patrons bringing beer into their ground. But the thirsty could still buy as much as they wanted from the Cricket Ground's bars, which led to many concluding the Trust's decision was more clever than considerate.

In the third Australia-West Indies one-dayer of the summer, at the SCG 12 days after the second, the Australians had defeated the West Indians by seven runs in a thriller, thanks mainly to the batting of the restored Ian Chappell, who scored 63 batting six, and the bowling of Lillee, who took 4-28. The Thursday night crowd was 11,406. Two days later, an attendance of 112 less saw the West Indies thrash the Englishmen by nine wickets in Brisbane's only one-day international of the season. In fact, only two of the 13 limited-overs internationals were played outside the Sydney and Melbourne Cricket Grounds, emphasising that the ACB had scheduled the games with the intention of maximising returns. However, the one game played in Adelaide, between England and the West Indies, drew the third biggest one-day crowd of the summer – 24,986 – a result which led to five matches (including one in Perth) being scheduled outside the country's largest two centres in 1980-81.

By January 18, 1980, the date of the 12th and final World Series Cup qualifying match, Australia's elimination from the Cup finals had been determined. But they left the competition with a flourish, defeating the West Indians by nine runs at the SCG. McCosker made 95 and Wiener 50 in the home side's 190 off 48.3 overs, before Lillee (3-17 off 10) and Pascoe (3-34 off 10) kept the West Indians short. So, while the West Indies went on to defeat England 2-0 in the finals, Australia looked back on a record of three wins from eight games – all over the eventual World Series Cup champions, who beat them 2-nil in their three-Test series.

During the 12 qualifying matches, Australia bowled 43 no-balls, in eight innings. Their opponents between them, in 14 innings (one England-West Indies match was abandoned because of poor weather), bowled just 16. Giving such opposition this kind of start defied logic, and suggested an inability to adapt to the one-day game. So too did some of the selections, such as the treatment of the Victorian all-rounder Trevor Laughlin, who was brought into the side for Australia's fourth Cup match of the summer, bowled reasonably and scored 74, and was then cast aside, apparently because the selectors wanted to keep the Test XI together.

Crowd figures for the one-day matches were adequate, but by 1990s' World Series standards mediocre. The total crowd figure was 259,133, the average match attendance just under 20,000, the average Sydney night crowd just under 16,000 (there were eight one-day internationals in Sydney in 1979-80). The total Test attendance for the summer was down more than 300,000 (437,635 to 776,802) on 1974-75, that famous, exciting summer, but only 67,000 up on the disastrous Ashes series of the season before. The administrators conceded that their program needed fine tuning, but a return to the old days, as some yearned for, was neither appropriate nor logical. It was extremely unlikely (many marketeers said impossible) to expect Test attendance figures to climb back to the halcyon days of '74-75 ... and that meant limited-overs internationals were here to stay.

In late February, the Australians travelled to Pakistan for a three-Test tour which did not schedule any one-day internationals. In August, they journeyed to England for a Test match at Lord's to celebrate the centenary of Test cricket in England and, as a preliminary, a two-match Prudential Trophy limited-overs series. Both matches (of 55 overs per side) were won by England, the first, at The Oval, by 23 runs, despite Lillee's 4-35 and Kim Hughes' unbeaten 73; the second, at Edgbaston, by 47, in a match in which Hughes scored 98, of 5-273, and Greg Chappell and Rod Marsh chose not to bat.

After the Test, which was ruined by rain but featured some extraordinary batting by Hughes, the Australians returned for a season the Australian Cricket Board looked to with some dread. Instead of the West Indies and England, the ACB welcomed the less marketable India and New Zealand. Those who feared that too much cricket was going to kill the game saw season 1980-81 as the ultimate test case. Would the fans who a few years ago had been satisfied with a five-Test series and the Sheffield Shield care for another program of almost non-stop sport? The answer was that those few-years-ago fans would continue to crave for a return to the good ol' days, but continue to stay in touch ... while the new fans and the young fans wanted as much of their heroes as they could get.

Despite the absence of Richards and Botham, Lloyd and Holding, Brearley and Boycott, season 1980-81 would be the summer when the new order finally established itself for good.

GREG CHAPPELL: FLYING IN THE DARK

Greg Chappell was at the heart of the most turbulent era in the development of one-day cricket. In the late '70s and early '80s the limited-overs game exploded, producing radical change and considerable riches for people who had previously struggled for their fair share. For Chappell the new era meant facing the twin challenges of adjusting as a player and also a captain. The first task, he said, was relatively easy. The second was a beast of a very different nature. It produced some of the most satisfying achievements of his career and his most notorious moment.

'It was very different from a captaincy point of view,' said Chappell. 'World Series Cricket was the crystalising of limited-overs cricket in a lot of ways. Until then it had been treated as a bit of hit and giggle. All of a sudden it became an important part of the program and we were forced to take it more seriously.

'It was a tough but exciting time. I'm delighted that I was lucky enough to be involved but once the changes started to come very quickly we were the meat in the sandwich. World Series Cricket and the four or five years following the end of WSC were the real evolvement of this modern era of cricket. There was a lot of experimenting that went on – some of it worked very well, some of it didn't work very well. All I know is a lot of it disadvantaged us (Australia). And as captain I was the meat in the sandwich, between the players and the administrators, trying to sort it out.

'We were the pioneers. We had to work things out by trial and error; there was a fair bit of pressure on us – not least of all myself coming to grips with all that was happening, working out the program. In those days we played two touring teams. We were playing three Test matches against each side and we were playing all the one-day double-headers. There were double-headers nearly every weekend and we were expected to play in both games. Two one-day games in a row was much harder than a five-day Test match. We were being killed because we were copping the rough end of the pineapple all the time – the other two teams we were playing against only had to play three Test matches, we had to play six, we were playing all the double-headers, they were playing none. All the pressure was on us and it really disadvantaged us.'

Chappell and his men never completely adjusted to the particular demands of one-day cricket and in the end failed to construct a record that truly reflected their abilities. It is a perception, current both at the time and since, with which Chappell has no quarrel. But he believes their reputation as poor one-day cricketers is as much a product of those tempestuous times and the demands that were placed upon them as the fault of the players themselves – maybe more so.

'I think it had a lot to do with our struggle to come to grips with one-day cricket,' he said. 'Had we had a format much as we see today I believe we would have been a much more consistent side. I've no doubt of it. We took the brunt of the experimenting in the transitional period and it caused a lot of problems for us. Two one-dayers every weekend was just murder.

'And it was very hard to change things. Everyone was flying in the dark. I'm not trying to denigrate them, because I think it was a very difficult job, but you had a group of administrators who'd come through one era all of a sudden into a new era. As captain I was out there copping the bullets. I had to go back and report that the fire was getting heavy and we needed some help. Unfortunately it took a lot of convincing that the fire was as heavy as it really was and we needed more support.

'We needed help to redefine the playing conditions and so on to make it more of an even contest. Obviously, as the home team – the Australian team – we were the big drawcards and if they could get us on every weekend that was going to draw better than if one of the days was the two non-home teams. It was just killing us from a physical, mental and performance point of view. If you're going to burn off your players it's going to be self-defeating.

'In the end they finally realised that and that's why we've got the program we've got today. The conditions for all teams are pretty even. I was doing a lot of battling off the field behind the scenes to get the format streamlined so we weren't on the rough end of the pineapple all the time and that was taking a huge toll. I had a big part to play in the support structure that was set in place for Kim Hughes and Allan Border – the team management, press liaison officer and cricket manager, which has subsequently become the coach – to take away from the captain some of that extra-curricular activity, which could only affect his performance on the field. Good captains are a limited resource and I could see good captains being burnt off

a lot sooner than they had to be if something wasn't done.

'I'm not too proud to say that I don't think Allan Border could have survived as long as he did if he didn't have that support system around him. If he had to go through what we had to go through he might still be playing but he wouldn't have been able to survive as captain for as long as he did.'

Chappell is just as proud of another blow he struck off the field that has had lasting ramifications on the way the one-day game is played. Ironically it was a 'one-day gimmick' with a traditionalist ethic behind it that went a long way towards retaining some excitement and pizzazz in the limited-overs version of the game.

'I had a bit to do with the setting down of the circles and fielding limitations,' he said. 'The one thing I felt then and I still feel now is that the more like real cricket it can be the better game it is both for the spectators and the players. What I didn't like was the idea that you put all the fielders on the fence. That was the reasoning behind the circles. You force captains to be a bit more attacking, not allow them to take the easy option of throwing everyone back and hoping the batsmen get out. I still feel very strongly that you've got to put the onus on the captains and the players to be positive and try to take wickets. The easiest way to restrict run-scoring is to keep taking wickets.'

Chappell appears to be one of the few players who began their Test careers before the eruption of one-day cricket who embraced the game and

Continued over page

FLYING IN THE DARK
Continued from previous page

enjoyed it for what it was worth. Too many of them approached the game in a flippant manner.

'There was certainly that feeling,' he said. 'A lot of blokes expressed the belief that this was rubbish, hit and giggle, only a token effort as far as we're concerned – it's really not an important part of the trip or season so why bother to take it seriously? I was disappointed with that attitude although I was guilty throughout my career as captain of always wanting the emphasis placed on the Test matches as far as selection of the team was concerned. I preferred to keep the Test team together as much as possible and I still believe that your best Test team is pretty much your best one-day team anyway – and the West Indies have basically proved that in their 20 years of domination of the limited-overs game.'

Chappell said he still had little time for those who demand a completely different line-up of players who are supposedly more suited to the frantic strokemaking of the limited-overs game. 'I would like to know what a one-day specialist is. I think most people think a one-day specialist is someone who goes in there and slogs the ball in the air all the time. But if he can't make runs in four- or five-day cricket he's not going to be successful on a regular basis in one-day games. The bloke most successful at the extended form of the game is going to be your best chance in the shortened version of the game as well. Ian Botham is as good a hitter of the ball as anyone I've seen but he didn't come off that

often. He had a reasonable technique in that when he was trying to hit them over the top he was still going straight but blokes coming in and heaving it over square leg or cover won't succeed on a regular basis.

'I don't think there is such a thing as a one-day specialist save for someone like Simon O'Donnell, who for the balance of the team played a very important part for the Australian team in the '80s. He wasn't a Test cricketer but he could play a very useful role in a one-day game – bowl well, field well and come in and lift the tempo in the middle order.'

For all his confessed traditionalist sympathies and classic technique Chappell loved playing one-day cricket. He enjoyed all aspects of the game – particularly the increased opportunities to get involved. 'It was a different challenge, placed different requirements on your skills, and as someone who batted and bowled one-day cricket was the ideal opportunity for me. I was never going to be a true all-rounder as far as Test cricket was concerned. Except for certain circumstances my bowling wasn't up to Test standard but it was good enough to be more than useful in limited-overs cricket.

'Batting was a great challenge not only to your technique but also your ability to score more quickly. I think one-day cricket did a lot for batsmanship. Fellows like New Zealand's Glenn Turner and Geoff Boycott, two of the most obvious examples, were very much grafting players as far as Test cricket was concerned and one-day cricket placed different requirements on them. I would certainly say so in Glenn Turner's case. He was almost surprised at how many shots he could play. He'd never really let himself go in Test cricket but he was forced to do it in one-day cricket and I think it helped his overall batting.

'We could say the same about all of us. One-day cricket made us experiment and do things we may never have tried in Test cricket. I loved it. You could make more of an impact more quickly than you could ever do in a Test match. That was exciting.'

Chappell is not a great disciple of the slog-and-hope approach to scoring runs in one-day cricket. 'I didn't have to alter my approach to batting much in limited-overs cricket. The same basic technique was involved, albeit that you had to get on with it a bit more. You didn't have as much time to build an innings. I still had the same basic approach to batting – give yourself a chance to see what's going on and then pick the run-rate up. Basically keep the risks to a minimum, but obviously in limited-overs cricket you took more risks than in five-day cricket. If you were going to take a risk you made sure the odds were in your favour. In other words if you're going to hit over the top the straighter you hit it the better. If you start to try and hoick them over square leg all day you're going to be in trouble. I enjoyed the fact that you had to take a few risks but you had to keep those risks within reason.'

Like many class batsmen – Allan Border and Mark Waugh to name two – Chappell dabbled with opening in one-day cricket. Usually it's an experiment with two objectives: (1) to replace a sluggish opener with a player capable of scoring more quickly and (2) to give that player, who is often the team's most talented batsman, the greatest possible opportunity to build an innings and, hopefully, a really big score. Those elements were certainly there in Chappell's case but there was also a third reason.

'I was finding it a bit tough in the early stages of limited-overs cricket batting at four, the waiting and the building up of pressure if the openers and top order got away slowly,' he said. 'The pressure started to build and I was getting anxious and Ian (Chappell) suggested that perhaps getting in early would be better. I was able to get the bad balls away pretty well so if you got me in early when the field was up and there were any loose balls around I was going to be able to take advantage of them. Generally speaking it gave me the chance to learn a bit more about batting in limited-overs cricket. Once I went back down the order again I was a better player because of it. I enjoyed the opportunity because it taught me just how much like real cricket it was. You didn't have to change your whole approach, you just had to shorten the time span for everything.'

Chappell has been quoted a number of times as saying that one-day games quickly became a blur for him and were hard to distinguish. Still, with a little prompting, he was able to remember a number of personal highlights. 'I got 120 or 130 against New Zealand at the SCG, I think it was the same season (as the underarm incident). I couldn't bat much better than that, and I got some runs against England at the MCG. We were in a tight situation and I got a quick 30 or 60. The run-rate needed a boost and I decided to take Botham on and hit a couple of lots of 20 in two overs. I enjoyed that. Then there was the 100 I

Continued over page

FLYING IN THE DARK

Continued from previous page

got at the Oval in 1977 when we finished up batting in the rain. That innings was one I remember because I batted well and because it was like looking through a dirty window. It was about seven o'clock at night, there was a break in the clouds and the sun was shining through behind the rain. It was very murky trying to pick the ball up but the bowlers were as handicapped as we were. The ball was slippery and they couldn't stand up.'

Aside from the underarm controversy one-day cricket was at the centre of Chappell's other great lowlight as a player – his string of seven ducks in the 1981-82 season. Four of those seven noughts came in limited-overs cricket but Chappell said neither the one-day game nor cricket itself was to blame. 'It was unrelated to cricket. It was as much a family matter that created the diversion. My wife was finding it harder and harder to cop the time that we were away. I was very aware of her anxiety about the coming summer. We had three young kids at the time. I wasn't ready to retire but I went into the season and my frame of mind wasn't quite right.

'Concentration has been the hall-mark of my batting really. From a physical point of view I don't think I was necessarily any better than a lot of other blokes but I'd got into a system of concentration that worked very well for me and was very important. Going into the season in the wrong frame of mind I struggled mentally to get started that summer and basically started a run of outs and then it all compounded. Anxiety set in – you wonder what's wrong, wonder if maybe there are some technical problems and you start looking for things that aren't there – and I also got some good deliveries.'

Chappell said he was finally rescued from the slump by Dr Rudi Webster, who had managed the West Indies during World Series Cricket. Webster made Chappell think about whether he was watching the ball and the Australian realised that while he was still watching it he wasn't focusing solely upon the ball and was thus being distracted by peripheral clutter like the sightscreen and the crowd. His wife also went to Adelaide for the Test match and told him that while she wasn't really happy with the situation if he was going to play he should play properly.

'Once my mind got back on the job everything fell into place,' said Chappell.

11

THE UNDERARM

One of the great but often unrealised joys of being at a major sporting event is simply being there, as an eyewitness to the action. To know that what you are watching is actually a piece of history. An event, not just to those at the ground, but also to those who are watching on television, or will read the next day's papers, or next year's books.

Unlike other forms of entertainment, like the opera or theatre or art, a sporting event is ever-changing and unpredictable. Opening night at the theatre may be a news story, but not the night after ... and the night after that. If you're in the crowd at a sports event you are watching incidents that matter to a lot of people. It's news and you're part of it. There is an inherent satisfaction in being part of the roar, part of the buzz, and then seeing the next day's back-page headline or the television highlights and thinking ... I was there.

From the opening limited-overs international innings of 1980-81 (when Rod Marsh smashed three sixes from the final over, bowled by the New Zealander medium-pacer Lance Cairns), the summer was a series of extraordinary, often crazy happenings. Most remembered, of course, is the infamous 'Underarm incident', when Australian captain Greg Chappell ordered his brother Trevor to deliver the final ball of the third (best of five) final like someone in whites on a bowling green. New Zealand at the time needed six to tie. But there was so much more than that, including the return to international cricket of Doug Walters, arguably the most popular of all post-war Australian cricketers, the success of the superb New Zealand fast bowler Richard Hadlee, who adopted the mantle of 'villain' worn by Mike Brearley the season before, the batting of Greg Chappell, Hughes, the Kiwis Bruce Edgar and John Wright, and the Indian Sandeep Patil, the bowling of Lillee and Kapil Dev, and the umpiring controversies that culminated in Indian captain Sunil Gavaskar walking off the MCG during the summer's final Test.

For the one-day internationals of 1980-81 the players wore genuine coloured clothing, rather than the ridiculous stripes they had been obliged to wear the year before. The Australians wore gold and green, the Indians blue and yellow, the Kiwis brown and black. The white ball was a feature of every match rather than just those under the Sydney floodlights, and the fielding circles, such a success in WSC but rejected by the Englishmen in '79-80, were here to stay. For the Tests, the ACB scheduled the three New Zealand matches to precede the Indian games, otherwise the schedule was similar to the previous year, although the three countries played five one-day internationals against each other before the finals, instead of the previous summer's four.

Without the one-day series, the 1980-81 season may well have been an unprofitable dud. The first two New Zealand Tests ended with emphatic Australian victories on the third day, and the third was an uninspiring draw on a slow Melbourne pitch suited to dreary cricket. The first Test against the Indians in Sydney was also over in three days, and it wasn't until the final Test, played after the one-day matches had concluded, that Australia's opponents managed to win a Test. And that result had much to with the home team's weariness and a poor fifth-day MCG wicket.

However, the one-dayers produced a series of shocks and highlights, right from the first match in Adelaide when, despite Marsh's last-over heroics, New Zealand battled to a three-wicket victory. The Australian team, which featured three men new to limited-overs international cricket – Geoff Lawson, Shaun Graf and Trevor Chappell – struggled against the tight, predominantly medium-paced Kiwi attack (Ewen Chatfield 5-34 off 10, Hadlee 0-25 off 10) ... until that 50th over, when Marsh went 6, 4, 6, 4, 6, out, to take Australia to 9-217. During the innings, a substitute fieldsman, John Bracewell, took four catches, the first time a non-wicketkeeper had performed such a feat. The New Zealand reply was built around a solid 60 by opener Wright, plus significant contributions from Hadlee and captain Geoff Howarth. The target was reached when Cairns cut Lawson for four off the first ball of the 50th over.

This result did much to allay fears that the New Zealanders would not be competitive, but by the new year the Kiwis were anchored at the bottom of the World Series table, with just two wins from six games. In fact, the confidence gained from that first win was quickly stifled by a masterly display by the Australian captain in Sydney, in front of nearly 20,000 fans, as he marched to 138 not out off just 109 balls. Australia reached 3-289 off 50 overs. The Kiwis' tame reply ended in the 43rd over, 94 runs adrift. Meanwhile, the Indians, with three wins from their first five games, looked much more likely to reach the finals, and had gained great heart from their comprehensive thrashing of Australia at the MCG on December 6, their first appearance in the competition. Their total of 9-208 had been based on a sensational innings by Patil, who rose above the inadequacies of the dying pitch to score 64 off 70 balls. After the Australians crumbled to 142, Greg Chappell slammed the Melbourne square and suggested the remaining MCG fixtures for 1980-81 be transferred elsewhere.

Perth's first-ever World Series Cup match, between India and New Zealand on December 9, drew less than 6000 fans, but resulted in a tight finish – the Indians home by five runs after the final New Zealand wicket fell off the fifth ball of the 50th over. Nine days later, an unbeaten 105 by makeshift opener Allan Border led Australia to an easy nine-wicket win over New Zealand in front of 27,622 at the SCG. This represented, to this point, the biggest night cricket crowd since the days of Packer. And the fact that the grandstands and Hill areas did not really fill up until after 5pm showed how many cricket fans were now prepared to enjoy a night at the cricket after a day on the job.

Western Australia's Graeme Wood, who played 83 one-day internationals between 1978 and 1989.

After Christmas, New Zealand's fortunes turned. Howarth had claimed his side's poor early-season form was a result of bad scheduling rather than lack of talent, and complained that it was only as the Test series ended that his side was running into form. This fact, and two remarkably poor displays by the Indians, led to many revising their earlier thoughts as to the make-up of the finals. First, in an all-day match in Sydney on January 8, Gavaskar's team were dismissed for just 63 off 25.5 overs (Greg Chappell 5-15 off 9.5 overs). Then, in Melbourne, they made just 112, which the Kiwis managed in just 29 overs, without losing a wicket.

The Australian win over India the following day, in front of 31,882 fans, assured them of a place in the finals, but left the Indians in huge trouble, especially after New Zealand somehow managed to win a nail-biter in Sydney two days later. This is a match that is well remembered, if only for one extraordinary moment under the floodlights when Marsh, in the process of trying to swing a ball far out of the ground beyond mid-wicket, saw his bat disintegrate. The blade flew in the direction of mid-on, the ball trickled away for a single, and the great Australian wicketkeeper was left with a rueful grin on his face as he stared at his naked bat handle.

This was one of the best limited-overs matches played at the famous ground. New Zealand had made 220 (Wright 78, Pascoe 3-37 off 10) before Australia stumbled to 5-123 after Trevor Chappell's run out in the 32nd over. National hero and local icon Doug Walters, whose highly successful return to international cricket had done much to attract people through the gate during the season, was 19 not out. Out to the wicket strode Marsh, and the pair proceeded to belt the home team back into the game. For many in the crowd it was a return to old times, or to times they had been told about by older brothers or uncles. Under a moonlit Sydney sky, with the flashing white ball as clear to all as could be, the pair gave the big, noisy crowd new hope. Then came a crucial moment. A Walters pull for four was intercepted by an over-eager young member in front of the Ladies stand, and the umpires ruled that only three had been scored. After Marsh, new bat and all, was caught behind for 49 in the 47th over, Walters and Graf pushed Australia to within two runs ... with just one ball to be bowled. Walters stepped away to leg, and slogged at Martin Snedden, but could only get the well-directed yorker towards Hadlee, running to his left from the edge of the circle at wide mid-on. By the time the ball was in hand, Graf was charging for the tie, but Hadlee's throw to the bowler's end was sure and the bails were off with the diving batsman just out of his ground. It was a thrilling end to a pulsating game.

New Zealand's subsequent defeat of India in Brisbane assured them of a place in the finals against the Australians. The first, of a possible five, under lights in Sydney, was a disappointment, both for the ACB (only 12,581 attended) and the Australians, who crashed to a Hadlee-inspired burst, and lost by 78 runs. The ordinary crowd figure was surprising, as eight days earlier nearly double that figure had attended a rain-threatened Australia-New Zealand encounter at the SCG that had meant nothing in terms of who qualified for the finals. Perhaps, some suggested, the poor attendance indicated the fans cared little for a best of *five* finals series, or that, after 15 preliminary matches, six of them at the SCG (including four in the previous three weeks), the Sydney public had had enough cricket.

The fateful moment ... Australia's Trevor Chappell (above) rolls the underarm ball to New Zealand's Brian McKechnie to prevent a six and a highly unlikely tie in the third final of the 1980-81 World Series Cup. The sensational aftermath to this infamous moment in cricket history proved that one-day international cricket did matter to a great many people – even prime ministers.

Below: The two batsmen, McKechnie and Bruce Edgar (in white hat), and the Australian keeper, Rod Marsh, leave the field after the underarm ball.

Kim Hughes, who played 95 one-day internationals for Australia between 1977 and 1985.

Australia's two finest fast men of the early 1980s.
Above: Dennis Lillee wins an lbw verdict from umpire Dick French in 1980-81.
Below: Geoff Lawson seeks a similar decision against the West Indies' Richie
Richardson in 1984-85.

The people's game lured all generations, and both sexes, to the cricket of the 1980s.

EXIT
simple SIMON
OZI
OBSESSION
MELBOURNE'S
CRICKET
GOD
SIMON
DONNELL
Enjoy

One keen fan of Australian captain
Allan Border brought a cardboard
cut-out of his hero to the second
final of the 1985-86 World Series
Cup, against India at the MCG.

Border completes the winning run in that second final, a triumph that meant Australia had a decisive 2-0 lead in the best-of-three finals series and had won the World Series Cup for the third time.

Craig McDermott at the MCG in 1985-86, the season after he was first chosen for the Australian XI.
By the end of the 1993-94 season, McDermott had taken more wickets (171) in one-day international cricket than any other Australian bowler.

If apathy was the reason behind the poor attendance in Sydney, such feelings had been extinguished by final No. 2. This was the first final the genuine Australian cricket team had *ever* been in since 1975, and the Melbourne sporting public, the most parochial in the country, responded appropriately. More than 30,590 people travelled to the MCG for the second final, which Australia won, by seven wickets with 10.3 overs to spare. This set the stage for Game 3, one of the most recalled days in modern Australian cricket, which drew the largest one-day cricket crowd seen in Melbourne since January 5, 1971.

Nearly 53,000 travelled to the MCG for the contest, which began with Greg Chappell winning the toss and electing to bat. Border fell early, to Hadlee, which allowed the home captain to come out and, with Graeme Wood, establish a platform for a big Australian total. From 1-8, they pushed the scoreboard past 100, to 130, when Chappell, on 58, was apparently caught by Snedden running and then diving in from the mid-wicket fence. TV replays showed that the catch was a brilliant one, but Chappell stayed at the crease (as was his right) and was given not out after the umpires, Peter Cronin and Don Weser, both admitted they had been watching for short runs rather than studying the flight of the ball. Many commentators and past players thought Chappell should have accepted the word of the fieldsman, although others counselled that fieldsmen in the past have not always been as honest as they could have been. Chappell went on to make 90 (caught by Edgar, diving in from deep mid-wicket, off Snedden), off 122 balls, and put on 145 with Wood, who made 72. The innings ended at 4-235, which left New Zealand the difficult task of just more than 4.7 runs per over on the still slow Melbourne wicket.

Edgar and Wright set about the distant target, and 85 runs came from the first 24 overs before Wright was caught by Martin Kent off Greg Chappell for 42. From there the Kiwis' attempt at glory was built around Edgar's brave defiance, but despite run-a-ball contributions from Howarth (18) and Cairns (12), they always appeared at least a fraction too far behind the run-rate. The veteran John Parker, in at 5-172 in the 43rd, added a brave 49 in six overs with Edgar (who reached his century during the partnership), but was out off the final ball of the 49th over, caught brilliantly by Trevor Chappell running back from extra cover. This left the visitors needing 15 from the final over, which the Australian captain assigned to his brother.

In days of old, there are stories of great cricket matches in which followers in the city have heard of the events at the SCG, or MCG, or Adelaide Oval, or the 'Gabba, and rushed to the ground to see the final moments. Word can travel fast. Thus people raced to to see Benaud and Davidson tie the Tied Test in December 1960. Or Mackay and Kline save the fourth Test that same season. On Sunday, February 1, 1981, things were the same only different, as word spread throughout the *country* that if you were any sort of cricket fan and you weren't watching the *television* coverage ... then you should have been.

Viewers all over Australia who tuned in for the first ball of the final over would have seen the new batsman, Hadlee (Edgar and Parker had crossed during Parker's dismissal), slam the first ball back past mid-on for four. In the commentary box, the former Australian captain Bill Lawry was geeing his audience up for a big finish. But in the middle, the younger Chappell's next ball was aimed at middle and leg, Hadlee

One of the most controversial moments of the 1980-81 season. During the third final of the World Series Cup, between Australia and New Zealand, Australian captain Greg Chappell (top) swung a ball high into the MCG outfield, where Martin Snedden appeared to make a spectacular diving catch. The New Zealanders were ecstatic (centre), but the two umpires ruled Chappell not out, because both had been watching for short runs, rather than outfield catches, when Snedden reached the ball. Kiwi captain Geoff Howarth could not believe it (right), but the umpires' decision stood and Chappell, who was 58 when the non-catch was made, went on to top-score for Australia with 90.

missed, and was given out lbw. Lawry and co-commentator Ian Chappell suggested Hadlee might have been unlucky, as the ball appeared to pitch outside the line. In many relieved Australian lounge rooms and public bars, viewers, after watching the slow-motion replay, knew they were right. Eleven to win, four balls to go.

The new batsman was keeper Ian Smith, who had distinguished himself earlier in the season by hitting the great Lillee for six at the SCG. From the first ball he gleaned two, and then two more, the second a desperate risk as the throw came back from the fine-leg boundary. Now, with two balls to go, it was seven to win.

In the back of the Channel Nine commentary box Richie Benaud was pondering why Trevor Chappell, and not one of the Australians' more experienced bowlers' was at the crease for this most important of overs. He came to the conclusion that Greg Chappell, as many captains had been prone to do, had got his calculations wrong, and by bowling Lillee at the wrong moment had left himself with few alternatives come the final over. Lillee's final over had been the 49th, and the captain's choices came down to his brother, who had been expensive, the once effective but now seldom used medium pace of Walters or the occasional left-arm finger spin of Border. Neither Walters nor Border had bowled an over in the final and could hardly have been expected to strike the perfect line at once. When the start of the final over began Greg Chappell had no real choice at all.

Bar the first ball of the over, which Hadlee had smashed for four, Trevor Chappell's line, length and choice of pace had been outstanding. With the match's penultimate ball he was right on line again, and Smith's hefty swing was unsuccessful. The middle stump, struck near its base, went back. Now, barring no-balls and wides, the Kiwis needed a six just to tie.

The game was nearly over ... but not quite. Onto the MCG strode Brian McKechnie, a former All Black five-eighth who had once won a rugby Test over Wales at Cardiff Arms Park with a late penalty goal. If anyone was perfect for the last-over madness it was a footballer. To Greg Chappell, McKechnie looked just the sort of man to put his brother far up into the crowd.

While McKechnie pondered Trevor Chappell's most likely strategy, Greg Chappell thought up his own. The Underarm. He put the idea to his brother, not as a suggestion but an order. Then he told the umpire, Weser, who raced to square leg to inform his colleague. Weser then told McKechnie, who stood back, stunned and appalled, to consider his position while the Australian captain slightly modified his field.

And then everything was set in place. In the commentary box, Lawry told the throng:

> ' ... Well, it looks to me as if they're going to bowl underarm off the last ball ... Rod Marsh is saying, "no mate", but I'm sure he's going to bowl an underarm delivery ... on the last ball, and bowl it along the ground and be sure it has not been hit for six. The umpires have been told, the batsmen have been told, and this is possibly a little bit disappointing ... Let's make sure it is an underarm ... but I've got the feeling, as an ex-Victorian skipper ...
>
> 'They're going to bowl an underarm ...
>
> ' ... Would you ever believe it?'

As Lawry asked if anyone believed it, Trevor Chappell rolled the ball to McKechnie, who, rather than be embarrassed by an abortive wild swing, blocked the ball and then spun his bat in the air. And the crowd booed. Not everyone – some sat in stunned silence – but enough. The bowler took his cap from the umpire and headed for the stand, as Howarth raced onto the field to claim the tactic was

Rod Marsh blazes away during the fourth final of the 1980-81 World Series Cup, at the SCG. Marsh's belligerent hitting was a feature of the summer.

illegal. But it wasn't. The ACB had not closed a loophole that had been slammed shut in English limited-overs cricket in 1979 (by the fourth final, the underarm was an illegal ball).

Australian officials headed for the New Zealand dressing room to apologise, while in the commentary box Richie Benaud put his 'sums wrong' theory to the nation. In doing so, he described Greg Chappell's performance as 'gutless'. Whatever the validity of Benaud's assessment, the fact was that he was just the first of many highly respected men, both in and out of cricket, to damn the Australians' strategy.

In the following 24 hours, the New Zealand Prime Minister, Robert Muldoon, called the Underarm 'an act of cowardice'. Australian PM Malcolm Fraser said it was 'contrary to the traditions of the game'. Ian Chappell, on the back page of the Sydney *Sun,* asked: 'Fair dinkum Greg, how much pride do you sacrifice to win $35,000?' Bobby Simpson wrote of '(Greg) Chappell's selfish action'. Bob Vance, the chairman of the New Zealand Cricket Council, said he had witnessed 'the worst sporting action of his life'. Newspapers across the country editorialised against the delivery, which had been tagged the greatest cricket controversy since Bodyline. The Melbourne *Herald* called it 'an all-time low in win-at-all-costs gamesmanship'. The *Australian* claimed that 'the Australian sporting image had been tarnished as never before'. The *Age* suggested Australian cricket was 'in disgrace' and that 'the country's reputation as a sporting nation (was) severely damaged'.

And so it went on. As the hours ticked by, however, and consideration was given for the stress Chappell was under (and the fact that the tactic was within the rules), the attitude towards the Australian captain mellowed. But for a while he was fair game, and the critics had a field day. Chappell later released a statement in which he conceded that his decision was not 'within the spirit of the game' and admitted it was 'something I would not do again'. Two days later, the teams entered the SCG for the fourth final, and Chappell played one of his finest hands, a cool, dominating 87 that won the game and the title. Significantly, the reaction of the Sydney crowd was more for Chappell than against. Those who waited to boo him onto the field were outvoted by those who cheered their support.

After the Underarm controversy, the former great Australian all-rounder Keith Miller had pronounced one-day cricket 'dead'. In fact he could not have been further from the truth. The underarm delivery was the culmination of what had begun under lights at the SCG on November 28, 1978, when it had become clear that there was a multitude of Australian sports fans who wanted to watch one-day cricket. The reaction to the Underarm, almost hysterical, and involving prime ministers, newspaper editorials and inevitably bar-rooms, breakfast tables, classrooms, building sites and office blocks,

The much-criticised Aussie skipper with the '80-81 World Series Cup after his side's 3-1 win in the finals. On the dressing room wall are a number of pre-match telegrams and messages that supported the team and the captain in the wake of the Underarm incident.

showed that one-day cricket *did* matter. This wasn't just a money-making exercise for the benefit of the ACB, PBL and Mr Packer. This was important. After the Underarm had been replayed over and over again, on news bulletins, sports programs, current affairs shows and the like, *everyone* had an opinion. And, significantly, the 50,000 who had been at the MCG, and the tens of thousands who watched the controversy live on television, had an advantage. They had been there. Their opinion counted that little bit more.

In the years that followed more and more one-day cricket fans would seek that advantage. Something brilliant, ridiculous, provocative or breathtaking was going to happen, and anyone who followed the game, or knew someone who did, would be taking a gamble by staying away. You could never be sure when the next great event was going to happen.

THE UNDERARM – GREG CHAPPELL'S VIEW

It is not exaggerating to say that the 'Underarm Incident' has become firmly entrenched as one of the most controversial – perhaps infamous – events in Australian cricket history. Certainly as long as there is one Kiwi able to draw breath it will never die. It outraged fans from all sections of the cricket community and brought untold wrath pouring upon the head of Australia's captain Greg Chappell. Even his brother, former Test captain Ian, took Greg to task in the press. Everyone had a view on the matter and all too few were standing in Greg Chappell's corner.

With New Zealand needing six runs off the final ball to tie the third World Series Cup final in February 1981, and new batsman Brian McKechnie coming to the wicket, Chappell asked his brother Trevor to bowl underarm. McKenchie dropped his bat on the mullygrubber, threw his blade away in disgust and all hell broke loose.

The fact that the action flagrantly contravened all the cherished ethics of a game that had long been exalted as more a moral imperative than a mere sporting endeavour was only the start of it. Chappell's decision enraged his detractors just as much because it was senseless. He didn't have to do it – and that is an aspect of the debacle that few are aware of but which, ironically, formed a key part of Chappell's motivation. 'I'll never be able to prove it, and it doesn't really matter, but I know that had New Zealand been able to win the game I wouldn't have asked Trevor to do it,' said Chappell. 'The chances of McKenchie hitting a six were remote and even if he did they couldn't win the game. I know in my own heart had they had a chance of winning the game I wouldn't have done it. The fact that there was nothing in the game for them meant I could make my statement – cop this, this is what I think of the whole damn thing. Maybe now you'll sit up and take some notice of what we're saying.'

Chappell was being driven to distraction by a combination of the gruelling playing schedule and his exhausting battles with officialdom off the field. He was being torn apart by the competing demands of administrators, players and fans while trying to maintain his form as a player. His complaints about the playing schedule and the condition of the MCG wicket were not getting anywhere. That frustration and anger and helplessness all boiled over late in the afternoon on February 1 in front of a then one-day world record crowd of 52,990.

'It really all culminated in that day at the MCG,' he recalled. 'Unfortunately I was the one who had to bear the brunt of the discussions and the arguments and the battles that went on – first of all to get the recognition that the conditions were no good and then do something about it. I'd had a gutful of it. I was mentally unfit that day, and probably for a fair bit of time leading up to it, to be captain of the Australian team because I was mentally shot from the battles that were being fought off the field. When everyone else could come off the ground, sit down, put their feet up and have a couple of beers I was off either discussing the poor condition of the MCG wicket or the fact that we were being shafted with the program and saying something had to be done about it. The frustration of all that came out in that game at the MCG. It was really just a protest to everyone, not least of all the administrators but partly to my own players for some pretty ordinary performances not only that day but throughout the summer.'

Chappell, therefore, was not a happy man when the game started but his mood had sunk even further by the time McKechnie walked through the gate. Australia had earlier placed themselves in a position where they should have won the game easily, but as the final overs ticked away the home side were in grave danger of blowing it. Chappell stressed that he never felt Australia was in danger of losing the game. Rather they were a chance of not winning it.

'I was fielding at deep mid-on that over,' he said. 'I was just looking foward to getting off the ground and I looked up and saw McKechnie coming through the gate. I hadn't seen him batting. I knew he was an all-round athlete, he'd played rugby for New Zealand, and he was a big, strong lad. If anyone was big enough, strong enough and talented enough to get in a lucky hit like Wayne Daniel did off Mick Malone at Football Park during World Series it was this bloke. It was a possibility. It didn't matter whether McKechnie could bat or not. Wayne Daniel wasn't the best batsman in the world. It could be done.'

Apart from his off-field woes Chappell was very much aware of the hurdles his tired team still had to clear. They, as much as he, had been worn out by the preceding months of combat and were digging into their last reserves of strength to finish off the summer. There was no way he wanted to add to their burden

unnecessarily. So if there was anything he could do to lessen the workload he was going to do it.

'We had, potentially, another two one-day games,' he said. 'By winning that one at the MCG we could get an extra day off before the weekend Test match if we won the next one-dayer in Sydney. I was just very concerned about the Test against India because we were jaded. Our best players were mentally and physically shot. I thought, "Dennis doesn't need another game, Rodney doesn't need another game, I don't need another game. We need to get a few days rest. If we can win this game it'll give us a chance of getting through the season. I'm sick of the arguments about the program, I'm sick of all the arguments about the MCG wicket. Bugger them, this is what I think of the whole thing."

'It was a spur-of-the-moment decision. It was something I knew wouldn't be well received but I was past caring. I just wanted to get off the ground. I just wanted to get away from Melbourne for a few days before we had to come back and play the Test match.

'I just walked in to Trevor and said "How are you bowling underarms?". He said, "I don't know, why?" I said "You're about to find out." He just shrugged. I went and informed the umpire who went and told the square-leg umpire and the batsmen and I walked back to mid-on and that was it.

'The next thing I remember is jogging off the ground and a little girl jumping the fence. I slowed down to let her pass because I thought she was running out to the middle but she ran up to me and tugged on the sleeve of

Continued over page

GREG CHAPPELL'S VIEW

Continued from previous page

my shirt. I looked down and at her and said "Yeah?" and she said "You cheated". And I think that was the first time I realised just what sort of effect it was likely to have. It had registered it wasn't going to be all that universally well received but I don't think I expected the absolute storm that erupted over it.

'Some of the reaction disappointed me. I had no problem with the general public or the general media. There were two blokes that I thought might have had a little bit more of an understanding of what I was going through. And yet when I think back they wouldn't have because they hadn't been through that sort of thing. They were both in the commentary box at the time. The one who made his comments straight on top of it, Richie Benaud, and then my brother Ian, who followed it up with a column in the newspaper the next day.

'I thought, well, if two blokes could have any idea of what the job was like these two blokes should have. Whilst it was very easy to be critical, and I'd given them plenty of opportunity to be critical, there was no balancing comment that we've been through the same situation and perhaps we've made the odd bad decision from time to time. There could have been some understanding from that corner.

'I've never taken it up with Richie (but) I took it up with Ian very soon afterwards. We were practising at the SCG No. 2 on the Tuesday. Ian arrived and parked his car at the No. 2 ground and had to walk past the practice area. Just at the moment he arrived the police band arrived in their band truck. I made the comment to Ian: "I'm surprised you came in the car." He said, "What do you mean?" I said, "I thought you should have been in the bandwagon." He said, "What do you expect me to do? I'm paid as a commentator and I've got to make my comments." I said, "A little bit of understanding wouldn't have gone astray." He said "Mate, if I'd agreed with you they would have locked us both up, they would have said the whole family's mad." That was the end of it as far as he and I were concerned. We've had a few laughs about it since.

'The support I got from the general public through the furore of the next couple of days was sensational. The avalanche of mail and telegrams I got – not necessarily agreeing with the decision but just saying, "We understand that sometimes these things happen. Don't let it get you down, we're right behind you." It was sensational.'

Prime Minister Muldoon may have led the blood-curdling chorus of condemnation from across the Tasman, where Australian tourists were reportedly sworn at and refused service in shops, but the Kiwi players themselves took the 'affront' in their stride.

'Geoff Howarth (the captain) and the bulk of the New Zealanders were terrific,' said Chappell. 'They weren't happy with the situation on the Sunday but there was a reasonable amount of empathy – particularly from Geoff. He was fantastic. He was fielding at mid-wicket or mid-on when I came out to bat on the Tuesday night in the following game. There was a mixed reaction, a fair amount of booing and hissing went on. Geoff walked up alongside me, didn't say anything, and gave me a pat on the bum as I went past. There was unspoken empathy with the situation and the understanding that there was nothing personal about the whole thing.

'It was just something that happened, there were no hard feelings – certainly from his point of view. There were a few of the New Zealand players who were angry about the whole thing and probably still are to this day. Most of them were pretty good about it. They didn't enjoy it but they accepted it and got on with the next game.'

As if committing the heinous act wasn't bad enough on its own there were those who, in addition to vilifying Chappell's character, also stuck the boot into his captaincy.

'I was accused of getting my sums wrong,' he said. 'They said that Trevor shouldn't have been bowling that last over. You've only got to look back through the records, not only of that season but of seasons leading up to it, to see that I did a lot of bowling at the end of games at the MCG. At my pace the ball didn't come onto the bat as well as it did with someone like Dennis Lillee.

'I found someone like myself was having more success at keeping the run-rate down at the end because the ball wasn't bouncing enough, the ball wasn't coming onto the bat fast enough for blokes to hit it hard. On that particular day I was bowling quite well in the middle of the innings. So rather than take the risk of coming off and bring Trevor in then and me coming back later on I elected to keep going with myself and save Trevor for later because he was like myself – not quite quick enough – and he tended to skid a lot more than I did because of our difference in height. He kept very low so he was the ideal finishing bowler at the MCG. So that accusation was quite incorrect.'

12

PACKING THE PEOPLE IN

I n his review of the 1980-81 season in *Cricket Year 1981*, *Cricketer* editor Ken Piesse wrote: 'The potential of cricket's popularity surge, and the changing wants of the average cricket fan, is underlined in the takeover by the one-day game of almost two-thirds of our cricketing dollar. The Packer revolution has been justified. Cricket has benefited and has only just begun to prosper ...

'The cricket crystal ball has never been brighter. When two reasonably lowly international Test teams such as India and New Zealand can attract more than 650,000 fans through the gate, what are the West Indies this season and England the next going to do?

'The general softening of attitude towards the revolutionary marketing and changes can easily be justified when yet another financially successful one-day season helped to temper the losses of the Sheffield Shield summer. The popularity of one-day cricket cannot be ignored ...'

Piesse's positive outlook was mirrored in the boardrooms and accounts of the ACB and PBL, but the future was not quite as attractive to many of the players, who found the constant demands of the modern game extremely stressful. But, as Dennis Lillee admitted, 'obviously we have to play a fair amount of cricket to justify the money we are now receiving'. The ACB had adopted a system of contracts for its star performers, who now appeared well looked after, but the fact remained that for many players who needed more than just their cricket incomes to survive, the pressures of constantly performing on the cricket field were relentlessly difficult.

At the conclusion of the 1980-81 Australian season, the Australian selectors chose a squad of 16 for the Ashes tour of England. That squad did not contain Greg Chappell (for personal and business reasons) or Pascoe (injured). Both withdrew at least partly because of the demands that had been placed upon them. After the Ashes tour, the Australians faced another season of home Tests and one-day internationals (against the West Indies and Pakistan) and then a short tour of New Zealand. The Australian team for England was captained by Kim Hughes. In addition to Chappell and Pascoe, the experienced Walters, Thomson and Laird were left behind, leaving the new skipper with a side that would depend a great deal on the skill and experience of Lillee and Marsh. The itinerary was basically the same as 1977, a three-match Prudential Cup series scheduled to precede the Test matches.

The English captain for the Prudential Cup was Ian Botham, who, on the retirement of Mike Brearley and in the space of 12 months, had led England in unsuccessful home and away Test series against the West Indies. Even so, Botham approached the one-day series against Australia in a positive mood boosted by the knowledge that England had won all six of their limited-overs clashes with Australia since the ACB-WSC compromise. However, despite a comfortable six-wicket victory in the first of the matches at Lord's, Botham's confidence proved ill-founded as Australia came back with a thrilling two-run win at Edgbaston (Yallop 63, Lillee 3-36, Lawson 3-42), and then a decisive 71-run triumph at Headingley, in which Wood scored 108 and Hogg took 4-29.

For much of the final session of the second match, England looked to be in control. Even though Hogg, Lawson and Terry Alderman had reduced the home side to 3-36 (chasing 8-249 off the maximum 55 overs), the No. 3 Mike Gatting had led a revival that had England 5-224 with five overs to play. Hughes then held a frightening skier off Botham, but with one over to go the target was six runs, with three wickets in hand and Gatting 96 not out.

Hughes had kept Lillee for the final over. The great fast bowler had been suffering from pneumonia, and had left hospital only five days before the one-day series began. But here he was, as belligerent if not as fast as ever, and off the first ball the Surrey fast-medium bowler Robin Jackman was run out trying to give Gatting the strike. Off the second Gatting swung hard towards long-off where Lawson took a well-judged catch. The third produced a single, the fourth two leg byes, and the fifth (bowled to Mike Hendrick) an inside edge that carried to Marsh for the win.

The series win was a boost for Hughes, who had been heavily criticised in England two years before during the second World Cup. Of the impact of the 'new' Australian captain during the Prudential Cup, Botham later wrote: 'I always felt that Greg Chappell was not particularly enamoured of limited-overs cricket. For the most part he still insisted on setting orthodox fields as he would for a five-day Test match, seldom making allowances for the ingenuity of batsmen in finding ways to score when none exist; he seemed unable to pick the right moment to change from attack to defence. Hughes was quick to pick up all these points from that first defeat (at Lord's).'

The Australians went on to lose the six-Test series 3-1, but only after Botham (who lost the captaincy after the second Test) produced a sequence of performances unprecedented in the history of Test cricket to win the third, fourth and fifth Tests. Following the tour, Hughes, whose leadership in the Tests had been criticised, handed the reins back to Greg Chappell for the 1981-82 Australian season.

In 1981-82, almost one million people walked through the turnstiles for the international matches. In the World Series Cup, the West Indies were victorious, winning the best-of-five finals by three matches to one over Australia, who had qualified over Pakistan through their superior run-rate during the qualifying matches (both countries won four of their 10 matches, the West Indies won seven). The Australians' qualification for the finals was extremely fortunate. In the final match before the finals, at the SCG, with Australia needing a win over the West Indies to

GEOFF LAWSON: 'IT'S A BATSMEN'S GAME'

Geoff Lawson has a well-earned reputation for saying what he thinks and the subject of one-day cricket quickly hits a nerve with Henry. It has long been an article of faith among the bowling fraternity, and a pitiful few of their enlightened batting brethren, that cricket is a batsman's game. Lawson said the axiom is doubly true of limited-overs cricket.

'I was always ambivalent about one-day cricket because it is a game designed by batsmen for batsmen,' said the Wagga-born fast bowler. 'I used to enjoy the game but not the way bowlers were treated. I played 79 one-day internationals (88 wickets at 29.45) and 35 domestic one-dayers (39 at 27) and I got man of the match once – and that was in India. The man-of-the-match awards went to a batsman who used to get 50 chasing 180. The game was so much slanted towards batsmen it was ridiculous. All the rules about how you've got to bowl and where you've got to bowl. Even the balls! One year they said the balls were swinging too much and they changed the balls.

'From that point of view it wasn't very enjoyable. You never used to get the credit for bowling your 10 overs and taking 2-25. I look back at 1982-83 when I got player of the Test series and had a great one-day series. I went for about 2.6 an over for 10 games and took 16 wickets and averaged about 16. David Gower got a couple of centuries and got lots of runs in the one-dayers and ended up getting the international player of the year. You knew that you were being discriminated against because of one-day cricket. I couldn't have bowled any better in the one-day games. I was going out, doing my job, getting early wickets and a couple later and not going for many runs. There was just no recognition of bowlers.

'One of my best games was one of the first games I ever played, in England in 1981. I was really a junior player on the tour, I'd only played one Test match. It was the second game at Birmingham and I took 3-42 off 11 overs, scored 29 not out, fielded my backside off and I took the world's best catch on the deep cover fence at nine o'clock at night to get Mike Gatting out for 96 and win us the game by two runs. I just did everything right that day – batted, bowled, fielded – but of course Gatting got ninety-odd, got dropped three times and got man of the match. That was typical. I couldn't have played any better. I still spew about things like that.'

That feeling of victimisation was derived not just from the television commentary, media reports and man-of-the-match largesse but often included recriminations from within the camp. Australia struggled for a long time to come to grips with the concepts and tactics of limited-overs cricket and when it came time for post-match post-mortems it was

edge out the Pakistanis, the home team was struggling to keep in touch in their chase for a 190-run target. But then a huge storm made an appearance, and before the rain arrived, Allan Border smashed 11 runs off one over to edge the Australians in front on run-rate.

all too easy to make the superficial connection between the margin of defeat and the number of sundries conceded by the attack.

'In the early '80s we didn't play one-day cricket very well, we didn't put a lot of thought into it,' said Lawson. 'We really should have won more games. We would lose by 10 runs and the bowlers would get blamed for bowling too many wides and no-balls when it was really our lack of thought in the middle order that was the problem. We'd go out and slog when we needed five runs an over instead of pushing it around. Then we'd have team meetings and the bowlers would get the blame for bowling too many wides and no-balls.'

As much as he felt like the hired help, making the hard yards and getting nothing for it while his 'betters' reaped the accolades and financial rewards, Lawson's view of one-day cricket is not completely jaundiced. 'It was great to be out there playing under the lights with the coloured clothing,' he said. 'It was a real spectacle and it used to be great to go out there and field at fine leg or third man, which are really a couple of the hot spots in one-day cricket, and virtually show off your fielding. I used to enjoy that part of the game.'

Lawson's reputation for being outspoken is, not surprisingly, matched by his reputation as a thinking cricketer. Although the team as a whole was having difficulty getting the hang of limited-overs cricket, Lawson did his best to make sure he was properly prepared. 'It

was very different from bowling in Test cricket,' he said. 'You couldn't use all of your attacking measures to get someone out, you needed to bowl a specific line and length and every move had to be a defensive one. Your mental processes were very different indeed. You couldn't bowl bouncers and you couldn't bowl big inswingers because it might slip down the leg side and be called a wide.

'The way I approached it was that I had 60 balls to bowl so I had to think a lot and concentrate hard on every ball I bowled. I used to be really focused on what I was doing. I didn't want to go for a boundary in my first spell. My idea was not to get hit through the covers and not to get pulled or cut. So I tended to bowl short of a length, a really good line on off stump.'

And as the team began to look to him as the key man in a crisis he had to develop new tools for the job.

'In the early '80s I became the senior bowler so I had to bowl the final overs,' Lawson explained. 'That's when I started to bowl the slower ball. When I started bowling it no-one else was bowling it in one-day cricket. It was just like an off break which came in to the right-handers which was easy to slog when they started picking it up. Since then Steve Waugh and Simon O'Donnell have developed a couple of great slow balls that are hard to pick up. They can bowl them a lot because they disguise them so well; it works well for them.'

The crowd for that Sydney match was a stunning 52,053, the highest official crowd at a Sydney cricket match since 53,001 saw the first day of the January 1976 West Indies Test. Thousands could not get in, or see the action if they did make it past the turnstiles. And tragically one 15-year-old fan went too far in order to catch the cricket, and fell 50 metres to his death from the roof of the adjacent Manufacturers Pavilion in the Sydney Showground. With changes to the ground in the '80s, including the introduction of plastic seating on the former grassy slope of the Hill, and the replacement of the old Bob Stand and Sheridan Stand with the Bill O'Reilly and Clive Churchill stands respectively, this crowd figure will remain an SCG record for limited-overs day/night matches.

The behaviour of sections of the Sydney crowd reached its lowest point during this match. For too many on the Hill, the night games had become an opportunity to drink a great deal in the afternoon, and then drink a good deal more and behave abominably under lights. Arrests for drunkenness and obscenity were many, beer can showers ridiculously common, and complaints from those there to see the cricket long and loud. The chorus to replace the Hill turf with seating gathered much pace in the aftermath of this match. Complaints about crowd behaviour were not restricted to Sydney, though it was in Sydney under lights that the problems were most intense. The SCG Hill at night was too close to a zoo. From 1984, the SCG Trust gradually reduced the extent of the Hill until, within a decade, it was gone. Few who had sat there for a night cricket match regretted its departure. The behaviour of those who couldn't stay sober and sensible under the moonlight had led to a famous landmark's demise.

The biggest crowd of 1981-82 came in Melbourne, on Sunday, January 10, when 78,142 packed the stadium to see the West Indies comfortably defeat the Australians by five wickets, 5-147 (off 47.1 overs) to 146 (42.5 overs) on a pitch that was dangerously below standard. More than one Australian was struck while batting, and Bruce Laird was lucky to survive with no more than a dented helmet following Michael Holding's opening over. In this match, Greg Chappell scored 59, his highest World Series Cup score during a season that saw him reduced to four consecutive ducks and five ducks in seven innings in Test and one-day internationals, and a run of very un-Chappell-like scores through the World Series Cup series. His scores in the Cup in 1981-82 were: 3, 1, 38, 0, 0, 35, 59, 36, 61, 0, 4, 1, 0, 10.

Early in the season, the Australians briefly had to do without Lillee, who was suspended for two World Series matches after a much-publicised altercation with the Pakistani captain Javed Miandad during the first Test, in Perth. Consequently, the great fast bowler was missing when Laird played the Australian one-day innings of the season, a superb, unbeaten 117 that steered the home team to an impressive seven-wicket win over the West Indies (8-236 off 49 overs to 3-237 off 47) in Sydney in the first clash between the two sides for the summer. The only other Australian limited-overs victory over the West Indies (other than the rain-abbreviated 15th Cup match of the season) came in the third final, at the SCG, when Australia won by 46 runs, thanks largely to the batting of Border (69 not out) and the bowling of Lillee (2-18 off 10). However, the local triumph gave false hope, and the West Indies prevailed in the fourth match by 18 runs, their first victory over Australia under floodlights, after six defeats. This was the last year of the best-of-five finals series. From 1982-83, the Cup decider reverted to a best-of-three format.

Following the Australian season, Chappell took his team (complete with one-day coloured clothing) to New Zealand, where he regained all of his old form and

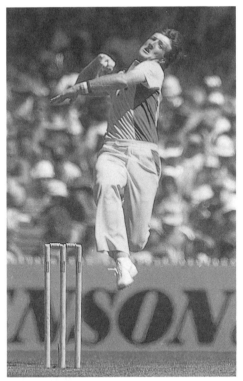

Four of best fast men to represent Australia in the early days of the World Series Cup. Clockwise from top left: Geoff Lawson, Jeff Thomson, Rodney Hogg and Len Pascoe.

was obliged to deflect countless references to the underarm delivery of Melbourne. The tour received extraordinary publicity in New Zealand, much of it a direct result of the controversy of the year before. Not long after the tour began, Chappell was informed local radio stations had received threats against his life. Interest in the tour was fanatical, and an unprecedented New Zealand cricket crowd estimated at between 41,000 and 43,000 crammed into Auckland's Eden Park for the first of three one-day internationals.

The veteran New Zealand cricket writer Dick Brittenden wrote of that match: 'Events in Australia a year earlier and a good promotion had made New Zealand a cricket-mad nation. It may be that disenchanted rugby union followers swelled the noisy throng.' Authorities had trouble with the size of the crowd, and the game was often held up while patrons spilled onto the playing area, or blocked the sightscreens. There were 74 arrests. The reception given to Chappell by the local fans was mixed, perhaps more jeers than cheers. When he batted a solitary lawn bowl was rolled out onto the arena, while a rather prominent banner suggested the Australians 'bring on Unkovitch', as in Vince Unkovitch, the local lawn bowls champion. But the tumult did little to disturb the captain's concentration as he made a masterly 108, of 194 as Australia went down by 46 runs. One potentially ugly moment came at the conclusion of Chappell's innings, when he was knocked to the ground by an over-enthusiastic cricket fan as he tried to make his way from the field. Chappell, though, made light of the incident when pressed by the media after the game.

Australia levelled the series with an emphatic six-wicket victory in Dunedin before a ground-record crowd, and then travelled to the Basin Reserve in Wellington where, in front of the first-ever sell-out cricket crowd in New Zealand and on a pitch that had lost its covers during a wild storm 36 hours before, Alderman (5-17 off 10) and Lillee (3-14 off 10) reduced the home side to just 74 in 29 overs, a target the Australians reached comfortably in 20.3 overs for the loss of just two wickets.

After New Zealand, the Australians had their first real break since the winter of 1980. In September, they travelled to Pakistan, for a disastrous tour under Hughes that saw three Test losses (out of three) and two limited-overs international defeats (out of three), with the third abandoned after missiles were thrown from the crowd. The tour was ill-timed. While the Pakistanis were coming off an extended tour of England, the Australians' preparation amounted to no more than winter net sessions and a pre-tour camp. Greg Chappell, Lillee and Pascoe were unavailable, while Marsh's arrival on the sub-continent was delayed.

After two drawn three-day matches, the Australians were soundly beaten in the first of the limited-overs internationals, played over 40 six-ball overs at Hyderabad. The match featured the first-ever hat-trick completed in this type of cricket, by the Pakistani first change, Jalal-ud-Din, in the side as a replacement for the injured Imran Khan, who took the wickets of Marsh, Bruce Yardley and Lawson with the final three balls of his seventh over. The Australians reached 0-104 (Laird 44, Wood 52) chasing a target of 230, but then lost 9-66 before their overs ran out. The second international resulted in another easy win for the locals (3-234 to 4-206, Laird 91 not out), before the chaos of the third match, played at the National Stadium in Karachi, when sections of the 30,000-strong crowd started tossing rocks, fruit, and even old batteries at or near the fine leg fieldsman, Geoff Lawson. The crowd apparently was making a protest over local water shortages. After Lawson was struck on the leg, Hughes chose to lead his team from the field. When they returned trouble soon flared again. The Victorian fast bowler Ian Callen (making his first Australian tour since 1978) and Greg Ritchie (who was making his debut tour with the Australian team) were struck, and, on the advice of the Pakistani veteran Zaheer Abbas, the visitors left the ground for the safety of the team hotel. Only 12 overs had been bowled. When, soon after, the crowd was informed that the Australians were no longer at the ground and the match had been abandoned, a full-scale riot erupted both in and out of the ground.

Back at the hotel, regular outfielder Lawson informed pressmen he intended to quickly develop his slip fielding.

The Australians arrived back home in late October, to prepare for a summer of a slightly different kind. For the tour of the England team captained by Bob Willis, the ACB scheduled a five-Test series, the first to be played from November 12 to 17, the fifth from January 3 to 7. Then, between January 9 and February 15, the World Series Cup, with New Zealand as the third nation, would be played. Many applauded the decision to separate the two contests, though others wondered at the wisdom of getting the Test matches over with by mid-season, and then staging a frenetic plethora of limited-overs action. If ever the fans were to get sick of the one-day phenomenon, it was suggested, this would be it.

The highest Test match crowd of the season came on the opening day of the fourth Test, Boxing Day in Melbourne, when 64,051 attended, though it was suggested that had queues at the various turnstiles not been as long as an estimated 90 minutes, as many as 80,000 may have pushed through the gates. For the one-dayers, the largest crowd came on Sunday, January 23, when an astonishing 84,360 packed the MCG to see Australia beat England by five wickets. Later, in the second final between Australia and New Zealand, 71,393 one-day fanatics crammed into the Melbourne ground.

During the World Series Cup, despite Australia's eventual triumph, two of the finest feats came during England-New Zealand matches. In Brisbane on January 15, David Gower produced a glorious innings of 158, which remains the highest score made by an Englishman in a limited-overs international in Australia. Two weeks later in Adelaide, after Gower had made another superb century, New Zealand reached a target of 297 with seven balls to spare thanks largely to Hadlee's explosive 79. This loss, and a later defeat by New Zealand, cost Willis' team a spot in the finals. Rain intervened after England had batted 17.3 overs for 3-45. Competition rules determined the match would be a contest of just 23 overs and New Zealand eventually needed 89 to win.

Australia, who were led by Kim Hughes throughout the Cup (Greg Chappell had captained the side during the Ashes series but then stepped down as skipper), were fortunate to make the finals. After winning their opening three matches, they stumbled to five defeats in six games, including a numbing 98-run loss to England under lights. The last nine Australian wickets fell in that match for just 37 runs, after 72 had been added in the first 15 overs. But a shaky 28-run win in their final

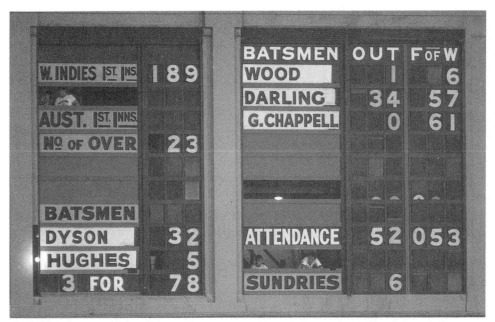

The SCG scoreboard tells the story of another of Greg Chappell's run of ducks during the 1981-82 season, and also of the largest official attendance to see a one-day international in Sydney. The match, played on January 19, 1982, ended in a victory (through a superior run-rate) for Australia over the West Indies and secured a place for the home team in the World Series Cup finals.

qualifying match, against New Zealand in Perth, sealed a spot in the decider. Once in the finals they dominated the Kiwis (minus the injured Hadlee), winning the first final by six wickets in Sydney (Hughes 63, Lawson 2-28 off 10) and the second by 149 runs (new opener Steve Smith 117, Wood 91, Lawson 3-11 off 8). A succession of leg-side sixes by Lance Cairns, who struck six sixes in 10 deliveries – two off Hogg, two off the West Australian bowling all-rounder Ken Macleay and two off Lillee – could not save the Kiwis in the second final.

However, despite the ferocity of Cairns' blows, perhaps the most stinging shot was fired after the trophies were presented. Safely back in Auckland, New Zealand's outstanding batsman Glenn Turner slammed the Australian team and the Australian crowds. Turner told reporters in New Zealand he 'felt like he'd been to Vietnam'. He dismissed the taunts and jibes of the Australian crowds as 'water off a duck's back', and said: 'What pleased me was that, as the tour went along, I got more and more boos as I went out to bat. That meant I must have been doing all right.'

In every season since 1979-80 the Australian cricket crowds had adopted a villain – in '79-80 it was Brearley, then Hadlee in '80-81, Pakistan's 1981-82 captain Javed Miandad and in '82-83, Turner, Hadlee and Ian Botham. At different times on the Ashes tour Botham, along with one or two of his team-mates, was criticised in the media over his weight. Finally the fans had their say. During the

Australia-England one-day international in Brisbane, someone let loose a pig onto the playing field ... with the name of Botham painted on one side of the animal's girth, and that of Botham's colleague, Eddie Hemmings, on the other. Players who lacked the athleticism of the game's best fieldsmen were being cruelly exposed by the one-day game, which had raised standards of throwing, catching and saving runs to previously unimagined levels. And the spectators, who in the past had taken great joy in recognising excellent moments in the field, now took it upon themselves to lampoon those whose inadequacies were exposed.

In 1982-83 in Australia, over 1.1 million people watched the Tests and one-day internationals. The average limited-overs international crowd was around 32,500, up 9500 on 1981-82. Of these Australian supporters noted author Alex Buzo wrote: 'When they weren't being arrested they were banging on fences, yelling for blood, and booing when opposition fieldsmen picked up the ball. They came equipped with signs, banners, styrofoam thumbs and fingers bearing legends which read "You're Out" or "Come on Aussie", and a thousand other objects d'art which PBL, the 'marketing arm' (as the jargonauts say) of the Australian Cricket Board, sells at its stalls outside and around the ground. Any one of these actions or props a few years ago would have resulted in the offending "mug lair" being told to shut up or get out by those around him. This is not to say that all these changes are for the worse; it is just that the rate of change outstrips everything else.'

Buzo also noted the introduction of the electronic scoreboard at the MCG. The replays, he wrote, 'produced the odd sensation of seeing a player booed some time after his transgression'. Sydney would not get its own magic scoreboard until November 1983.

It had long been accepted that the excitement and huge media coverage of one-day internationals had brought cricket to the attention of more children and many more migrants than had been the case in past eras. Studies in the early '80s showed that more and more future Greg Chappells were playing and watching the game. What was also becoming clear was that more and more ladies were joining the cricket crowd. In the *Sun-Herald* of January 28, 1983, Jill Mullens wrote that while very few women cared for the Test matches, for World Series Cup games ... 'from long-on to deep fine-leg the oval is ringed with women of all ages, shapes and sizes'. This she put down to three factors – that the cricketers, because of the saturation TV coverage, had joined the ranks of the daytime soap opera stars; that the cricket gave women real-life heroes; and that there was an 'overt sexuality' about the game that 'constitutes pretty heady stuff to the female watcher'.

The ladies who chose to venture into the outer at Australia's major cricket grounds had to encounter the heavy chauvinism that pervaded the area. Patrons on the Sydney Hill and Bay 13 at the MCG were always made aware, by the wolf-whistles that filled the air, that a good sort was walking by. And few considered their language or their looks as they might at a dinner party. This, quite clearly, was a male domain. But it was not a place where ladies could not go, and could not have a good time; after all, when the place got ugly it was ugly for all – male and female. Newcomers to the cricket soon learnt there was no discrimination when the cans were flying.

PHIL RIDINGS: ONE GAME, ONE TEAM

Phil Ridings was a national selector from 1972 to 1984, a period that almost exactly paralleled international one-day cricket's birth and explosive growth. He retired in 1984, having become chairman of selectors, and also served a term as chairman of the Australian Cricket Board. As such he is able to offer a valuable insight into the selectors' view of the one-day game.

While he never played a Test match Ridings was a talented batsman who played first-class cricket for South Australia for 21 years and was captain of the Croweaters for 13 summers. He did tour as vice-captain to Bill Brown on the 1949-50 Australian tour to New Zealand when the Test team was in South Africa, and was considered certain to make the 1953 Ashes touring squad but made himself unavailable for business reasons. So there is no doubting his credentials.

Ridings said that during his term the only criteria he and his fellow selectors followed was to pick the best team – never did they take into account whether it was a Test match or a limited-overs fixture. 'In the main you stick with your best players,' said Ridings. 'Unless there was some in-form player that stood out who would have been useful in a one-day game. That doesn't happen very often. You get a fellow like Dean Jones and like David Hookes and from there you draw the line. The odd ones are head and shoulders above the others. They give the impression that they could be good one-day cricketers. But there was never a player selected purely on the fact that they'd be suited to one-day cricket.'

Many players of the mid-'70s era have confessed to finding it difficult to take one-day cricket seriously but Ridings claims he and his cohorts on the selection committee were under no illusions as to the importance of the game. 'We treated

Glenn Turner had not been alone when he criticised the nature of the limited-overs crowds ... and he was not just critical of the spectators. He also blasted the Australian players: 'Their batsmen don't have the method to confront and adjust to the demands of one-day cricket,' he said. 'Some of their batsmen are simply block-bash merchants – in particular Kim Hughes and David Hookes, on whom they rely heavily to score runs. What's been happening is that they dead-pat the ball for five balls an over and then they think they have to whack the next one for a boundary.'

The Australians *did* have their problems. In one embarrassing episode during the

it pretty seriously,' he said. 'We treated it as another international game. We were very firmly of the impression that one-day cricket was here to stay. We treated it with a lot of thought. It wasn't going to go away and it never will either.'

The speculation that surrounded the Australian captaincy before Allan Border's retirement, and the perceived weakness that his successor Mark Taylor was alleged to have in one-day cricket, prompted debate over whether it was desirable, or even possible, to have separate captains for the Test and one-day teams. Most, if not all, respected critics rejected the concept and Ridings is no different.

'No, it's not a viable proposition, of course not,' he said. 'We never discussed it in my time on the panel.' Ridings said the selection panel was aware early on that not too much could be read into an innings that had crumbled under the pressure of the chase for quick runs late in the piece. He said the selectors were looking for more than simple scores and cut a little slack for batsmen who sacrificed their wicket in the hurly-burly of a one-day match.

'You had to make allowances under certain circumstances because people might have gone out there and been in a position where they had to throw the bat and got out cheaply,' he said. 'You put that in the back of your mind and didn't take it into account. You were looking for other things. To some extent you had to forget some performances that required a player to throw his wicket away.'

He does not agree with the old chestnut that the frenetic batsmanship of limited-overs cricket has corrupted players' games. 'I don't agree that one-day cricket has ruined players' techniques. Good players can adjust their techniques as simple as ABC,' he offered. In fact, he believes that limited-overs cricket has had a positive effect on modern cricket, particularly in the way it has sharpened up the art of fielding.

first final in Sydney, Lillee and Hughes had had a very public slanging match after Lillee wasn't given the field he wanted. It appeared the fast bowler's intention was to humiliate his captain. Many doubted whether Hughes had the respect of his players and the tactical acumen for the captaincy. But the ACB were committed to Hughes as their leader. As the team flew off for the 1983 World Cup in England, minus Greg Chappell, many critics doubted the ability of the team to function as a unit.

These fears would prove spot-on. The Australian team was about to enter the darkest hour of its one-day life.

13

ALL TIED UP

'*Hughes was deficient in one very important aspect of captaincy: the ability to communicate and liaise with his players. He didn't mix well with them on that tour and he tended to put Kim Hughes first and the team second. A few of the guys were talking behind his back and muttering things about what they'd like to do to him if they caught him in an alley on a dark night. That sort of stuff. It wasn't a happy camp and the unhappiness was reflected starkly in our performances on the field.*' – Rod Marsh, on Australia's 1983 World Cup campaign, from G*loves, Sweat and Tears* (1984).

The Australians embarked on a short tour of Sri Lanka in April 1983, for the first Test and first four limited-overs internationals between the two countries. Hughes, Marsh, Lawson and Thomson were unavailable for the trip, so Chappell stepped back into the captaincy breach, with David Hookes as his deputy and the Tasmanian Roger Woolley as his wicketkeeper.

The Australians won the Test easily, but lost the one-day series 2-0 after the third and fourth matches were rained out. The Australians lost the first by two wickets (9-168 off 45 overs to 8-169 off 44.1), and the second by four wickets (5-207 off 45 to 6-213 off 43.2). Greg Chappell was the bowler when the young Sri Lankan No. 5, Arjuna Ranatunga, hit the six that clinched the second match, and, as it proved, the series. The Sri Lankans had needed 90 with just 72 balls remaining. The first one-day international was played the day after the Australians arrived in the Sri Lankan capital, Colombo.

When the Australian selectors chose the team for the 1983 World Cup to be staged in England, they relied in the main on the team that had won the 1983 World Series Cup final for the basis of their squad. Of the 12 players who appeared in the two finals matches against New Zealand, only Greg Chappell and Steve Smith were missing. Chappell withdrew with a neck injury. Smith, the young NSW right-hand opening bat who had made such an impression in the latter stages of the World Series Cup with his batting and fielding, was a notable omission from the World Cup squad. The full team was Kim Hughes (captain), David Hookes (vice-captain), Allan Border, Trevor Chappell, Tom Hogan, Rodney Hogg, Geoff Lawson, Dennis Lillee, Rod Marsh, Ken MacLeay, Jeff Thomson, Kepler Wessels, Graeme Wood and Graham Yallop.

Hogan, a left-hand finger spinner from Western Australia, had been surprisingly preferred to his state team-mate, the off-spinner Bruce Yardley, in the World Series Cup qualifying matches in '83, despite Yardley's impressive form in the Test series against England. Both Hogan and Yardley had played in the Test match in Sri Lanka. Wessels, the South African-born opening batsman who had made his name in Australia in World Series Cricket, had become eligible for the Australian team at the beginning of the 1982-83 season, and marked his first Test appearance in Brisbane in the second Test with a resolute 162, just three short of the Australian record for the highest individual innings on Test debut. He had lost his place to Smith for the final qualifying match of the World Series Cup and the finals, but was surprisingly preferred for England, apparently on the basis of his superior form in Sri Lanka. Trevor Chappell was seen as the replacement for his elder brother, while Hookes was given the vice-captaincy after Marsh indicated he would rather not have the job.

As in previous World Cups, the eight teams were split into two groups of four, with matches over 60 overs. However, instead of each team playing their group rivals once, this time they would play twice, after which the two top teams in each group would go through to the semi-finals. Once again, the umpires were instructed to apply a stricter interpretation to wides and bouncers. There were no fielding 'circles'. The pre-tournament favourites for the World Cup were the West Indies, at 11-8 on, with England at 7-2, Australia and Pakistan at 6-1, New Zealand at 9-1, and India all but unwanted at 33-1. The outsiders of the field, at 1000-1 were Zimbabwe.

Australia's first opponents were the men from Zimbabwe, who were playing their first-ever limited-overs international. For the Australians the match became something of a game of milestones – Marsh completed his 100th catch in one-day internationals, Lillee took his 100th wicket ... and Australia suffered perhaps their most embarrassing one-day defeat, by 13 runs. Duncan Fletcher, the Zimbabwean captain, with 69 not out and 4-42, became the first man to take four wickets and score 50 in a limited-overs international.

Hughes had given the opposing batsmen first use of the Trent Bridge wicket, and by lunch the score was 5-94 off 33 overs. But in the afternoon session the bowling and fielding deteriorated (five catches went down), and Fletcher's intelligent hitting saw Zimbabwe reach 6-239. Wood and Wessels then started confidently, adding 61 before the West Australian was caught behind for 32. Hughes then fell for a duck, Hookes for 20 and Yallop for 2. Wessels became bogged down and was then run out, and the task was left to Marsh (who finished 50 not out) to try to redeem a lost cause. The Australians, as their captain admitted, had been 'outplayed'.

Two days later, at Headingley, Australia faced the West Indies who themselves had lost their opening match to India. In a match that was extended over two days because of poor weather, the outsiders were thrashed by 101 runs. The West Indian paceman Winston Davis became the first man to take seven wickets in a limited-overs international, the Australians conceded 11 no-balls and 10 wides in the West Indies 9-252, and Wood was taken to hospital after being struck by a ball in Michael Holding's second over. The Australians were bowled out for 151 in the 31st over.

For the side's third match, against India at Trent Bridge, the Australians dropped

Dennis Lillee for Tom Hogan. Lillee had missed most of the previous Australian season because of a knee injury, and by his high standards was below his best against Zimbabwe and the West Indies. But the sacking was still a bombshell, as was the Indians' decision to drop their greatest batsman, Sunil Gavaskar. Wood's replacement was Trevor Chappell, who stepped out and scored 110 as Australia reached 9-320 off their 60 overs. Then Ken MacLeay, who had replaced Thomson for the West Indies game and held his place here, came on as second change and took 6-39 off 11.5 overs, the best bowling by an Australian in a one-day international since Gary Gilmour's famous 6-14 at Headingley in 1975. India collapsed to be all out for 158.

That victory, and a somewhat fortunate 32-run defeat of Zimbabwe at Southampton – with eight overs remaining the Africans had needed 61 with five wickets in hand – pushed the Australians back to equal second on the group ladder with India. One win from their remaining two qualifying games would put them in the semi-finals. An injury to Lawson had given Lillee a reprieve (strangely MacLeay was dropped for Thomson) while Wood had come back to score 72 against Zimbabwe, but against the West Indies at Lord's, Australia were beaten again, 6-273 off 60 overs to 3-276 off 57.5. The batting effort was commendable – Hughes made 69, Hookes 56, Yallop 52 and Marsh 37 from 26 balls – but the bowling, with the brave exception of Hogg (1-25 from 12) was slaughtered by Haynes, Greenidge and Richards. Lillee went for 52 from 12, Thomson for 64 from 11, and near the finish Lloyd was clearly trying (albeit unsuccessfully) to manipulate the strike so Richards could reach his century.

Even with this defeat Australia were only a win away from the semi-finals. But Hughes, who had batted with a runner at Lord's, withdrew from the side (it was later suggested he had decided to rest the leg for the semi-finals) to be replaced by MacLeay. Lawson also returned, for Lillee. The match was played at Chelmsford, in Essex, and India batted first, for 247 from 55.5 overs. Yashpal Sharma, with 40, was top score. Second-top score was extras, with 37, including 15 no-balls and nine wides. The Australian reply was a disaster. From 1-46 to 7-78; only Border managed more than 30, and the innings ended in the 39th over with Australia 119 runs from the semi-finals.

While India went on to stun the cricket world by winning the whole thing – defeating first England in the semi-final and then the West Indies in the final – the Australians snuck home to reflect on a Cup gone wrong. Team harmony was clearly not what it could have been. One player, Trevor Chappell, confirmed that there was still a 'hangover' from the days of World Series Cricket. Rumours spread that negotiations had been taking place during the Cup concerning a proposed 'rebel' tour of South Africa, which involved some players but not others. Hughes returned to Australia without the rest of his team, and to criticism from media and players alike, including his vice-captain Hookes, who was fined $1200 by the ACB for suggesting on an Adelaide radio station that Marsh would be a better Australian captain. When Lawson later called Australia's '83 World Cup tour a 'disaster' he was being kind. It was one of the sorriest chapters in Australian cricket.

Hughes retained the captaincy over Marsh after an ACB vote that preceded the

Steve Smith of NSW, who scored two one-day centuries for Australia, one each in 1982-83 (against New Zealand, in the second World Series Cup final) and in 1983-84 (against Pakistan), but disappeared from Australian first-class cricket after touring South Africa with a rebel Australian side in 1985-86 and 1986-87.

Dean Jones, during his debut in Australia's colours, an innings of 40 not out against Pakistan on January 30, 1984, at the Adelaide Oval. Australia won the match by 70 runs.

1983-84 season, with the support for Hughes of the two West Australian delegates proving crucial. The season's structure was identical to the previous summer with five Tests, this time against Pakistan, preceding the World Series Cup which would involve Pakistan and the West Indies. Marsh decided he would accept the vice-captaincy, while Greg Chappell announced his availability for the Test series.

Australia won the Test series easily, 2-0, though the matches would undoubtedly have been closer had Pakistan's superb but injured captain Imran Khan been able to play in the first three Tests. Following the fifth Test at the SCG, which Australia won by 10 wickets, Greg Chappell and Dennis Lillee both announced their retirement from international cricket. They were soon joined in the 'past greats' ranks by Rod Marsh, who announced during the World Series Cup that he too was departing, after the Cup, a tournament that provided few highlights, bar some massive attendance figures, until the finals series.

The Pakistanis could win only one game, a shock 97-run defeat of the West Indies in the third qualifying match, while Australia's only win over the West Indies came in the final qualifying match, an 18-run win in Perth. But the main talking point was the fantastic crowds – 72,610 at the MCG to see the opening match of the Cup, between Australia and the West Indies, and then 86,133 at the Australia-West Indies match at the MCG on Sunday, January 22. Those at the latter contest saw a memorable display by Viv Richards, who smashed 106 in 96 balls. Crowds in Brisbane, Perth and Adelaide were also huge. In fact, from this season on, crowds for Sunday limited-overs internationals involving Australia were almost inevitably sell-outs.

For the one-day matches at the MCG, officials had decided, as their Sydney colleagues had already done, to ban the bringing of alcohol into the ground by spectators. They then went one step further, and limited the purchase of beer to two (opened) cans at any one time. After more than 70,000 had attended the first international of the summer, the highly respected Melbourne writer Keith Dunstan applauded this move: 'The yobbies with their sea of empty stubbies around their ankles, the cascades of bottles down the concrete steps, weren't there. It was good to be at the cricket again without a brawling drunk at your elbow.'

There was a marked improvement in crowd behaviour in 1983-84. The police still had their problems, and newspaper and cricket magazine editors continued to receive letters of complaint from aggrieved or abused patrons, but the depths of obscenity and drunkenness had been reached the previous year. The decision by television producers not to train their cameras on the crowd invaders led to a sharp decline in such invasions. The invaders had lost their audience. The introduction of surveillance cameras was also effective. Gradually, from this season on, the question of crowd control became less of an issue, less of a back-page (or front-page) headline. The issue, however, would not disappear completely. As late as 1993-94, the SCG Trust commisioned NSW's highly popular Mike Whitney to plea, via the electronic scoreboard, for good behaviour from the masses.

The first final went the same predictable way as most of the qualifying matches, a brutal nine-wicket demolition by the West Indies over the home team under lights in Sydney. A feature of the thrashing was a sensational, undefeated 80 by a new star, Richie Richardson, who opened the batting with Desmond Haynes.

During the finals, the Australian team became involved in a dispute with the ACB over the contracts for their upcoming tour of the West Indies. A meeting of all 16 players and ACB officials was held at 7.30 on the morning of the first final, and Hughes was seen in discussion with his lawyer just half-an-hour before that game. The area of contention concerned a clause that would have tied the signing players to the ACB for two years from the commencement of the tour (with no financial guarantees), a move by the Board that was a direct result of the rumours concerning a rebel South African tour that had existed since before the 1983 World Cup. After that early-morning meeting the Board's legal people went away and modified the tour contracts, which were then signed by the players in the days between the first and second final. Hughes later claimed the Australians' improved showing in the second final was a direct result of the issue being settled. Others suggested that Lawson's actions in the field, where he was reported by the umpires for dissent, were also a result of the negotiations. The fast bowler had been the last to sign on the morning of the second final, after a frustrating delay.

Lawson was the central figure in the exciting finish to the second final, on Saturday, February 11, at the MCG. Most expected the West Indies to clinch the finals with another decisive victory but, as the afternoon wore on, the crowd of nearly 40,000 suddenly realised the locals were in with a chance, despite having lost two batsmen, Greg Ritchie (knee) and Steve Smith (dislocated shoulder) through injury. The West Indies, even with Jeffrey Dujon smashing 14 from the 50th over, had been restricted to 5-222. Hogan, Marsh and Hogg had each completed brilliant catches. Then, after Wessels and Hughes had added 109 for the second wicket, with seven overs to go, Australia need 47. Lawson was in at No. 7, and with Marsh he took the score to 192 before the keeper was out, bowled by Joel Garner, for 16, off just 13 balls. But, even with Marsh's hitting, 31 were now needed from the final four overs.

In the Nine box, the commentators were as close to the game as the fans in the outer. The on-air team, made up of some of the greats of the game – Benaud, Ian Chappell, Lawry, Greig, Tyson, Walker, Stackpole – had, through their sometimes biased, sometimes absurd, sometimes provocative and always excited descriptions, become as much a part of the summer as the cricket itself. In the final overs of this gripping second final, the Victorian pairing of Lawry and Stackpole was at the microphone, calling the action and avidly reflecting the hopes of the MCG.

In the 47th over, Holding dropped Lawson off his own bowling – an absolute sitter. Then Richards, who was acting as captain with the injured Lloyd off the field, had to bring himself back to bowl the 48th over so Garner could be saved for the finish. Lawson smashed him through the covers. 'You little beauty, Geoff Lawson!' screamed Bill Lawry as the ball raced to the boundary.

The crowd had really got into the game while Hughes and Wessels were in control. But the quick dismissals of Wessels, Ritchie and Border had put the brakes on. Then Marsh had pressed the accelerator again. Now, with Hogan, Lawson added

The final ball of the thrilling second final of the 1983-84 World Series Cup. Australia's Geoff Lawson has swung and missed at the last ball of the 50th over (bowled by the West Indies' Joel Garner), and Carl Rackemann has just begun his sprint for the potentially winning run.

17, before the spinner was caught by Gus Logie off Holding from the third ball of the 49th over. Hogg came out to add three more before the return of Garner. Eleven to win, six balls to go.

Off the first ball, Hogg scrambled a single. Then Lawson sliced away an overpitched yorker to the backward point fence.

'That's four!' yelled Lawry. 'That's racing out to the boundary. That's desperate runs for Australia. Well played, Geoffrey Lawson!'

The crowd was now on its feet, chanting 'Henry! ... Henry! ... Henry!' scarcely believing what they were seeing. It had been assumed the Windies were invincible. 'Take your time, Geoffrey Lawson,' advised Lawry's co-commentator Keith Stackpole. 'Six runs from four balls. The challenge is now down a little.'

To the third ball, Lawson stepped to the off-side and lobbed a leg-stump yorker behind square leg. 'Two!' the crowd roared in unison, like a football crowd demanding a free kick, and the batsmen took off. On the square-leg boundary was the great fast bowler Malcolm Marshall who threw to the bowler's end, to where Hogg was struggling. Garner's hands were sure as a wicketkeeper. Hogg was out by inches. Australia, now eight down, needed five off three.

THE 12TH MAN: YOU'VE GOTTA LAUGH!

In the years since 1983, *'The 12th Man'* and his send-ups of the cricket has become a summer institution – every bit as much a part of the season as Richie Benaud's measured tones, Tony Greig's key-in-the-pitch routine and Bill Lawry's flustered enthusiasm. Actually the *12th Man*, or more accurately Billy Birmingham, the man behind The Man, has become an integral part of the Australian summer BECAUSE of Benaud's measured tones, Greig's key routine and Lawry's flabbergasted proclamations.

Not only has everyone heard the 12th Man, they have been bored witless by a 'mate' who knows each record off by heart and is more than willing to recite the funniest bits at the cricket, at parties, on the bus, at work, at the drop of a hat – in fact just about anywhere or anytime. South African fast bowler Allan Donald is a huge fan and not a bad mimic. He was heard entertaining his team-mates with generous *12th Man* extracts on the South Africans' tour of Australia. But who is The Man?

'I'm a media junkie but I'm not as interested in the game or as keen on the game as everyone thinks I must be,' said Birmingham. 'Everyone has got me sitting down there with three VCRs and a clipboard, taking notes and planning my next assault on the boys in the commentary booth. If a game is boring I'll just walk out on it. A lot of people think I'm a rabid bloody fan but there's no way in the world I'm going to be annoyed because I've got a dinner engagement and there's a game of cricket on. It's water off a duck's back. I'm not that big a fan to say "do we really have to go out to dinner?" I'm more likely to say that about a footy game.

'I played the game right through school. I left in 1970, and had a vague interest in the international scene. Like all of my school chums I was a modest fan. I wouldn't call myself or any of my mates really rabid cricket fans who

The Queensland fast bowler Carl Rackemann came to the middle. Lawson, stepping away, sliced another full toss to third man.

'He hits it!' shouted Lawry as Lawson made contact, and then, after the batsmen had scampered three, he added breathlessly ... 'Aw ... what a finish!'

One to tie, two to win, two balls to go. Garner bowled, Rackemann edged the ball into his feet, and, as the crowd roared as surely no Melbourne Cricket Ground cricket crowd had ever roared before, Lawson ran through ... the game was even.

'Beauty!! One run to win!'

The crowd was in a state of near hysteria. All were standing. Lawson called Rackemann to him to explain the obvious. Richards moved to short forward square, and beckoned his troops in to stop the one. Beyond the fence the chant was for Lawson, for Australia, for the single. Garner stopped at the end of his mark.

'Look at the field around Lawson,' said Stackpole. 'He's surrounded. Carl Rackemann ... back up, son.'

'They'll run for anything as Joel Garner comes in,' yelled Lawry. 'The crowd's

couldn't wait to swap a card or sit down at lunchtime and read the latest player profile book. It was really only the fact that I was playing the game that drew me to any interest in the international scene at all. So once I left school and I wasn't playing the game I didn't give a damn about it and nobody else did. Certainly amongst my friends it wasn't a game that anyone discussed that much.'

That might have been the end of it. But Australia's richest man, Kerry Packer, ensured that a great comic talent would not go to waste when he opened his wallet and bankrolled World Series Cricket.

'The rejuvenation of the game for me was World Series Cricket,' said Birmingham. 'When the game was Packerised in 1977-78 myself and a whole lot of people who quite liked the game really got back into it at both a one-day and Test level. That's fair to say of a lot of people who didn't dislike the game but didn't find it that attractive as a spectator sport or as a TV sport. It was always presented in such a dour fashion.

'All of a sudden our television screens were filled with blow-by-blow coverage of these games. Kerry Packer and John Cornell and the various other people who were the instigators of the whole thing realised that this was a great game. That if someone wanted to grab it by the balls and present it in all of its gladiatorial light, man hurling rock down at man at 100 miles an hour, and give it a bit of Hollywood pizzazz, coloured uniforms, whatever it takes, then there's no reason why it shouldn't enjoy the same sort of public interest that all the other sports are enjoying.

'Those guys were 150 per cent right. One-day cricket, the fact that people could come along and watch the excitement during the course of one day and get a result, was a very important stepping stone in dragging people back to the game. Subsequent years have proven that it didn't have an adverse effect on the Test game. If anything, by drawing people back to the game

Continued over page

all standing here at the Melbourne Cricket Ground.' Garner bowled ... Lawson swung, and missed. And set off for the win. Keeper Dujon, who had been standing closer than normal behind the stumps, gloved the ball, took four hurried steps forward and fired at the keeper's end ...

'He's out!' cried Lawry. 'He's run out! ... And the West Indies win. What an end to a magnificent final. A tie! So the West Indies win the Benson and Hedges World Series Cup ...'

It truly had been a magnificent ending – the first tie in international limited-overs cricket. Later in his review of the game for Channel Nine, a calm and assured Richie Benaud recalled that he had seen two ties in Australian first-class cricket, one in a Sheffield Shield game in 1956, the other the famous Tied Test of 1960-61. But this one-day tie differed from those other two great finishes. This one had occurred in front of 40,000 fans, who had worked themselves into a fever pitch usually reserved for football finals.

Sadly the game had a disappointing epilogue. Most at the ground, and all who

THE 12TH MAN: YOU'VE GOTTA LAUGH!

Continued from previous page

generally, Test cricket has benefited from it.

'Test cricket has been swept along in the slipstream of the ever-increasing popularity of one-day cricket and Channel Nine's coverage of it, the style of commentary the boys developed, the different camera angles, the competitions, the whole masterstroke of 50 overs a side, the coloured uniforms, lights, all of those things. They had a whole swag of ideas when they started and to their credit they kept chipping away and chipping away and coming up with more and better and improved ideas. Because of that one-day cricket continues to be the most popular form of the game in terms of TV ratings and that's where I enjoy most of my cricket. I don't go to the game much.'

Television is a recurring theme in the Birmingham odyssey. 'The fact that World Series Cricket received such good coverage on TV was instrumental in luring me back,' he said.

Well, the 'why' one-day cricket gave birth to the *12th Man* seems fairly clear, but what about the 'how' the whole thing developed?

'I'm not specifically saying that the one-day game is all I'm interested in,' said Birmingham. 'It was the whole Channel Nine coverage thing that got me in. It was an evolution. It was probably after seeing Richie and the boys for a couple of years that I found myself sitting in the lounge room on a Sunday afternoon watching a game with my mates.

'During a boring passage of play while hearing Richie waffle on or pad the show out I started doing impersonations of him.' Birmingham said there was no doubt that one-day cricket was 100 per cent responsible for his success.

'You'd have to say the bulk of my inspiration comes from one-day cricket. My records wouldn't have existed without Richie and the boys doing the job that they do on Channel Nine's cricket

listened to the commentators on the television coverage, had assumed that the West Indies had won the Cup, having finished top of the qualifying ladder and then won and tied the first two finals. Or because they had conceded fewer wickets in reaching 222. A few, though, believed the finals were still unresolved, including, it seemed, some members of the Australian Cricket Board. Amazingly, they had no provisions for a tie in their rules. So, after four hours of behind-closed-doors debate they decided to make them up as they went and ruled that the third final had to go ahead. If Australia won the third final the prizemoney would be shared. To most critics, it seemed the Board's decision was motivated by one thing. Money. The West Indies certainly believed so, and refused to play unless they were guaranteed a percentage of the gate from the third final, which the Board duly promised.

So the game was played, in front of a disappointing and disappointed crowd of 19,210. When Malcolm Marshall strolled out and bowled the first over off a very

presentation and the show having become so popular. The success of my records is a direct result of World Series Cricket being launched, Channel Nine picking up the television rights and choosing the style of presentation and style of commentators they have.

'From my point of view Max Walker leaving the team was a real blow because he has a voice that is larger than life and easy to rip into. There's something you can latch onto there. Unfortunately he was replaced by a guy like Greg Chappell. It's like chalk and cheese. That's the difference between what Max offered me in terms of material and what Greg gives me because his style of commentary is straight up and down the wicket, hermetically sealed and not too much flair about it. His voice is as bland as you could ever get – and that's not a putdown, it's just that God hasn't given him a voice that is larger than life.'

Birmingham has now reached the stage where he's got to wonder if there is anything left in the tank. If there is anything else which he can squeeze a laugh

out of. He is very realistic about what the future holds for the *12th Man*.

'I don't feel one-day cricket is an infinite source of material but then I don't feel inclined to say I've done my last record,' he said, adding that finding new jokes isn't getting any easier.

'It probably gets harder every time because there are a lot of things about their coverage that they haven't changed. I have found it reasonably difficult in the past when the world was my oyster, when it hadn't been done, when it was a totally unmined area. Now having done four or five records I'd have to say it's become more and more difficult.

'I'm absolutely thankful for the fact they've been so successful and have made me a decent sort of living over the last 10 years I've been *12th Man*. I'd like to broaden my horizons but it's a bit hard not to do another one when the last one was so successful. It was the most successful that I've done so rather than the joke wearing thin it seems to be gathering momentum.'

---

short run, at less than half pace, it appeared the game was being reduced to a parody. But the West Indies (without the 'injured' Lloyd and Richards) still won, and the Board had their extra gate. What should have been a highly dramatic end to the limited-overs international season was instead reduced to farce.

It was not the sort of farewell Rod Marsh would have preferred. But he left the game as one of the sport's true greats. His contribution to the development of one-day international cricket, like that of Greg Chappell and Dennis Lillee, was enormous. Their style, charisma, passion and skill were the focus of all that attracted the new fans to the game.

Significantly, their international careers had all started in 1970-71, the year the first limited-overs international was played. Now, in the season they departed, crowds of 86,133 and 72,610 had come to the MCG to watch such a game, and the sport relied on such matches for its livelihood. They had been part of a revolution. Without them, the game would never be the same.

THE FIRST TIE: 'WHAT DO YOU THINK, HENRY?'

The controversial tie in the second World Series Cup final against the West Indies in 1983-84 caused the biggest ruckus in Australian cricket since the 'Underarm Incident'. This time it was not a player or players who were the villains but officialdom. Fast bowler Geoff Lawson was one of the key participants but he was spared the recriminations that followed the Australian Cricket Board's decision to play the third final. The home side could not have won the Cup after their nine-wicket thrashing in the first final in Sydney so the Board was the sole whipping boy, enduring a merciless bucketing from the media for its alleged greed and cynicism.

According to Lawson the atmosphere was already tense before the Melbourne match and it had nothing to do with the hiding Australia had suffered at the SCG. 'A lot of things happened around that game,' said Lawson. 'We were in the middle of drawn-out contract negotiations with the Board and we were supposed to be leaving for the West Indies on the Wednesday after the Saturday and Sunday in Melbourne. It was a very tumultuous period and the players were far from happy with the ACB.'

Lawson recalled that the Australians bowled well and restricted the Windies to a 'pretty gettable total' on a wicket that he said was very good for the MCG of that era. But, as happened all too often in those days, the wheels fell off, and because of Steve Smith's shoulder injury, Lawson went in at No. 7 with five wickets in hand and a target of around 40 runs in six overs.

'When I went out to bat Rod Marsh said, "Well, Hen, what do you think?" and I said, "We've got no chance". Holding was bowling well, Garner was bowling well and Marshall was bowling well. It was going to be a big ask. When Marsh was out, and Tom Hogan had been and gone, Rodney Hogg trudged out to the crease. Hoggy came over and said, "What do you think, Hen?" and I said, "We've got no chance of winning this game, Garner's got an over left".

'The last over came and we needed 11. So Hoggy and I came together again and I said, "What do you think ace?" and he said, "We've got no chance of winning this. When was the last time Joel Garner got hit for 11 off an over?" And I said, "Yeah mate, no chance. We'll just give it our best shot. Just run hard and see what happens. You just get a one and I'll try to hit 'em".

'He just blocked it on the leg side somewhere and we took off and got a single. I thought Garner was going to bowl five yorkers. First ball I stepped away outside leg stump and he bowled a full toss outside of off stump and I swatted it to backward point for four. Next ball I thought "don't go outside leg stump" so I jumped outside off stump and he bowled a yorker on leg and I flicked it really high down to backward square. It almost went for four. Malcolm Marshall jumped and pulled it down, it nearly bounced over his head. I was running to the danger end and Hoggy got run out at the non-striker's end. I couldn't believe it. Marshall made a perfect throw to Garner and Hoggy was out by about six inches.

'That cost us the game, Hoggy not

getting back for two when the ball went to the boundary at the MCG. The next ball I stepped outside leg stump and he bowled another full toss and I hit it down to third man. Winston Davis came belting around the fence and just stopped it going for four. That brought Big Carl on to strike.

'All of a sudden we were back in the game and the crowd was going absolutely berserk. Carl and I had a conversation and I said, "Mate, whatever you do get in front of the stumps and wherever it goes we're running". He just moved back and across and flopped it down in front of the stumps, the ball lobbed down the leg side and we took a one.

'It's tied with one ball to go so we had another mid-wicket conversation and I said to Carl, "Mate, I don't care where this goes you've got to run, get out of the blocks early, cheat. If he wants to Mankad you in front of 50,000 at the MCG don't worry about it. Even if it goes to the keeper we've got to run. I'll just try to get something on it and we'll take the odds that no-one is going to throw the stumps down." I thought he's got to bowl it at the stumps so I was prepared to just get in behind it and try to run it on the off-side somewhere. So he bowled it and it was bloody short of a length outside off stump. My eyes lit up and I tried to cut it quite hard but the ball didn't bounce and it went underneath the bat. It went to Dujon and he threw the stumps down.

'I got halfway up the wicket and turned around to see Mocca getting run out. You could just see the ball coming towards the stumps and you think "is it going to hit? is it going to hit?" and it did. And it was a tie.

'Of course the West Indies thought they'd won because they lost less wickets and they were carrying on like pork chops. I remember Viv running off and giving the black power salute. I remember thinking "that was a chance to make a name for yourself and it didn't quite turn out". I look back at the replays and think if only I'd just tried to nudge it down to third man instead of trying to hit it hard. But you get one shot and you try to do your best. I was pretty happy getting 10 off Garner's last over.

'As that over went on Garner was just losing it. He used to be such a tough guy to get away and very unemotional but as the over went on you could see he and Viv really losing control. When we needed one run to win off the last ball there was a look of panic in their eyes which was something they hadn't had for some time.'

Lawson recalled that the Australian team spent quite a long time sitting around in their playing gear while the ACB's representatives first worked out if there was to be another game and then tried to persuade the West Indians, who thought they had already won, to play the third final. Needless to say, no-one was happy with the solution.

'Everybody was totally crooked on it,' said Lawson. 'We were heading off to the West Indies so it was a big anti-climax in some ways. It didn't impress us because we couldn't win the Cup, we could only tie it. We'd had a long hard season and that was supposed to be the last day before we headed off on another tough tour. It was something that no-one really wanted.'

14

KEEPING THE
GAME ALIVE

The Australian team's first assignment in the post-Chappell, Lillee and Marsh era could not have been more daunting. Under the leadership of Hughes the team travelled to the Caribbean, to meet the West Indies at the absolute peak of their powers. The West Indies were just about invincible – possessing a pace attack of Marshall, Holding and Garner, a batting line-up of Richards, Lloyd, Haynes, Greenidge and Richardson, and a wicketkeeper/batsman in Dujon who had taken from the retired Marsh the mantle of most valuable keeper in the world.

Hughes' team was slaughtered, with only Border coming away with his reputation enhanced. In the five Test matches, the home side did not lose one second-innings wicket. The Australians' sole success in the four limited-overs internationals came in Trinidad, where they won a rain-tampered game by four wickets off the second-last ball. The Australians' three losses, by eight, seven and nine wickets, gave a true indication of the gap between the sides. The crowds for the one-day internationals far outweighed the Test match attendances. In the opening one-dayer in Guyana, the strain of more than 14,000 fans trying to squeeze into a tiny ground caused the main scoreboard to collapse under the weight of those illegally perched upon it, while more than 30,000 saw the exciting conclusion in Port-of-Spain.

For all its disasters, this tour was the confirmation of Border's greatness. He produced two Test innings of supreme courage and ability in the second Test in Port-of-Spain (98 not out and 100 not out), and in the third limited-overs international in St Lucia he blasted 90, the best Australian batting effort in the one-day series. The Australians limped home to prepare for a short tour of India, then a five-Test series against the West Indies in Australia, a World Series Cup involving the West Indies and Sri Lanka, and the World Championship of Cricket, a limited-overs extravaganza scheduled for Melbourne and Sydney in February/March to celebrate the 150th anniversary of the founding of Victoria. By this time, Border, the Queensland captain, was universally recognised as the best batsman in the land.

The Indian trip – confined to a five-match series of one-day internationals – was staged as part of the celebrations of the Golden Jubilee of the Ranji Trophy, India's equivalent to the Sheffield Shield. Australia won the series against the World Cup champions 3-nil, with two matches abandoned due to rain. Perhaps the 'highlight' of the tour was a comical incident in Jamsehpur, where the start of the third international was delayed for three hours because the truck delivering the uniforms and equipment of the two sides went missing. No sooner had play finally begun when the rain tumbled down, ending the match. The crowd was not amused, and India's cricket officials, who had recently been handed (with Pakistan) the opportunity to stage the 1987 World Cup, were severely embarrassed. The first match at New Delhi's Jawaharlal Nehru Stadium took place under lights, the first time an official limited-overs international had been played under lights outside Sydney.

Following this tour, several of the Australian team members met up in Singapore with four other Australian players, Dr Ali Bacher from the South African Cricket Union, and the former Australian opening bat and now businessman Bruce Francis

Australian captain Allan Border (left) with Australian Prime Minister Bob Hawke at the opening ceremony of the 1985 World Championship of Cricket.

to discuss a rebel tour of South Africa. The meeting was highly secret, but it was later revealed that a level of payments had been agreed to and contracts signed. The resounding impact of the cricketers' decision would be felt at the end of the '84-85 Australian season.

When the 1984-85 World Series Cup began in early January, Border was the Australian captain. Hughes had quit amid batting collapses, dropped catches and tears after the second. The West Indies had won each of the first two Tests ruthlessly. A consolation victory in the fifth Test on a spinners' paradise in Sydney promoted hopes of a revival under the new leader. But in the World Series Cup the West Indies were their all-powerful selves and won all of their qualifying matches, usually in front of big crowds, and often with ridiculous ease.

The Sri Lankans were competitive and even managed to win one match against Australia in Melbourne (9-226 off 50 overs to 6-230 off 49.2), an occasion also memorable because it was Border's 100th limited-overs international – a milestone no other cricketer had reached at the time. The Australians' revenge for that loss came in the third of three matches played in Adelaide over the Australia Day weekend, when victory was won by 232 runs, and the Victorian right-hander Dean

Jones (99 not out off 77 balls) and Border (118 not out off 88) completed an unbroken third-wicket stand of 224. This remains the highest Australian partnership in limited-overs international cricket.

Jones had made his debut late in the previous year's World Series Cup and started with an enterprising 40 not out against Pakistan. But he had made little impact in that season's finals, and then, after reaching 43 not out in the first of the limited-overs internationals in the Caribbean, had struggled. He missed the short tour to India and was left out of the Australian team for the first three World Series Cup matches of 1984-85. The unbeaten 99 was his first score above 50 in an international.

Jones was not the only new face to emerge for Australia during this season. The Tasmanian batsman David Boon had made his limited-overs international debut in the ill-fated third World Series Cup final match of 1983-84 – Rod Marsh's farewell. He missed the side for the West Indies but made his first Test appearance in the second match of the '84-85 home series in Brisbane. Boon played in eight of Australia's 10 qualifying matches that followed the Tests in '84-85, batting anywhere between three and six. He missed the finals, and was then omitted from the Benson and Hedges World Championship squad. He would be back the following season – this time to stay.

Two other players had a greater impact on the Australian one-day side of 1984-85. The teenage Queensland fast bowler Craig McDermott and the 21-year-old Victorian all-rounder Simon O'Donnell made their debuts together in the opening World Series Cup match and went on to impress throughout that competition and the World Championship. O'Donnell, a medium-fast right-hand bowler and free-swinging batsman with an openly aggressive nature, appeared a player made for the limited-overs game. In two matches – the third final of the World Series Cup and the World Championship match against Pakistan – he produced innings of rare power and courage, even though he was fighting lost causes on both occasions.

Australia went into the World Series finals as the longest of outsiders, but stunned even themselves in winning the first game by 26 runs, on the back of an unbeaten 127 by their leader, and consistent bowling efforts from McDermott and the South Australian Rod McCurdy. Four days later, it appeared at the change-of-innings break that the locals were about to provide a stunning clean sweep. Australia had totalled 3-271 from their 50 overs (Smith 54, Wood 81, Border 39, and the left-handed keeper/batsman Wayne Phillips 56 not out from 37 balls, including a colossal 15 off the 50th over, from Joel Garner). The 40,000 crowd suddenly brimmed with confidence, but though Lawson was superb, and the Windies stumbled to 5-179 in the 37th over, Logie and Dujon saw the champions home with four balls to spare. Sadly, the third final was an anti-climax. Australia needed O'Donnell's swashbuckling 69 to take the score from 7-89 to 178, but this was never enough, especially as Haynes (76 not out) and Richards (76) were in excellent touch.

The World Championship of Cricket was something of a mini-World Cup, involving the seven Test-playing cricketing nations. England and India flew in from India, where they had been Test rivals; similarly New Zealand and Pakistan crossed the Tasman, to join the three teams that had competed for the World Series Cup. All

Patrick Eagar

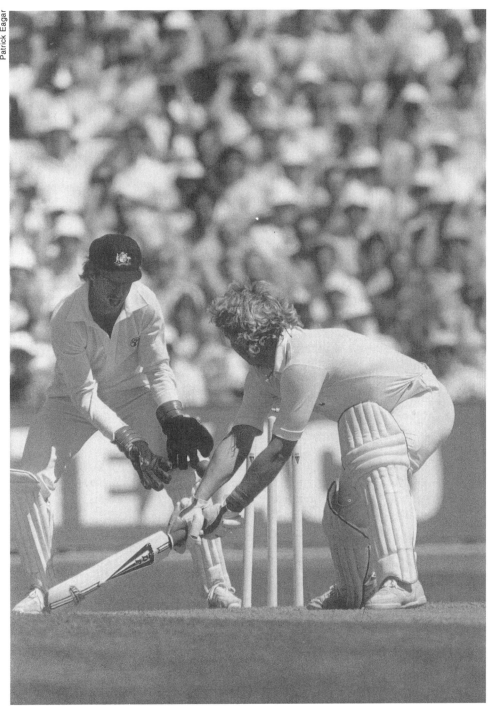

England's champion all-rounder Ian Botham is bowled by Greg Matthews after attempting a reverse sweep in the first Texaco Trophy match of the 1985 Australian tour of England. The keeper is Wayne Phillips.

but three of the matches were held under floodlights, including the opening encounter between Australia and England which marked the first occasion a limited-overs match was played under the newly installed $3 million lights at the MCG. The game attracted a bubbling, highly patriotic crowd of 82,494. They saw an emphatic local victory by seven wickets, spearheaded by an unbroken fourth-wicket stand of 157 between Jones and the Queensland opener Robbie Kerr, who was subsequently named man of the match.

However, only a further 162,808 people watched the remaining 12 matches in the tournament. After their excellent beginning thc Australians surprisingly crashed out of the tournament after successive losses, firstly to the pace of the exciting Pakistani left-arm fast man Wasim Akram, and then to the skill of Kapil Dev and the teenage leg spin of Laxman Sivaramakrishnan of India. Only O'Donnell, who smashed an unbeaten 74 against Pakistan (after the score fell to 5-42) and Phillips, who managed 60 against the Indians (after coming in at 4-17), made it past 50 in these two games. The Australians played like a team in need of a break, as did the fans, who had been watching one-day internationals almost without fail for 10 solid weeks. Although some critics described the tournament as an instance of Australian cricket officials trying to kill off the gold mine that was one-day international cricket, the administration could point to the new MCG floodlights as justification for their efforts. Melbourne needed the World Championship of Cricket, and the sponsorship the contests attracted, to fund the lights that matched those of Sydney. India went on to win the Championship, beating Pakistan in the final.

Two weeks after the Championship final in Melbourne, the Australians were in Sharjah in the United Arab Emirates. This most unlikely of cricket locations was the result of the efforts of a local wealthy businessman, Mr Abdulrahman Bukhatir, who had fallen for the game during his days as a student in Pakistan and then raised over £2 million to construct a 12,000-capacity stadium in the middle of the Great Arabian Desert. Soil had been transported hundreds of kilometres by lorry to make the oasis possible and create a pitch that Tony Lewis in *Wisden* described as '(one) on which the ball turned a lot but was level and fair'.

Playing for the 'Rothmans Four Nations Trophy' (the competition involved two 'semi-finals', Australia v England and Pakistan v India, a consolation final and a final) Australia scraped through their semi-final with a last-ball, two-wicket victory over an understrength England, but then lost the final to India by three wickets. Personal highlights were rare – Wood's 35 against England was the highest Australian score in either game, while the NSW off-spinning all-rounder Greg Matthews' 1-15 from 10 overs in the semi-final was the pick of the bowling spells. The Indian captain Sunil Gavaskar was named man of the series, which featured neutral umpires, including the Australian Mel Johnson.

The Australian squad for the 1985 Ashes tour had been announced on March 20, two days before the team left for Sharjah. However, the XVII that finally left for England in late April bore strong differences to the side originally chosen. The Sharjah squad arrived back in Australia on April 4, and nine days later the *Australian* and the Adelaide *Advertiser* broke the story of a rebel Australian tour to South Africa. It was soon apparent that seven members of the Ashes team – Terry

Greg Matthews (centre) threads his way through the fans after scoring an unbeaten 46 and steering Australia to a four-wicket victory over India at the Gabba on January 12, 1986. After a highly successful '85-86 season in Australia and then New Zealand, in which he scored three Test centuries, was named the player of the World Series Cup finals and gained much exposure because of his non-conformist, rock'n'roll image, Matthews was arguably the most popular cricketer in Australia.

Alderman, Murray Bennett, Rod McCurdy, Wayne Phillips, Steve Rixon, Dirk Wellham and Graeme Wood – had signed with the SACU. Bennett had sought a release from his South African contract before the storm broke, and, after the Ashes squad was announced, Phillips, Wood and Wellham also reneged, allegedly after receiving lucrative offers from PBL Marketing. Alderman, McCurdy and Rixon were replaced by the Queenslanders John Maguire, Carl Rackemann and Ray Phillips, but Maguire and Rackemann were also packing for South Africa, so Jeff Thomson and David Gilbert were measured for Ashes blazers instead.

On May 19, Kim Hughes announced he would captain the rebels in South Africa. Hughes had been the only member of the team in Sharjah who had not been chosen for England and had not been sought as a stand-by player when the South African story broke. His linking with the Springboks effectively ended his 'official' Australian career, and ensured that the enduring memory Australian fans would have of him would be his tearful resignation as Australian captain. Hughes was a

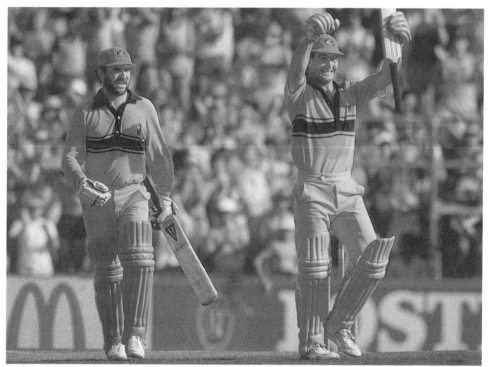

Geoff Marsh acknowledges the home dressing room after scoring 125 against India at the SCG on January 21, 1986, the first of nine hundreds he would score in one-day international cricket. The other batsman is Allan Border, who slammed 52 as Australia totalled a massive 6-292.

cricketer whose contribution to the Australian cause was much maligned. However, at his best he was a superb batsman who for much of his career was considered the equal of Allan Border. He played many fine hands in his 95 limited-overs internationals (in May 1985, only Border and Viv Richards had played more), including 17 fifties and a highest score of 98, against England at Edgbaston in 1980, and was one of the main players in the seasons when limited-overs international cricket in Australia developed into an extraordinarily popular sport.

Hughes' rebels completed two tours of South Africa, in 1985-86 and 1986-87. On the first trip they played six one-day 'internationals', for one win and five defeats; on the second they won two and lost five of eight such matches. But despite their final record they were always competitive and never once in those two seasons did an 'international' one-dayer draw less than 10,000 people. The largest crowd was 31,000 at the Wanderers Ground in Johannesburg in February 1987.

Border's official side arrived in England as outsiders, but surprised by winning the Texaco Trophy one-day series which preceded the Test series. The first two matches were exciting affairs. The first at Old Trafford went to Australia when Matthews hit the first ball of the 55th and final scheduled over through mid-wicket to take Australia to 7-220. Border had earlier scored 59 and Lawson taken four wickets. The second match, at Edgbaston, was won a ball earlier, Australia reaching 6-233 in reply to the Englishmen's 7-231. Border this time made 85 not out, while Wessels reached 57. In the final match, at Lord's, Wood scored a century, Border 44 and Boon 45 as Australia reached 5-254, but this was easily surpassed, as captain David Gower (102) and Graham Gooch (117) added an unbroken 202. England won by eight wickets with six overs to spare.

This third defeat was an ominous portent to the Test series, where, with the exception of Lord's where the veteran NSW leg-spinner Bob Holland bowled his country to a famous victory, the Australian bowlers were totally ineffective. Holland, who played in the first of the Texaco Trophy matches, had become in the previous Australian summer the first wrist-spinner to play for Australia in a one-day international since Bobby Simpson in the West Indies in 1978 (the only other specialist wrist-spinners before 1985 were Terry Jenner in 1974-75 and Kerry O'Keeffe in 1977). Holland took 2-49 from 11 overs at Old Trafford, but it was the off-spinner Matthews, with some help from a celebrated rival, who turned the game. Ian Botham had smashed his way to 72 and his side had reached 5-160 in the 40th over when, having just hit a colossal six, he tried a highly risky reverse sweep and was bowled. Lawson and McDermott then returned to control the tail, and the Australians were given a target much below what might have been.

The Australians' Texaco Trophy victory was scarcely remembered by the end of the Test series, which the home side won 3-1 after crushing innings' victories in the final two Tests. Border apart, the batting lacked consistency, while the bowling, after Lawson and McDermott, was below standard. The team experienced further problems when it returned to Australia for Test series against New Zealand and India. Lawson, after an English tour in which he was troubled by a bronchial complaint, suffered a severe back injury and dropped out of cricket. Wessels was omitted, amid a contract dispute and rumours of his involvement with the South African rebels. Others lost already ordinary form, or were injured, and despite the continued batting excellence of Border, and the runs of Matthews, Boon and Ritchie, Australia lost a Test series to the Kiwis for the first time. India had much the better of three successive drawn Tests which followed.

Australia won the World Series Cup, however, defeating India 2-0 in the finals. It was a series that still attracted healthy crowds, despite the poor Test form of the home side and the lack – except for Hadlee, Gavaskar and Kapil Dev – of box-office stars in the two overseas sides. For the Australians it was perhaps more significant for the emergence of another exceptional young cricketer ideally suited to the one-day game.

Stephen Waugh, aged just 20, had come into the Australian side for the final two Tests against India but achieved little. However, from his first limited-overs international innings – a crucial 40 in Brisbane – he became a key member of the Australian one-day side. A right-hand batsman of exquisite timing, he had been named man of the match in his fourth appearance against India under lights in Melbourne, despite the fact Australia lost by eight wickets with almost 10 overs to spare. His unbeaten 73 off 104 balls, after coming in at 4-40, was the one-day innings of the season. Waugh also bowled medium pace, though Border for this series at least used him sparingly.

To win the Cup the Australians had to regroup after one of their poorest ever displays. Against New Zealand in Adelaide they were bowled out for 70 in 26.3 overs after their opponents had reached 7-276 off their 50 overs. But two days later under lights in Sydney they hammered the Kiwis by 99 runs, the final three wickets of the night presenting a hat-trick to the tall West Australian left-arm quick Bruce Reid, who had come into the Australian side after Lawson's back gave way. Australia's innings in this match had begun with a 98-run partnership between Boon and Geoff Marsh, a right-hander originally from the WA country town of Wandering. Earlier in the competition they had contributed a 152-run stand in Sydney, when Boon made 83 and Marsh a stirring 125 off 145 balls. In Australia's final qualifying match, they added 146 and were not separated until the 33rd over. Then they began the first final with a stand of 69. Both openers, battle-hardened by years in the Sheffield Shield, were sensible men who knew the value of a stolen single and a platform for the batsmen who followed. If Australia still had problems after the World Series Cup, and a late-season tour to New Zealand indicated they did, their opening partnership was not one of them. In fact, in the young players who had come into the side since 1983 – Boon, Jones, O'Donnell, McDermott, Waugh, Reid and Marsh – Border had found the raw material for another potentially outstanding Australian XI.

In New Zealand, Australia played four one-day internationals, losing the first two, but coming back to square the competition. The crowds were particularly rowdy. Matthews, who in Australia had become something of a cult figure with his brave batting and rock'n'roll image, especially had struck a Kiwi nerve. However, the taunts and slander from the outer had little impact on the NSW all-rounder, who remained one of his team's key men throughout the tour. The one-day matches followed a three-Test series (which the home side won one-nil, Australia's sixth straight unsuccessful series), and after the second one-dayer, a depressed Border told reporters he was thinking of resigning as captain. The constant stream of losses and batting collapses had taken their toll. He later described his comments as a 'frustrated cry for a better effort from the team', and it appeared to have the desired impact. The Australian highlight of the one-day internationals in New Zealand came in the first match after Border's press conference, when a fantastic fifth-wicket partnership between Wayne Phillips and Waugh saw their side home by three wickets with three balls to spare. Australia had fallen to 5-142 in the 39th over, then added 80 in 62 balls. With one Hadlee over to go, a solitary run was needed. Phillips, after a superb 71, was lbw to the first ball and then Waugh (53) was run out chasing the win. Local hopes lifted for an outrageous escape, but McDermott came in to slice the third ball square to the boundary.

As the Australians were returning home, the 1986 *Wisden* was hitting the shelves of bookshops in England. It included an essay by Sir Donald Bradman, entitled 'Whither Cricket Now?', in which, as part of an overview of the future of the sport, he looked in some detail at the phenomenon of limited-overs cricket. Sir Donald referred to what he called the 'Achilles heel' of the one-day game – 'the premium placed on defensive bowling and negative and defensive field placing' – but then

The Aussies celebrate their victory in the 1985-86 World Series Cup. Left to right: Greg Matthews, Geoff Marsh, Steve Waugh, Dirk Wellham, Ray Bright, Simon Davis, Allan Border (with Cup), Craig McDermott, Dave Gilbert, Tim Zoehrer.

looked at the positive aspects of the game.

'It rids the game of the utterable bore who thinks occupancy of the crease and his own personal aggrandisement are all that matter,' Sir Donald wrote. 'It demands fieldsmen of great speed and agility with good throwing arms. The standard of fielding at all levels of cricket has undoubtedly been lifted. Running between the wickets, too, has taken on a new dimension. Risks must be taken to maintain the essential run-rate. Umpires are put under enormous pressure, having to adjudicate frequently on split-second issues; to their credit, I believe they have responded in a very positive manner and improved their standards ...'

Sir Donald went on to suggest that umpires would benefit from the use of slow-motion replays for run outs, and even stumpings and disputed catches. He also cast doubt on a theory that many cricket experts had put – that the emergence of the one-day game was destroying batting techniques. The editor of *Wisden* had suggested this was the main cause of the failures of Border's 1985 Australian team in England. Although he accepted that the theory may have some validity, Sir Donald pointed

GREG MATTHEWS: BOWLING 'DOTS'

Greg Matthews has achieved a lot in his 12 years on the first-class cricket scene but he is still dissatisfied. Many people would be happy to have pulled on the baggy green – or yellow – cap just once but Matthews, who, to the start of the 1994-95 season, had played 33 Test matches and 59 one-dayers for Australia, still feels he has more to achieve.

'Of course not,' said Matthews with a laugh when asked if he had played as much one-day cricket as he would have liked. 'I would love to have played as many games as AB.'

Matthews contends he has yet to perform to his potential in limited-overs cricket. 'I had a couple of great years in 1985-86-87. I was really starting to get my act together in 1987. I was very positive and confident. During the 1986-87 series when England won absolutely everything I was second in wickets and tops in runs per over and that was against the West Indies and England. That gave me a hell of a charge and a lot of confidence but unfortunately I haven't played a lot since then.'

Matthews said it took him a long time to come to grips with the demands of bowling in limited-overs cricket and is frustrated that at the very moment he got on top of his game he lost his place in the side.

Despite his unconventional personality and exuberant approach to cricket Matthews is very much a traditionalist and, like the majority of first-class cricketers, his heart is forever pledged to Test cricket. But it is not just that Test matches are 'the way cricket is meant to be played' as he puts it. Matthews believes the challenges and demands of the five-day game are of a purer and more elemental nature than the helter-skelter of one-day cricket. To him Test matches equate to running a marathon, where a competitor has to reach deep into himself and conquer his weaknesses while trying to out-think his opponents at the same time, and one-dayers are like the 100m sprint, a furious dash where the athlete goes hell-for-leather for the finish line and barely takes a breath.

'The difference between the two games is that Test cricket is a test of the man, that's what I've always loved about the game of cricket,' said Matthews. 'By watching a guy play cricket you can really glean a lot about his character from the way he performs on the field, the way he carries himself. 'The one-day game is not a test of the man. It's a different type of intensity. It's very intense while you're out there, very fast, very quick. There is less time to think, less time to contemplate options.' One of Matthews' favourite parts of the limited-over game is the crowd. In one-day cricket the fans switch from passive observers to being part of the action. And for a born showman like Matthews, who spends so much time toiling in front of minimal

out that the best players had no difficulty making the necessary adaptations to each form of cricket. Border, for example, had had few problems. And Sir Donald also rejected the argument that spinners could not cope with the limited-overs game. '*Top* quality spinners can and will survive any challenge,' he explained.

crowds with NSW and his grade club Waverley, the rush of playing in front of a full house should not be underestimated.

'There is much greater crowd participation, there are much greater crowds,' he said. 'One-day games are the same throughout the world. The crowds don't tend to go to appreciate the cricket, they tend to go for the spectacle – the wham, bam side of it. It's very much like the West Indian game. It's almost a community outing for people where a Test match is not. People go there to appreciate the game, what's happening on the field – they pay greater attention to detail. In a one-day game it's like "wow, there's a four", "bam, there's a wicket", "zap, there's a runout", "let's see a replay".'

As a young man Matthews gave scant regard to the percentage approach, preferring instead the adrenalin rush of all-out attack. That was as true in limited-overs cricket as it was for first-class cricket. 'Initially my ideas were to take wickets and I tended to bowl very much like that. I was never afraid to toss them up and be hit for runs in order to secure wickets.'

Matthews said that all changed when he played with Worcester while on an Esso scholarship in 1983. 'It was all about bowling dots over there – bowl around the wicket to a 6-3 field, fire them in at leg stump and bowl dots. And while it took me some time to adjust to that when I got back here I still tended to toss them up. It wasn't until the latish '80s that I started to really think about bowling dots instead of wicket balls.'

The battle to find his place batting-wise, by contrast, is still going and probably will never be completely resolved because of the very nature of where he bats in the line-up. 'Without doubt the worst places to bat are six, seven and eight because six, seven and eight tend to be all-rounders and you're expected to go in there in the last few overs and belt at least two or three a ball. For an all-rounder it's very difficult.

'The higher you bat in one-day cricket the easier it is to score runs and opening amplifies that. You get time to set yourself, the field's up, yet you can be a bit belligerent with your strokeplay and it's still cool.'

Like many of his peers Matthews said that one game tends to blur into another but he did not have to struggle to name the highlight of his limited-overs career for Australia.

'It's not my career highlight but it's definitely in the grand final. It was when we won the one-day series against India and I was named player of the finals. At the SCG in that particular series I took 3-27. It was a capacity crowd and it was just an incredible charge, the crowd teeing off. I got Azharrudin and I bowled Kapil Dev first ball. I had Armanath out handled the ball, which is very rare, and I took a hot caught-and-bowled off Srikkanth in the other match. That was without doubt the highlight of my one-day career to date.'

He concluded with a warning, and in so doing spoke for all the people who followed the game – in all its forms: 'It remains for players and administrators to accept the challenge to keep cricket alive and vibrant, and not to shrink from the decisions needed to ensure that end.'

15

TURNING THE CORNER

The Australians returned to Sharjah in April 1986 for the first staging of the 'Austral-Asia Cup', but the trip was not a successful one. Five countries were involved – Australia, New Zealand, India, Pakistan and Sri Lanka. A week earlier on their home turf the Sri Lankans had won the 'Asia Cup', a one-day tournament that also involved Pakistan and Bangladesh (India had rejected an invitation to compete). For the Sharjah event, the winners of the Asia Cup were seeded automatically into the semi-finals where they were joined by the two first-round winners and the 'best' of the two first-round losers. Sadly the team to miss the semi-finals was Australia – their defeat by Pakistan by eight wickets with five balls to spare (7-202 to 2-206) was deemed worse than New Zealand's three-wicket loss to India, even though India reached their target with 16 balls in hand.

With Border unavailable for the short tour, the Australians were led by the veteran Victorian captain Ray Bright who became the ninth man to lead Australia in a one-day international (after Lawry, Ian Chappell, Greg Chappell, Simpson, Yallop, Hughes, Hookes and Border). Five months later, Bright was Border's vice-captain when the Australians returned to the world stage on a tour of India that will always be remembered for the tied first Test in Madras. *Wisden*'s correspondent later compared the home team's chase on the final day of the tie as being 'in the limited-overs manner of a charge launched on the foundation provided by the first three men'.

The first two (of six) one-day internationals scheduled for the tour were played before the first Test. In the first at Jaipur, Boon and Marsh started with centuries and a 212 opening stand, but the innings ended at 3-250 after 47 overs (instead of the intended 50) when the allotted time ran out. It appeared – not for the first time in a one-day international – that the team fielding first had slowed the over-rate. There was no penalty or fine built into the tour conditions to guard against such a tactic. The Indians needed only 41 overs to reach 3-251. In the second match at Srinigar the Australians returned the compliment bowling only 47 overs and eventually winning by three wickets with six balls to spare. Border, who scored an unbeaten 90, was named the man of the match.

The third one-dayer at Hyderabad was scheduled between the first two Tests, and attracted considerable interest after the heroics in Madras. But the game was ruined by the rain. Kapil Dev put the Australians in 'so that he could apply the strategy of rationing the overs' suggested *Wisden* and once again only 47 overs were bowled by

Bruce Reid, bowling on his home turf at the WACA Ground during the limited-overs Challenge tournament that involved Australia, England, Pakistan and the West Indies and was staged to coincide with the 1987 America's Cup.

the team fielding first. Australia's total of 6-242 was due largely to a blazing 75 off 53 balls by Greg Ritchie, who hit 22 runs from one over. The Indians were 1-41 in the 11th over when the thunderstorm intervened.

The final three matches were played before the third Test. In the first in New Delhi Kapil's delaying tactics were appalling, and the visitors received only 45 overs. The Indian captain had clearly not read Sir Donald's essay in *Wisden*. Australia finished with 6-238, and owed much to a dashing, unbroken stand of 102 in 76 balls between Waugh and reserve keeper Greg Dyer. The Indians, who smashed Matthews for 54 in five overs, eventually won with nine balls to spare. Three days later they clinched the series in front of a crowd of more than 60,000 with a decisive 52-run victory in Ahmedabad, despite the fact that Australia required 102 from the final 25 overs with eight wickets in hand. Border, Ritchie and Dyer were all run out, and the match ended with six-and-a-half overs still available. In the final match, Kapil Dev struck a fearsome half century from only 26 balls, including 24 from one McDermott over, but Australia sailed home on the back of a sparkling unbeaten 91 by their captain, winning with seven wickets and nine balls to spare.

This tour of India was the first genuine outing for Bob Simpson as Australia's coach. Simpson had received much credit for NSW's Sheffield Shield wins in 1984-85 and 1985-86, and had been seconded to the Australian team for the 1986 tour of New Zealand, where on the surface it seemed he had little effect. But he was not officially appointed to the national team coaching role, under the title of 'cricket manager', until the 1986 off-season. Simpson was appreciative of the talent in the team. The tour of India he saw as a valuable preparation for the coming Ashes series in Australia and for the 1987 World Cup (to be played in India and Pakistan). Of his charges, Simpson told reporters: 'I believe we have the nucleus of a team already in place which will go a long way to being the team which will eventually take Australia back to the top of the tree.'

This was not always apparent during the 1986-87 Australian season, when the team was beaten comfortably in the Test series, the World Series Cup, and also in a four-team limited-overs 'Benson and Hedges Challenge' tournament staged in Perth over the new year to coincide with the staging of the America's Cup yacht races. Like the previous four summers the season was split, with the Test series preceding the World Series Cup. The 'America's Cup' competition was squeezed between the fourth Test (which England won easily to retain the Ashes) and the fifth. It also involved the West Indies and Pakistan who had squared a Test series in late 1986 in Pakistan though the Windies had won a five-match one-day series 4-1. There were signs during that tour that the mighty West Indies machine was on the wane, never more so than in the first Test when Imran and Abdul Qadir bowled them out in the second innings for just 53. Viv Richards, now the regular captain following the retirement of Lloyd, was twice dismissed first ball in the limited-overs internationals while his great fast-bowling battery seemed more and more prone to injury.

The competition involved a round-robin of the four sides, followed by a final involving the top two teams. All matches were played at the WACA Ground where floodlights had just been installed. The first international teams to use them were

Simon O'Donnell, who first played for Australia in the opening match of the 1984-85 World Series Cup, and in the seasons that followed found himself labelled, more so than any other player of his generation, as predominantly a limited-overs cricketer. Certainly his batting and bowling talents were perfectly suited to the shorter game. Only Craig McDermott and Steve Waugh have taken more wickets in limited-overs internationals, and of all the Australians to play one-day international cricket, perhaps only Dean Jones has produced as many spectacular, big-hitting adventures as the charismatic O'Donnell.

SPIN BOWLING: THE RISE OF PETER 'WHO'

Off-spinner Peter Taylor burst into international cricket with a magnificent debut Test. The headlines following his selection for the final Test of the 1986-87 Ashes series had screamed 'Peter Who?' but there were no doubts about his identity after he collected 6-78 with his first spell in Australia's colours.

Taylor enjoyed commendable success thereafter in his 13 Test appearances without ever truly cementing his place in the team. Where he really made a name for himself, at a time when the majority of his slow-bowling brethren were struggling even to get a game, was in one-day cricket. Dean Jones, no slouch at the one-day game himself, in 1991 rated Taylor the best one-day spinner in the world.

Ashley Mallett, along with commentating doyen Richie Benaud and former NSW and Australian leg-spinning all-rounder Peter Philpott, is one of this country's most respected authorities on spin bowling. Mallett was an avid student during his playing days and since retirement has been involved in maintaining the rage through his 'Spin Australia' clinics, where he has helped oversee the development of the best spin bowlers in each state around Australia, and his writing, his most recent success being a biography of legendary leg-spinner Clarrie Grimmett. He is thus eminently qualified to comment on off-spinner Taylor's legacy in one-day cricket.

'I thought Peter Taylor was a bit under-rated as a bowler,' said Mallett. 'Basically his strategy was wrong in the first-class arena. A lot of people said he was just a one-day bowler but I believe if he had bowled the same line in Tests as he did in one-day games he would have been a very good Test bowler. He was useful in the first-class game but probably not as effective as he should have been.

'In one-day games he bowled a line outside off stump as an offie should bowl. So he was giving himself a chance

the West Indies and Pakistan, and the Pakistanis were triumphant by 34 runs in front of nearly 12,000 fans. Forty-eight hours later, in front of a ground record 27,125 people on the afternoon and evening of New Year's Day, England defeated Australia by 37 runs. Despite a superb century by Dean Jones, the man of this match was Ian Botham who slammed an unbelievable 68 off 39 balls, including 26 from one Simon Davis over. Davis, a fast-medium bowler from Victoria, had made something of a name for himself as a miserly one-day bowler during the World Series Cup of the previous season. Although never a contender for the Test side in 1986-87, he was an automatic selection for the Australian one-day team ... until Botham got hold of him. His eighth over went for 26 – 4, 4, 2, 4, 6, 6 – and Davis was not seen in the remainder of the tournament.

Even with these first two victories, few believed England and Pakistan would be the Challenge's finalists. However, a curious sequence of events followed. Australia finished without a win, after a heartbreaking loss to Pakistan and an inglorious

of bowling a bloke through the gate or getting him caught at slip. He also seemed to like two blokes out. A fielder at forward square leg on the fence and a bloke at wide mid-on or mid-wicket. He seemed to have the confidence to bowl in one-day games the way he should have in all forms of cricket.'

Mallett believes that Taylor paid a heavy price for his defensive approach in first-class cricket – a game that cried out for aggressive bowling.

'In the first-class game his line changed,' said Mallett. 'He started to bowl the line of off stump turning into the pads and he couldn't get anyone out at all. It was sad but something that should have been worked out. He retired prematurely. He was a very good bits-and-pieces cricketer and he should have done better in the first-class arena than he did. I firmly believe that he wasn't just a one-day bowler.

'In one-day cricket he always looked as dangerous as anyone. He spun the ball hard and his flight was good. He got good loop and he bowled a particularly good ball that fizzed on straight.'

Peter Taylor, who was labelled 'Peter Who' when first selected for the Australian team in 1986-87. Although Taylor never cemented a position in the Test XI, he developed into a key man in the one-day combination and more than any Australian bowler before Shane Warne proved there was a place for a spin bowler in limited-overs international cricket.

crash against the West Indies. In the competition's third match, Pakistan were all but thrashed when they fell to 6-129 in the 30th over chasing the home team's 274. Jones had made his second successive hundred, this time a dazzling 121 off 113 balls, and Waugh 82 (the stand for the fourth wicket was 173) and then Waugh and Ken MacLeay had broken through the top order. But things went horribly wrong. Border took off Waugh to save him for the final overs, and the Pakistanis, led by the little-known left-arm spinner Asif Mujtaba, counter-attacked. The seventh-wicket partnership added 52, the eighth 43 and the ninth 43. The second-last wicket fell on the first ball of the 50th over, seven short of victory. Waugh bowled this tense final over, but after having Wasim Akram caught at long off, his next four balls went for 1, 1, 3 and 2. One ball remained when the target was achieved and Australia had fallen to an infamous defeat. Two days later, the Australians collapsed for 91 chasing 256 in a meaningless match against the West Indies, who themselves had crashed to a defeat against the Englishmen the previous day.

Much of the home team's outcricket during the Challenge was lambasted by the critics, and often lampooned by the fans, who on occasions cheered competent pieces of fielding in recognition of their perceived rarity. Peter Roebuck, in his book of the English tour, *Ashes to Ashes*, wrote of the first match: 'Australia were incredibly incompetent in the field, conceding overthrows, bowling wides and no-balls, dropping catches. They played like a badly coached school rugby team, all gung-ho and no direction.'

England won the Challenge final and then proceeded to win the World Series Cup as well to complete, as the English correspondents described it, the 'Grand Slam'. In the final of the World Series they played not the West Indians as everyone had assumed, but Australia, who topped the qualifying table by winning five matches, including their last four. But this feat was overshadowed by one extraordinary event under lights in Sydney ... the final over of the Australia-England match on January 22. This was the fourth match of the series, each team at this point having won one match. The Australians' total of 8-233 had been built around Dirk Wellham's diligent 97 and seemed sufficient all the way to the final over, when the visitors required 18 to win. Bruce Reid (1-26 off nine) was the bowler, and Allan Lamb, the nuggetty, South African-born right-hander, was on strike on 59 not out.

Lamb had been struggling to keep his side in touch and managed just two from the first ball, keeping the strike only because of a wild throw from deep extra cover. The second ball was swung for four to deep square leg, reviving English hopes, and then the third was smashed to where the Hill had once been, beyond deep mid-wicket for a stunning, fantastic six. The silence was broken only by the few loud British supporters who sang, danced and annoyed as if England had won soccer's World Cup. Six was now needed in three, and then four in two when Lamb guided the ball to cover for one, but got two through an ordinary return and a Reid fumble near the bowlers'-end stumps. The chants of the English fans built to a crescendo as the home fans sat stunned. Reid's fifth ball was pitched on leg stump again, and Lamb already knew where the vacant square-leg fence was. He ran from the field very much the hero, having completed one of the greatest last-over rescues in the game's history. The immediate home-town reaction to this over was the lowest point of the summer. A feeling of helplessness and hopelessness consumed the home fans.

This debacle was the Australians' only loss in the qualifying matches to the Englishmen, and at times they did look like a very good one-day side. But they were prone to putting in a 'shocker', usually just as their followers were beginning to believe they had turned the corner. Jones' hundred in their opening match in front of a full house in Brisbane was outstanding, as was O'Donnell's brilliant bowling display against the West Indies in Sydney (4-19 from 10 overs). More than 63,000 at the MCG saw one magic moment, when the local favourite O'Donnell struck the imposing Malcolm Marshall straight for a massive six. With one stroke, the concept that few dared believe – that the West Indies were genuinely vulnerable – had been confirmed.

The English victory in the finals was clear-cut. They won the first final by six wickets, an all-day contest in front of 51,589 at the MCG in which Ian Botham scored 71. The second under lights at the SCG ended in English victory by nine runs after O'Donnell had failed to do a 'Lamb' as he chased 18 off the final over. The Victorian cavalier, who ended with 40 not out off 27 balls, had struck two more truly imposing sixes during his solo assault after the Australian run chase lost its way. The first was an extraordinary, advancing cross-bat slash over long-off off the fast-medium bowler Phillip de Freitas that ended many rows back under the Bradman Stand. The second was a brutal drive over the sightscreen from the same bowler that threatened the members 30 metres from the boundary in the lower section of the M.A. Noble Stand.

Within two seasons, these bold, often breathtaking hits, like the aggression and strength of Jones and the consistency and quality of Border, Marsh and Waugh, had become extremely positive aspects of the Australian one-day scene. The fans were beginning to recognise new heroes to replace the likes of Chappell, Marsh, Lillee and Walters – but what they craved was a trophy-winning team as well. A disappointment for Simpson was the apparent demise of Boon and McDermott, who both struggled in 1986-87. Also of concern was the form of Ritchie and Matthews, who were now not sure of places that had been theirs to keep just 12 months before. Matthews' problems multiplied in Sharjah at season's end, when he was involved in an incident at a team barbecue that led to a highly publicised fine. In Sharjah, the Australians, without only an injured Jones for all matches and Border for one (Marsh led the side in his absence), lost all three of their games in what had become a round-robin competition. The only solace was the return to form of Boon, who scored 71, 62 and 73.

When the Australian selectors sat down to choose their XIV for the fourth World Cup, they did so with the axe ominously near the table. Matthews, Wellham, Ritchie, Davis and the wicketkeeper Tim Zoehrer did not survive. The Cup squad included three players new to international cricket – the South Australian off-spinner Tim May, the WA batsman Mike Veletta and the young South Australian medium-pacer Andrew Zesers – plus Greg Dyer and the NSW off-spinner Peter Taylor. Taylor had come into the side, unheralded but successful, for the final Ashes Test and kept his place for the World Series and Sharjah. Boon and McDermott were there as well, the latter fortunate that no-one had stepped forward to claim his spot. The full squad was Border (captain), Marsh (vice-captain), Boon, Dyer, Jones, McDermott, May, Moody, O'Donnell, Reid, Taylor, Veletta, Waugh and Zesers. London bookmakers rated them 16-1 chances, but the off-season preparation was shrewdly planned, and the experience on the sub-continent a year earlier had been invaluable.

Though few outside the squad realised it, the Australians were ready for the greatest month in their one-day cricket history.

SIMON O'DONNELL: THE ONE-DAY SPECIALIST

It has never been particularly fashionable for a player to pledge undying love for limited-overs cricket. One-dayers have still not quite shaken of the stigma that they are 'not proper cricket'. Players are now treating limited-overs cricket much more seriously but, almost to a man, they will still state a firm preference for Test cricket. That's where the prestige and credibility are. But players are beginning to be recognised for their contributions in the one-day game. Victorian all-rounder Simon O'Donnell is perhaps the prototype of the player who is found wanting in Test cricket, but becomes a heavyweight when he steps out under lights.

O'Donnell played just six Test matches in his 10-year career but turned out for Australia's limited-overs side 87 times. In many of those games he was a pivotal member of the team. So important was he to the Australian cause that many felt it was his omission from the 1992 World Cup squad – because of injury and poor form – that cost Australia the title. The big Victorian, known to his team-mates as 'Sod', is ranked fourth on Australia's international limited-overs wicket-taking list with 108 victims at 28.72 apiece, with best figures of 5-13. He scored 1242 runs at an average of 26 with nine half-centuries and a top score of 74 not out.

O'Donnell has no illusions about the effect one-day cricket had on his career. 'I think it played an enormous role,' he said. 'The majority of the cricket I played on an international basis was one-day cricket. I suspect the way I played the game probably suited that course of action more than it suited playing Test cricket.' All of O'Donnell's Test matches occurred in a span between 1985 and 1986, after which he never really got a look-in. The fact that he was living a dual life – discarded Test player one week and one-day linch-pin the next – had the potential to make him bitter, but O'Donnell said he did not resent the situation.

'It didn't bother me all that much. I think it's more the way Test cricket has gone these days. Test cricket is played a lot more on the percentages whereas in one-day cricket a bit more flair and adventurousness comes in. When you get to that level you always play to your strengths and I believe my strengths were being aggressive and a touch adventurous at times. And I don't think that style overly suited the way that Test cricket has gone. If I tried to be Geoff Marsh I wouldn't have survived either. He had his strengths and I had my strengths and mine were very different. You adjust mentally and tone your game down for four- or five-day cricket but I believe if I had tried to tone it right down it would have been no good to anybody.'

That's not to say that he ever wrote off his chances of winning another baggy green cap. 'No, I never gave up hope of playing Test cricket. You always look to find the shining light at the end of the tunnel and I always thought there was one. I think if you give up and resign yourself to one thing, you are doing yourself and your ambitions a disservice. You've always got to believe that you're good enough to get there. While I played I always believed I was good enough to play Test cricket. I didn't play much of it – that's the way it worked out – but you would always keep it in mind because if an opportunity arose you would jump.'

O'Donnell believes the reason he was so successful at one-day cricket comes down simply to mental approach rather than strength or timing or courage. 'I treated all the opposition the same whether it was Wasim Akram or Phil DeFreitas,' he said. 'I had respect for their ability but I was never overawed or intimidated by what people said or what their record was or how much experience they had. I always had to walk out there believing I could do what I wanted to do and I'd have confidence in my own ability. I never believed that the guy at the other end was no good but I always believed I was better than him. That enabled me to have that sense of adventure, that confidence that a ball pitched in such an area could be dispatched over the fence.'

As the side's genuine all-rounder O'Donnell was regularly thrust into the pressure cooker of the final overs. If he wasn't trying to score quick runs as the overs evaporated he was bowling those final overs and trying to choke the life out of the opposition's bid for crucial runs. But one man's ulcer farm is another's utopia. 'I loved the pressure,' said O'Donnell. 'Ate it for breakfast. That was a great motivation. As an all-rounder you've got such an opportunity to have an enormous influence on every single game you play. And that went back to a football mentality; I liked to be in the action all the time and moving quickly. As an all-rounder that opportunity was created – especially in one-day cricket because you're on the go all day.'

O'Donnell had no preference between the thrills of batting and bowling and said if pressed he would not be able to choose. 'They were both a lot of fun,' said O'Donnell. 'A lot of pressure and a lot of satisfaction if you could do them in a top-quality manner.' Many middle-order batsmen complain of the difficulties of being thrust into the cauldron and having to score quick runs without any time to settle in but O'Donnell had no gripes in that regard. 'I think my natural game was suited to the middle order so it didn't bother me where I batted. If I was batting anywhere in the top seven I was happy and thought it gave me an opportunity to do my job.'

Similarly O'Donnell said he never had trouble with his enthusiasm despite the sometimes crushing limited-overs schedule of an Australian summer. 'If there was a day I felt flat I'd do something stupid to get myself up, make myself annoyed. That might have been a confrontation in some shape or form with the opposition or maybe sometimes even with the umpire. If I felt I was flat and needed something to gee me up and get my mind right on the job I'd try and make myself, within reason, angry and pump up a bit of aggression inside me. Sometimes it might even be the drinks waiter.'

Although O'Donnell believes the correct mental attitude was one of his most potent weapons he did not neglect either technical practice or analysis of techniques and trends. He said he gave himself the foundation to improvise when the pressure was on by rigorously practising the skills he was going to need in the thick of the one-day rush.

Continued over page

THE ONE-DAY SPECIALIST

Continued from previous page

'In pre-match practice you bat differently for Sheffield Shield, Test and one-day cricket,' he said. 'You practice the range of shots you take into a one-day game differently compared to a four-day or five-day game. You're more on your toes and looking for opportunities, so you bat accordingly in the practice lead-up. There was definitely a difference when it came to practising my bowling. I'd practise my change of pace a lot more leading into a one-day match than I would before a five-day game.'

O'Donnell was constantly trying to develop that new delivery that would give him an edge. 'I think part of people's success is adjusting to what they see will happen in the future. You've got to read what the game requires to be successful in the future, putting extra strings in your bow. You can never be stereotyped and say I'm going to bowl this way and bat this way and that's it. You've got to make subtle adjustments along the way to make sure you stay competitive. You can't go out onto the field with the batsman or bowler knowing exactly what you do and how you do it. You've got to adjust those things and try to stay a step ahead.'

O'Donnell said analysis formed a major part of his preparation and was all-pervasive. 'It can happen in lots of different ways. It can happen lying in your bed watching telly, it can happen in the lounge room watching telly, it can happen having a few beers with the boys after a game. I spent a fair bit of time talking tactics and technique with other players. Any time you're away on a cricket tour it's really 90 per cent cricket. You're always thinking, talking, learning about the game. You spend most of your time retracing your steps.

'Steve Waugh and I used to talk a lot, especially out on the ground during one-dayers, I suppose because we're similar types. A lot of times we'd end up bowling the last six or seven overs together so we'd always communicate a lot to ensure we had the right plan.'

O'Donnell said there were many games and exciting finishes he could recall but when pressed named a World Series Cup game against England as his finest performance in Australia's colours.

'We were in a fair bit of trouble and I got 70-odd not out and then took 1-15 from five or six overs,' he recalled. 'That was probably as close as I got to my optimum in having an influence on the game, in giving the side some direction under a fair bit of pressure. But no one stands out where I could say: "That is the best day of my cricketing life and that's the best I could ever play." You always search for that. If you ever reach that I think you'd find it pretty dull afterwards. You always want to better yourself no matter what.'

16

THE WORLD'S BEST

The members of the ICC had decided on July 19, 1984, by a vote of 16 to 12, that the fourth World Cup would be held in India and Pakistan in 1987 rather than, as the previous Cups had been, in England. Originally the organisers from the sub-continent had wanted to hold the tournament in February/March, but, after discussions with Australian, English and New Zealand delegates, it was shifted back to October/November. Another key component of the India/Pakistan bid was the financial guarantee offered to the competing countries, which was almost twice that put forward by the TCCB.

In August 1986, it was announced that the Indian company Reliance would sponsor the competition, and that the teams would be playing for the 'Reliance Cup', a trophy which turned out to be an extraordinarily elaborate piece – 60 centimetres of 24-carat gold plating protecting pure silver with a re-creation, in diamonds, of the Reliance logo sitting at the cup's pinnacle. Initially the Indian Board had been seeking a multinational sponsor, to avoid potential foreign ex-change difficulties. But after the Indian Government was approached and agreed to turn the proceeds from a local deal into the necessary foreign monies, the organisers accepted the Reliance sponsorship offer and set forth to make the Cup the success it would eventually become. Matches were scheduled only for towns and cities with suitable accommodation, facilities and playing conditions, and each location had to gain the approval of a representative of either the TCCB or the ACB before it was added to the fixtures list.

The vexatious South African hurdle rose angrily in the months before the tournament. At the 1986 annual general meeting of the ICC, delegates representing the West Indies and Zimbabwe had attempted to move a motion that would have effectively banned from big-time cricket any player who had any sporting contact with South Africa. Nothing was done at that meeting, but the Australian Board resolved to support the resolution, provided the question of sporting contacts was not applied retrospectively. However, there was soon after a change of mind, and the ACB decided to accept that individuals who travelled to South Africa to coach or play should not be legislated against. New Zealand and England had taken a similar stance.

The Indian External Affairs ministry told the Reliance Cup organising commit-tee in India that under no circumstances would visas be granted to players with

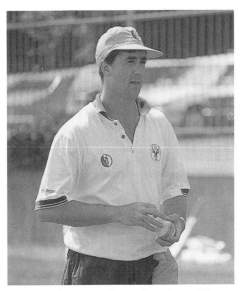

The South Australian off-spinner Tim May who edged out the other slow bowler in the squad, Peter Taylor, for a place in the Australian starting line-up for the latter stages of the '87 World Cup.

sporting links with South Africa. Pakistani cricket authorities were told by their government that they should follow the lead of the Indians. Such moves meant that the odds of England being involved in the tournament were lengthening by the day, as many of their finest players had held coaching or playing positions in South Africa. Some had just completed suspensions after being involved in a rebel tour. The ACB told the Cup organisers that if any player from any nation was barred in such a way then that was the end of Australia's involvement in the Cup. New Zealand's policy was the same. With the real possibility of a split in the cricket community looming, World Cup organisers began making plans for a five-nation round-robin competition.

In the run-up to a crucial ICC meeting in London in June 1987, less than four months before the scheduled start of the Reliance Cup, newspaper columnists saw such a division in the cricket world as almost inevitable. Inside the hallowed halls of Lord's, strong and passionate views were put on the justice and legality of the West Indies/Zimbabwe resolution, which many in the meeting were determined to see passed. This meeting, of course, involved not just delegates from the Test-playing nations, but also officials from the ICC's associate members. It soon became clear that the split was not simply along 'colour' lines. Delegates from the USA, Canada, Holland, Bermuda and Hong Kong all spoke in favour of the principle of the resolution, though some questioned its wording. The President of the Hong Kong Cricket Board then suggested that an alternative resolution be put, which suggested that the problem be handed over to a special committee made up of one member from each Test-playing country and three associate members, with that group being required to produce a report to the ICC by March 31, 1988. Such a motion was eventually put by the West Indian delegate, and seconded by Australia, but only after further passionate debate, and a delicious irony. The passing of this resolution meant that the Reliance Cup, in all its glory, would go ahead. But the only delegate not to vote in favour of the Cup-saving motion was the man from the Indian Board, who had been instructed by his prime minister not to support anything but the original less-conciliatory resolution.

Following this meeting, the Indian government chose to soften its own stance on this issue. Visas would be granted, but only after the players with South African links agreed to publicly denounce apartheid. The English newspaper, the *Independ-*

ent, looked at the 'solution' to the South African issue and the coming Reliance Cup and wrote: 'What we have here is the equivalent of a game of football on Christmas Day, after which it's back to the trenches.'

Not all the teams who eventually arrived for the Cup were at full strength – among the unavailable were Botham, Gower, Hadlee, Marshall, Garner and Greenidge. The eight countries involved were split into two groups. India, Australia, New Zealand and Zimbabwe were in Group A, with all matches to be played in India. Group B, whose matches were programmed for the cricket fields of Pakistan, was made up of the pre-tournament favourites Pakistan, the West Indies, England and Sri Lanka. The matches were of 50 overs, with no bowler allowed more than 10. Boundaries throughout the Cup would be a uniform 75 metres from the pitch. The umpiring panel was made up of the top officials from all over the world, and included the South Australian Tony Crafter, who stood in four qualifying matches and the semi-final in Bombay. As had been the case in 1983, the teams in each group played their fellow group members twice, with the top two teams going on to the semi-finals. And, as had been the case in the one-day internationals of the previous Australian summer, any riser that sailed over the batsman's shoulders was to be deemed by these 'neutral' umpires to be a no-ball.

In the days leading up to the Cup, many critics observed that none of the six visiting teams had adapted better to the stresses of the local conditions than the Australians, who, of course, had been in India playing a tied Test match 12 months before. This approach was reflected by the outcome of the opening match of the Cup, a thrilling one-run Australian defeat of India on October 9 in front of more than 50,000 stunned fanatics in Madras, the scene of the tie. The win came about through a century by Marsh, the resilience of McDermott, and Steve Waugh's coolness in the final over as India failed to gather the six runs they needed for victory.

Australia's total of 6-270 owed much to the 110-run start given by Boon and Marsh after Kapil Dev had won the toss. Jones then strode out to hit 39 from 35 balls, before the bearded McDermott's first four overs went for 31, as Gavaskar and Srikkanth began with a flourish. However, he came back to rip through the Indian middle order. When the 50th and final over began, India's last-wicket partnership needed six. However, Waugh was too controlled and conceded just a pair of twos off the second and third balls to Maninder Singh, before ripping out his off-stump with the fifth.

This match set the scene for Australia's nerve-wrenching passage through Group A. After Zimbabwe were handled comfortably in match two (9-235 – Border 67, Marsh 62 – to 139 off 42.4 overs – O'Donnell 4-39, Waugh six overs, three maidens, 0-7), New Zealand were edged out in a rain-shortened thriller at Indore. Australia's total of 4-199 from their permitted 30 overs owed much to Boon's 87 from 87 balls, but the New Zealanders, led admirably by the supreme batting skills of Martin Crowe, reached 6-193 with a single Waugh over to go, and Crowe unconquered on 58, from just 45 balls. But, as it had on opening day, Waugh's nerve held; Crowe lofted the first ball to Marsh at deep cover, the next, a yorker, shattered Ian Smith's stumps, and the remaining four balls brought no more than three singles and the run out of Snedden. The Australians, with three wins out of three, were all but in the semi-finals.

Next came a hiccup, a 56-run loss to their hosts in New Delhi, where Australia went in with an all-seam attack but were beaten by the left-arm finger spin of Maninder Singh. But another Marsh hundred, which included two sixes in the innings' final over, saw Border's team through by 17 runs in the return against New Zealand. With this innings, Marsh became after Gavaskar and Glenn Turner the third man to bat through an entire World Cup innings. In the Australians' final qualifying match, against Zimbabwe at Cuttack, Boon and Jones scored half-centuries as the Australians reached 5-266 on a pitch that had been dampened by overnight rain. This proved sufficient for a 70-run victory.

The Australians were left with a nervous wait to see whether they would be travelling to Bombay in India as Group A winners or Lahore in Pakistan as Group A runners-up. The certainty was the team that travelled to Lahore for their semi-final would be facing Imran's rampant Pakistanis, who had clinched the top spot in Group B and were everyone's favourites to win the whole thing. More than wanting to avoid Imran and his men, India desperately yearned to play their semi-final in front of their fanatical countrymen. Their final Group match, against New Zealand, was played 24 hours after the Australians' fifth win, and the mathematicians' calculators showed that India needed to win, and score at a run-rate of 5.25 an over, to book their passage to Bombay.

In the end they did this comfortably. New Zealand won the toss and batted, but were kept to 221 from their 50 overs. This meant the Indians had 42.2 overs to top the group, but they needed just 32.1, as Gavaskar smashed a hundred off 85 balls.

The Cup organisers had always hoped for an India-Pakistan finale. Now India faced England, who had surprisingly eliminated the disappointing West Indies, while Pakistan prepared to overrun the Australians at the Gaddafi Stadium. For Border's team, after such a barren 1986-87 home season, reaching the semi-finals was an achievement in itself. The team took strength from the close wins it had gleaned, and the toughness and demeanour of Waugh and Marsh which had been so vital. As victories, especially close victories, are wont to do, the team's success had built up a team spirit not experienced since the days before WSC. They believed they had a real chance. And they bristled at the comments of the former great Pakistani batsman, Zaheer Abbas, who sneered through his newspaper column that the Australians were no more than 'schoolboys; mere club cricketers'.

The Pakistanis had lost only one match, their last, meaningless (in terms of the final group standings) match against the West Indians. But the match was rumoured to have been far from insignificant, for their superb bowling all-rounder Wasim Akram had apparently chipped a small bone in his foot and was thought to be out of the tournament. The Australians were further heartened by the news that the two excellent English umpires, Dickie Bird and David Shepherd, would be in control.

The match, like all those in the tournament before it, began at 9am, to ensure the cricket finished in daylight. However, the early starts had had surprisingly little effect on the behaviour of the pitches or the new balls. Nor had they prevented the fans from being there for the start. Martin Johnson, writing in the *Independent*, described the atmosphere at the semi-final as the players first appeared on the field as being 'a bit like an open-air Beatles concert in the Sixties, a cacophony of noise

The former Australian captain, Bob Simpson, whose role as coach was a crucial one as Australia moved towards its ultimate World Cup triumph.

augmented by the screams from Imran's teenage girl fan club packed inside the ladies' section'.

'(But) by the end,' Johnson added, 'you could almost have heard the sound of the nib scratching Australia's name on the winner's cheque.'

More than 40,000 people watched the semi-final. Imran had indicated this would be the last home match of his career (he was, however, cajoled into continuing after the match), which lent even more emotion to the day. Border won the toss, and though Wasim Akram played, he did not take the new ball. Instead Saleem Jaffer began with a wayward spell and Boon and Marsh took full advantage, adding 73 from the first 18 overs before Marsh was run out by Salim Malik's precise throw from near the square-leg umpire. Boon went on to 65, Jones scored 38, and Veletta 48 from 50 balls as the momentum continued. Imran, though, came back to slow the run-rate, until Waugh, Lamb-like, took a stunning 18 from the 50th over, bowled by the hapless Saleem, and Australia finished at 8-267.

In the press-box, Pakistan were still slight favourites, but not for long. Rameez Raja's lust for a single saw him run out by a throw by Border to the bowler's end in the first over. Mansoor Akhtar and Salim Malik added 35, before the former was bowled by McDermott. Then Waugh came on as first change and from his first ball, Salim chipped a catch to McDermott at mid-off.

Imran strode out to great, almost hysterical, acclaim, but Waugh, brave and realistic if not diplomatic, shouted for lbw straightaway, and then again, which the crowd quickly and passionately indicated was not the done thing. This jittery start over, Imran and Javed Miandad set about saving the hopes of the nation. But the Australians' outcricket, so poor when the sides had met in Perth 10 months before,

TIM MAY: A PURSUIT NOT SO TRIVIAL

Australia's against-the-odds triumph in the 1987 World Cup was the classic story of an underdog, full of fight. Insulting pre-tournament cracks about the team's ability served to harden the players' resolve, but the glue that helped bind the team together was the unique challenge of the sub-continent. It produced an avenue of male-bonding perhaps unequalled in professional sport.

Winning a thriller in the first game against co-hosts India helped; at that stage traditional Australian beer was at hand to ensure things worked smoothly. But the magic ingredient that bound these men and held them together as they defied the odds was not some trendy piece of esoteric sports psychology, nor a 'New Age' fruit-and-nuts diet — a simple board game did the trick.

Off-spinner Tim May, one of cricket's true individuals and a man with a sharp sense of humour, said the reason behind the side's reliance on children's games was simple. 'India is a place where you play cricket and that's it – there's absolutely nothing to do,' said May. 'They have a few bars but they're not worth going to so we all just had to make our own fun. We played Trivial Pursuit, Steve Waugh brought a game called Othello ('a minute to learn but a lifetime to master') and the Uno championship of the world was the biggest game that we played. That's how boring it was.

'It was always a good laugh to play a little game that you played when you were 10 or 11. A lot of games get washed out and all the lads try to show how intelligent they are and how much they know about the world. It's always quite a

Continued on page 185

was now outstanding. The two great Pakistanis added 112, but only at four an over, and the ask per over when Imran edged Border to Dyer was up to more than seven. Wasim Akram came in and struck two colossal sixes, to universal, banner-waving joy, but then had his stumps shattered by McDermott. The contrast in the emotions of the crowd when things were right or wrong was stark and bizarre. While Javed remained there was always hope, but his fall, bowled swinging at Reid in the 44th over with still 56 required, was the final blow. The silence as he trudged to the pavilion told the story much more clearly than the scorebook.

As the sun faded behind the grandstands, the last three wickets all went the same way – caught Dyer bowled McDermott, which left the fast bowler with the first five-wicket performance by a bowler in the tournament. Afterwards, the Australians celebrated their triumph while making a long and awkward journey, via stadium, hotel and airports, to Calcutta in India to prepare for the final. Next day came the Cup's second huge upset, as the Indians crashed out to England, by 35 runs, on the back of a Graham Gooch century. Gooch, as captain of a rebel team that played in South Africa in 1982-83, had had as much trouble as anyone getting a visa for the tournament. Now, the Indians were left wondering why they had ever let him in.

In the betting shops of London, the Englishmen were favourites for the final. In

*The gallant and exciting Victorian
Simon O'Donnell bowling in the 1987
World Cup final between Australia and
England at Eden Gardens, Calcutta.*

Allan Border, on the shoulders of team-mates Dean Jones (left) and Craig McDermott, holds aloft the Reliance Cup after the '87 World Cup final, which Australia won by seven runs. Australia's triumph in India was a significant landmark in the history of Border's side. In his first two years as captain the team had struggled. However, building on the confidence gained by this surprise victory, they were by 1989 one of the most formidable combinations in world cricket.

Australian Picture Library
(Chris Cole – All Sport)

It is unlikely any cricketer has ever been more at home with the fans in the MCG's outer than the charismatic local fast man, Merv Hughes.

Top: Australian wicketkeeper Ian Healy attempts to run out West Indian opener
Desmond Haynes during a World Series Cup match at the SCG in 1988-89.
Below: Opening batsman Geoff Marsh, on the way to one of his
Australian record nine one-day international centuries, at Lord's
during the third Texaco Trophy match of 1989.

Below: Patrick Eager

Queensland and Australian paceman Carl Rackemann on his home turf at the Gabba during a 1989-90 World Series victory over Pakistan.

Above: Australian opener Tom Moody swings a boundary at the Gabba in 1989-90.

Below: The Australians after their victory in the 1990-91 World Series. At back: Errol Alcott (physio), Steve Waugh, Mark Taylor, Bruce Reid, Peter Taylor, Carl Rackemann, Simon O'Donnell. Middle: Ian McDonald (media manager), Ian Healy, David Boon, Terry Alderman. Front: Bob Simpson (coach), Dean Jones, Allan Border, Mark Waugh (obscured), Geoff Marsh.

laugh finding out how much they don't know. The Trivial Pursuit was stationed in my coffin (cricket bag) and was brought out many times with quite hilarious results. It's certainly an easy way to work out who's dumb.'

Although Uno, Othello and Trivial Pursuit were the team's life support off the field, the World Cup was strictly business when game time came.

'They weren't brought out during games,' said May. 'The World Cup, being one-day cricket, was pretty dynamic in the dressing room. You haven't got time to put your feet up like you have in Test cricket so we did nothing in the dressing room except sweat, drink bisleri water and watch the cricket. Once the games were over we were out of there, you didn't take the chance of having a shower. Back to the hotel and you'd have a couple of beers in the manager's room – if there were any floating around that some kind soul from the consulate had

provided – have a quick dinner and then play cards.'

However much the Trivial Pursuit helped team morale, May believes the catalyst for Australia's stirring march to victory was the post-match celebrations following the thrilling first-up win over India. 'Those little things help but I think probably the biggest thing that brought us together was the first game against India which we won by one run,' he said. 'You wouldn't expect to see too many Australians in Madras, it's a bad place, but it seemed like half of Australia converged on the hotel we were staying in and we had one of the greatest parties of all time.

'There was a lot of alcohol consumed, a lot of laughs and a lot of singing. I think that is what brought us together. We knew we had something special. Any Australian travelling in India at the time got there. It was a big moment. A very, very large night.'

the streets of Calcutta, the support was clearly with the Australians. Once the locals came to terms with the profound disappointment of their own loss, they adopted Border's side as their own – a tribute to the Australians' underdog status, and the side's leader, who, despite his own ordinary form, was seen in this cricket-mad country as a cricketer worthy to carry the cloak once worn by Bradman, Benaud and Ian and Greg Chappell.

In his preview of the final, the veteran English writer Henry Blofeld wrote: 'Boon and Waugh are the two England have to fear. Their vibrant form is symptomatic of the way the whole of this Australian team are functioning and another sure sign that all is well is that they are fielding as Australian sides are traditionally expected to field. Surprisingly, Border has yet to make much of a contribution with the bat, but he is such a fine player that his best form is never more than one innings away.'

Eden Gardens – the site of the final – next to the MCG is the largest cricket ground in terms of crowd capacity in the world, and more than 70,000 people were there on November 8, 1987, for the fourth World Cup final (and the first for the Reliance Cup). Around the stadium, amid the advertising hoardings and the banners waved by the fans, were huge templates bearing the names of all the nations involved in the Cup, and digital clocks featuring the time in each of these countries.

The umpires appointed to the final were India's Ram Gupta and Mahboob Shah from Pakistan, though it had been rumoured that Border, with Gatting's support, had asked unsuccessfully for Crafter and Bird.

The Australian captain won the toss and batted, as most leaders had done during the Cup. Eighteen of the 26 matches before the final had been won by the team batting first, which reflected a change from the long-held belief that it was easier to chase rather than to defend, and an admission that the sub-continent pitches were at their best for batting before the day was long. Boon and Marsh started briskly and 48 runs came from the first nine overs. But then they slowed as the fast-medium Neil Foster produced a miserly spell and when Marsh was bowled, as much by frustration as Foster, the score was 1-75 in the 18th over. Jones and Boon consolidated, but the run-rate was kept in check, and the murmured feeling through the packed grandstands was that the 76-run second-wicket partnership had taken too many overs. By the time the 150 was reached both captains would have been planning for 220, or perhaps 230 at most, especially when Jones (38 off 57 balls) and Boon (75 off 125) were dismissed within 15 runs of each other, and McDermott, pinch-hitting at No. 4, was bowled for 14 at 168 late in the 39th over. But then Border and little Veletta changed the game. Their partnership lasted only 10 overs, but was worth 73 as Australia suddenly accelerated towards 250. It was a figure no team batting second had reached in the tournament. Veletta's innings was his best ever for Australia – an unbeaten, cavalier 45 from just 31 balls – and was completed amid much excitement as he and Waugh nabbed another 11 off the 50th over. Australia finished at 253.

Significantly, England had bowled seven no-balls and five wides – 12 extra deliveries – twice as many as the Australians would give them in return.

In 1975, Australian cricket followers throughout the land had been able to sit up through the night and follow the fortunes of the first World Cup final live on television. Sadly, this was not the case in 1987. Channel Nine, who had the rights to the telecast, chose instead in Sydney and Melbourne to stick with the regular Sunday night entertainment. Fans could go to the pubs and clubs where the match was being shown on SKY Channel, but this was no use to the fans under 18 who were not allowed by law into these venues. As the giant digital clock at Eden Gardens showed the time on the Australian east coast was 8.30pm, Channel Nine began showing a movie entitled *Unfaithfully Yours*. For the cricket fans prevented from watching the exciting end to one of the great days of Australian sport, the title could not have been more apt. The movie's final credits would be rolling over the screen just as the Cup final reached its gripping conclusion.

Although Nottingham's Tim Robinson had fallen lbw in England's first over in reply, by the 31st the chase had reached 2-135. Gooch had gone to O'Donnell, but Gatting and Bill Athey had steadied and then attacked. The English captain rode his luck, especially when Waugh, hands above his head, caught him at long-on, but in the process trod on the boundary rope. Athey was almost run out by a direct hit by May, then Gatting edged a catch centimetres wide of the despairing Dyer. But mixed in were shots of quality, and with May having been smashed from the attack, Border was running out of options and ideas when he brought himself on to bowl the 32nd over.

Early on, the Australians' fielding had been superb, with O'Donnell, Jones and Border all responsible for stirring saves. By the 32nd over, O'Donnell wore the grass stains of battle as he had when he played in the VFL for St Kilda. Once, after diving headfirst along the boundary rope to prevent a four, he had been slow to rise, and Jones, too, seemed troubled by his knee for a period. Then the Australians' standards dropped. Waugh, as if trying to prove that he *really* was 22 years old, threw away four runs with an unnecessary shy at the bowlers' end, and then Dyer fumbled a leg-side delivery and conceded two more. If the game had been in the balance for most of its life, it seemed now to be slowly tilting England's way.

Border's first ball was innocuous enough, a slow turner that lobbed just outside the line of Gatting's leg stump. He could not have realised that the English captain had decided, before the ball was bowled, that he was going to 'reverse-sweep' the ball to the vacant area behind point. This was a shot that had been played with some success during the competition, notably by Javed Miandad, but on this occasion it did not work. The ball went from the top edge, to Gatting's shoulder, and spooned in the air for Dyer to take one of the easiest catches of his life. The Australians could scarcely believe it. In the press-box, the English writers had their scapegoat. In the space of one ball, one 'masterpiece of bad judgement' as Blofeld later called it, the entire game had changed.

Gatting's place was taken by Allan Lamb, who through the tournament had the been the fastest-scoring Englishman. Within three overs he had two fours – one a fierce pull from a Waugh no-ball, the other a lob over mid-on off Border. The target had dropped below 100, and Athey had reached his 50. But the mood had changed, and the Australians had new verve in the field, even though Lamb shaped as potentially an even more destructive foe than Gatting. In the 39th over, with the score on 3-168, Reid bowled to Athey, who pushed the ball past a diving Border within the circle at mid-wicket. Waugh, from mid-on, gave chase and reached the ball on the practice wickets, about 15 metres from the boundary. The fieldsman slipped as he grabbed for the ball, and Athey, seeing this, set off for a third. But Waugh was balanced in a flash, and his throw arrived at the bowler's end as Athey began to dive for the crease. It was a desperate moment. Video replays showed the Englishman might have been given the benefit of the doubt by Mr Gupta, but he was not, and he left the field an angry man as the Australians formed a vibrant huddle.

Athey's replacement was the wicketkeeper Paul Downton, who almost immediately lofted Reid over mid-wicket for four. Then he tried to put Border over extra cover, but was caught by O'Donnell nearer to long-off. The variation in the crowd reaction to these two shots was clear. The boundary was greeted with polite applause, the dismissal with great cheers and outstretched hands punching the air. And with each dismissal the Australians ran to each other, fists clenched like Wimbledon champions after a crucial point in the fifth set.

Lamb was the key man for England. With the required run-rate edging to almost eight an over, everyone waited for the final assault. With eight overs to go, the target was 63 runs away. Lamb was 29, the new batsman John Emburey 1. The 43rd over, from Reid, cost five, including a wretched no-ball, but also a featured a brave save at the bowler's end by the lanky paceman after Boon had shied at the

BOB SIMPSON: THE COACH'S ROLE

Whether you love him or hate him, Bob Simpson is a man who provokes extremes of reaction in times of success as well as failure. But he has been at the centre of Australia's maturing into a global limited-overs power, and Australia's winning percentage in one-day matches since Simpson took over the reins as coach is excellent. Many will debate how much credit he deserves for the improvement but there can be little argument that Australia's one-day teams have developed a consistency that eluded their predecessors despite the talents of players like Dennis Lillee, Greg Chappell and Rod Marsh. The respect that Australia finally garnered in the one-day arena was sparked by the side's startling performance in the 1987 World Cup.

Simpson said he had worked to turn things around from the very moment he was put in charge of the team. The heart of the rebuilding plan was extensive research which he said only reinforced his firm ideas on how limited-overs cricket should best be played. It was also the start of Simpson's much-discussed partnership with Australian captain Allan Border.

'When I first came in Australia hadn't had a great record in one-day cricket,' said Simpson. 'We basically constructed what we thought was the best way for an Australian team to play. Obviously in those early days and since I've had a fairly big input into what Allan and I believe is the best way to tackle one-day cricket. Everything that happens within the team structure is discussed between ourselves and the senior players.

'It's my belief that one-day cricket is probably the simplest form of cricket there is and as such I think you've got to attack it in a simple way. If you score a run a ball you're going to win 99.9 per cent of cricket matches – certainly one-day cricket matches. If you go back through the records you'll find that invariably the team scoring the most singles wins.

'There was a fair amount of research and thought went into what we believe is the best way for us to play the game. A lot of theories abound that are different to the way we do it but we believe the way we do it is working very well.

'I looked at a lot of other results from other games. We looked at why Aus-

stumps from extra cover. Before the 44th Border faced a dilemma. He, the sixth bowler, had bowled six overs. With May's four overs, the fifth bowler's requirement had been completed, so Border could quite easily have handed the ball to his quicker men to finish the job. But his six overs had gone for just 30; his sixth had cost only four and brought the wicket of Downton. He decided to give himself at least one more.

Emburey pushed the first ball for one, to set up Border versus Lamb. This was great theatre. To the second ball, the batsman gave himself just a little room and slashed the ball with great force for four to extra cover. Veletta, patrolling the off boundary, didn't even move. To Border, the extra over was suddenly verging on

tralia was losing in the past. Really when you look at old-time one-day cricket, and by old-time I mean in the early days of it, I don't believe those teams could live with this (1994) Australian side. I think we'd just be too professional and planned for the way they were doing it back then.'

The seeds of the limited-overs renaissance were to quickly bloom in the harsh environment of the sub-continent where Australia's much-maligned one-day squad triggered a rebirth in our cricket which eventually extended to the Test arena.

'We started working on the 1987 World Cup from the time we first took over, because I'd only been appointed the year before,' said Simpson. 'We were lucky in as much as we had a brilliant build-up. We were down in Madras for two weeks where we practised and played in very trying conditions and I think in that two weeks we hardened up and had a chance to really get together and formulate what we wanted to do. In many cases it's probably easier when you're away from your own country. You travel with the team, that's all you think about. Probably on tour you get a better spirit going.

'After the first couple of games we had great expectations. We got up against India by one run in the first game which was a sensational match and we got up against New Zealand in the rain-affected match. In those two games the team showed a tremendous amount of spirit in really tough conditions. We fancied our chances for the semis then, and if you get into the semis anything can happen.

'That team spirit and confidence was all-important. We were the unfashionable side in the competition and as it went on people started to respect us more for our toughness and the simplicity with which we were playing the game and the professionalism we were showing. We were really pleased about the fact that we weren't fancied. We could go at our own pace without a huge amount of attention being given to us.'

When asked to describe his own emotions at the time, Simpson had replied: 'Great satisfaction – I'd come in at a time when Australian cricket hadn't been doing as well as it should have been doing. There were a few under-achievers around but we built a good solid core of 100 per cent triers. So I was absolutely thrilled to see these guys come through and win the competition.'

suicide. He looked down the wicket to see Lamb sizing up the boundaries. But the Australian captain refused to yield, and a sweep to backward square brought only a single. Emburey got the next to long-off for one, but then Lamb missed with a mighty heave to leg, then was satisfied with a single to long-on to keep the strike. Border took his hat from the umpire and got out of there. McDermott saw his captain's signal and began to limber up.

The target was 50 in six. Far from easy, but 15 less than the Australians had belted from their last 36 balls earlier in the day. Reid bowled the 45th over, his 10th, and conceded just five runs. Twice Lamb was kept scoreless, which must have satisfied Reid no end after his last-over problems under lights in Sydney 10 months before. Forty-five needed in five. Lamb took a single to McDermott's first ball, and then Emburey stepped away and sliced to deep cover point. Veletta, running to his left, had the dying sun making an easy catch murderous and he could do no more than stop the four. The batsmen ran two. The remainder of the over brought four singles, leaving the required run-rate, with four overs to go, at 9.5.

Border spoke with Reid's replacement, Waugh, and vice-captain Marsh, while Lamb and Emburey decided the time had come. Singles on their own were no use now, there had to be boundaries. Waugh, precise as ever, was on line straightaway and, after two runs had been added from the first two balls, Lamb aimed a huge pull-drive but lost his off-stump. The bowler punched the air, and Border did a little jig at mid-wicket while the crowd roared as loud as if Kapil Dev had struck this vital blow. Waugh conceded just two from the rest of his over. Emburey slogged but missed the first ball of the 48th, and then took on Boon at mid-wicket and lost off the second. Thirty-four were still needed from just 16 balls. The game, all agreed, was won. Or was it? In a frenetic two minutes de Freitas desperately and gallantly swung McDermott for 4, 6, 4, and finally one to keep the strike. With 12 balls to go, the target was 19. Reliance's World Cup just refused to die.

Waugh to De Freitas. The first ball was a slow leg cutter, which all but bowled the totally deceived but still swinging batsman. The second brought a confident, extended appeal for a catch behind, as Dyer dived forward to grab a ball that had been aimed about six inches down the leg-side and still induced an attempted heave over extra cover. For a while a cluster of Australians stood near mid-pitch, asking de Freitas why he wasn't out. To the third, de Freitas slogged again, but was fooled by the pace and length and could not clear Reid at long-off. This was quite superb sport by Waugh, who, at a time of potential crisis, produced an over of nerve, precision and skill. In all, just two runs came from the over, and though 11 came from the last, the Aussies were able to savour their triumph and the atmosphere it created during the final six balls, rather than dread the consequences of another last-over disaster.

After Foster had sliced the final ball for two meaningless runs, the Australians' reaction was spontaneous and joyous. It was a win they had coveted greatly. Jones ran from long-on to his captain, snatching two stumps from the ground along the way. Everyone in the team knew what this result meant to Border, and to each other. McDermott stood in mid-pitch, tired arms raised in triumph, while Boon, Marsh and Waugh, with an eye for history, grabbed for stumps as well.

Soon the players were engulfed near the pitch by a sea of team-mates, opponents, photographers, tournament organisers and well-wishers. It was a momentous occasion for a side that had been ridiculed by many less than 12 months before, and for a captain whose suitability and temperament for the job had been questioned by many, including some disenchanted members of the ACB. In the space of the World Cup month, Border had affirmed his place as the leader of Australian cricket, Simpson had demonstrated the value of his role, and the key members of the side – Border, Boon, Marsh, Jones, Waugh, O'Donnell, Reid and McDermott – had shown they had the character and ability to match it with the very best.

Although injury and illness would prevent a couple of these men from contribut-

Australian Picture Library – Chris Cole (All Sport)

The man of the match in the '87 World Cup final, Tasmania's David Boon, sweeps England's Eddie Hemmings during his innings of 75. The batting of openers Boon and Marsh during the tournament was one of the major factors in the team's success.

ALLAN BORDER: LEADING FROM THE FRONT

The grit and determination that fuelled Allan Border's defiant rearguard actions during the dark days of Australian cricket in the late '70s and early to mid-'80s also drove him to amass a hoard of Test cricketing records that is simply awesome. Most runs ever scored, most half-centuries, most scores over 50, most catches, most Tests, most consecutive Tests, most Tests as captain, most innings – it has justifiably made him a legend in his own lifetime. His performances in one-day cricket, while on the surface probably not as statistically outstanding as his Test achievements by virtue of the fundamental differences between the two games, are also out of the ordinary.

But it is his achievements as captain, his role in the much-belated maturing of Australia as a one-day cricket power and the subsequent rebirth of Australia as a leading Test nation, in which he takes greatest pride. Given a choice he would like that to be his legacy in the one-day arena. Apart from his tactical innovations Border finished his career with a winning record second to none – leading Australia to 107 wins in 178 outings.

'My role (in the resurgence) was finally realising that one-day cricket was very important not only to the Australian people and the Australian players but on a world stage,' said Border. 'It was here to stay, it was very important and we'd been letting ourselves down by not being competitive enough.'

Border said the genesis of the turnaround was newly appointed coach Bob Simpson's commitment to cricketing fundamentals and the platform Simpson's unswerving belief in the gospel of good fielding gave the side.

'I think one-day cricket for us really did turn things around in that 1986-87 period,' said Border. 'We'd been going through a particularly tough period and been inconsistent in one-day cricket. Bob was very insistent on getting the basics right in general. We worked very, very hard on the fielding and fielding as everyone knows is a vital part of the one-day game. We became excellent in the field. We developed our other tactics as we went along but particularly in the field I saw that we went from being very sloppy to very, very professional and quite ruthless and that's probably where we turned it around.'

That attitude and approach soon paid off. So successful did the Australians become at limited-overs cricket that they were soon considered among the best in the world. It is a ranking Border feels was justified and which was formally endorsed when the Australians, as 16-1 outsiders, won the 1987 World Cup. But

ing as much as they would have wanted in the seasons that followed, for the Australian cricket team as a unit this result was a desperately important one. Even Ian Chappell and his men had not been able to win the World Cup. Not only had Border's team won the respect of their rivals and their own supporters, they now knew *themselves* how good a side they could be. This newly won confidence owed a

it was not merely the simple win-loss record that Border believes earned Australia their No. 1 ranking. He believes the Australians fundamentally changed a number of areas of the one-day game. The fact that many teams then copied their successful program endorsed that view, imitation being the sincerest form of flattery.

'We went through a period where we were arguably the best nation,' he said. 'We revolutionised certain areas of the one-day game with our field placings and our tactics. The way we went about our batting in that we had the Geoff Marsh and David Boon era at the top of the order, and of course we had Jonesy with his running between wickets and the way he approached the game. The use of spinners and the different tactics. That, I suppose, was not all my doing, but I had a big part in formulating those tactics. So rather than just a player, I'd like to be remembered more as a tactician. I enjoy the tactics of one-day cricket. The hit and miss, the fact that everything's got to happen so quickly."

Despite an admitted preference for Test cricket Border said the difference between captaincy in the two different forms of the game was not so clear-cut. 'Both are very satisfying if you do things right and have a good tactical day,' he said. 'Test cricket is probably slightly harder because it's a more drawn-out process getting people out. It's obviously a lot harder to build up pressure because the game goes over five days. It's not as intense.'

Border has no doubt about the link between Australia's one-day triumphs and the eventual fightback in the Test arena. He said there could have been no recovery in Australia's Test fortunes if they had continued to struggle in one-day cricket.

'It went hand in hand,' he said. 'We started to convert some of the good things we were doing in one-day cricket to the Test match arena. It had a snowball effect and it was basically the one-day game that got us going. It gave us a bit of confidence, a bit of self-belief, and then we'd say "hang on, we can do well in one day so why can't we convert that into the five-day game?" and that's basically what happened.'

Border's respect for limited-overs cricket and its importance in the scheme of things came slowly. He broke into the Australian team during the transitional period and played for some time with a lot of senior players who have admitted to harbouring a less-than-professional attitude to the one-day game. It is hardly surprising that Border adopted that same attitude in his youth and took a long time to shake it.

'My attitude to one-day cricket has changed over the years,' he said. 'In the initial stages I don't think Austral-

Continued over page

lot to the integrity of the Reliance Cup and the fervour and passion of the Indian and Pakistani cricket communities. As the sun set on this famous day and the huge crowd stayed to clap and cheer, the Australians indulged in a victory lap ... and hoisted their captain high on their shoulders. From way up there, Border could look down and accept that the cricket world was, after all, a friendly place.

LEADING FROM THE FRONT

Continued from previous page

ian teams ever took it that seriously. It was a bit of a fun game, a bit of hit and giggle, but the real McCoy was Test cricket. Obviously over the years we've changed our attitude to it to the point where we regard it as very, very important – almost equal to the Test series. Worldwide it's taken on more importance; there's a far more serious attitude to one-day cricket. It took Australia probably a lot longer to come to grips with it than most of the other teams.'

Australia's disregard for the compressed format was reflected in a refusal to prepare diligently for games and in a lack of concern about the eventual outcome of each contest. 'Initially we struggled to have any particular game plans,' said Border. 'We just went out there and played. If we won, great; if we lost we weren't that upset about it.' Needless to say that mindset has long been buried.

'It's developed into a game where everyone has developed particular skills that are unique to the one-day game,' Border said. 'All the better players are able to adapt. Guys over the years have sorted out what's required for one-day cricket as against Test cricket and adjusted their games accordingly. Now we take it very seriously.'

That's not to say that one-day cricket has finally deposed Test cricket for the prime place in our cricketers' hearts. 'I think most of the guys really enjoy one-day cricket but we don't place the same emphasis on one-day cricket as we do on Test cricket,' said Border. 'It's still second to Test match cricket. Whether that attitude changes over the next 10 years remains to be seen.'

When you've played more than 260 one-day games, four World Cups, hoisted aloft many trophies and accepted hundreds of thousands of dollars of prizemoney, it can be a little difficult to nominate a highlight. Border, like many of his peers, has admitted that the passing parade of limited-overs matches quickly becomes a blur. Still, he had no trouble pin-pointing his proudest moment. 'The World Cup campaign in 1987,' he said. 'Everything just turned to gold from the first game against India. They were the red-hot favourites and we were the underdogs. We made a good score and won the game by one run. It snowballed from that point. We just got better and better and ended up winning the thing. It was a huge game.'

Border said a key point in that game surrounded a six hit by Dean Jones which was incorrectly signalled four by the Indian fielder, Ravi Shastri. The umpire took Shastri's word for it and four runs instead of six were added to the Australian score. Fortunately team manager, and now chairman of the Australian Cricket Board, Alan Crompton saw the incident on television and appealed for it to be changed from four to six during the break between innings. Umpire Dickie Bird reversed his decision, Australia got an extra two runs, and eventually triumphed by one. 'It was quite a vital decision so Crommo got a few pats on the back that night,' said Border. 'I do remember that game and the impromptu party afterwards as a big turning point for that campaign and the team. We became a very good one-day team from that point on.'

The difference in emotions surrounding the 1987 campaign and the 1992 defence could not be sharper. The prevailing mood post-1987 was euphoria at a most unexpected triumph while the dominant emotions after the bungled 1992 defence were of angst, disbelief and regret. As much as 1987 thrilled him the failure in 1992 disappointed Border. He, the team, and Simpson came under heavy criticism for their shocking loss of form but Border does not blame the press nor the public for the backlash.

'I suppose it was justified in that we played very, very ordinary,' he said. 'There are many reasons but no excuses. We'd just come out of a particularly grinding season where we'd played reasonably well and we didn't really target the World Cup like we should have. We probably should have gone into a camp and played a few lead-up games against good opposition. We came out of our season, had a bit of a break and just got together and went over to New Zealand for that first World Cup game. We hit a submerged log over there, found it hard to pull things back and it wasn't until the end of that World Cup that we started to play well.

'In 1987 we got over to India early. We really worked hard on our particular one-day game and things that we wanted to do. Our preparation was excellent. We were together for a while and we really went in with a specific purpose, whereas in 1992 we were favourites but we didn't do that preparation. We just expected to go out there and play well and when we started to play ordinary we found it hard to pull back. We were chopping and changing the team and did all the things

you do when people push the panic button. It was just a frustrating time because we knew we were arguably the best team but we just couldn't put it together.'

As far as individual performances go Border said it was not as easy to isolate a particular innings. In his case in particular the trail stretches back a way and the sameness of the terrain can play tricks on the memory.

'I think when you start talking about Test cricket the statistics are there and I guess over five days you've got a greater chance of remembering how the game panned out and your individual performance. Whereas you play so much one-day cricket day after day after day. You're travelling interstate and sometimes you wake up and you don't know where you are. It is hard to remember specifics. I think all of us remember if we had a particularly outstanding day but if you made 20 or 30, bowled a few overs and took a wicket or a catch and it's been 220 plays 180, a convincing win or loss, it's just another day at the office.

'There are times when someone plays an extraordinary innings like a couple of Dean Jones' or Steve Waugh's or Viv Richards' or Robin Smith's or David Gower's. All these blokes played particular innings that just stick in your mind so you remember them but the majority of the time it all gelled into one. It's hard to remember if that happened in 1980 or 1990.

'I've made three one-day hundreds and probably the best was my 127 in the first World Series final against the West Indies in Sydney in 1985. We ended up winning that game but los-
Continued over page

LEADING FROM THE FRONT

Continued from previous page

ing the next two. I batted as well as I've ever batted in one-day cricket against a pretty formidable attack so that sticks in my mind as something special.'

Border's defining characteristic as a batsman has been pragmatism. He honed his game down to the basics and made the best bowlers in international cricket play day after day for 16 seasons in the international arena. His cut shot, pull shot and cover drive may not have had the elegance of a Greg Chappell or a Gower, and no-one is ever going to be moved to poetry by a nudged single, but the simple effectiveness of Border's shot-making repertoire had a beauty all its own and the sheer mountain of runs bears eloquent tribute to their quality. Border's pragmatism again revealed itself in limited-overs cricket, albeit in a different form.

'My own game has chopped and changed over the years,' he said. 'When I was playing at my best I just played my normal game. You were good enough to adjust without doing too much to your technique. Over the years you might bat in different positions, the higher in the order the more normally you can play. As you get down the order you find you've either got to swing the bat or be looking to knock the ball down and hustle between the wickets. Batting in one-day cricket is a lot more difficult than it looks. Test match cricket you can go out with a certain frame of mind and you can be defence-oriented and build an innings

based around a good, basic technique. You can't do that in one-day cricket. You've got to be able to either get off strike with ones or be able to play a couple of big shots where you can take to the bowling.

'It's a tough game in that you can see over-rates and runs required per over creeping up. It's a high pressure game and it does affect the way you approach your batting.'

Many of one-day cricket's critics have vilified it for an alleged perversion of pure techniques in Test cricket. The link has never been conclusively proven, life being far more complicated than that, but traditionalists continue to insist that one-day cricket ruins techniques for the 'proper' game. Border, while admitting that there is some truth in the allegation, said there are two sides to the coin.

'It's an amazing thing that you can be performing badly in one and not the other. It can get blokes in and out of form. You might be struggling in the Test arena and go out and play a hit-and-giggle-type of innings in a one-day game where you're just swinging the bat and it gets you back into some sort of form for the Test match. It happens more and more and the reverse can happen that you start playing a few one-day shots and it creeps into your technique as far as Test match cricket is concerned. You get a few flaws showing up.'

Border's other great trademark, particularly in one-day cricket, has been his unparalleled ability to hit the stumps. Many a batsman has chanced Border's arm and come away a sadder but wiser man. It is no exaggeration to say that Border is deadly from within the circle. It is a skill that has given him much pleasure over the years.

'I think it came from my baseball background,' he said. 'I know how to throw a ball, I know how to throw the ball accurately and I know how to get rid of the ball quickly from my baseball upbringing. So that was a combination of things that I've been able to put into practice in one-day cricket. You see a lot of blokes who are a hell of a lot quicker to the ball than me but they either take too long to get rid of it, or when they do throw, they're not accurate. That's an area that I've really enjoyed, that I can use baseball skills in a cricketing sense.

'You'll find more and more guys will be working on this area. One of the best examples is South Africa's Jonty Rhodes. He spends a lot of time practising getting to the ball, picking the ball up and getting rid of it quickly and accurately. He's one of the best and most refreshing blokes I've found for fielding. Especially for one-day cricket; if he gets a couple of run-outs and saves 20 runs he doesn't really have to bat.

'I think the fielding really has become a lot better. You get guys fielding in the circles that are like jack rabbits. They get to the ball quickly and there are always run-out chances on. It's creating a lot more pressure on batting sides. That's why you'll find the scoring is a lot less than it was in certain eras.'

The growth of one-day cricket in particular, and cricket generally, has seen an international cricketer's workload expand exponentially in the last decade. Sir Donald Bradman played just 52 Test matches and a total of 234 first-class games in a career which started in December 1927 and did not end until March 1949. When the years of World War II are taken out Bradman's career spans roughly the same number of seasons as Border's – who played 156 Test matches, 363 first-class fixtures, 273 limited-overs internationals and 38 domestic one-dayers.

Border believes today's workload, which sees international cricketers now on the verge of true full-time professionalism, is making unprecedented demands on players' fitness levels. Cricket has never demanded rigorous athleticism but Border says that day is fast approaching. 'Everyone is starting to realise that their fitness levels have got to be better and they've got to do a greater amount of work in that area,' he said. 'We flirted with fitness levels but we've never been totally fair dinkum about it and I suppose the time's come – particularly when you look at the future program. It's going to be a nine-month season for an Australian cricketer and if he wants to play Test cricket and one-day cricket and go on all the tours and be competitive he's going to have to have a greater fitness level. That's an area we've toyed with over the last four or five years but never really got fair dinkum about.'

Speculation surrounded Border's retirement plans for the four or five years before he finally called it a day in May, 1994. His longevity is all the more amazing because of the unprecedented burden one-day cricket placed on him, but he said shortly before he made his announcement that it was never a factor in deciding whether or not to keep on playing. 'At my age you don't want to be like the fighter who fights one or two fights too many,' Border said. 'You want to get out at the right time and for the right reasons.'

17

STRETCHING WITH MERV

Three months after the World Cup, Border won his first Test series as captain, a three-match home contest against New Zealand that went down to the final over of the final day as Australia's No. 11, the left-arm fast-medium bowler Mike Whitney, saw out Richard Hadlee at the MCG to preserve his captain's 1-0 series lead. Much was made of Whitney's batting effort, and that of his last wicket partner McDermott, as few had expected them to survive against the might of Hadlee during the tense final overs.

Just four days later, Whitney again found himself in a last-over drama. The third Test had reached its exciting conclusion on December 30. On January 2, in Perth, the first of the World Series Cup matches resulted in an 81-run win for the Australians over Sri Lanka. The following night in Game 2 with three balls to play Australia were nine wickets down and needed two more runs to defeat New Zealand. The man at the striker's end was Michael Whitney.

New Zealand had made 9-232 from their 50 overs, and the Australian reply was built around Dean Jones' 92 from 91 balls. But when he was run out off the second ball of the 49th over, the home side required 12. Whitney and the more qualified Tony Dodemaide secured 10 of them. But off the fourth ball of Martin Snedden's final over (the 50th), Whitney lost his nerve and swung hopefully but tamely to wide mid-off where John Bracewell held the catch.

This ending, coming so soon after the dramatic finish in Melbourne, highlighted one of the major differences between the Test match and the limited-overs international. At the MCG, Mike Whitney had only to defend to attain an honourable draw. His was not to win, only to prevent his opponent from winning, which he was able to do with a straight bat and a steely nerve. But Whitney was never a good batsman, and in Perth he needed more than just defensive skills. With three balls to go and two runs to win ... or lose ... there was nowhere to hide. This is not to denigrate Whitney's achievement in Melbourne. There can be great glory in a Test match draw, especially if both teams have spent the entire match striving for a win as was the case at the MCG in that third Test. This has been shown time and again through the game's history. Limited-overs cricket is a different game, one in which the players and fans know that one team is going to succeed and one is going to fail.

An example of the 'Mexican Wave', which first appeared in Australian cricket grounds in 1986-87 after gaining exposure in American college football and then in the 1986 World Soccer Cup finals in Mexico. This was a way for the fans to be involved in the game (or, perhaps, to indicate, without realising, that the cricket was occasionally less than exciting), but the habit of throwing cans, plastic cups and paper in the air became a nuisance and more than one game had to be delayed while the playing area was cleared. Many believed the fans would quickly become 'waved out', but eight seasons on, the wave is still a part of the game, and the fans in the outer are still booing when the conservatives in the Members Stands refuse to get involved.

Because of this, it can emphasise contrasting skills and play havoc with elements of a cricketer's psyche that are rarely under stress during a five-day Test match.

Tony Dodemaide's rise to the Australian team in 1987-88 was one of the stories of the season. Before the third New Zealand Test he had been seen as no more than an above-average member of the Victorian Sheffield Shield side. However, injuries to Bruce Reid and the Victorian fast bowler Merv Hughes had given Dodemaide a chance in the Melbourne Test, an opportunity he grabbed with glee. After scoring 50 from No. 9 in Australia's first innings, he took six New Zealand second-innings wickets for 58, to become the second Australian (after A.E. Trott in 1894-95) to score 50 and take five wickets in an innings on Test debut. He followed that by taking 5-21 from 7.2 overs on his limited-overs international debut in the opening

MARK WAUGH: A BRUTAL BLEND OF ELEGANCE

There are very few cricketers of international standard who will admit to preferring one-day cricket to Test cricket. The baggy green Test cap is still the dream of virtually every Sheffield Shield player in the country and if they are lucky enough to break into the Australian limited-overs squad along the way they are grateful – but their eyes are still on what they see as the first prize.

Elegant strokemaker Mark Waugh is an exception. Waugh was made to wait what seemed an eternity before he was finally given his chance in the Test team, but he was thrilled to be named in the Australian one-day side. He made his debut against Pakistan in Adelaide during the 1988-89 season – two years before he finally won his first Test cap against England. 'I just wanted to play for Australia,' said Waugh. 'I didn't care what team. It's still international cricket. I think it's just as respectable to play one-day cricket as Test cricket. I wasn't even thinking about that. I was just happy to be there in the canary yellow. It's better than watching.'

There was no doubt Waugh considered it a positive sign as far as his Test hopes went but it is just as true that he recognised and valued the limited-overs cap in its own right. Having grown up when one-day cricket was part of the international scene he was much more willing to accept it on its own terms.

'At the time I was doing quite well for NSW and I was glad to at least get a foot in the door,' said Waugh. 'Your name's in the Australian side and that's a good feeling.' It is also true that Waugh is temperamentally suited to the pace and improvisation of the abbreviated game. He may possess an elegance and grace that evoke memories of the game's classic era but he is also blessed with the courage and flair to pull out a shot that breaks all the rules. More often than not it has the desired effect and still sends critics into raptures. The unquenchable thirst for sport and competition that nurtured Mark's and brother Steve's talents in their youth is still very much in evidence. There is no doubt that he has a lot of fun playing a game that too many players often view as a chore.

'I enjoy limited-overs cricket,' said Waugh. 'I think it's part of being a professional cricketer to play both forms. I enjoy the atmosphere and tempo of the game. I enjoy it just as much as Test cricket; there's the crowds and it's always exciting.'

Waugh agrees with the majority of players about the unique demands that Test cricket places on a player's charac-

World Series Cup match. A steady all-rounder who bowled outswingers and seamers at slightly more than medium pace, Dodemaide kept his place for the remainder of the summer, and for the tour of Pakistan that preceded the 1988-89 season. But from the moment he was left out of the Australian Test side for the third Test of the home series against the West Indies in '88-89, Dodemaide became nothing more than an occasional feature of the Australian one-day side.

ter and mental toughness, but he also believes that limited-overs cricket presents challenges of its own. 'Mentally Test cricket is a lot tougher because you're out there for five days and there are so many ups and downs to cope with,' said Waugh. 'But one-day cricket is tough to play because you've just got to be quicker in everything you do. I'm naturally a fairly positive player so it suits my batting. I don't have to change my batting too much to switch to one-day cricket. It hasn't improved my game but it's definitely sharpened it up. You definitely take a few more risks. You're looking for a run a ball whereas in Test cricket you're looking to survive and just let the runs come.'

There is still a tendency to judge a batsman by first-class cricket's traditional benchmark – his average runs per completed innings – but Waugh thinks that is an outdated yardstick given the different demands of the two games. He regards the strike rate as more important. Waugh's aggressiveness and ability to improvise, and the breathtaking array of strokes he has at his disposal, are potent weapons in the one-day arena. But Australia's recent success has been built upon a more workman-like approach. Waugh said he sometimes finds playing within coach Bob Simpson's very structured team-oriented approach difficult, particularly in the middle of the order.

Waugh was given the opportunity to open the innings during the one-day series on the tour of New Zealand at the end of the 1992-93 domestic season. He jumped at the opportunity and made every post a winner. He said New Zealand in particular had shown the positive virtues of improvisation and flexibility. 'There is room in the game for individual flair and a bit of something different,' he said.

Waugh's bowling is one area that thrives on the peculiar demands of one-day cricket. He is a gambler when he has a ball in his hand, prone to bowling six different deliveries in an over. Skipper Allan Border used him when regular members of the attack failed to make inroads and, more often than not, Waugh responds with one or more wickets. 'Quite often when I get a chance to bowl it's usually to break a partnership so I'll be looking to take a wicket. I'll change my pace a bit more than in Test cricket, mix it up and keep them guessing.' His best-ever performance with the ball was during a World Series match against the West Indies at the MCG on December 15, 1992, when he grabbed 5-24 off six overs in a spell that truly snatched victory from the jaws of defeat. Towards the end of the spell the crowd of 74,450 was chanting 'Mark Waugh, Mark Waugh', just as the fans had serenaded paceman Dennis Lillee when he was in his prime.

Five of Sri Lanka's eight matches during the World Series Cup in 1987-88 attracted less than 10,000 people; their largest attendance was the 28,818 who saw Australia win by 38 runs in Melbourne on January 14. But crowds of 61,316 and 48,802 (Melbourne) and 41,813 and 29,356 (Sydney) arrived to see Australia-New Zealand fixtures. Crowd figures for Australia's matches in the other centres were also exceptional, despite the fact the Cup in '87-88 was the least exciting to date, as

Australia were simply too powerful for their two opponents. The defeat in Perth was the home team's only loss of the summer, and their superiority was clearly shown in the Cup finals, which were won 2-0, by eight and six wickets respectively.

Highlights of the Cup included the first match played in Tasmania, between New Zealand and Sri Lanka at Bellerive Oval in Hobart (Sri Lanka won by four wickets), a colossal six struck by McDermott in Adelaide which cleared the Cathedral end mound, Allan Border's 100th appearance in a World Series Cup match (out of a possible 101), and a bizarre sequence of events at the 'Gabba, when curator Kevin Mitchell, armed with local knowledge and information from the weather bureau, ran onto the field while the 41st over was being bowled and, with the help of his groundstaff and to the astonishment of players and umpires, removed the stumps and covered the square. Within seconds a torrential rainstorm blew over the ground, but Mitchell's covers held firm and only 37 minutes were lost.

After the World Series Cup, Australia played a Test match and a limited-overs international against England to celebrate Australia's bi-centenary. The Test, played at the SCG in front of a five-day attendance of 103,831, was a great occasion, but the cricket lacked imaginative captaincy and degenerated into a boring draw. Two days after Australia had batted more than eight hours for 2-328 to ensure the Test-match stalemate, over 54,000 journeyed to the MCG to see Australia defeat England by 22 runs in the one-day international. This, too, was not a dramatic contest, and it appeared the visitors were far from their peak after an arduous and controversial tour of Pakistan.

This win meant the Australians had won their past nine limited-overs internationals, and 17 of the 19 they had played since the beginning of the '87 World Cup. Following the bi-centenary celebrations, the Australians had their longest break between limited-overs internationals (eight months and 10 days) since the ACB and World Series Cricket had come together in 1979. The Australians' 'return' to one-day cricket came in October 1988, in Lahore. They lost a thrilling struggle to Pakistan, because the Pakistanis had lost one less wicket (seven to eight) in reaching 229.

Pakistan in September/October 1988 was a nation in turmoil. The country's president, General Zia ul-Haq, had died in a plane crash in August, and fears of sustained civil unrest were evident. Ethnic violence had poisoned the atmosphere in Karachi and Hyderabad and resulted in the cancellation of one-day internationals in the two cities. A third limited-overs match was abandoned after floods ruined the playing fields at Gujranwala. In addition, local cricket fans had been shattered by the decision of Imran Khan to miss the Tests and one-dayers as a protest over the decision to schedule the tour for a time of year he believed unsuitable. They were then further dismayed by the Australians' fervent criticisms of the umpiring during the Test series.

The limited-overs international in Lahore was the first for young Queensland wicketkeeper Ian Healy who had been selected for the tour after just six first-class appearances. His contribution in the one-dayer in Lahore was minimal, but it was his good fortune to commence what would prove to be a lengthy limited-overs career in such a thrilling encounter. Also in the Australian team was the Victorian

The Australians celebrate a wicket to Simon Davis during the 1987-88 World Series Cup. Left to right: Mike Veletta, Greg Dyer, Davis, Allan Border and Geoff Marsh.

batsman Jamie Siddons, who scored 32 from 37 balls. The game was played on a 45-overs-per-side basis on the pitch that had been used for the drawn third Test, which had finished three days before. It came down to a final over with Pakistan needing just two runs to win with four wickets in hand. A single off Dodemaide's first ball levelled the scores, but Wasim Akram was unable to find the winning run from any of the following three deliveries and was then caught by Border at silly mid-off off with one ball left. Abdul Qadir was well aware he needed to do no more than survive for Pakistan to 'win'. Qadir and all in the 20,000 crowd held their breath when the Australians went up for an unsuccessful lbw appeal on that final ball, but Qadir's survival meant Pakistan had lost one wicket less than Australia and could therefore claim victory.

Back home for the '88-89 summer, the Australians faced a revised season plan, with the World Series Cup matches intertwined with the Tests, as had been the case in the years between 1979-80 and 1981-82. However, in 1988-89 the Test match season involved five Tests with the West Indies, rather than twin three-Test series with the two overseas sides in the country that summer. Pakistan, captained once more by Imran, came only for the limited-overs internationals, but were again a disappointment and won just two matches, one each against Australia and the West Indies.

Steve Waugh's twin brother Mark made his debut for Australia in this series – the first time twins had played in the same international match. Also back in the side was Dean Jones, who had missed the one-dayer in Pakistan after suffering a wretched run of form in the three Tests. Before the season was through Simon O'Donnell would also make his return to the side. After the World Cup triumph,

O'Donnell had been diagnosed as suffering from lymphoma and was obliged to suffer the agony of chemotherapy treatment to rid his body of the disease. His courage and dignity through the ordeal were inspiring, and the emotion in a record crowd when he strode onto the WACA Ground in Perth on January 2 underlined the sporting community's appreciation of his bravery. He was cheered all the way to the middle when his turn came to bat, and all the way back after top-scoring with 46.

Three days later, O'Donnell's home fans had the chance to welcome back their hero. Over 66,000 people packed the ground to see an exciting match which ended with the Australians' first victory over the West Indies in Melbourne in a limited-overs international. The final margin was eight runs, after Australia were all out for 226 in the daylight, and the West Indies fell behind under lights. The action after dinner featured some ordinary fielding by the Australians, who dropped Viv Richards four times, but also a truly remarkable catch by Steve Waugh. With three overs remaining, the West Indies, with six wickets gone and Richards still at the crease, needed 27. Roger Harper swung at McDermott, and sent the ball flying high back over the bowler's head. Waugh turned and sprinted, straight for the sightscreen, and held the catch at full pace, despite the possibility of a sickening collision. Many in the huge crowd were not sure that the dismissal had been completed until Waugh emerged unscathed from behind the black screen holding what was surely one of the greatest outfield catches ever taken in international cricket.

This was the second of three stirring Australia-West Indies matches during a season of record crowds and high excitement. On December 13, Australia had just failed to beat the West Indies in Sydney in a match the home team would probably have won had Steve Waugh not been run out while batting with his brother for the first time in international cricket (the same thing would happen again the next time the two were together in the middle). McDermott needed a single to tie and two to win off the final ball of the match, but swung a full toss to a relieved Richards on the edge of the circle at mid-wicket to send a full house home disappointed.

If this was a thrilling match, the first clash of the finals was a one-day classic, which had as its leading man the charismatic Merv Hughes. Prior to 1988-89, Hughes had been seen as below international class by fans and critics alike. With a physique that wouldn't have been out of place in a public bar and an outrageous handle-bar moustache, Hughes had caught the eye of those seeking something out of the ordinary, but his performances, though valiant, had lacked results. However, in the second Test of the West Indies series in Perth, he produced an epic effort of guts and persistence. After fellow paceman Geoff Lawson had been flattened by the latest fast bowling star from the Caribbean, Curtly Ambrose, Hughes returned fire – and finished with eight second-innings wickets to give him 13 for the match, including a hat-trick. Suddenly great courage and skill had been added to his vibrant character, and Australian cricket had a new folk hero.

Australia batted first in the opening finals match, and reached 9-204. The innings featured a fine 78 by Border, and an outstanding exhibition from Ambrose, who took 5-26 and conceded just one run from his and the innings' final over. The West Indies started their reply disastrously. Hughes, with 73,575 Victorians roaring their support, had Greenidge caught behind in spectacular fashion by Healy and then had

Haynes, plumb lbw to reduce them to 2-16. With the total at 23, Gus Logie was lbw to Alderman, and then Richards tried to drive the same bowler past square leg but the swinging ball took the leading edge to be caught by Border running from slip to the edge of the circle on the angle of gully. Richie Richardson and Carl Hooper mounted something of a recovery, but when Richardson fell to O'Donnell and Hooper to Peter Taylor, the match appeared to have slipped beyond the West Indians.

Hooper fell, caught pulling a rank long hop to Dean Jones at deep square leg, in the 29th over with the score on 108. Dujon and Marshall were left with the salvage job, and took the score to 129 before the game took a controversial turn. Dujon pushed Taylor to Border's right hand at mid-wicket and called a single. Marshall took off, but Border was too quick and his return to the keeper's end had the great fast bowler short of his ground. Healy smashed the stumps, the bails went flying, and umpire Steve Randell's arm shot into the air. And Marshall refused to go.

The TV replay showed Border's alertness, his crisp pick-up and perfect throw, bail-high to the side of the stumps. But then came the cause of Marshall's displeasure. Healy had dropped the ball. A second replay showed that the ball may have dropped onto the stumps. But whether it had struck the stumps before Healy's gloves was unclear. From the replay, Marshall should clearly have been given the benefit of the doubt. Randell may have had a clearer view. Whatever, Marshall had to leave, and slowly, and then finally, he trudged towards the dressing room.

Border's fielding at mid-wicket had become a feature of Australia's one-day performances, and would continue to attract great admiration and respect in the seasons ahead. Quick singles to this region were taken at great risk, as the Australian captain's aim was sure and true. No fieldsman, in any form of cricket, had ever hit the stumps as often as Border from mid-wicket. When he picked up and shied at the stumps, it appeared that the stumps were as wide as the winter's goalposts. Marshall, however unluckily, was just another victim.

At 148, Dujon swung at Taylor but was conned by the change of pace and lobbed a catch to Jones who speared the ball into the crowd like a wide receiver at the Superbowl. Taylor was in the latter stages of a superb spell. The crowd, always animated, was now in a state of wild excitement and roared for every ball that edged Australia closer to their victory. Rarely, if ever has a cricket crowd ever been so much part of the occasion. Earlier, the patrons in the outer had created a marvellous, spontaneous scene. As Hughes went through an elaborate series of exercises before his turn at the bowling crease, his followers behind the fence mimicked his every stretch. Nine's camera caught perfectly the sight of Hughes and his aerobic class in the middle of their session – in all likelihood there were toes being touched and hamstrings loosened in lounge rooms right across the country. The fans could not have been closer to their hero if he had been ruckman near the boundary line. This really was the people's game.

However, the people's game still had another dramatic turn. Ambrose and his fast bowling colleague Ian Bishop were not outdone, and they smashed and snicked the score to 190 with two overs to go, as the crowd's mood slowly ebbed from glee to fitful prayer. But then O'Donnell produced the perfect yorker to upset Ambrose,

GEOFF MARSH: GIVING IT EVERYTHING

Geoff Marsh may have been more modestly credentialled than many of his illustrious colleagues in the powerful Australian batting line-up of the late '80s and early '90s. But in a team that blossomed into the leading power in international limited-overs cricket he was an indispensable cog. Although considered by many to be a slow batsman with a limited shot repertoire, Marsh plugged away until he scored more one-day hundreds than any other Australian batsman. It is a distinction he still holds.

Marsh, ever the team man, said the role he was allotted and the support he received from his team-mates were the reasons behind his success. 'I was lucky in a sense that my role in the Australian side was to play a certain way,' said Marsh. 'There was no way I was a Dean Jones or a David Boon or a Viv Richards. I had my own role to play and I had to play it. By doing that I took a lot of criticism but I knew that I had to do that job, and if I was to survive in the Australian side I had to accept the criticism. It was very hard getting out and people abusing you for being too slow. But in the end the players in the team knew that I'd done the job they wanted. That's all that counted. I couldn't care less what the media, what Tony Greig and Co were saying. I had a job to do for AB and the boys. I tried to do the best I could and you just had to look at the record. In that time we had a pretty successful period.'

Given the fact that he was so successful at converting long stays at the crease into centuries it was natural to ask whether Marsh began every innings focused on making a hundred. His reply reflected his outlook: 'Every time I walked out the gate I was just praying that I'd get off the mark and get moving before the crowd would start abusing me.' Marsh was quick to add that he also received a lot of support. 'Most of the crowds around Australia probably understood. People in Sydney and Melbourne love their cricket, they understand the game. Especially in Melbourne they knew what I was there for. I always got great support from the Melbourne crowd.' Whatever the reception from the crowd Marsh knew it was important to stick to his guns and the gritty right-hander had only to look at the team's results for vindication.

'People go to one-day cricket to see sixes and fours, but at the end of the game if they don't get that and Australia wins they don't care,' Marsh went on. 'I knew that if I could just set it up they were going to see some outstanding batting anyway. Most of the time Boonie was always going or Deano was going and I just quietly went along and no-one ever really noticed what was happening at the other end. People were always going away happy and that was what counted. There was a packed house everywhere we went.'

Inside every 'anchor' is a 'glory boy' striving to get out and Marsh was no exception. He doesn't deny that as he tucked and glided and nudged and bunted in support of his glamorous batting partners he longed to wrench the spotlight in his direction. 'I always dreamed of going out there and belting it all around the ballpark but unfortunately I knew if I did that and got out I would have let the side down, so I had to do what I had to do. I had to build an innings.'

Marsh did not have an easy answer when asked why he was so successful in tallying limited-overs centuries. 'I don't know,' he said. 'I would have thought that David Boon, being an opener and being the player he was, would have scored a lot more at the time but he had a different role to play. He was the striker who had to get the score ticking over. It was my job to rotate the strike. The same when I had to get Dean Jones on strike and Steve Waugh. It was my job to just hold an end and rotate the strike.'

Marsh did suggest, though, that the criticism of his strike rate acted as a powerful incentive to succeed in the one-day arena. 'When I first started playing Test cricket everyone said I'd be a good Test player and I wouldn't make it in one-day cricket,' he said. 'I guess if they'd have told me I'd be a good one-day cricketer and a poor Test cricketer I'd have probably had a better Test record than a one-day record. There was (that incentive) but I tried very hard in Test cricket. It's just a fine line. I would have loved, obviously, to have finished with an average of 40 and done a lot better (in Test cricket) but I enjoyed every minute, every second I played for Australia. Whether I averaged 30 or 40 or 60 I gave it everything I had. I would like to have had nine Test hundreds and four one-day hundreds but that's obviously not the way it goes.'

Marsh said his success and that of the team during its golden run was a function of the selfless attitude of the individual players and the way they combined as a unit. 'We had people like Steve Waugh and Allan Border and Mark Waugh who just accepted the fact that their job was to average 30 in one-day cricket,' he said. 'We enjoyed each others' success and we didn't worry whether one got a hundred and one got six off six. We all did it as a team. We had a very good side. A team that got on well together. We knew exactly what we had to do and we did it. You can't beat togetherness.'

The vast majority of middle-order batsmen consider their top-order brethren privileged when it comes to one-day cricket. They envy the time and freedom that openers and No. 3 batsmen have to construct and shape an innings. More than a few are jealous. While he does not deny the advantages of facing up first, Marsh does not have much time for the middle-order grumblers.

'There's no doubt that opening the batting in one-day cricket is a good position,' he said. 'But those sort of players always come out and say yes they'll open in one-day cricket, but you go and ask them to open the batting at half past five on the first day of a Test match and you can't find them, they're running out the back, going back to the hotel. I think that opening the batting is a very, very tough game. I'm not just saying that because I'm an opening batsman. In one-day cricket I accept that it's the best place to bat but there's a lot of people that have tried opening the batting that haven't been good opening batsmen and the team has failed.'

Marsh had little trouble nominating his best innings in one-day cricket. 'I think that hundred I got in Madras
Continued over page

GIVING IT EVERYTHING

Continued from previous page

against India in the World Cup, the first game that we won by one run. Because of the fact that we won and it got us off to a good start. From then on we never looked back. We had the best party that night as a team. From then on we really clicked. There was a good spirit. We just worked hard and we won the World Cup. Also the hundred against New Zealand in the '87 World Cup, I played well then, and in the World Cup final. I think I only made 20-odd but Boonie and I put on a good start. Not all your best innings are your highest scores.'

For much of his one-day career Marsh opened the innings with David Boon. He did not deny that Boon had a vital role to play in his personal success. The nature of their partnership is best illustrated by the way it was born. 'Boonie and I got on really well off the field, and on the field it just clicked,' said Marsh. 'We sat in the bar one night after my first couple of Test matches. At the time Australia had struggled for openers and we just said, "let's open and let's really make a go of it". I think the thing that we did well was run between wickets.' Most players believe that combining Test and one-day cricket has very little effect on their technique but Marsh said there was one area where he had problems.

'If I've got any gripe about playing one-day cricket and Test cricket it's in one-day cricket I ran the ball a lot,' he said. 'When it came to Test cricket you run the ball and you've got five or six slippers there waiting for it and I think at times that got me into bad habits. But that's the way it goes. It never really caused Desmond Haynes or Gordon Greenidge or anyone like that any problems, so no excuses. I know in Test cricket I let myself down at times. I played some lazy shots. I should have made a lot more runs than I did but everyone makes those mistakes.'

He had no hesitation when it came to naming the best one-day bowler he had faced. 'Curtly Ambrose. He's the best bowler I've ever faced. Him and Malcolm Marshall. Richard Hadlee was a good bowler but Ambrose late in the innings was awesome.'

and set up Hughes for the final over, off which nine were required. Hughes stuck solidly to a policy of yorkers at middle stump, and the batsmen could hit no more than ones and twos. Four were needed from the final ball – shades of Daniel, Lamb and McKechnie – but, though Walsh's cover drive was well struck, it was straight at Border, and the Australians were home by two runs.

The West Indies recovered to win the Cup, though their title-sealing second victory was achieved after the weather had reduced the match to farce. Boon and Marsh opened with gusto and Australia were 2-83 in the 24th over when Sydney's rain forced the players from the field. When they returned, to bat for 14.5 overs more, Jones was absolutely brilliant. He raced to 93 not out, to leave the West

Indians needing 227 to win at almost six per over. Another storm was imminent, and Richards and Haynes took risks to charge to 47 in the seventh over after Greenidge and Richardson had been dismissed in the opening over. Then the weather forced the combatants from the field. Not long after 9pm, the rain stopped and the umpires' calculators showed that the requirement of 180 off 31.2 overs had been reduced, under the conditions of the tournament, to a meagre 61 from 11.2. The advantages of the rules to the side batting second had never been more clearly shown. Richards and Haynes achieved the victory in just 40 more balls.

While most newspaper columns lambasted the lopsided rulebook, most conceded that the Windies had showed once again they were a superior side – this was their fifth World Series Cup win from six starts – although it had also been proved that the marked contrast in ability that had once existed between them and the Australians had been substantially reduced. Although the West Indies missed the fast bowling of Holding and Garner in '88-89, in Ambrose they had a substitute of comparable class, while what the batting lacked through the absence of the great Lloyd was largely compensated by the skill and belligerence of Richardson. What is unarguable is that whenever the West Indies were at full strength during the 1980s they were the best one-day side in the world. And an extremely strong argument can be put that their best XI – probably the '84-85 combination – was the best team ever to play limited-overs international cricket.

At the end of that season the Australian selectors named their side for the Ashes tour of England. As well as omitting the season's leading first-class wicket-taker Michael Whitney, they also left out two of the regular members of the Australian one-day side in '88-89 – O'Donnell and Taylor. While Whitney's misfortune was greeted with howls of derision, few cries were heard for the latter pair, which reflected the lack of importance placed on the limited-overs internationals scheduled for the tour. Also missing from the squad was Craig McDermott, whose decline during the season had been so pronounced that, after playing for Australia in two Tests and six World Series Cup matches, he had been dropped from the Queensland Sheffield Shield team for their final match of the season. Beating McDermott and Whitney for places were Terry Alderman and Carl Rackemann, available again after completing the suspensions that resulted from their travels to South Africa with Kim Hughes' rebel team. Also in the squad was a third rebel, the Queensland leg-spinner Trevor Hohns.

Once more only three 55-overs-a-side matches – for the Texaco Trophy – were played on the Ashes tour. Even if in the days leading up to the one-day contests tickets were as scarce as centre court tickets at Wimbledon, few in England or Australia saw the matches as anything more than an entertaining entree before the Test match battle. As had occurred in 1981 and 1985, the team that went on to win the Ashes was beaten in the one-day series, Australia going down on a countback after losing the first, tieing the second and winning the third. The circumstances of the second result – England losing five wickets in scoring 226 while Australia lost eight – meant that the trophy stayed in Great Britain.

Inevitably the tie at Trent Bridge was the most exciting of the three matches, although the final match was not far behind. The Australians' afternoon run chase in

DAVID BOON: LIFE AT THE CUTTING EDGE

David Boon is widely considered the most valuable member of the current Australian batting line-up. Whether he bats at No. 3 in Test matches or opens in one-dayers he is the rock any competitive total is built upon. He combines a blue-collar work ethic with a distaste for affectation and unstinting devotion to the team cause in a package that can be summed up in one word – reliability. It is an approach which has made him one of the premier batsmen in world cricket.

Whenever there is hard work to be done Boon is one of the first at the coal face and usually the last to leave, happily getting his hands dirty if it means his team will benefit. Although not a big man physically he is as tough as they come and certainly stands tall whenever he is facing the West Indies and their four-pronged pace attack – the most testing challenge in world cricket.

The Windies have dominated Test cricket because of their unparalleled pace battery. Their excellence is such that they have found a way to remain effective in one-day cricket – a game whose nature reduces the strike power of bowlers. Despite the odds being loaded against them Boon said the West Indies pacemen were no easier to handle in one-day cricket.

'I don't think one-day cricket neutralises the advantage their fast bowlers give them,' said Boon. 'They definitely still have an advantage with the fact that they have four fast bowlers, the same as they would in a Test match, and the class that they are. It can be difficult – especially against guys the calibre of Curtly Ambrose who are going to bowl straight, a good length and with a couple of fielders on either side who make it very difficult for you to run ones as in Test cricket, if you can score runs against the West Indies it's very satisfying.'

Not even the limited-overs bouncer rule, which directs the umpires to no-ball anything that passes above shoulder-height of a batsman, can restrict the West Indies attack. 'No. I don't think it makes too much difference at all,' said Boon. 'That sort of pace, the sort of bowlers they have, the ball that concerns you more is the one that is coming through at chest-height. They're allowed to do that and they're so good at continually getting the ball to come through at that height.'

Because of the difficulty of maintaining a decent run-rate against the West Indies Boon said it was vital that a batsman and his partner work well together. 'In all one-day cricket and especially in situations against the Windies your partner is very important to your running

Game 2 was built around solid contributions by the top five in the order, of which the highest was Steve Waugh's 43. But when he was run out after Healy had slipped turning for a third run, the score was 6-205 in the 52nd over. With three overs to go, the target was 18, which Healy and Lawson reduced to 12 from two. In the 54th, Lawson sliced Foster to Gooch at deep cover as the ask became seven from six balls. Then de Freitas started the 55th over with a wide and two full tosses. But his

and turnover of strike. You've got to be very positive and aggressive and have a good attitude against them.'

When asked to name the best of the Windies quicks Boon wasted no time in answering – with a name that is by no means a surprise. 'They've had a few obviously over the years but I've got to rate Curtly Ambrose up there as one of the best bowlers in Test and one-day cricket and Malcolm Marshall as well.' On the other hand it was not as easy for him to pinpoint an Australian batsman who had consistently met the West Indian fast bowlers and bested them. 'Everyone has their own day but over the years you'd have to say that AB (Allan Border) has played them very well in one-day cricket.'

Apart from the 1987 World Cup victory Boon's favourite one-day memory is Australia's convincing series victory in the West Indies in 1991 when they dominated the rubber to such an extent that they almost pulled off a clean sweep. Only rain and the local rules restricted them to a 4-1 result. 'It was great – especially in their own countries,' said Boon. 'We played good cricket and beat them convincingly.'

Boon said he hardly altered his game when he switched from Tests to the more hectic pace of the one-day game.

'Basically my job is to open and try to get the guys off to a good start, but obviously you're looking to be more positive than you are when you first go in at Test level. But your job is still the same. It doesn't change too much.

'The way Australia plays one-day cricket we try to build the score up rather than just go out and try to belt one. Personally I think that's the reason for our success over the years at the one-day game.'

Boon is justly famous for the no-nonsense way he approaches his batting. Although capable of playing the full range of strokes he has polished and pared his game down to the bare essentials. As he said, that approach remains much the same in one-day cricket although he does employ a more varied arsenal of strokes when the situation demands it. Even then he is responding more to his team's needs than his own self-indulgence.

'It just depends on the day,' said Boon. 'Over a longer period of time you're going to go out there and one day things are just going to happen for you. I still stick within my shots and if I bat through the innings to a certain extent I start to improvise more. You've got your bread-and-butter shots; Mark Waugh is very strong on his legs, and I suppose with mine it's leg side and a cut that I do a lot of scoring with. But the rest of the shots ... if it's dished up there I try to play everything.'

fifth ball bowled Tim May, leaving Rackemann with the task of finding two from the final ball to keep the series alive. De Freitas delivered just wide of the off-stump, Rackemann swished and missed, and Healy raced up the pitch and beat a direct hit from the keeper, Stephen Rhodes, to tie the scores.

Had the throw from Rhodes been to the bowler's end Rackemann would surely have been run out. But Rhodes could hardly have believed that Healy would reach his end in such a hurry. Earlier in his innings, the Aussie keeper had pulled a thigh muscle and sought a runner. The England captain David Gower readily agreed until Healy, forgetting he had Dean Jones to do the job for him, sprinted off for a two. Gower (and the bemused umpires) then decided that Healy, strained muscle and all, could complete the quick singles on his own. Afterwards, the English press labelled the affair the 'Ben Johnson incident', a result of Gower suggesting Healy had sprinted faster than the disgraced Canadian 100-metres champion.

The final match at Lord's was a high-scoring affair and featured another Geoff Marsh hundred (111 not out), a match-winning 53 off 46 balls by Border, and a brilliant 35 by Steve Waugh as the Australians passed England's 8-278 with four wickets down and three balls to spare. When Marsh and Waugh came together 81 were needed at seven per over, but Waugh put Foster twice into the crowd at deep mid-wicket, and when he left in the 54th over another 10 runs were required at a run a ball. Marsh's innings was typical of his role in the one-day internationals to provide a platform for his fellow batsmen and at the same time take advantage of his own solid start by batting through the overs. It was a role both he and Boon readily adapted to, and was not fully appreciated by observers until Marsh's decline in form in the Australian summer after the tour of the West Indies in 1991.

The afternoon's proceedings at Lord's in 1989 were interrupted by a spectator who dashed onto the field. *Wisden* described the incident this way: '(It was) the longest and most stylish streak on an English cricket ground, by a shapely young lady from the Essex-Suffolk borders. It started from the Mound Stand and finished by the Warner Stand and included an excellent cartwheel ...'

Border's heroes went on to totally dominate the Ashes series, achieving a status in Test cricket they had promised since the World Cup victory in 1987. They returned to Australia to general acclaim, before heading back to the scene of the Cup triumph for the 'The Madras Rubber Foundry World Series for the Jawaharlal Nehru Cup', a tournament that also featured India, Pakistan, the West Indies, Sri Lanka and England. Staged to commemorate the centenary of the birth of India's first prime minister, the Nehru Cup was a disappointment for the Australians, who included O'Donnell, Peter Taylor and Greg Matthews in their party but won only two of their five matches. They were restricted by general fatigue after their arduous Ashes tour, and also by a back injury to Waugh, who was unable to bowl. But they did manage to provide the innings of the tournament, played by Border, an extraordinary 84 off just 44 balls in the match against England at Hyderabad. At one stage during Border's flurry 42 runs came in two overs, bowled by the fast-medium Gladstone Small and Angus Fraser. In all he hit five sixes and eight fours, but even this was not enough to ensure a victory. The Englishmen replied with 3-243 to Australia's 3-242.

Victories came against the West Indies (Marsh 74, Waugh 53 not out off 46 balls, Border 3-20 from 10 overs) and Sri Lanka (Jones 85), but matches were lost to India (in front of 50,000 people in Bangalore) and Pakistan, as well as that first match against England, and the Australians missed a spot in the semi-finals. The Nehru Cup was eventually won by Pakistan, who defeated the West Indies in front of more than 70,000 people in the final in Calcutta.

The ever-popular Victorian fast man, Merv Hughes, loosens up with his mates in the MCG crowd during the first final of the '88-89 World Series Cup. This was one of the most exciting one-dayers played on the famous ground, and was finally won by Australia over the West Indies by just two runs, after Hughes had held his nerve while bowling the final over amid great tension. The support and passion of the Melbourne crowd was a key factor in the win.

The newly crowned Nehru Cup victors were scheduled to return to Australia for the 1989-90 season, to play three Tests and join Sri Lanka in the battle for the World Series Cup. The Australians faced a difficult program of six Tests, the World Series, a tour of New Zealand and finally the Austral-Asia Cup in Sharjah in May. After a five-month hiatus, season 1990-91 would involve an Ashes series in Australia, the World Series and then a tour of the Caribbean.

Every cricket board around the world acknowledged that the staging of limited-overs internationals guaranteed big crowds and lucrative pay-days. And all, with the exception of the TCCB in England, had by 1990 responded by scheduling as many limited-overs internationals as they dared. The consequence for the world's best cricketers was that they would be making more money in the 1990s than their brothers of earlier generations had ever dreamed of. Unlike their predecessors in international cricket, the Australian cricket stars in the '90s would be fully professional, relying on their talents, their form, and their celebrity status to pay the bills. The pay-back was that they would be seeing more airports, more hotel rooms, more practice nets and less of their families and friends. As international limited-overs cricket headed towards its 21st birthday, cricket followers could only sit back and wonder at the rich and colourful cricket world that the one-day game had brought.

Patrick Eagar

Everyone seems happy with the result of the final ball of the second Texaco Trophy match of the Australians' 1989 tour of England. Before the ball was bowled Australia, one-down in the three-match series and with Carl Rackemann on strike and Ian Healy at the bowler's end, needed two to win. The final delivery was missed by Rackemann and went through to the keeper, Stephen Rhodes. Healy charged through for the bye, and just beat Rhodes' throw but, unfortunately, the celebrations of the Australian wicketkeeper (far right) were premature. The match was declared a tie, and because England had lost fewer wickets during the match it was ruled they could not lose the Texaco series.

18

UNSTOPPABLE!

The 1989-90 World Series was a competition of milestones. Allan Border played his 200th one-day international, the first man to achieve this figure, and also became the first Australian to pass 5000 runs in international one-day cricket. He captained his country in a limited-overs international for the 100th time, in the same match in which Imran Khan racked up match No. 100 as the leader of Pakistan. On the debit side, Steve Waugh was dropped from the Australian team for the first time since 1985, while against Sri Lanka in Perth on December 30, Australia dropped a ridiculous 11 catches, including the Sri Lankan captain Arjuna Ranatunga five times before he passed 21.

This was the first season that the Pakistanis reached the World Series finals, but this owed as much to the Sri Lankans' lack of competitiveness as it did to their own expertise. Australia lost only two matches as they sailed to the Cup for the fifth time in 11 years (the West Indies had also won five times, and England were successful in 1986-87). Despite the one-sided nature of many of the matches, and the realisation not long after a ball had been struck that the final would be between Australia and Pakistan, the crowds continued to roll in – to bask in Australia's re-emergence as a genuine world cricket power. For the first time, an Australia-Pakistan match attracted an attendance above 50,000 – 52,813 to see Australia win by seven wickets at the MCG on January 3, and 55,205 for the first final, which Australia won by seven wickets at the MCG. After the thrashing of England in the 1989 Ashes series, the defeat of Pakistan in the World Series and in a three-Test series left only the West Indies ahead of Border's men at the top of the cricket tree.

The demise of Steve Waugh was the disappointment of the summer, coming so soon after his triumphant tour of England. His back injury meant he hardly bowled (just 16 overs), while his run-getting in the World Series was reduced to a meagre 104 runs from eight innings (including two not outs). As compensation, O'Donnell returned as a one-day cricketer of great influence, while Jones had another brilliant season. Also prominent was the West Australian Tom Moody, who was pushed into the opening batsman role after Boon and Marsh were injured and responded with some marvellous innings, the pick of which was an 89 from 82 balls against Pakistan in Brisbane that included a six which landed among pedestrians walking along nearby Stanley Street. Australia scored 5-300 that day, only the second time 300 had been reached in a one-day international by the Australians at home (the other had been against Sri Lanka in Adelaide in 1984-85).

Following the 1989 Ashes tour, NSW's Mark Taylor (above) was firmly established as his country's leading Test opening bat. However, with David Boon and Geoff Marsh a proven success at the top of the order in one-day cricket and Dean Jones a fixture at No. 3, Taylor found it impossible to guarantee himself a place in the Australian one-day side. Even so, he has had many rewarding days in the limited-overs game, especially in 1990-91 when he was named the player of the World Series finals and in 1992-93 when he twice won Man-of-the-Match awards.

The NSW left-hander Mark Taylor, who had been so dominant in the Test matches in England (scoring the third-highest series aggregate in Test history), opened the batting in all but one of Australia's World Series matches. However, despite his run-getting in the Ashes Tests, which continued through the five-dayers of '89-90, many would-be selectors questioned his place in the one-day side. A superb slip fieldsman, some thought him too slow near the fielding circles and in the outfield, while others felt his batting style too inflexible for the 50-over limit. After moderate efforts in the first two matches, he was left out to make way for an extra bowler in Game 3, but after Boon's injury Taylor came back for the remainder of the competition and played a crucial hand in the second final in Sydney with an innings of 74 that set up his team's match-winning total of 6-255.

After that second win sealed their Cup victory, the Australians' next assignment was in New Zealand, where they played in a triangular one-day tournament with their hosts and India, who had just completed a Test series. The Australian selectors were faced with a difficult poser. With Boon and Marsh available, and O'Donnell having established himself at No.6 in the one-day side, there were too many quality batsmen to fit into the one XI. The unlucky Moody was the one left at home, and Taylor and the recalled Steve Waugh were preferred to Marsh for the opening match, which Australia won by 18 runs against India. For the match against New Zealand, which Australia won by 150 runs in front of 20,000 at Christchurch (Jones 107, O'Donnell 5-13 from six overs), Marsh was brought back for Taylor. Then, in the return match against India, Jones was rested. After Australia won this contest by seven wickets (Marsh 86, Taylor 56, O'Donnell 0-62 from nine), to ensure their place in the final, Border gave himself the day off, and Marsh was in charge in the fourth match. Australia won this on run-rate after rain first delayed play and then ended New Zealand's reply to Australia's 6-239 off 47 overs (Jones 59, O'Donnell 52) in the 35th over. The Kiwis had reached 2-167.

Mark Taylor was the unfortunate man left out of the final, along with Hughes who had been struggling with injury since late in the Australian season. His place went to the Tasmanian paceman Greg Campbell, who took three wickets as the Kiwis were restricted to 162 from 49.2 overs. At one point, the scoreboard read 5-33, but Richard Hadlee, playing his last international match in Auckland, smashed 79, including 22 off two overs from Peter Taylor. Carl Rackemann also took three wickets (for 22) but the key spell came from O'Donnell, who finished with 1-12 from eight overs. Jones then strode out and made New Zealand's small total look dismal. In 94 balls he struck 102, and Australia won the Rothmans Cup with more than 10 overs to spare.

In the Austral-Asia Cup in Sharjah, Pakistan gained revenge for their failures in Australia by defeating Border's team in the final on May 4. The Australians had been drawn in Group A, with New Zealand and the inexperienced Bangladesh, and moved through to the semi-finals without worry, defeating the Kiwis by 63 runs and the men from Bangladesh by seven wickets. Sri Lanka faced Australia in the semi-final and had no answer to an awesome batting display that included another Jones century, 68 from Marsh, and a quite remarkable 74 off just 29 balls by O'Donnell. O'Donnell's first 50 came off *18* balls – a new record in international limited-overs

MIKE WHITNEY: 'IT'S A TOUGH GAME'

All the highly popular NSW fast bowler Mike Whitney ever wanted to do was play Test cricket. In the end Whitney only played 12 Tests in a career that ended in retirement in February 1994. Ironically it was one-day cricket, a game which he had dismissed as lightweight for the greater part of his career, that threw him a lifeline when it appeared he would tally far less than a dozen. Whitney's hopes of adding to his four Tests looked dim after he was controversially omitted from the 1989 Ashes tour, but he won a place on the 1991 tour of the West Indies and limited-overs cricket was the crowbar he used to break back into the Test side. That prompted a radical rethink in his attitude to the game.

'At first I really didn't think one-day cricket was important to my career at all,' said Whitney. 'In fact in the early days, being a purist, I had very little regard for the game. But when I went on tour to the West Indies I got picked in the first one-dayer at Sabina Park. Bruce Reid had already had a couple of back problems early in the tour so it was a great chance for me to break into the Test team through the one-day series, and that's exactly what happened. I played the first two Tests and all the one-day games so it was fantastic.

'My whole perception of the thing changed then. I realised it wasn't just this pyjama game that I'd considered it to be. It was still a game of extremes and enormous skill but also different techniques and different strat-egies. I really got off on it then, I really enjoyed it because it's 50 overs of pure adrenalin. It's such a whole different scene to playing Sheffield Shield or Test cricket. And the razzamatazz involved – I never used to like that – but being part of a team and being out there in front of 70,000 people in a one-dayer we won by five runs was fantastic.

'Cementing my spot in the limited-overs team revived my Test career. I nearly became a permanent member of the one-day team for the West Indies campaign, the home one against India and the Windies, the World Cup, the tour of Sri Lanka and then against the West Indies at home in 1992-93. It was great. I thought even this year before I retired I was probably a very, very good chance of playing in the one-day series where my chances of playing Test cricket had probably dwindled.'

Once he had removed the blinkers, Whitney threw himself into the task of becoming an effective one-day bowler and quickly carved out a niche for himself. 'I developed slower balls. I probably became, in that regard, a little more stereotyped. For probably 30 of my 38 limited-overs games "Billy" McDermott and whoever would open the bowling, and I'd come on and bowl my 10 overs straight. I had a specific role, I had to try to keep it down to so many runs and eight out of 10 times I was bowling with Stephen (Waugh) as well which used to be fantastic.'

For a man used to taking the new ball the switch to the workhorse role would seem difficult, but Whitney said his yearning for the glamour role of impact player did not last long. 'I did miss taking wickets as a strike bowler at first, but at the end of the day, no I didn't, because I realised quickly that the name of this game was the team which conceded the least runs won the game. If I had 0-20 off 10 I'd done my job equally as well as someone who took 2-45 off 10. And a lot of times the only reason the bloke at the other end got wickets was because you were keeping it tight.

'I really used to get turned on – a maiden over was sensational. It was as good as a wicket over sometimes – and as important pressure-wise coming to the money end of the game in the last five overs. I bowled on a few occasions when I can remember thinking "wow, I've got to bowl a maiden" and it was a huge conquest to get that maiden over out – or a couple of maiden balls even.'

Whitney admits that for him, one-day games tended to blur into one another. 'It's not as specific as Test matches. I remember much more vividly my whole first-class career. Of the 72 domestic and international one-day matches there's only a handful that I would remember.'

Nevertheless, he had no trouble reeling off the highlights. 'Australia v India during the 1991-92 World Series (M.R. Whitney 2-22 off 10 overs in the six-wicket win), I remember bowling really well that day; Australia v Zimbabwe in Hobart (2-15 off 10 in the 128-run win) and, of course, against India in the second World Series final at the SCG in 1991-92 (three catches and 1-32 off 10). I took three outfield catches and a wicket and we won the series that night. That was a huge game for me. I'll never forget that. Allan Border made me bowl

the final over of the match and they needed about a dozen to win. Playing on my home turf, I'd had a good summer – it was big, really big. My family was sitting in the stand and I had the World Series in my claws holding it up.'

The relentless schedule of one-dayers in an Australian summer is thought to pose a significant threat to players' motivation but Whitney says the issue is simply one of tiredness.

'I don't think that attitude was ever a problem but fatigue, mental and physical, definitely was,' he said. 'One-day cricket is a tough game and it's very tough on the bowlers in particular. If you play a couple of games in quick succession you get very tired and you just have to keep pushing yourself and pushing yourself. There's a number of factors why the players want to do that. Obviously the money comes into it, the slice-up of the prizemoney and your match fee, you don't want to miss out. And then there's your personal profile in one-day cricket. You want to keep all those things high.'

Whitney may be a convert to the one-day way but that does not mean for one moment that he has spurned Test cricket, which still holds a special place in his heart. 'Test cricket is the ultimate game. One-day cricket's been great for the profile of the game and in bringing people to the game who previously wouldn't have come – women in particular and people who don't want to sit there for five days and watch a Test match evolve. For purists, which I am – I'm a cricket fanatic – Test cricket is the bottom line.'

cricket – and the final Australian total of 3-332, off 50 overs, was the best by an Australian team in international one-dayers, beating the previous best of 5-328 scored off 60 overs by Ian Chappell's team against Sri Lanka during the 1975 World Cup.

In the final, the Australians ran into a whirlwind called Wasim Akram, who was perhaps an even more devastating one-day cricketer than O'Donnell. Three months earlier in the first World Series final Wasim had played a brilliant innings of 86 off 76 balls (out of a total of 162) that included one of the biggest sixes the MCG had ever seen. In the final in Sharjah, he belted an unbeaten 49 off 35 balls, and then ended the contest with a hat-trick in the 47th over to give his side a 36-run win. The Australians had needed 267 after Wasim's attack with the bat, and although Taylor and Steve Waugh passed 50, the loss of Boon (37), Jones (0) and Border (1) in the space of two runs after Boon and Taylor had added 62 for the first wicket proved too big a hurdle to overcome.

The Australians were handicapped in the final by the absence of Marsh, but were heartened by the return to form of Steve Waugh, who bowled without mishap throughout the tournament and batted with much of his former style. With Waugh and O'Donnell in form, Australia were able to write in their scorebook a one-day batting line-up superior to any other in the world. Marsh, Taylor, Boon, Jones, Border, Waugh, O'Donnell and Healy added up to a top eight of diversity and skill. In Jones, Australia had arguably the best limited-overs batsman in the world in 1990, better even (if only marginally) than Haynes, Richardson, Richards and Javed Miandad. Yet, as early as the beginning of the 1990-91 home season, the Australian selectors were obliged to restyle that imposing batting order. Their hand was forced by the magnificent early-season form of Mark Waugh, and for the first match of the World Series it was the unfortunate Taylor who watched the entire match from the dressing room.

By the start of the 1990-91 Cup, which featured England and New Zealand, changes had been made to the much-criticised regulations for rain-interrupted matches that had so hindered Australia in the 1988-89 finals. Instead of the new requirement of the team batting second being calculated on the overall run-rate of the team that batted first, only the *best* overs of the team with the runs on the board were considered. The first instance of the rule being used in the World Series came in the opening fixture of the 1990-91 competition, when rain washed out Australia's innings at 9-236 after 43.5 overs and then reduced New Zealand's reply to 40 overs. Their target was measured by Australia's best 40 overs, rather than calculated on the run-rate over their entire innings. So the target became 236 off 40, rather than 216 as it would have been under the old rule. Everyone rated this system superior, although the future would reveal alternative injustices. But these faults were not apparent at the time.

For England, the 1990-91 tour was a far cry from the 'Grand Slam' adventure of four years before. Graham Gooch's team lost the Test series 3-nil, and failed to reach the finals of the World Series, which the Australians won in two straight matches over the Kiwis. In fact, Australia won nine of their 10 matches during the competition, their only setback being a bizarre loss to New Zealand before a record

David Boon (above) and Geoff Marsh (below), who shared in an Australian record eight century partnerships in one-day international cricket, and who between them hit 14 of the 39 individual centuries scored by Australians in limited-overs internationals.

crowd of 11,086 in Hobart in the first World Series match featuring the home team that had been played in Tasmania. The Kiwis, batting first, had managed 6-194, and so confident was Border that he rearranged his batting order. Eighty-four were needed from 20 overs with six wickets in hand, but then Healy and O'Donnell fell within a single of each other, and Jones was run out to leave Australia at 7-154. Border, batting eight, and Greg Matthews took the score to 177 before the captain ran himself out. Then Alderman was run out as well. Matthews reduced the target to two from the final six balls, but Bruce Reid, a terrible batsman, had the strike to the medium pace of Chris Pringle and could not even find one for the tie.

This hiccup excluded, the Australians were superb throughout the competition. Jones' century in Brisbane, 145 off 136 balls including four sixes, was the highest by an Australian in limited-overs internationals. *Wisden* described him as 'unstoppable'. Marsh was remarkably consistent, his scores before his first-ball duck in the second final being 46, 45, 37, 51, 82, 61, 29, 7 and 70. But perhaps the batting highlight of the one-day season was a partnership of 112 between the graceful Mark Waugh and the belligerent O'Donnell in Sydney on New Year's Day. the *Australian*'s Terry Brindle described Waugh that day as having 'played with the timing of a Swiss watch-maker ... as near to perfect a one-day innings as makes no difference'. Waugh's form was such that Taylor did not get a look-in until the finals, when Border dropped out to rest a groin strain, but the left-handed opener took his chance and was named the player of the finals after scoring 41 and 71. Matthews and Peter Taylor wrestled for the spin bowler's job, Matthews' superior claims as a batsman eventually being outweighed by Taylor's bowling economy. And Steve Waugh, back bowling in every match, returned as a limited-overs cricketer of great importance. His partnership with Healy in the final qualifying match against England, which ended the British hopes of a finals berth, realised 95 runs in 12 overs and exemplified the value of both men's batting in an innings' turbulent final overs.

Following the conclusion of the international season in Australia, Border's team climbed aboard for the testing flight via Bangkok and London to the West Indies for what amounted to the cricket championship of the world. At Test level, these two sides stood out; as far as the one-day game was concerned only Pakistan, as winners of the Nehru Cup in 1989 and the Austral-Asia Cup in 1990, could match Australia's and the Windies' claims to the world title. But the Australians pointed to the manner in which they had dominated Pakistan in the 1989-90 World Series – for most critics and all the players the tour of the Caribbean involved the best two teams at both Test *and* one-day level.

Although the Test series was eventually lost (two Tests to one), the Australians were superb in the five-match limited-overs contest, losing only the third encounter in Trinidad after the home team's target was reduced because of a rain delay. This was the first time the West Indies had been defeated in a one-day series at home. And the decisive manner in which Australia achieved this triumph suggested, perhaps even above the '87 World Cup, that this was the greatest performance by an Australian side in the first 21 years of international limited-overs cricket.

The Australians went into this one-day series without O'Donnell, who had done

The Australians after winning the World Series in 1991-92. Back row: Errol Alcott (physio), David Boon, Bob Simpson (coach), Tom Moody, Craig McDermott, Mark Waugh, Paul Reiffel, Ian McDonald (media manager). Front: Dean Jones, Geoff Marsh, Allan Border (captain), Mike Whitney, Peter Taylor, Steve Waugh, Ian Healy.

enough in the World Series to win the International Criceter of the Year award for the 1990-91 Australian season, but could not win a reservation on the plane to the Caribbean. He was the only member of the team which had thrashed New Zealand in the Cup finals not to make the Windies tour, although Terry Alderman would play no part in the one-day matches once in the Caribbean.

The two vacancies in the one-day side were filled by Craig McDermott and Mike Whitney. McDermott's renaissance in Shield cricket in '90-91 had led to a Test recall and 18 wickets in the final two matches of the Ashes series. Whitney proved highly effective against the West Indies' stroke-makers in the one-day matches, all of which were played in front of full, colourful houses. In the first match in Jamaica, the tough New South Welshman bowled seven overs for just 16 runs as the visitors kept the West Indies 35 runs from their target of 4-244 (Jones 88, Mark Waugh 67). McDermott, too, was a key man in the victory. In his match-winning final spell he dismissed Richardson, Dujon and Tony Gray as the final six wickets fell for just 19 runs. This was the West Indies' first loss in a limited-overs international at home for almost five years. The tenacity and confidence of the Australians in this form of cricket was perhaps never better illustrated than by Steve Waugh, who greeted the king of the Caribbean Vivian Richards with a bouncer first ball.

After the weather had ruined the first Test, the Australians flew to Trinidad, to go two-up in the one-day series. This time the winning margin was 45 runs in a match

CRAIG McDERMOTT: FIGHTING THE ODDS

Bowlers are the oppressed under-class in any form of cricket, but in limited-overs cricket their role reaches its absolute nadir. Most rules are loaded against bowlers but in one-day cricket the game's powers-that-be turn the screws even tighter. The whole ethos of the abbreviated game is stacked against cricket's honest toilers. A good game is where the batsmen on each side score a truckload of runs while a bad game is when the bowlers of one or both sides dominate. They just can't win.

Aussie quick Craig McDermott says Test cricket is his ideal game but, surprisingly, he has no beef with one-dayers. 'One-day cricket is there for the public,' said McDermott. 'It's a good spectacle to watch.' He certainly has no illusions about the role he is being asked to play. 'It's definitely not a bowler's game. One-day cricket is designed for runs to be scored. They've made most of the rules so that batsmen can score runs. To get people interested they need to score runs so that's fine. We've just got to find the best way around it to keep the scores low.'

McDermott, however, is opposed to any attempts to give bowlers a fair shake by putting some life in the heart-breaking concrete strips on which the bowlers are usually asked to toil in limited-overs cricket. 'I tend to agree that you shouldn't have a wicket that's seaming all over the place for a one-dayer,' McDermott said. 'If it does a little it's not too bad but if the wicket is seaming around in a one-dayer it's not an even contest because invariably it settles down in the second innings. That's why you have to have a wicket that's got very little grass, so it's fair for both teams.'

that was originally reduced by rain to 42 overs per side. Whitney (3-41) and McDermott (3-29) were again major players, after the Australians were limited to 9-172 (Jones 64). So slowly did the locals go through their paces, that when the allotted time ran out, the Australians had faced eight overs less than they had originally expected. Whitney, never an ace with the bat, was obliged to defend all but the sixth ball of the final over (from which he was caught) to ensure his opponents faced just as many overs as they had managed to fit into their time frame. Only Reid batted after Mike Whitney. Had the Australians been all out, the locals' tardiness would not have mattered, and McDermott and company would have had to bowl their full 42 overs. The Windies came out, reached 1-47, and then lost their last nine wickets for 80, with only Haynes and Richards getting past 13.

More rain the following day reduced the home team's target in Game 3 to 181 in 36 overs, after the Australians had scored 7-245 from 49 overs. The tour conditions had the revised target being calculated on the basis of the team batting first's overall run-rate. Marsh made 81, while Steve Waugh and Healy (33 off 23 balls) scored most of the 54 that came from the final six overs. The reduction in overs was to the West Indies' benefit, and Richardson's 90 and Logie's quick-fire 24 at the end were enough to get them home with time to spare. However, three days later, in

McDermott said even though the game and his assignment may change for a one-dayer his approach doesn't. 'I don't really try to do a lot different because you're trying to bowl a good line and length and hopefully pick up one or two early wickets so you're really trying to do similar things. Your line may be a little different than in a Test match but not much. You bowl a bit straighter in one-dayers.'

In a limited-overs match bowlers have to give everything in an allotment of 10 overs that may be broken up into three or four spells. The hectic atmosphere would seem to deny bowlers a chance to develop and maintain the rhythm they rely so heavily upon but McDermott said that is not so. 'I don't think it's harder to maintain your rhythm because everything's on the boil every ball whether you're in the field or bowling. I think that helps you keep your mind on the job and makes the three hours go pretty swiftly.'

Still, he confesses the adrenalin rush is a transient experience, without the afterglow that nourishes his memories of outstanding Test performances. 'No-one remembers one one-dayer from the other,' he contends. 'You might remember when you got 5-50 or 5-30 but they all pale into insignificance beside Tests. You can remember a lot of Tests you played.'

The one thing that stands out from the many games that Australia's leading limited-overs wicket-taker has played is Australia's sole World Cup victory. 'The World Cup in 1987 definitely is top of the tree by a mile. We played great cricket every game. I took 5-40 in the semi-final and bowled well the whole series. I got 18 wickets which is actually a record.' He said the reason for his success then was simple. 'I trained very hard. I was very fit. I worked really hard so I was ready for the heat.'

Barbados, Australia clinched the series when the home team was beaten in an international match (Test or limited-overs) at the Bridgetown ground for the first time since January 1935. Batting first for the fourth time in a row, the Aussies amassed 6-283 on the back of Marsh's eighth one-day international century. With Border (79) he added 146, then with Mark Waugh (49) a further 87 in 12 overs, after Taylor and Jones had fallen cheaply at the barrier. Although Reid conceded 52 from seven overs, McDermott, Whitney and Steve Waugh were superb with the ball, and a Windies revival was never likely. The final margin in favour of the Australians was 37 runs. The celebrations in the away dressing room, which continued long into the night, provided the players with some of their best memories of the tour.

Marsh was once again the man of the match in the fifth game. Although the series had been decided, the Australians were relentless, while their rivals' lackadaisical approach was reflected by the 11 wides and 24 no-balls they bowled as the man from Wandering batted through the innings for 106. Australia eventually passed the West Indies' 251 with six wickets and nine balls in hand. One feature of the West Indies' innings was the run out of Greenidge, who was defeated by a throw bulleted from the boundary from Mark Waugh. Later, Waugh received an award valued at US$400 as the fieldsman of the match, which reflected the quality of that one piece of brilliance. He had, he commented later, fielded only three balls during the entire innings.

McDermott had once again been outstanding, taking 3-29 from his 10 overs. He received sterling support from Merv Hughes (3-33), who was playing his first limited-overs international since his solitary appearance in the World Series back in December. Hughes, somewhat strangely, had become perceived as a five-day rather than a one-day cricketer, a rating he found difficult to shake. With few exceptions, the Australian selectors had seen their strongest one-day side as being their Test XI. Hughes was one of these exceptions. In the period between November 1990 and February 1992, he would play in 14 Tests (out of a possible 15) but only two one-day internationals (out of 25). For some it worked the other way. In the same period, Mike Whitney would play five Tests and 13 one-dayers, while the off-spinner Peter Taylor would play three Test matches and 21 limited-overs internationals. Later in his career, Dean Jones would be an automatic selection for the one-dayers (often at the expense of Test vice-captain Mark Taylor), but not the Tests. Simon O'Donnell wore the 'one-day' tag for most of his career.

Most players had talents that the selectors judged translated across both styles of the sport. This was shown once again during the 1991-92 World Series, when Australia defeated India and the West Indies. Only Hughes and Mark Taylor of the XI that played in the first Test against India (which included Whitney and Peter Taylor) missed out on the one-day matches, being replaced originally by O'Donnell and Steve Waugh. O'Donnell, who was battling a loss in form in the Sheffield Shield, was dropped after the first two matches, a humbling loss to India in Perth when the batting fell apart for just 101, and then a simple eight-wicket demolition of the same side in Hobart. During this game Jones had the time and political acumen to manage the strike so that Boon was able to score a hundred in front of his home fans. O'Donnell's omission came before the first Cup encounter with the Windies, now captained by Richie Richardson and without Richards, Greenidge and Dujon. This was the first international cricket match played at the MCG since the construction of the immense Great Southern Stand, and few in the crowd of almost 60,000 appreciated the sacking of O'Donnell, even if his replacement Tom Moody's 51 was the highest score in the Australian innings of 9-173. This total proved enough, but only because of the all-round skill of Steve Waugh, who took two catches, two wickets and completed two run outs as the Windies fell 10 runs short of victory.

Moody's good form in the World Series eventually led to his return to the Test team for the fifth Test. By this stage of the season, the Australians were the World Series champions, and favourites for the World Cup, to be held in Australia and New Zealand in February/March. In the World Series they had defeated India 2-nil in the finals – the first a comfortable 88-run victory, the second a nail-biting six-run win. This second triumph, achieved amid great excitement at the SCG with the local boy Whitney the hero, was won despite some mediocre moments for the Australians. The batting in the middle order, Border apart, appeared fragile, while Jones and Steve Waugh dropped easy catches as India tried to reach 208. At times, the Australian captain looked angry and frustrated in the field, and in the commentary box Greg Chappell observed, with a comment that brought back memories of that

STEVE WAUGH: A CLASSIC ONE-DAY CRICKETER

Steve Waugh's many and varied talents place him consistently at the heart of the multi-coloured maelstrom that is limited-overs cricket. Waugh can turn a match with bat, ball or in the field.

Often it is not just scoring runs or taking wickets either, as was illustrated during a World Series match against South Africa at the SCG during the 1993-94 season. Waugh hammered a series of ferocious cut shots to ace fieldsman Jonty Rhodes at point, eventually forcing him to retire from the game with a fracture above the little finger on his left hand. When middle-order batsman Rhodes eventually marched bravely out onto the SCG to bat at No. 9 the game was all but over.

Waugh is the classic one-day international cricketer, and as such points the way to the future. He himself believes that the influence all-rounders have on limited-overs cricket can only increase.

'It's a game for all-rounders. Anyone who bats and bowls is suited to one-day cricket,' said Waugh. 'One or two specialist batsmen and bowlers – I think that's the way the game is

Continued over page

controversial 1980-81 underarm summer, that the home team seemed desperate to avoid a third final and get some rest instead. Late into the evening, with India's new teenage batting sensation Sachin Tendulkar at the crease and beyond his half century, a surprise looked possible, but Whitney at deep cover took a brilliant running catch in front of his disciples in the Brewongle Stand and Australia sneaked home.

After the fifth Test, in which Moody scored 50 and 101 and Whitney took 11 wickets, the Australian selectors announced their squad for the World Cup. In keeping with their established loyalty to the Test players, Hughes and Mark Taylor were included. So too were Mark Waugh and Marsh (who had both been dropped for the fifth Test), and Bruce Reid, who was available now after missing a fair slice of the season with back problems. As was expected, Peter Taylor won the spinner's job over Matthews, who was in the middle of another prolific Shield season with bat and ball, and the young Victorian leggie Shane Warne, who had played in the third and fourth Tests. The shock was the omission of O'Donnell, judged the best one-day player in the land a season before but now not good enough even for the squad.

After the triumph in the Caribbean and the World Series success, who was going to match the Australians in the World Cup? To read some of the more jingoistic previews, this was a World Cup already won. But, with hindsight, it is clear that the chinks that ever so slightly revealed themselves in that second final in Sydney were actually the beginnings of large cracks that were going to appear in Border's ship. At a time when the Australian cricketing public was preparing to put the World Cup crown proudly on their heroes' heads, the Aussie team was heading for a fall.

A CLASSIC ONE-DAY CRICKETER

Continued from previous page

going. They'll be picking completely different sides for Test and one-day cricket.'

The ultra-competitive Waugh thrives on the pressure of being in demand. 'I'm always involved which I like,' he said. 'Generally you're more relaxed because you know you're going to have a good time, be more involved, so there's less pressure. You can try a few things without worrying about whether or not it will come off. You can't stick by the textbook. You've got to think on your feet.'

Ironically Waugh's contributions with the ball in one-day internationals often overshadow his efforts with the bat – even though there is no doubt where his principal strengths lie in Test cricket. He believes it is the opportunity to relax and improvise that has enabled him to shine with the ball. Along with the fact that the demands of limited-overs cricket on a bowler like himself are not as strenuous.

'The skill factor is there but not as high as Test cricket,' he said. 'You don't have to be as good a bowler because the batsmen are having a go. It makes it more interesting.'

Waugh certainly thinks like a bowler when the conversation moves on to the merits of the game and the philosophy behind the rules and regulations. 'It's probably a little easier for the batsmen because the rules are made for the batsmen. Wides are ridiculous. Bowlers are told where to bowl so the batsman is virtually waiting for the ball because he knows where it has to be bowled.' Waugh said his aims when bowling in a one-day match are to bowl a good line and length, not swing the ball, try to contain the batsman and perhaps pick up a wicket or two. Unusually, it is the demanding task of bowling the final overs in an innings, a job which has found many a class Test bowler wanting, that particularly enthrals him.

'For me the best part of one-day cricket is bowling those last few overs,' said Waugh. 'It's a big challenge to try to win a game for the side and hopefully not lose it.' Steve has thrived on being Australia's man in a crisis despite unfortunate events like Pakistani Asif Mujtaba's last-ball six off his bowling to clinch an improbable tie in Hobart during the 1992-93 season. 'I tend to think I can win a game rather than lose it,' he said. 'You've got to be positive. I think there is more pressure on a batsman than a bowler when they are trying to win a game. If you keep your head it is going to be very hard for a batsman to hit fours or sixes to win the game. So I've always fancied myself in that situation.'

'You've got to back yourself. You can't go into those last few overs not thinking that you can do it. If you're scared you're not going to do well. I really enjoy it so if there's a chance I always say "give the ball to me. I'll give it a go. I'll back myself." I think over the years I've probably come out in front. Bowling-wise I never feel under too much pressure. I'm not the world's greatest bowler but if it gets down to the last couple of overs I'll back myself against any batsman.'

Waugh believes his stunning 1987 World Cup, undoubtedly a turning point in his international career, is the best series he has played in one-day cricket. He dismissed tailender Maninder Singh with the second-last ball of the match to clinch a thrilling one-run win over India at Madras, picked up three wickets in the final over against New Zealand for a four-run win, scored 16 runs off the final over in Australia's semi-final victory and coolly took the wickets of Allan Lamb and a rampant Phil DeFreitas in the 47th and 49th overs of the final to give Australia the World Cup by seven runs. In a comment which says as much about himself as the team Steve said: 'I think the good thing about Australia is that we never give up. You've really got to hang in there because anything can happen. We've always backed our ability under pressure.' NSW team-mate Greg Matthews summed up his contribution succinctly: 'Steve carried that Australian side during the World Cup in 1987. The resurgence of the team as a one-day side dates back to then.'

Apart from shatterproof nerves, Waugh's most famous weapon has been his slower ball. That, like his 'Iceman' role, came about more by accident than design. It was during a training session for NSW before a Sheffield Shield match against Western Australia in Perth. 'It was a long session in which I had been bowling for a fair while and Greg Matthews wanted a few extra minutes,' Steve recalled. 'I was mucking around a bit and bowled a slower ball out of the back of my hand. He was stunned. "That was a winner that ball," he said. "I couldn't pick it. You want to bowl that in a game, it's going to be a winner for you." I tried it the next day and got a wicket with it first ball (Mike Veletta) and I've stuck with it ever since. And really it came about by accident. Now I just try to work on a few variations because the guys are always looking for it.'

As crucial as his strokeplay and steady nerves have been to Australia in the dying overs of their one-day innings, Waugh admits a sneaking dissatisfaction with his role in the middle order. Not unreasonably he is a little envious of the time at the crease enjoyed by the top-order batsmen. 'I'd enjoy batting in the first three or four because you've got the opportunity to build an innings,' he said. 'It's frustrating but pleasing when you get 30 off 25 balls and do a job against the fast bowlers. One-day cricket is just for the top four batsmen. The rest just fill in the gaps and try and get as many runs as they can.'

Despite his flair and effectiveness in scoring quick runs on demand Waugh said he does not alter his approach with the bat in one-day cricket. 'When you're batting you basically stick to the same principles as you do in Test cricket. Generally you're better off just playing the way you do in Tests, playing straight.'

THE FALL OF '92

'Playing in the '92 Cup on home soil was a great buzz. I think all of us had a sense of history in the fact that the South Africans made their re-appearance in cricket's international family in that tournament. My memories are fragmented, but mainly of tough, enjoyable competition, big crowds, and a mix of fierce rivalry and the mateship of shared experience among the teams.

'But for the Australian team the Cup proved a major disappointment.'

– Mike Whitney, in his 1994 autobiography *Quick Whit*.

In the months before the World Cup, the possible involvement of South Africa was the main talking point. Eventually, the changes in that country's political philosophy since the release from jail of the head of the African National Congress, Nelson Mandela, made possible the return of the once-feared South Africans to the international cricket stage. In October 1991, after the advice of Mandela had been sought, the South Africans' invitation was sent, to be accepted with great joy, while observers wondered what impact cricket might have on the white South African electorate, which was due to vote in a crucial referendum on the question of all-race elections eight days before the World Cup final.

The late decision to invite South Africa necessitated a re-draw. For the first time the Cup would involve nine countries, instead of eight. But such an innovation was not out of place. After all, the Cup would also feature for the first time coloured clothing, day/night matches and a complete round-robin draw (with the ninth team that meant 39 matches in total). It would also feature the ACB's rules that covered rain interruptions – time did not allow for rain-affected matches to go onto a second day, as they had in past World Cups. Sadly, the imperfections of this rule would arise to haunt all who swore by them. The Cup was sponsored by the ACB's long-time ally, the Benson and Hedges company, and spread itself over 33 days, from the Australia-New Zealand launch in Auckland on February 22 to the final at the MCG on March 25.

Australia were firm favourites before the matches began, but rank outsiders within the first week. After the World Series finals ended on January 20, the players had returned to the Sheffield Shield before two one-days trials were played, a tie against NSW at North Sydney Oval on February 18 and a 62-run defeat of an Auckland XI in Auckland three days later. However, in the World Cup's opening match they were beaten comfortably by 37 runs in front of a packed Kiwi crowd which took great delight in a century by their captain Martin Crowe and the success of Crowe's unorthodox tactic of opening the bowling with the off-spinner Dipak Patel. Just 19 runs came from Patel's first seven overs, as Boon and Marsh struggled with the slow pitch. Boon went on to an even hundred, but Crowe's constant changes confused the Aussies. In the late overs the required run-rate climbed up near double figures, even with Steve Waugh's quickfire 38, and proved unreachable.

Many critics put down this loss to the pitch, the patriotic crowd or to one of those days. Just one change – bowler Whitney in for batsman Mark Waugh – was made for the second match, the historic encounter with South Africa in Sydney, which drew a capacity crowd. The South Africans were making their Cup debut, and were led by Kepler Wessels, the former Australian player who had become the first man to play for two different countries in limited-overs international cricket. The match quickly developed into a great occasion for South African cricket, but a forgettable one for the home side, who were thrashed by nine wickets after a spiritless display. The highest score in the Australian innings of 9-170 was 27, by both Boon and Waugh, Border was out first ball, Healy tore a hamstring while running between wickets, and the bowling was generally inconsistent and uninspired. Afterwards, the South Africans received messages of congratulations from their President F.W. de Klerk and from Mandela. Only the bookmakers had kind words for the Australians.

Hughes and Taylor came in for Reid and the incapacitated Healy for Australia's third match, a must-win encounter in Brisbane with India, whom Australia had beaten five times out of six during the World Series. Boon kept wicket as the Australians prevailed – by a solitary run, after Jones had scored 90 in their 9-237 and the Indian innings had been reduced by rain from 50 to 47 overs. India's target became the total of Australia's most productive 47 overs – two maidens and one two-run over were negated. But despite this extra handicap, their captain, Mohammad Azharuddin, played gallantly for 93, and with one over to go, to be bowled by Moody, 13 were needed.

Moody's first two deliveries were terrible, directed outside leg-stump and swung away for boundaries by the little Indian keeper, Kiran More. However, the third took middle stump. The new batsman Manoj Prabhakar managed a single but was then run out after the striker Javagal Srinath changed his mind about a single. To the final ball, Srinath connected and sent the ball out wide of long-on, where Steve Waugh had to race around the boundary. Waugh spilt the catch but prevented the four. In the middle the two Indians were sprinting for the tie, but the fieldsman's throw to Boon was precise and Venkatapathy Raju was short of his ground. But it had been a near thing. As the crowd sat down for a breather, the realists among them acknowledged the Australian performance was not that of a team with serious aspirations to the World Cup title.

This was underlined back in Sydney four days later. Marsh was left out and Moody pushed up to open with Mark Taylor. Healy returned, Reid came back for Hughes, and the home team was humiliated by England by eight wickets. The selections reeked of panic, or at least a lack of alternatives. One wondered over the treatment of Mark Waugh, and how desperately the selectors were yearning for the inspiration of O'Donnell. In the afternoon session, the Australian middle order collapsed when pressured by Ian Botham's cunning and medium pace, and then, after McDermott was seen off by Gooch and Botham, the rest of the night went exactly the same way as the South Africans' celebration of a week earlier. England won (171 to 2-173) with 9.1 overs to spare.

Mark Waugh and Marsh came back, for Mark Taylor and Reid for the match against Sri Lanka, which was won comfortably by seven wickets, to revive hopes of a semi-final spot. At this point, the Cup front-runners were the unbeaten England and New Zealand. South Africa had defeated Australia and the West Indies, but lost to Sri Lanka and New Zealand. The West Indies, too, had two wins from four matches, Imran Khan's Pakistan just one win from four. India were not good enough. Sri Lanka and Zimbabwe were making up the field. When, the day after Australia's defeat of Sri Lanka, Pakistan lost again (to South Africa after another example of the inadequacies of the rain rule) and slumped to second-last place, hopes of Border's team reaching the final four became increasingly bright.

The key match was Australia v Pakistan in Perth. The Australians this time left out Peter Taylor, and brought back Reid, whose bowling figures for the competition stood at 1-129 from 26 overs. But his home track, it was argued, would suit him. In the game's second over, after Imran had won the toss and batted, the left-handed Aamir Sohail was caught behind off Reid. But it was a no-ball, and the first wicket did not fall until 78. Sohail went on to 76, Reid finished with 0-37 from nine overs, and the innings ended at 9-220. When Australia batted in the evening, the ball swung more for Imran, Wasim Akram and Aqib Javed than it had for the Australians in the afternoon, and the run chase never recovered from the loss of Moody and Boon in the early overs. Marsh batted 34 overs for 39 and even with Jones' adventurous 47 and Mark Waugh's desperate 30, the Australians were never in the race. The end came, amid a bitter on-field exchange between Whitney and the Pakistani keeper Moin Khan, with Australia 48 runs away from staying in the Cup chase.

Even with Australia's thorough defeat of the 1983 nemesis Zimbabwe (6-265 off 46 overs to all out 137) in which the Waugh twins added 113 for the fifth wicket in 69 balls, the prospects of a semi-final spot were obliterated when Pakistan defeated Sri Lanka and then New Zealand. An Australian defeat of the West Indies could do no more than end Richardson's team's tournament and get the Pakistanis into the last four. And so it proved. Boon scored his second hundred of the competition, and even with Brian Lara's exciting 70, Whitney's four wickets broke the West Indies reply, giving Australia a too-late victory by 57 runs. The win left the Australians fifth on the final qualifying table, and ruing the fact that the point Pakistan had gained when rain had prevented a massive victory by England (England were 1-24 chasing Pakistan's paltry 74 when the match was curtailed) was the point that kept the home nation from fourth spot.

The World Cup suggested the Australian team was not of the same quality as it had been 12 months before. Only Whitney and Boon were consistently effective. Marsh was a shadow of the opening batsman who had scored two limited-overs centuries in the Caribbean. Jones was still more than worthy of his place, but no longer the most effective one-day batsman in the game. By his own high standards,

Just two of the many banners that have appeared over the years extolling the virtues of Steve Waugh.

BOB SIMPSON: THE REASONS WHY

The retribution for Australia's poor showing in the 1992 World Cup was swift and savage and ultimately targeted just one man – coach Bob Simpson. Australia had started the campaign as defending champions and strong pre-tournament favourites, but quickly stumbled, recovering only when events had all but passed the home team by. Although the Australian players came in for their fair share of criticism for the way they performed – the batsmen in particular struggled to bat with the authority expected of them – most of the recrimination was aimed at Simpson and the tactics he had championed.

From the very first loss to New Zealand in Australia's opening game, critics alleged Simpson's conservatism had been exposed and counselled that it should be altered before it was too late. The fact that our modestly credentialled little brother from across the Tasman was putting us to shame with flair, intelligence and the courage to experiment and improvise only raised the temperature of debate.

While Kiwi captain Martin Crowe was profiting from the gamble of opening the bowling with Dipak Patel and promoting middle-order slugger Mark Greatbatch to the top of the order, where he consistently created havoc, Simpson and skipper Allan Border refused to be stampeded into changing the Australian team's tried-and-true approach.

Simpson stoically defended his team's tactics, claiming it was the implementation and not the plan itself that was at fault, and stands by that defence to this day. He puts Australia's woes in the '92 Cup down to a combination of faulty planning, principally by the ACB, and of a natural, but poorly timed, slump in the team's form cycle.

'We went straight out of Test cricket into the one-day series and while we didn't think that it would affect us – at the time we had been playing great one-day cricket for four years and were the dominating force – we really just went

Border's impact had declined. And, perhaps most crucial of all, O'Donnell was no longer in the side. The reduction in the effectiveness in the top order had placed pressure on the middle order that it had not been used to. Without O'Donnell to stride in at No. 7 and right the ship, the returns the bowlers were asked to achieve were not possible. The runs of Marsh, Boon and Jones, and the accuracy of McDermott, Whitney and Steve Waugh had been able to mask the significance of O'Donnell's absence in the West Indies. But not in the '92 World Cup, or at least not until the semi-finals were out of reach.

The tables prepared by the statisticians after the World Cup made interesting reading. No Australian batsmen made the top 10 strike rates (runs per deliveries faced). Only Boon (fourth) and Jones (15th) made the top 20 run-scorers. Boon's efforts in the Cup were a continuation of his quality form through the entire one-day international season. In all, he scored 800 runs during 1991-92, from 17 innings which included two not outs, three centuries, four fifties, 75 fours but no sixes.

off the boil and didn't get back into it until too late,' said Simpson. 'On reflection we probably should have had a week's break to go out and get into a camp. We had so many good players who just weren't performing as they normally did – particularly in the batting.

'We were caught napping but Australian programming may have been caught napping too. We expected to do better, we should have done better and I don't think the programming, and our preparation because of that, allowed us to perform as well as we should have. And that's not dodging the issue because the end result is we didn't play well.'

Simpson was subject to some pretty personal criticism at the time, criticism that only got louder and more pointed as Australia's miseries worsened, and while he is not, even now, inclined to reply in kind there is an unmistakable message behind his views on the media and their effect on the team at the time. It would be fair to say he doesn't believe the various newspaper critics, in particular, were much help.

'I don't think the media spotlight ever really helps you in your preparation,' said Simpson. 'It's an extra lot of attention that you have to give to fulfil the needs of the media. We didn't do very well and we deserved some of the media criticism, but sometimes, like anything, they go overboard.' He still has no time for any suggestion that he and his tactics were misguided.

'There were a lot of theories going around from people who suggested that we try to change tactics but I didn't believe, and the team didn't believe, the tactics were wrong. It was just the way we were putting the tactics into operation. Sometimes I wonder about the media's knowledge of exactly what's going on.' In fact, Simpson believes timing had a lot to do with the end result and pointed to Pakistan and their eventual success by way of illustration.

'In the 1992 World Cup we didn't play very well but we were just starting to come good and I think if we'd have made the semis it could probably have been a very good result for us,' he said.

Boon, the dependable accumulator at the top of the order, left the big hitting to those below him. The next best one-day aggregate by an Australian during the season was Jones' 478. No Australian bowler took 10 or more wickets during the World Cup (13 men did, the best Australian was Whitney, with nine). Whitney (second) and McDermott (fourth) made the top 10 economy rates (runs per deliveries bowled).

The World Cup was eventually won by Imran's Pakistan, who defeated England in an entertaining final at the MCG. Organisers had hoped the occasion and the Great Southern Stand would provide a world record cricket crowd for the final, but the final massive figure of 87,182 was marginally short of the 90,800 who witnessed the second day of the fifth Australia-West Indies Test in Melbourne in 1960-61, and also ranked below the estimated 90,000 who saw the India-Pakistan and India-South Africa one-dayers in Calcutta in 1987 and 1992 respectively. On those occasions in India, no official crowd figures were given, and some media estimates put the attendance as being more than this official estimate. At the time of the 1992 match, Eden Gardens officially had 90,452 seats. If there was one vacant for the South Africa match – their 'return' to international cricket – then the ushers were not aware of it.

South Africa's assault on the 1992 World Cup had ended at the semi-final stage. Unfortunately it came in ludicrous fashion, when the weaknesses in the rain rule were brutally exposed. With overs running out in the semi, the South Africans were involved in a desperate run chase against England at the SCG. To add to the tension, rain began falling, and with 13 balls remaining and 22 runs needed the umpires, Randell of Australia and Aldridge of New Zealand, took the teams from the field. This was umpiring of the poorest kind. Surely the pressure and excitement demanded that the match reach its natural conclusion, despite the rain. It was hardly teeming. Not long after the players left the field, the scoreboard told that South Africa now needed 22 from seven balls. As the players went back to their positions, the scoreboard showed a new adjustment – an absurd, scornful 22 from one ball. England, in the 12 minutes they had sat in their dressing room, had won their place in the final.

Gooch's side, under normal circumstances, would probably have won anyway. But justice had not been seen to have been done. Surely, everyone asked, the match could have been extended a further 15 minutes into the night. Rules aren't that rigid. And if it couldn't have been, what right did the umpires have to decide the result of the match with their stupid rain delay. The inconvenience of a slippery ball could not have been as unfair as the impact of the rain rule. That Aldridge, despite the widespread criticism of the fiasco, was appointed to umpire in the Cup final was one of the outrages of the summer.

By 1992-93, the ill-fated rain rule had been revised once again. The formulae became more complicated, but hopefully fairer. Nobody wanted a repeat of the semi-final fiasco, but nobody was sure a situation of a similar kind would not raise another different ramification. The fact that in 30 years of limited-overs cricket no genius had been able to come up with a solution (other than providing for extra time to complete the match) implied that, whatever the cosmetics applied, the impact of foul and forbidding weather would remain the single biggest blot on the playing of the one-day game.

20

BORDER'S FAREWELL

During the one-day international series that preceded the 1993 Ashes Tests in England, the veteran cricket writer Robin Marlar, in the *Sunday Times*, penned an article headed 'ONE-DAY GAME IS FIRST-CLASS'. In the piece he asked why a game as popular as limited-overs international cricket was classified as not being of the same class as the more traditional game.

'What sub-class are they then, these often thrilling contests for which people have established a black market in tickets while staying away in millions from the Tests?' he questioned.

For a writer of Marlar's considerable status to push the credibility of one-day cricket was rare, especially in England. By way of contrast, Matthew Engel, the editor of the cricketers' bible *Wisden*, wrote in the 1994 edition of the 'gimcrack appeal' of one-day cricket. As Marlar put it: 'The plain fact is that cricket's upper crust – players, officials and critics – all look at the one-day game with disdain at best and contempt at worst.' And he continued: 'This deliberate and careless attitude towards the most popular form of the game is utter madness.'

Unfortunately, most commentators who stand up and praise the limited-overs style are immediately labelled as enemies of Test cricket – a throwback to the days when some Australian marketeers spoke of the imminent (though, in reality, impossible) death of the Test match as though it would be a good thing. People with an eye for the one-day game are quickly told by the Test match's most devoted advocates they do not know what they are talking about. This is unfair.

In the case of Marlar, he was not being critical of the five-day Test match (which he had covered with enthusiasm for more than 30 years). Nor was he critical of the cricketers' efforts in the abbreviated version of the game. 'The players, naturally, do their damnedest, just as they do in the two-innings fixtures,' he wrote. 'Personal pride and the collective purse are sufficient incentive and such deficiencies we see reflect lack of skill rather than inadequate motivation.' What Marlar was seeking was a more realistic balance in attitudes between the two forms of cricket – a balance that reflected the passions of the sport's entire support base.

Marlar found it strange and dangerous that many in cricket's highest offices could not recognise any of the qualities of limited-overs cricket (other than its ability to attract rich gate takings), and the significance of the huge crowds who continued to pack the stands. And this at a time when, even more so than had been the case in the 1970s, limited-overs cricket quite readily reflected society's frantic, hurried lifestyle.

In the 1992-93 Australian season, sports fans saw the best of Test match cricket and some more invigorating one-day cricket as well. The Australia-West Indies Test series, coming after Australia's pre-season tour of Sri Lanka, was one of the most dramatic in years – arguably the best since Ian Botham's extraordinary conquest of Kim Hughes' team in England in 1981. The batting of Brian Lara, the leg-spin of Shane Warne, and the fantastic one-run finish to the Adelaide Test were modern gems the like of which the game had not seen for years. And the World Series, involving the two Test teams and the World Cup champions Pakistan, provided a sequence of thrilling finishes – one was tied and four others decided by less than 15 runs.

The Sri Lankan tour, involving three Tests and three limited-overs internationals, was a mixed bag for Border's men. Without the retired Peter Taylor and the omitted Marsh, Hughes, O'Donnell and Steve Waugh, Australia lost the one-day series 2-1. Only in the third match, a day/night encounter in Colombo, did the visitors prevail, after a telling partnership between Boon and Mark Waugh. In this match, Australia wore what Mike Coward described as 'a rich salmon strip with a broad grey band'. The Test series went 1-0 to the Australians, although the Sri Lankans had genuine victory chances in all three matches.

Richie Richardson's young West Indies side returned to Australia keen to make up for their disappointing efforts in 1991-92, when they failed to make the World Series finals and the World Cup semis. This they would do in style, but only after a stuttering start that had critics wondering whether the absence of Richards, Greenidge, Dujon and Marshall was having a similar impact as the retirement of Greg Chappell, Lillee and Marsh had had on Australian cricket a decade before. But in Ambrose, the West Indies had a paceman equal to any of his predecessors and in Lara a batsman of unequalled promise. Richardson, in his first full series as captain, proved himself an inspiring and clever general, and the Frank Worrell Trophy was retained, albeit by the narrowest of margins, while the World Series finals were won in a canter over the team that had topped the qualifying table – Australia.

Crowds for the Test series averaged 16,000 per day, the best result in years, but still almost half the World Series average. That one-day tournament quickly became a battle between Australia and the West Indies, as the Pakistanis without Imran were far below their standards of the season before. Only in Hobart, where they needed 92 in 10 overs, 46 in four and then 17 off one, from Steve Waugh, did they create bold headlines. The Pakistanis were still seven from victory when Waugh bowled his final ball, but instead of a yorker he bowled a shin-high full toss and Asif Mujtaba swung him into the crowd at deep mid-wicket.

In Australia's first match, in Perth, the home team was booed by the WACA crowd, who were infuriated by the absence of any local players in the national side. 'I doubt if any Australian cricket team has ever been given more hostile treatment by a "home" crowd,' wrote Mike Whitney in his autobiography. 'Every Australian player who fielded on the boundary was ridiculed and abused.' The crowd's main

One of the four catches taken by stand-in Australian captain Mark Taylor at the SCG on December 8, 1992, when the West Indies were bowled out on a poor wicket for 87 chasing 101. The batsman is Gus Logie, the keeper Ian Healy. Taylor won the man-of-the-match award, for his safe hands and enterprising captaincy.

target was Healy, who they thought inferior to their own Tim Zoehrer. Allan Border led Australia that night, but missed the next four World Series matches through injury. The temporary captain was Mark Taylor, whose initiation as Aussie skipper came in a rain-shortened, eccentric 30-over-a-side match at the SCG on December 8. This was a quite bizarre contest. Richardson won the toss, sent Australia in and watched his bowlers keep Australia to 9-101 from their allotted overs. Almost immediately it had been apparent that the batting surface was unreliable, almost perilous, and in reply the West Indians could do no more than 87 all out. Dean Jones' 21 was the highest score of the match. Taylor, who took four slip catches, two of them brilliant, and led his men with aplomb, was judged man of the match. His captaincy record for the competition ended at three wins and a tie, and his batting during his brief tenure was the best it had ever been in one-day cricket.

Taylor's third victory came in Melbourne, when the West Indies fell four short of Australia's 198 total after being 3-173 with 5.1 overs in hand. Six of the last seven wickets fell to the Waugh brothers (the other was run out), five of them to Mark, who finished with 5-24 from six overs. The crowd that night was 74,450. The other tight Australia-West Indies one-dayer came before a capacity crowd in Brisbane on January 10. The winning margin was seven runs to the West Indies after Whitney was run out off the last ball of the 49th over. The run out was a costly one

MARK TAYLOR: SEARCHING FOR STABILITY

The Australian cricket team's hectic summer of Test and World Series matches, like so many other things in the stressful race of modern life, has spawned a confused and troubled sub-class – cricketers whose fortunes swing wildly and repeatedly between rejection and acceptance. One minute they are the best in the land and the next out on their ear. Newly appointed Australian captain Mark Taylor is one who has suffered the false hopes and disappointments that are a fact of life for those few considered pivotal to the Test team's success, but perversely a liability in limited-overs cricket – or vice versa.

Until recently Taylor was caught up in the demoralising push and pull of being wanted then unwanted and wanted again as the national team switched backwards and forwards between five-day and one-day cricket.

For a long time he battled even to get a look-in and although he tried to make the best of a bad situation he doesn't deny it got him down. 'It certainly wasn't much fun,' said Taylor. 'You feel like you're doing the job for your country in what many people feel is the hardest form of the game. It does hurt a bit. I didn't talk to too many people but the general feedback

was that I had some very good opposition in Geoff (Marsh) and David (Boon) and the selectors didn't want to play three openers.'

Taylor was at least able to draw some comfort from the presence of a fellow traveller. Paceman Merv Hughes, although finally recognised in recent years as a key member of the Australian attack, still has not completely rid himself of the 'not quite right for one-day cricket' tag. 'We made a few jokes about it,' said Taylor. 'Halfway through a Test match we'd be asking each other who our next Sheffield Shield game was against. But it was never that serious. Both Merv and I were disappointed when we didn't get in and strived to make the team. I felt for Merv against the West Indies during the 1992-93 summer and he congratulated me when I broke back into the side.'

Although it may seem like the perfect opportunity to get some much-needed rest, given the many complaints about the Australian squad's gruelling schedule, getting caught in the revolving door – into the Test team, out of the one-day squad, into the Test team and so on — can do just as much harm as good.

'It does hurt your confidence because you come back into the side when the team's been together a month and you

for the popular paceman, who was struck on the foot by deliveries from the paceman Kenneth Benjamin twice during his brief innings. X-rays later revealed a broken bone, an injury which cost him most of what was left of the season and, in reality, his last chance to tour England with an Australian side. Not long into 1993-94, Whitney broke down with a severe knee injury, which hastened his retirement.

The first match of the finals, at the SCG, belonged to Ambrose, and is chiefly recalled for an incident involving the great fast bowler and Jones, who had been

haven't been there,' said Taylor. 'You lose that little bit of continuity, that little bit of camaraderie because they are talking about the game they played last week and you haven't played for a month. There's nothing better than recognition from your peers, when a teammate walks up and pats you on the back. You don't get that when you haven't played for a month so you lose confidence. You also lose a bit of rhythm and feel for the game.'

Hughes' and Taylor's outsider status was even more puzzling given the fact that despite limited opportunities both had produced a number of impressive performances in one-day cricket. Taylor was man of the finals in Australia's 2-0 whitewash of New Zealand in January 1991 despite missing all of the qualifying matches. He came in as a replacement for skipper Allan Border, who had strained a groin in the warm-up for the first final, and contributed 41 off 40 balls and 71 in Australia's six- and seven-wicket wins. A number of other impressive knocks did him no good until he finally forced his way into the squad full-time during the 1992-93 season.

Ironically it was not his batting so much as his captaincy that signalled he was there to stay. Again substituting for an injured Border, the rookie Australian captain was robbed of a perfect four-from-four World Series record during the 1992-93 season by Asif Mujtaba's last-ball six off Steve Waugh which tied the match against Pakistan in Hobart. Taylor impressed commentators, critics and Border himself with a confident, aggressive and intelligent performance at the helm. Official recognition came in the form of two man-of-the-match awards.

Typically, though, Taylor admits that he was not entirely blameless for his earlier woes. And the cause was not technical but purely mental. Curiously, for a man some portray as dour and one-paced at the crease, Taylor confessed that his problem rested with a devil-may-care attitude. 'At first I thought it was a bit of a hit-and-miss game. You have a swing and if you miss who cares? Sort of like a Sunday League game in England. I tended to think that 60 or 70 was a good score but since then I've realised that if someone goes on and makes a big score you'll make 250 plus which is obviously very hard to chase.' Which leads to the final piece of the puzzle. 'I still haven't got that one-day 100 which still leaves me some work to do. It's something I've got to do and something I need to make a lot of to become a really good one-day player,' Taylor offered.

Attitude, rather than technique, has *Continued over page*

unable to find a spot in the Test batting order but remained a key component, at No. 3, in the one-day line-up. Ambrose had dismissed Boon with the score on 41 after the Windies had scored 8-239, to bring Jones to the middle, whereupon the Victorian star insisted Ambrose remove a white wristband from his bowling arm. Ambrose had been wearing the band all season. Whatever Jones' logic, the move backfired completely as Ambrose shifted through the gears to produce as fiery and superb a spell as had been witnessed under the Sydney lights. He finished with 5-32,

SEARCHING FOR STABILITY
Continued from previous page

been modified. Taylor is now much more conscious of turning over the strike so his free-stroking team-mates can let loose on the bowling, and also of the need to hit the bad ball hard when the opportunity arises. 'The only thing I try to do is be more aggressive in the first 15 overs,' Taylor said. 'That doesn't mean hitting over the top, just looking for a few more balls to hit. I think I've improved my knowledge of the game since my first 20 matches. Mentally I think I'm a better one-day player. I feel much more relaxed. It's a great feeling from an opener's point of view if you get to 30 because there are only four blokes in the circle and a medium-pacer bowling, so you've just got to push the singles. There's no pressure. The only way you can get out is if you do something stupid. From an opener's point of view it's a great game.'

Taylor believes that the rules, and almost uniformly flat batting strips, free up a strokemaker and encourage the chase for runs. And, despite his slowcoach image, it is a challenge he is more than happy to take up. 'I'm not the sort of player who likes to bat 20 overs for 20 runs and think I've done a good job. I enjoy playing one-day cricket. I find it generally less pressured than Test cricket. The crowds are great and it's good for you personally because it gives you extra exposure.'

Taylor believes his appointment as Australian captain will be the turning point for him as a one-day player. He made it clear at his first press conference as captain that he had received an iron-clad guarantee from the selectors regarding his place in the limited-overs line-up. 'I'm going to be an automatic selection which is going to be a weight off my shoulders,' said Taylor.

'Hopefully it'll give me a chance to feel settled in the side and to put some good performances on the board. I've played 50-odd one-day games but I haven't played that many in a row. I found it difficult to get some sort of continuity with my game. Every time I've batted, especially in the last couple of years, I've felt probably the same as Matthew Hayden's felt and Michael Slater's felt ... that this is a selection trial for me ... if I make runs this game I'm in the next game. That doesn't always lead to your best cricket.'

and followed up with 3-26 in the second final to be named the player of the finals.

The Australians preceded their Ashes tour of England with a tour of New Zealand, which included three Tests and five limited-overs internationals. The Tests were completed before the one-day series, and Jones and Tony Dodemaide were flown over to boost the squad once the five-day matches ended. For the first time in an international series involving Australia, the third umpire (stationed in the grandstand with a video replay handy) was used in the one-dayers and the first to fall victim was Boon in Game 2, in Christchurch. Later in the same match, Healy and Dodemaide fell the same way, Healy in amusing circumstances after he was involved in potential run outs at both ends off the same delivery. Both appeals were referred to the video, which showed that the first instance of the stumps being broken had been enough. During that Christchurch match, which Australia won by one wicket after the match had to go to a second day, a TV cameraman had to be taken to hospital suffering from hypothermia.

This icy match was not the only tight finish of the series. In Game 4, in Hamilton, New Zealand levelled the series with a win with two balls to spare. With 60 balls remaining they had needed 76. The following day in Auckland, the fate of the trophy was not decided until the final ball, bowled by Hughes, which Chris Pringle could only hit for two. Before the ball was bowled, Hughes (back in the one-day side for the matches in New Zealand) had mimicked an underarm delivery. This match, like the four before it, had been watched by packed crowds – not even the cold of the South Island could keep the fans from the first two encounters.

Boon had missed the first match of the one-day series, which gave Mark Waugh the opportunity to open the innings. The experiment was a total success. Waugh would open in each of the five games, for returns of 60, 57, 0, 108 and 83. His role in the three one-day internationals in England (again for the Texaco Trophy) was even more vital, as Jones was not in the touring party – left out for younger men such as NSW's Michael Slater, Queensland's Matthew Hayden and Damien Martyn of Western Australia, who were seen as more likely to play in future Test matches. Waugh was given Jones' pivotal role at No. 3, and responded with 56 in the first match at Old Trafford (which Australia won by four runs off the second-last ball) and then 113, at Edgbaston where a stirring 168 fourth-wicket stand between him and Border took Australia to a 2-nil lead. Steve Waugh later called this win 'one of the greatest one-day victories I've been associated with'. At the change of innings, after England's Robin Smith (167) had dominated a total of 5-277, many in the energetic and highly charged crowd had been thinking in terms of an English victory.

It was during the Texaco Trophy matches that Merv Hughes first became acquainted with the 'Sumo! Sumo!' chants that would follow through the English summer. The big fast bowler, who would establish his reputation as one of his country's best and most courageous quick men, originally thought the chant was just another of the songs more regularly heard in the football terraces. Only later did he realise the fans had likened his physique to that of the famous Japanese wrestlers.

Australia completed a clean sweep of the one-day series with a 19-run win at Lord's, a prelude to another Ashes triumph, this time by four Tests to one. But by the end of the Test series, the bowling attack was in severe disrepair. McDermott, after being judged the best Australian player in the one-day series, had to return home after undergoing abdominal surgery during the second Test. Hughes was told by his doctors after the tour that he needed at least three months away from the bowling crease. Not surprisingly, prior to the 1993-94 Australian season, the ACB advised the selectors they could 'rest a jaded or slightly injured player from one-day internationals, while (the player) still received full pay'. With a full domestic season to be followed by a two-month tour of South Africa, it was seen as essential that the players' engines were kept reasonably oiled. Fortunately, McDermott recoved fully to lead the Australian attack through the 1993-94 season. Even more fortunately, by the start of the campaign Shane Warne had evolved into something very, very special.

During the England tour, Warne had developed into a phenomenon. A stocky leg-spinner from the suburbs of Melbourne, complete with bleach-blond hair and an earring, he had performed admirably in Test cricket since taking the vital last three wickets in the first Test of the 1992 Sri Lankan tour. His second-innings 7-52 had won the second Test against the West Indies, and then in New Zealand he had taken 18 wickets, the most by an Australian in a Test series in that country. Just 23 years old when the squad for England left Australia, he started his Ashes series with an astonishing leg break that pitched well outside leg stump but took the off-stump of a bemused Mike Gatting. From that moment, Warne was the talk of the cricket world. His ability to spin the ball great distances was as amazing as his superb control. And allied to this was a difficult-to-pick 'flipper' – the ball that appears harmless as it leaves the hand but then spits through much quicker seeking bowled and lbw dismissals. He was undoubtedly the player of the Ashes tour, and returned home to read his first unauthorised biography. Yet for all his quality and mystique, by the time of the first World Series match of 1993-94, when he had taken 82 wickets in 20 Tests and 69 in his last 13, he had played just one limited-overs international.

Press reports in the lead-up to the 1993-94 Australian summer suggested that Warne would again be left out of the Australian one-day side, at least for a while, to keep his secrets from the South African batsmen he would be fooling in the Test matches. The original strategy was to leave Warne out of the first four one-dayers, which preceded the first two South African Tests, but play him in the lead-up to the World Series finals.

On December 7, Australia wrapped up the third (of three) Tests against New Zealand to take the rubber 2-0. Warne was once again the star, with 18 more wickets in the series. 'He's a bit brash, the Aussie way,' remarked Kiwi captain Ken Rutherford. To young cricket fans he was an idol, sex symbol and champion rolled into one. He was the face of cricket in the '90s, bowling leg-spinners – the art long thought dead. So veterans who remembered Grimmett and O'Reilly loved him as well. But the selectors were concerned – they did not want their prized asset exploited – so he was added to the one-day squad, rather than be made to bowl extended spells in the Sheffield Shield in the weeks between the Tests.

However, circumstances were such that Warne *did* play in the early matches ... with stunning effect. Having been included in the squad for the first four World Series games (though there was no intention of playing him), Warne was obliged to appear in Game 1, against South Africa at the MCG, when Tim May was a late withdrawal with a hamstring strain. Before Warne's name was finally and reluc-tantly written on the team sheet, the option of Border becoming the fifth bowler was considered, but ruled out. This was a decision that made the night for the Melbourne fans who gave their new hero an extraordinary reception when first he strode out to bat late in the afternoon, and then came on to bowl the 25th over of the South Africans' innings, even though by that late stage the game was all but lost.

The attendance that night was 58,030, almost that which watched the entire New

Patrick Eagar

Allan Border on the Lord's balcony with the Texaco Trophy, after Australia had completed a clean sweep of the 1993 limited-overs international series.

MIKE WHITNEY: THE POWER OF THE FANS

One of the reasons for the enduring popularity of one-day cricket is the fact that it offers the crowd an opportunity to be part of the entertainment. One-day cricket is an event and the crowd, because it becomes virtually a single entity, is a major player – just as much as the batsman who hits the winning run or the bowler who wreaks havoc. When a full house is in full cry the adrenalin surge in the players is almost visible. Fast bowler Mike Whitney, a crowd favourite wherever he went, never underestimated the impact a crowd could have on the game.

'Crowd support is extremely important in one-day cricket,' said Whitney. 'It goes from one end of the scale to the other. There is absolutely nothing like bowling at the SCG, taking the ball first change after McDermott and Reiffel or whoever, and the 40,000-strong crowd chanting your name – it was hair-standing-up-on-the-back-of-your-neck stuff. Then there's playing a game in Perth where we got beaten by the West Indies and were booed off the ground. I can't remember too many times feeling so low. Getting back to the dressing room and saying: "Hang on, we got beat but we really tried to do the business and we just had a bad day." Quite bizarre.'

Whitney said the aftermath of that match at the WACA when the Australians were walloped by nine wickets rammed home the power of a supportive

Zealand Test series that had preceded it. Those who counted the gate takings wondered how many would have come if all had known Warne was playing. The other two local box office stars, Hughes (injured) and Jones (dropped), were in the grandstand. It is not always wise to tell the market your leading actor will not be appearing. And, mused some, at least a bit unfair to let people pay big money through the gate to see less than the very best.

The omission of Jones was another of the selection controversies of the summer. His place in the squad had gone to Hayden, Queensland's opening bat who had scored 708 runs (including four centuries) in four Shield matches that season. Hayden was 12th man for the match in Melbourne, but then came into the side for Taylor for Game 2, against New Zealand in Adelaide. Hayden was out again for Australia's third match, an absurd affair in Sydney ruined by a dreadfully inappropriate pitch that saw the visitors dismissed for 69. For the second New Zealand match, Test opener Michael Slater (who had established himself in England and scored 73, 8 and 10 in the first three World Series matches) was relegated. Then, after a break for Tests in Melbourne and Sydney, Jones was finally recalled and Slater and Hayden dropped altogether.

Through the first four matches Warne had taken 9 wickets for 87 runs, including returns of 4-19 and 4-25. His flipper had almost instantly become one of the most effective weapons in international one-day cricket, as had his unique ability to spin the ball on any surface. Those who contended that effective players in Tests were

crowd. 'Very soon after that one-day game where we got booed off in Perth we played a one-day game in Melbourne and the crowd really got behind us because it was in the press that these guys (in Perth) had given us a gobful and how disappointed the team was. We won a real tight one against the West Indies and "Tubby" Taylor, who was captain for that game, made a statement in the press saying that we won because of the crowd, that they really helped the team get together. That was a huge win that night and it was true. Everyone was lifted because of the support.'

Whitney always made a point of showing his appreciation for the crowd's support. 'When I was down on the fence fielding in Melbourne or wherever I always used to go down there and say: "How are you going, folks? Hope you have a good night." And they'd say: "This is going to be great, give it to these blokes." They enjoyed it, everyone enjoyed one-day cricket. People go in groups to see one-day cricket but only fanatics do that for Test cricket. Mates of mine won't go to the Sydney Test but they go to two or three one-dayers at the SCG. It's a big night out, that's the mentality of it and there's nothing wrong with that. It's cricket and it's supporting the game.'

Whitney rated the MCG and the SCG as his favourite venues. 'To play a big game in Melbourne is always enormous but to play in Sydney was extremely special but that's because it's my home ground. The crowds were just fantastic – usually it was a packed house and they knew the game.'

effective in one-dayers saw Warne as the ultimate living proof. It was simply a matter of being good enough. And Warne, more so than any leg-spinner in 23 years of limited-overs internationals, was certainly that.

Jones' return to the Australian XI was a triumphant one. He scored 98 as Australia beat the South Africans by 48 runs before a full house at the 'Gabba. Afterwards, Border was quick to pay tribute to the Victorian. He described himself as a 'biased Jones fan', and looking forward to the coming tour of South Africa, said: 'We play eight one-dayers in South Africa, and to not have your best one-day player in the team seems a bit strange.'

Warne was rested from the Brisbane game, but returned to take 2-27 from 10 overs in a rare Australian loss to the New Zealanders in Sydney. This was a match of some controversy, especially when Rutherford was clearly caught and bowled by Warne. Healy and his bowler were 15 metres from the pitch celebrating when they realised Rutherford was not walking, and furthermore, the umpire was not going to give him out, apparently because he thought it was a bump ball. The Australians' reaction was clear and inflammatory, and the negative press reaction a precursor to worse things to come. Replays confirmed what everyone knew about the out, but the third umpire, who had been introduced to Australian cricket for the 1993-94 season, was there only to adjudicate on run outs, stumpings and boundaries.

It appeared after this Kiwi victory that they would join the Australians in the finals. The South Africans had not won since the competition's opening day. But,

IAN HEALY: ALONE BEHIND THE STUMPS

Ian Healy is an intensely competitive cricketer whose enthusiasm, work ethic and attention to detail make him an outstanding example of the modern-day keeper. That energy and intensity make him perfectly suited to limited-overs cricket. Although his selection for the 1988 tour of Pakistan was a major shock he has grown so much in stature over the years that, dare we say it, the job now fits him like a glove.

Respected cricket scribe Mike Coward wrote in 1992: 'Within the Australian and Queensland teams his conscientiousness is seen as exemplary. He goes to great lengths to prepare his mind and body and maintains a diary to detail the strengths and weaknesses of opponents. And these days he takes a particular interest in sports psychology.'

His Australian team-mate Mike Whitney, writing a column for the *Sunday Telegraph* while sidelined with a broken foot during the 1992-93 season, gave cricket fans an interesting insight into Healy as part of a piece detailing what goes on in the Australian dressing room during play. 'Ian Healy is one of those guys who can never sit still for a minute. He's always doing something – taping his fingers up, mucking around with his gear or throwing a golf ball against the wall to sharpen up his keeping skills. He just likes to keep himself occupied and I don't think I've ever seen him sit down for longer than half an hour.'

An important part of the Australian wicketkeeper's obsessive fine tuning and reshaping of his game has been a radical redefinition of a keeper's priorities in limited-overs cricket. Traditionally the two principal criteria for judging a gloveman's performance have been the number of dismissals he has completed and the number of byes he has allowed. But Healy dismisses those two yardsticks out of hand, claiming they have no relevance to the job as it has evolved. He said the most important things for him are being a good fielding captain – that is, being a positive influence on the fielding side as well as policing the angles of the individual fielders – and a lack of errors.

'In one-day cricket you often go without a dismissal – it's just the nature of the game – and byes mean nothing, you can always get a bad ball,' said Healy. And the way he explains it being a 'good fielding captain' is a lot more complicated than you think. 'It's a shorter period of time but the intensity is higher in

Continued on page 249

now captained by the admirable Hansie Cronje (Wessels had returned home because of injury), they won their remaining two matches to sneak into the decider on run-rate. This was confirmed in the final qualifying match, when Jones scored 82, Warne took 3-28, and Australia beat New Zealand by 51 runs. In many ways this final qualifying match was a celebration of Victorian cricket, as the local seamers Paul Reiffel (3-35) and Damien Fleming (2-15) were also prominent. Of the ovation he received when he walked to the wicket, Jones told the *Sydney Morning Herald*:

Above: Mike Whitney celebrates with his local Sydney crowd after taking one of his three crucial catches in the second final of the 1991-92 World Series, against India, which Australia won by six runs.

Below: David Boon during his 100 in Australia's opening match of the 1992 World Cup, a shock 37-run loss to New Zealand in Auckland.

Below: Australian Picture Library
(Joe Mann – All Sport)

Two shots of Dean Jones, who in the seasons between 1986-87 and 1992-93 led Australia's chase for one-day runs from the No. 3 spot. Above: A glide to third man creates the chance for a quickly-run two at the SCG in 1991-92. Below: Providing an autograph for one fan among a packed house at the Gabba a season later.

The Victorian fast-medium bowler Paul Reiffel, who first played international cricket in 1991-92 and became an integral member of the Australian one-day line-up in the seasons that followed.

Mark Waugh, during the second Texaco Trophy match of 1993, at Edgbaston, where he scored a century and with Allan Border won a famous Australian victory.
Patrick Eagar

Above: The Ladies and Members stands at the SCG, flanked by the light towers erected in the WSC years, during a World Series match in 1993-94.

Below: Allan Border, chaired by Craig McDermott (right) and Shane Warne, after the third World Series final of 1993-94, against South Africa. This proved to be Border's last one-day match in Australia, and although that fact had not been officially announced, the SCG crowd sensed the occasion and gave the long-time Aussie captain a rousing and emotional send-off.

The superb Victorian leg-spinner Shane Warne, who proved conclusively in 1993-94 against South Africa and New Zealand that a spin bowler could be successful, even dominant, in one-day international cricket.
Clifford White

*Mark Taylor batting at the Newlands
Ground in Cape Town, South Africa,
during the third day/night international
of Australia's historic 1994 tour of the
Republic. After the tour, and following
Allan Border's retirement from international cricket, Taylor was named as
the new Australian captain.*
Australian Picture Library (Thomas Turck – Touchline Media)

a one-day match because it's crucial that you're up to the stumps or backing the stumps up – as soon as the bat hits the ball your job isn't over. The dynamics of fielding are much, much more intense.'

Healy said the percentage of takes is actually lower for a wicketkeeper in a limited-overs match because the bowlers bowl much straighter in an effort to stem the flow of runs and the batsmen are, conversely, eager to play more shots in an effort to lift the run-rate.

In May 1994 he was appointed vice-captain in the wake of Allan Border's retirement but working on the fielding angles has always been an important part of his job because, more often than not, the captain is patrolling the outfield which means he does not get a good view of the action.

Not surprisingly the physical and mental drain of limited-overs cricket can be brutal. 'It's the same sort of feeling when I finish a one-day international as when I finish a full day's play in a Test match,' said Healy. 'It takes a lot of mental energy to switch between the two games. A good week at least. We always play pathetically in Perth when we're coming off a Test match.'

But that's not to say he doesn't enjoy it. 'I think it's fun,' said Healy. 'It's entertaining for the public because it's a little easier to play than full-length cricket. There's a little bit less skill and that's probably why it's more fun. A full-length match is far more skilful. People say it's more boring but that's when the skills cut in – persistence, patience, concentration. That's when the best sides show the most skill.'

Healy said one-day cricket hadn't particularly enhanced his skills, but it certainly hadn't hurt them. As far as preparation goes, Healy does not alter his build-up greatly before a limited-overs series.

In fact he works more on his mental approach than skills. 'I probably do a little bit more running-up-to-the-stumps practice but mainly just think about it a little more. In the nets I'll hit over the top and practise strokes to hit boundaries. It's best to pick one or two areas where you can hit a four and channel all your energies into those areas. Otherwise I just push singles because you can't hit boundaries everywhere.'

Healy is a much better batsman than a lot of people give him credit for and indulging his passion for strokeplay in the frantic final overs of a one-day innings is pure pleasure for him. 'There's not as much pressure batting down the order. It suits me because I can have a hit and a miss and not get blamed for it.'

'That's the bit you probably miss. They're very good the Melbourne crowd. They've got the Australian Open (tennis) over the road and there's still 61,000 here.'

By the time of the finals, Taylor was out and Hayden back, after another string of big scores by the Queenslander in the Sheffield Shield. Warne had his worst return of the one-day summer in the first final (1-45 from 10), as South Africa won by 28 runs at the MCG before a crowd of 69,384. But in Sydney two days later, he took three wickets after Jones (79) and Mark Waugh (107) had given him more than enough runs to play with. Waugh's first 50 had taken 65 balls, the second just 39. During this match, Warne was presented with the award for the outstanding player of the World Series qualifying matches. Thus the finals went to a third game, for only the fourth time since 1982-83. Hopes were high for an exciting finale, but the decider developed into a one-sided Australian victory. However, it will always be remembered as a special night for Australian cricket.

Much speculation had been given to Allan Border's future, and more than one newspaper column during the summer had been filled with theories as to Border's plans. For his part, the Australian captain gave little away, other than to confirm he had not made up his mind, but many saw 1993-94 as his 'farewell' season. Consequently there was much misplaced criticism, especially from the Channel Nine commentators, when it appeared a section of the Melbourne crowd had irreverently booed when Border walked out to bat during the first final. In fact, the crowd's attentions had been distracted by an over-zealous security guard. In Sydney, Border was cheered all the way to the wicket when he batted in the two remaining finals, but this was nothing to match the tribute the crowd gave him during the final overs of the series.

After he had been dismissed for a rapid 30 late in the afternoon, he had acknowledged the Sydney crowd like a man farewelling the stage. A few hours later, as the South Africans' required run-rate climbed over double figures and the overs remaining declined, the crowd, none of whom had left, began chanting Border's name and demanding he come on to bowl. Border, for his part, joined in the fun and began warming up at mid-wicket. The crowd roared its approval, and chanted their captain's name once more. During the second last over, Mark Taylor (12th man, vice-captain, and on the field because Boon had strained a groin) ran to his leader and implored him to bowl the final six balls. Border did so, amid a cacophony of roars as every spectator tried to say thank you just a little bit louder than their sister or brother in the seat beside them. Soon after Border was cradling the World Series, and being carried, among his team-mates and on the shoulders of Warne and McDermott, on a victory lap. Throughout it all, the cheers, the applause and the chants continued. 'Border's a Legend' sang through the air. The following day was January 26 ... Australia Day. For the capacity crowd who travelled to the SCG that night, and for the tens of thousands watching on television, Australia Day had come a day early.

Twenty-four hours earlier, at a tribute dinner, Border had looked back on a first-class career which had begun in the second half of 1976-77, the season before World Series Cricket. 'I'm quite indebted to Kerry Packer for his involvement and giving cricket a good kick up the backside,' Border said. 'In a strange way, he is responsible for my being here tonight. Who knows where we would have all ended up without that impetus?'

Australian Picture Library – Joe Mann (All Sport)

Mark Waugh slams a ball to the leg-side boundary at the SCG during his superb century against South Africa in the second World Series final of 1993-94. This was Waugh's third one-day international century in the space of 10 months.

21

WHERE DO WE GO FROM HERE?

Soon after the Australians had defeated the South Africans in the third of three Tests in Australia in 1993-94 to level the series, the two teams travelled to South Africa to resume hostilities in another three-Test series, and an eight-match limited-overs competition. Then it was on to the sands of Sharjah. By the time the adventure finally ended, on April 19, the Australians had played 22 one-day internationals since December 1, 1993. Soon after, they were a team with a new leader after Allan Border finally announced his retirement. NSW's Mark Taylor, who had been omitted from eight of Australia's one-dayers in '93-94, was handed the reins for the trip to Sri Lanka and Pakistan which would commence in early September.

Taylor's rise to the top job in Australian sport was not without controversy, and the claims of Healy, Boon and Steve Waugh were also considered. Never in doubt was Taylor's capabilities as a leader – his captaincy of NSW and (on the occasions when Border stood down) Australia, in both two-innings and one-innings games, had inevitably been shrewd and effective. However, his indifferent form in the limited-overs internationals of 1993-94, which on more than one occasion led to his omission from the side, suggested a situation may arise in the future where the Test captain was dropped from the one-day side. Before Taylor's promotion, the thought of having two Australian captains – one for the Tests and another for the one-dayers – had been considered and rejected.

The team was going through a period of uncertain transition. Bob Simpson had been re-appointed as coach before the team left for South Africa, despite murmurs in the media as to his continued effectiveness. The squad for the September tour did not include Paul Reiffel, the only man to play in all of those 22 one-dayers in 1993-94. Also missing was arguably Australia's greatest ever one-day batsman, the brilliant Dean Jones, who at age 33 had announced his retirement from international cricket. On the South African tour, Jones had played in no Tests but batted at No. 3 in the first seven of the eight one-day internationals, a selection philosophy that had frustrated him for too long.

Australia came from 3-1 and then 4-2 down to level the one-day series in South Africa. The end result came down to the final ball of the final match, in Bloemfontein, bowled by the Victorian Damien Fleming, who had arrived in South Africa after McDermott had broken down late in the Test series. The South African keeper David Richardson could manage only two when three were needed for a tie, and the series was deadlocked.

The matches had been split into two groups of four – the opening half all-day contests, played before the first of three Tests, the final four played under lights after the Test series was completed. In the early exchanges, the home team, spearheaded by the graceful power of their finest batsman, Hansie Cronje, were too good, winning the first, second and fourth matches. Cronje's battles with Shane Warne were a feature. In Game 1, in Johannesburg, the leg spinner went for 56 from 10 wicketless overs as Cronje belted 112; a day later Warne (1-41 from eight) was swung for three sixes by Cronje during a majestic innings of 97. But Warne came back to take 4-36 in Game 3, after Australia had amassed 6-281 (Boon 76, Jones 67, Mark Waugh 60, Border 40 off 17 balls) and Steve Waugh had dismissed Cronje for only 45. That win was the 12th in a row for the team batting first in a one-day international involving Australia. However, the trend was broken two days later in Durban when South Africa lost only three wickets in passing Australia's mediocre 154, a total which owed much to Border's sterling 69 not out after his team had crashed to 4-23.

In the four day/night matches, Cronje was restricted to 10, 11, 37 and 18, and Australia prevailed everywhere but in Port Elizabeth, where there was much criticism of the lights under which the visiting team had to chase 228 for victory. In that match, they crashed to 7-77 before Warne and Reiffel added a gallant but eventually fruitless world-record 119 for the eighth wicket. Two days earlier, Steve Waugh had produced one of his greatest one-day innings, a dynamic 67 off 60 balls, as his team won easily by seven wickets (158 to 3-159) in East London. Waugh had joined his brother at the wicket with the score 3-71, and then out-scored him at an extraordinary rate. In Game 7, a 36-run victory, Mark Waugh scored 71 and Warne took 3-31 to set up the exciting finale in Bloemfontein. After the thrilling conclusion, Steve Waugh was named the man of the one-day series. The trophy would sit with those he was awarded as the player of the Australia-South Africa Test series in both Australia and South Africa.

During the tour, the Australian squad for the Austral-Asia Cup in Sharjah was announced. Like Border, Jones and McDermott, Ian Healy was not available but the selectors strangely decided not to replace him with a specialist keeper. Whether the selectors were suggesting there was no keeper of the required standard, or that a specialist keeper is not necessary in one-day cricket, or whether they simply forgot to pick a fair-dinkum gloveman was not clear. It was expected the new keeper would be the captain Taylor, but in the end Justin Langer, the left-handed batsman from Western Australia, volunteered for the job. Besides Langer, the other new face in the squad was another left-hander Michael Bevan, who had enjoyed a second consecutive season of prolific run-scoring for NSW in the Sheffield Shield.

The Australians reached the semi-finals in Sharjah, where they were beaten by India. Warne took another nine wickets, and Taylor, Mark Waugh, Hayden, Boon and Steve Waugh all had at least one significant innings. Then, finally, the ex-

DAVID HOOKES: THE GAME AS HE SEES IT

Inevitably, there are a number of critics of the influence and spread of one-day international cricket. One of the most vitriolic is David Hookes, a man who was arguably the most attacking Australian batsman of his time. Hookes has never been short of an opinion, is ever-ready to state it and, to his credit, stand by it. During his playing career his candour and honesty were as much Hookes trademarks as his flashing blade and crowd-pleasing philosophy. These days he remains true to that stance in his work in the media.

One issue that had him fired up when he was interviewed for this book was the retirement of Dean Jones from international cricket and how that reflected on the prevailing attitude of players, press and fans to limited-overs cricket. He believes the pendulum had swung so far towards limited-overs cricket that it had overwhelmed traditional values to the extent that an outstanding player was, in Hookes' eyes, insulted.

'The epitome of that swing is Dean Jones retiring as the world's best one-day player – he probably vied only with Viv Richards and probably Desmond Haynes and Javed Miandad over the last 15 years,' he said. 'Suddenly we've got a person who has retired recognised for his one-day performances. The fact is he made 11 Test hundreds, played 52 Test matches and averaged 47. I think it's disgusting that Dean Jones will be remembered now as a great one-day player when his Test record is outstanding. If he played 52 Tests and averaged 31.4 and played 160 one-dayers and averaged 50 I can see where they can say he was a better one-day player, a great one-day player, but to ignore and just sweep under the carpet his 52 Tests at 47 with 11 hundreds is just totally abhorrent to me.'

Jones himself is disappointed he came to wear the 'one-day' label. When he returned home to Australia after announcing his retirement from international cricket on the tour of South Africa in 1994 he said if he could he'd swap every one of his 164 one-day matches for another Test match. He also expressed the hope that he had inspired kids to play Test cricket. They were interesting comments from a man many consider to be one of the finest, if not the finest, one-day player in the history of the game.

'It's all very well to play one-day cricket for Australia and I love that but I've always wanted to play Test cricket for Australia,' said Jones at the time of his retirement, after he had played seven of the eight one-dayers but none of the three Test matches on the South African tour. When asked what he hoped his legacy would be he said: 'I'd like to be

---

hausted Australians returned home, to continued speculation about Border's future, the likely captain if Border did quit, and the make-up of the one-day international cricket program. In late April, the ACB announced that a second Australian XI, tagged Australia 'A', would be involved in the World Series in 1994-95. Although the Board suggested the move was designed to provide an opportunity for talented

remembered as a guy who had a go, hopefully, as a good Test player and a guy who gave it all, a guy who liked his cricket and lived his life to the full.'

Hookes was stinging in his criticism of what he calls the 'new wave – the new mentality of journalists and players'. He believes the modern era of cricket, with its emphasis on giving the public large doses of one-day international cricket, has bred a new type of fan who is unwilling or unable to discriminate. 'You can turn the lights on at the SCG or the MCG and you pack it out,' he said. 'You can play Mickey Mouse versus Donald Duck and they'll be there. I think that probably the most damning tour of recent times has been the '94 Australian tour of South Africa where they played three Tests and eight one-dayers,' Hookes continued. 'How far the Australian Cricket Board has allowed the pendulum to swing is disgusting really. I know South Africa will say that we've been out of the game for years and we need the money but for the Australian tour to go ahead with three Tests and eight one-dayers is beyond me. People say to me that we play five Tests and 15 one-dayers here but it's played over a period of six months and it's a far different structure.'

Hookes was a member of the World Series Cricket squad that toured the West Indies in 1979. That tour consisted of five Super Tests and 12 limited-overs internationals but Hookes said the attitude and the circumstances were again different to the situation in South Africa. 'Our emphasis from a playing point of view was really on the Test matches,' he said. 'There were a few of us younger players but the older players – Ian Chappell, Greg Chappell, Rod Marsh and Dennis Lillee – were very much cricket traditionalists so our emphasis was on the Test matches and the one-dayers were totally subservient.

'Allan Border would say the same thing but unfortunately the majority of his team has been brought up on one-day cricket whereas in my case it was the other way around. The majority were brought up on Test cricket so I approached the limited-overs matches in the West Indies in 1979 as being subservient to the Test matches. It was the Test matches we were there for.'

Hookes claims the effect the 'new wave' is having on the values of the country's youth poses a serious threat to cricket. He believes their value systems have been thoroughly twisted by heavy promotion of limited-overs series.

'The sad part of that is you speak to the best 15-year-old kids playing cricket in the country and they'll know AB's one-day game yesterday but they won't know how many he scored last week in the Test match. You can't get the best 15-year-old kid to a Test match but you can't stop him from going to a one-dayer.'

players on the fringe of the genuine Australian team, most saw it as a move designed to prop up a series that for the first time would involve the latest arrival in international cricket, Zimbabwe. The marketeers did not like the idea of too many England-Zimbabwe matches on national television. The critics' response to the ACB's decision was swift and conflicting, the most publicised negative being the effect the innovation would have on the Sheffield Shield competition.

Border's future finally was resolved when he announced his retirement on May 11. His was a career of unprecedented longevity. His top-class cricketing life had really begun in 1979-80, when the WSC-ACB compromise came into effect and Border, who already had two Test centuries under his belt, walked into the Australian side to bat at No. 3. He was dropped for one World Series match that season, but from that point Border was only out of the Australian team if he felt he needed a rest, which he rarely did. His ability to adapt to any situation was remarkable – he was always a tough, doughty battler unless flair and power were needed, which he then provided. Like all the great champions, he was at his best when things were roughest. His batting in the three years before the '87 World Cup triumph was magnificent, the victory in Calcutta a just reward, and the success of the Australian team in the years that followed a credit to him and the loyal lieutenants in his unit. He remains a great Australian, a sportsman in the same league as icons such as Bradman, Fraser, Elliott and Cuthbert. For much of his career, Allan Border striding onto the field was the badge of the Australian cricket team, more so than the coat of arms on the green and gold caps or the ACB logo on the cricket shirts.

And the fans loved him ... and respected him. When AB was fighting for Australia, he was fighting for them.

International one-day cricket enters its 25th year as the most popular summer sporting entertainment in Australia. Inevitably, every Australia-England limited-overs international in the 1994-95 season will be sold out – envious entrepreneurs would kill for such a product. However, the game retains its critics, especially those who deplore what they perceive as the predictability of much of the play. There are, the game's opponents argue, too many matches of a similar style. And that sameness is exacerbated by the rules that limit the options for bowlers and fielding captains. Those who support the game point to its quite often great excitement, its thrilling finishes and its often fantastic sport. And they highlight the packed grandstands – the market-place where the game has been judged a winner season after season.

Cricket's administrators have been reluctant to tamper with the one-day game in the past 15 years, no doubt motivated by an 'if it ain't broke don't fix it' philosophy. Once major innovations such as white balls, floodlights, coloured clothing, black sightscreens and fielding circles were introduced all in one go, the rule-makers have been doing little more than reacting with cosmetics when problems such as inappropriate rain rules and over-rate slowdowns arise. Even the changes in the design of the players' coloured clothing has been cautious. Why are these alterations from year to year so minor, and why do all the teams wear predominantly one colour?

The view of cricket's administration has always been that the one-day game should always try and stay as close to the core of Test match cricket as it possibly can. However, it should never be forgotten that limited-overs international cricket is now very much part of the entertainment industry, fighting with soap operas and cinemas, basketball and baseball, for the consumers' dollars. At the moment, one-

Australian Picture Library – Thomas Turck (Touchline Media)

Steve Waugh, the man of the limited-overs internationals on Australia's 1994 tour of South Africa, during the third day/night match, in Cape Town. By the end of the 1993-94 season, Waugh was ranked fifth on the list of Australian run-getters in limited-overs internationals, second on the list of Australian wicket-takers, and had caught more one-day catches than any Australian bar Allan Border.

THE 'A TEAM': A CHANGE FOR '94-95

The Australian Cricket Board sparked an energetic debate among the country's cricket fraternity when it announced in April 1994 that an Australian 'A Team' would play in the 1994-95 World Series limited-overs competition. Many welcomed the innovation, which offered Australia's second-tier players an extra chance to push for selection in the Australian side, but there were those who raised their voice against it, predicting doom for Sheffield Shield cricket and bemoaning the sullied prestige of the Australian cap.

NSW coach and former Australian wicketkeeper Steve Rixon believes the 'A Team' concept is the ultimate step in a long-term program to reduce the status of the Sheffield Shield. 'It's exactly as I've been indicating the last five years,' said Rixon. 'To me this is the ultimate in as much as they're denigrating Shield cricket even further. I just think it's a disgrace. It's not a commonsense decision to me. It's a little demeaning to the Australian cap for a kick-off and it's more demeaning to the Sheffield Shield which is the strongest domestic competition in the world. Shield cricket is slowly being chewed away by poor management.

'I'm ropeable. I think it's a poor performance. I just can't understand where they're coming from. If they haven't got good enough sides coming over to draw crowds then just have a domestic season. Get back to a State of Origin effect. You can't tell me if there's no other cricket to be played fans are not going to watch

their Shield sides run around – especially at full strength.'

Rixon said the ACB's justification that the new team would affect only one Sheffield Shield match and one Mercantile Mutual Cup match cut no ice with him. He said that at the end of the day they would be ripping the guts out of his side by taking as many as five or six key players on top of the seven who were selected for the Australian tour of Sri Lanka and Pakistan. 'Let's assume they take Phil Emery, Brad McNamara and possibly a Richard Chee Quee and a Neil Maxwell, who all become potential selections, and Phil Alley and Wayne Holdsworth,' he said. 'It leaves a grade side playing first-class cricket.'

Rixon did a superb job in lifting what was essentially a Second XI side to the 1993-94 Sheffield Shield-Mercantile Mutual Cup double. To do that two years in succession would be an incredible feat but he is ready to shoulder the burden. 'If it means we've got to start again with another half-a-dozen new faces it really is drawing on depth and attitude,' he said. 'That's not to say that I don't think we can still win it from there because I do. It does make it awfully hard though. You don't have to be a Rhodes Scholar to work that out. I'm just unhappy for the competition. It's a terrific brand of cricket, Sheffield Shield, for those who watch it regularly.'

Former Test star Norm O'Neill is also a vocal opponent of the concept but for different reasons. O'Neill believes the new 'A Team' will devalue the worth of an Australian cap. 'I'm not for it,' said O'Neill. 'I think if you reach a situation like that you're going to run into problems. To me it's unbelievable. I think they're going in the wrong direction. I think it's really stupid.

'In an international competition the best side should take the field and that should be it. Apart from anything else there's one aim in life as far as cricketers are concerned and that's to play for your country. The selectors should pick the best side and leave it at that.'

O'Neill has no time for the argument that the 'A Team' will encourage and nurture talented players who are being frustrated by the good form of the Test incumbents. 'That's been going on forever,' he said. 'I know lots of players who could have played for Australia. They had to suffer, why the big change now? If the selectors think these guys are good enough to play for their country I'm sure they could find a spot for them somewhere along the line.'

He also dismissed the suggestion that it is intended to make up for the poor drawing power of Test minnows Zimbabwe. 'If it is, as rumour would suggest, because of revenue then why have Zimbabwe?'

As vocal as its opponents are, there is plenty of strong support for the 'A Team' concept. Queensland Cricket Association chief executive Barry Richards is one supporter. Richards welcomes the chance it will give young players to strut their stuff and shoots down the argument that it is bad because it will hurt Shield cricket. 'It's disappointing from a Shield point of view but the prime function of a state association is to have a strong national team and your aspiration for your players should be geared towards trying to attain national recognition and selection,' said Richards. 'Anything that devalues the Sheffield Shield is disappointing but in this case the positives outweigh the negatives. It does give the opportunity for younger players to get the incentive of playing at that higher level, to find out exactly what's required. It's a good opportunity for a lot of younger players who are probably good enough to play Test cricket but in this era haven't been given the opportunity. There are just so many players around who deserve to be playing at the higher level. Overall it's a good move for Australian cricket.'

Mike Whitney is an unabashed admirer of the concept and even admitted to being a little bit jealous that it hadn't been introduced when he was playing.

'I think it's fantastic,' said Whitney. 'I can't see it detracting at all from our cricket and what a great opportunity for our young guns! It's got to be a platform for some of them. I wish I was a young bloke; I never had an opportunity like that. What if our second XI knocks off our first XI? That'll be huge. I think you'll get an absolutely sold-out crowd. It's more cricket and it's the players the public wants to see. That's got to be a stronger base for Australian cricket.'

Whitney did offer some advice for the ACB. 'I don't think it should be restricted to young blokes only. It would be great to have someone like Geoff Marsh to help them along.' His great mate Greg Matthews was in complete agreement with Whitney. 'I can't see any negatives,' said Matthews. 'It'll be great to see the interaction between the two sides. To see if the same intensity will be there – the bite, the niggle.'

day cricket is right at the top of the charts and, with cricket so much a part of the Australian psyche, there seems little likelihood of that status changing. But if the door is slammed shut on possible innovations, one-day matches may well be risking the loss of the part of its audience that cares as much for the history of cricket as it does for the fate of the disco music of the late 1970s.

We are not suggesting a major overhaul for the game as it is stands as a tremendous sporting contest, but, as an example, an innovation such as baseball's double play would be perfect for one-day cricket. Limited-overs cricket's massive contribution to the standard of fielding has been one of its most precious gifts. To introduce the double play – where both batsmen could be dismissed off the same delivery – would reward these extraordinary fielding standards even more, and create the possibility of a sudden change in the shape of the game. Picture this: Australia all out 199 in 50 overs, the West Indies 2-120 in the 30th over. A full house under the MCG lights, Richie Richardson and Brian Lara both 50 not out. They need 80 in 20 overs. Four an over, eight wickets in hand, and little the Australian captain Mark Taylor can do! Then Lara superbly cover drives a Steve Waugh slower ball, but Mark Waugh dives full length, his body parallel to the ground, to take a remarkable catch. Then he rises quickly, and fires a brilliant throw to his brother. Richardson has backed up too far and is run out. The Windies are now 4-120; Australia, and the home crowd, are right back in the game, and a wonderful piece of fielding has been totally rewarded. It might not have been cricket as we know it, but it was fantastic.

Situation substitution is another concept worth considering (and one that has already been introduced in some matches in South Africa, the country where fielding circles were born). The captain or coach would have the ability to replace a batsman, bowler or fielder with a substitute off the bench, which could open up a multitude of possibilities. Imagine a World Series involving Australia, England and the West Indies. Before the competition begins, each team has to nominate their 14-man squad, and in every game each of the 14 would be available. The starting elevens would not be nominated until after the toss was completed. In a game at the SCG Australia is playing England, and the home team is in trouble. Eight wickets down with six overs to go, and still 50 runs needed for victory. The batsmen are Warne and Reiffel, with just proven No. 11 Glenn McGrath to come. The disappointed fans are heading for the exits. But then there's a roar – Australia are to make a change. Michael Slater, surprisingly left out of the starting XI, is striding to the wicket as a replacement for Warne. Suddenly the game is alive.

Once a player is replaced he's out of the game, so those behind the substitutions would have to think very hard before making a switch. Such a rule change could create an entirely new style of player – a cricketer with a very specific role. He could be the one-day equivalent of baseball's closer, a bowler who comes into the game only in the crucial final overs of the innings. Or he could be the man injected into the middle order, at the expense of one of the bowlers, if it was judged that a big hitter was necessary to boost the run-rate. In Port Elizabeth, on the Australians' tour of South Africa in 1994, Border had sent out Craig McDermott at No. 5, with the instruction to swing at everything. Afterwards the captain told reporters: 'I've

Mark Ray

The beginning of a new era for Australian cricket. On May 19, 1994, Mark Taylor answers the questions of the media after being named as the new Australian captain following the retirement of Allan Border.

tossed around the idea of a pinch-hitter for years (McDermott had batted at No. 4 in the 1987 World Cup final). If he does succeed, it can give you the springboard to something special.'

It would be a moment of great sporting theatre if the fielding captain responded to the sight of a dangerous pinch-hitter by bringing back his finest bowler. But, under the present rules, if that man had already completed his allotment of overs, this would not be possible. Fans enjoy a contest, and like to see a batsman and bowler go toe-to-toe. Why are the great bowlers limited to a certain number of overs? To restrain a bowler in such a way can, in certain circumstances, truncate the drama. Should a champion bowler be restricted when a batsman is permitted to bat the whole innings? Craig McDermott or Shane Warne should not have to stop bowling just when they are tearing the heart out of a batting line-up (and entertaining the crowd). It seems unfair and even unnecessary that bowling excellence is often obliged to take a back seat to the production of runs.

It is possible that at some point officials will look at the number of players on the field, and even the number of overs bowled. Matches over 40-overs-per-side would be less like traditional cricket than the present 50 overs, but would still provide the big hitting and close finishes that are such an attraction to the fan. Mike Whitney is one prominent figure who has suggested that reducing the overs per side to 40 might improve the game, by getting rid of what he called 'that 10-over-or-so period when nothing much happens'. In some internationals there has been a tendency for the

ONE-DAY CRICKET: AN EYE FOR THE FUTURE

Inevitably, one-day international cricket has aroused much comment as to its future, its place in the sport and its impact on Test cricket. All the men we interviewed for this book have strong views on the game and the way it is played at present and the way it will be played in the future. Here is a sample of the opinions expressed.

'Australia is one of the most cosmopolitan countries in the world and 40 per cent of its population wouldn't know what cricket was all about. But a tremendous percentage of those people still come to what they called the pyjama game because it's fun. Not only fun but it has a longer period of excitement than any other game played on television – even football.' – **Bob Parish**

'I'm not as pessimistic about the future of Test cricket as a lot of people seem to be as there are more people watching Test cricket now than ever before. They're just not doing it at the ground – they're doing it via the television set. What Test cricket is becoming is basically a television sport. You only have to look at the TV ratings. The interest in Test cricket is still great but if you have a limited budget both financially and in time the majority of fans are going to take the one-day game over the Test match.

'I think Test cricket and one-day

middle stages of innings to become something of a stalemate, with the fielding captain happy to give away singles and the batting team content to take them.

It was revealed in June 1994 that the Australian Cricket Board was looking at introducing bonus points for teams that score quickly in the early overs of one-day innings in the interstate limited-overs competition in 1994-95. Such a concept may well come to the international stage as well. The Board is also keen to stage a 'sevens' competition, though this concept is as removed from one-day cricket as one-dayers from Test matches. The intention is to conduct such a tournament (involving teams of seven-a-side) in the north of Australia during the Australian winter. Such an event, with innings of as little as six overs (one from each player, bar the keeper), would feature all the stars, and be over in a weekend, or even a day. Such an event would be a natural for television. Already an annual six-a-side competition is staged annually in Hong Kong. 'It is in no way intended that cricket sevens would operate in opposition to existing cricket,' ACB Chairman Allan Crompton told the *Sydney Morning Herald*'s Philip Derriman during the '93-94 Australian season, 'but I do believe it has enormous potential.' Crompton saw such an exhibition as an ideal vehicle to introduce the game to Asian countries who at present know less than a little about the sport.

But for all the possible modifications, and the critics who refuse to believe the game's extraordinary popularity, the fact is limited-overs international cricket is an amazingly successful product. The rise of one-day cricket in the past 16 seasons, from the moment the lights were turned on at the SCG on November 28, 1978, to

cricket complement each other very well. Without one you haven't got the other. If they kill off Test cricket they'll have killed off one-day cricket because they won't be producing cricketers who can play it the way it's meant to be played.

'If one-day cricket becomes too predictable it will lose its attraction. I'd like to see captains being encouraged to be more positive, to try and take wickets, to keep fielders in attacking positions longer. If that means you have to do it by legislation then do it by legislation. We have the restrictions up to 15 overs now. I'd like to see that extended. There's not as much pressure on the batsmen when the field's back. They can get six an over. So why not keep attacking? If a bloke is good enough to keep whacking it back over the bowler's head or through mid-wicket then the bowlers aren't doing their job and you have to find some other bowlers who can do a better job. Then it becomes more of a contest, it becomes less predictable, you'll get scores climbing into the high 200s and the game will become even more attractive to the general public. – **Greg Chappell**

'People, particularly from the country areas, will continue to be more willing to bring their kids to see both sides bat and bowl on the one night and then go back home rather than watch four or five days of a Test match. They do that once or twice a year and the kids are happy ... everyone's happy.' – **Doug Walters**

Continued over page

the glitter of Allan Border's farewell season, has been one of the great phenomena of Australian sporting life. It has produced heroes and drama, glory and despair. And it has led to some of the most memorable and controversial moments in modern Australian sporting history. The cynics may wince every time the white ball goes up in the air, but at the same time the fans are cheering, and waving their flags and banners as one.

In December 1993, the ACB's chief executive, Graham Halbish, commented on the future of cricket in Australia. 'I feel it would be extremely risky for us, and quite wrong, to go through any summer without five or six Test matches,' Halbish said. 'Also I think it would be wrong to reduce the number of one-day internationals.

'Brisbane, Perth, Adelaide – there are only two there a year. People tend to look at the whole program and say: 'What an enormous amount of cricket.' But there are only two days of one-day internationals in those three cities. Hobart gets one. Melbourne and Sydney get three or four depending upon how we schedule the finals. This is not an enormous amount of cricket compared with Australian rules football, for example, or rugby league, over a full season.'

But what about the masses who watch the extensive coverage of cricket on television but don't go to the ground? Surely their perception is that there is too much international cricket in an Australian season.

Not so according to the Australian Cricket Board.

'The perception of those people,' commented Halbish, 'is that they can't get enough of it.'

AN EYE FOR THE FUTURE

Continued from previous page

'At Test matches in the 1990s slow play is tolerated more so than in the past. Back in our day slow cricket used to get the hand clap and the jeers. But the people that used to hand clap and jeer are no longer going to Test cricket. They're the ones at the one-day cricket who want action.' – **Keith Stackpole**

'One-day cricket is absolutely vital. The future of the game financially is more dependent on one-day cricket than Test cricket.

'It's a vital part of modern-day cricket. It's the promotional arm of the game. It's the game the general public has taken an enormous fancy to and obviously it's important to do well in it. I think it's good for the players, too, because they can show their flair and the drive – it gives them a great chance to be real entertainers.

'Test cricket will be threatened only if the players themselves lose their enthusiasm and skill for the five-day game. I think Test and one-day cricket will live comfortably together for many years.' – **Bob Simpson**

'I've come to grips with the amount of one-day cricket played. There was a period when I was a bit worried about killing the golden goose and maybe just overdoing it a bit as far as the players are concerned. It is hard to peak all the time, to keep bringing the team to a 100-per-cent level. That's why you'll see teams play well for a couple of weeks then go off the boil.

'As long as the program doesn't get any longer then I think it's okay because the international cricketers now have a more professional attitude. If they want to be professional, play full-time cricket and earn a good living then they have to give the time back into the sport.

'There is one area in which one-day cricket can be improved. We've seen some tremendous games played but in Australia our boundaries are very big, particularly at the MCG and SCG, and I wouldn't mind seeing those boundaries brought in. That would encourage more big hitting. You would get rewarded for a good strike, and guys would take on blokes on the fences and hit sixes or be caught out. It would generate higher scoring. We should never forget it's basically a game for entertainment. If you could change a game from 200 plays 201 to 240 plays 241 it has to be better for the game. Some of the games we played in South Africa were very good in that you could take on a bowler, particularly in the last 10 overs, and if you hit a ball in the air and hit it well you got six. Some of the blokes had days out where they scored 40 off 20 balls.' – **Allan Border**

'I like the mix (between Tests and one-dayers). People say we play too much cricket in Australia but it's not so much that we play too much cricket. It's the fact that Australia is a damn big country. You have to do so much travelling – that's what tends to knock you round. I don't agree with this stuff that we're playing too much cricket ... you could never play too much Test cricket because I love it so much. And I'm sure everyone appreciates the importance of the one-day game from the financial point of view.' – **Greg Matthews**

'I think there's a renewed enthusiasm for Test cricket, and there's an element of predictability about one-day cricket at the moment. Especially the volume of games we play here in Australia. People keep seeing the same thing. There's not much difference from game to game. They're going to have to put more innovations into the one-day game because a bad one-day game, and there are plenty of bad games floating around at the moment, is a hell of a lot worse than a bad game of Test cricket.' – **Tim May**

'I don't think for one second you should play so many one-day internationals that they become just like going to the office for another day. The secret for the administrators is to get the right balance so the players still feel enthusiastic about playing. I think that Australia's balance at present is pretty right with the triangular series.

'To me one of the most important things they have to try to do is come up with a decent white ball. Not just for one-day cricket because it would flow on to four-day cricket and probably eventually to five-day cricket. You can't get a ball that will last 50 overs at the moment. I can't believe we can do all the things we can do on this earth but we can't find a decent white cricket ball. If they do that then it opens up Sheffield Shield cricket under lights which eventually opens up Test cricket under lights.

'It doesn't matter what sort of cricket it is you're playing, I object to the thought of a new ball at each end. It's giving far too much advantage to the pace bowlers. Especially when we see now what Shane Warne can do in a one-day game – why would you not be doing everything in your power to encourage more teams to pick not only more spinners but leg-spinners as well?

'I detect a bit of an undercurrent about the team batting second under lights not having quite the same opportunity to win as the team batting in daylight. If it is felt that it is a problem, well I would have thought that competitions like the Mercantile Mutual Cup would be ideal to test out theories like having 25 overs of batting from one side and they retire, the other side has 25 overs and then you do the same thing again at night. There's only one way to find out whether it's any good or not and that's to try it.' – **Ian Chappell**

'I really haven't got many problems with the current program. I think there are lots of complaints, and the argument will still be going on until we've passed on and left the game, that there's too much one-day cricket and there's not enough Test cricket and they're not in the right spot. One-day cricket is now an integral part of international cricket and I think it's time people started accepting it as a code and the most popular cricketing code in the world.

'The foresight Kerry Packer showed in bringing one-day cricket to its optimum level for the entertainment sake of the game was a fantastic piece of thinking.

'People have to adjust their own minds and players have to adjust their own games because it's now an integral part of cricket and the sooner they come to grips with that the better.' – **Simon O'Donnell**

22

STATISTICS

Compiled By Ian Russell — As at August 1, 1994

1. AUSTRALIA IN INTERNATIONAL LIMITED-OVERS CRICKET

Game	Date	Venue	Australia	Opponent	Score	Result
1	Jan 5 1971	Melbourne	5-191	England	190*	Won by 5 wkts
2	Aug 24 1972	Manchester	8-222*	England	4-226	Lost by 6 wkts
3	Aug 26 1972	Lord's	5-240	England	9-236*	Won by 5 wkts
4	Aug 28 1972	Birmingham	9-179*	England	8-180	Lost by 2 wkts
5	Mar 30 1974	Dunedin	3-195	New Zealand	9-194*	Won by 7 wkts
6	Mar 31 1974	Christchurch	5-265*	New Zealand	6-234	Won by 31 runs
7	Jan 1 1975	Melbourne	190*	England	7-191	Lost by 3 wkts
8	Jun 7 1975	Leeds	7-278*	Pakistan	205	Won by 73 runs
9	Jun 11 1975	The Oval	5-328*	Sri Lanka	4-276	Won by 52 runs
10	Jun 14 1975	The Oval	192*	West Indies	3-195	Lost by 7 wkts
11	Jun 18 1975	Leeds	6-94	England	93*	Won by 4 wkts
12	Jun 21 1975	Lord's	274	West Indies	8-291*	Lost by 17 runs
13	Dec 20 1975	Adelaide	5-225	West Indies	224*	Won by 5 wkts
14	Jun 2 1977	Manchester	9-169*	England	8-173	Lost by 2 wkts
15	Jun 4 1977	Birmingham	70	England	171*	Lost by 99 runs
16	Jun 6 1977	The Oval	8-246	England	242*	Won by 2 wkts
17	Feb 22 1978	St John's	7-181	West Indies	9-313*	Lost on run-rate
18	Apr 12 1978	Castries	8-140	West Indies	139*	Won by 2 wkts
19	Jan 13 1979	Sydney	1-17*	England	-	No result
20	Jan 24 1979	Melbourne	101*	England	3-102	Lost by 7 wkts
21	Feb 4 1979	Melbourne	6-215	England	6-212*	Won by 4 wkts
22	Feb 7 1979	Melbourne	4-95	England	94*	Won by 6 wkts
23	Jun 9 1979	Lord's	9-159*	England	4-160	Lost by 6 wkts
24	Jun13/14 79	Nottingham	197	Pakistan	7-286*	Lost by 89 runs
25	Jun 16 1979	Birmingham	3-106	Canada	105*	Won by 7 wkts
26	Nov 27 1979	Sydney	5-196	West Indies	193*	Won by 5 wkts
27	Dec 8 1979	Melbourne	9-207*	England	7-209	Lost by 3 wkts
28	Dec 9 1979	Melbourne	8-191	West Indies	2-271*	Lost by 80 runs
29	Dec 11 1979	Sydney	192	England	7-264*	Lost by 72 runs
30	Dec 21 1979	Sydney	6-176*	West Indies	169	Won by 7 runs
31	Dec 26 1979	Sydney	6-194*	England	6-195	Lost by 4 wkts
32	Jan 14 1980	Sydney	163*	England	8-164	Lost by 2 wkts
33	Jan 18 1980	Sydney	190*	West Indies	181	Won by 9 runs
34	Aug 20 1980	The Oval	8-225	England	6-248*	Lost by 23 runs
35	Aug 22 1980	Birmingham	5-273	England	8-320*	Lost by 47 runs
36	Nov 23 1980	Adelaide	9-217*	New Zealand	7-219	Lost by 3 wkts
37	Nov 25 1980	Sydney	3-289*	New Zealand	195	Won by 94 runs
38	Dec 6 1980	Melbourne	142	India	9-208*	Lost by 66 runs
39	Dec 7 1980	Melbourne	6-159	New Zealand	156*	Won by 4 wkts
40	Dec 18 1980	Sydney	1-183	India	9-180*	Won by 9 wkts
41	Jan 8 1981	Sydney	1-64	India	63*	Won by 9 wkts
42	Jan 11 1981	Melbourne	3-193	India	5-192*	Won by 7 wkts
43	Jan 13 1981	Sydney	7-219	New Zealand	8-220*	Lost by 1 run
44	Jan 15 1981	Sydney	8-242*	India	8-215	Won by 27 runs
45	Jan 21 1981	Sydney	180*	New Zealand	1-23	No result

Game	Date	Venue	Australia	Opponent	Score	Result
46	Jan 29 1981	Sydney	155	New Zealand	6-233*	Lost by 78 runs
47	Jan 31 1981	Melbourne	3-130	New Zealand	126*	Won by 7 wkts
48	Feb 1 1981	Melbourne	4-235*	New Zealand	8-229	Won by 6 runs
49	Feb 3 1981	Sydney	4-218	New Zealand	8-215*	Won by 6 wkts
50	Jun 4 1981	Lord's	7-210*	England	4-212	Lost by 6 wkts
51	Jun 6 1981	Birmingham	8-249	England	247*	Won by 2 wkts
52	Jun 8 1981	Leeds	8-236*	England	165	Won by 71 runs
53	Nov 21 1981	Melbourne	9-209*	Pakistan	6-210	Lost by 4 wkts
54	Nov 24 1981	Sydney	3-237	West Indies	8-236*	Won by 7 wkts
55	Dec 6 1981	Adelaide	208*	Pakistan	8-170	Won by 38 runs
56	Dec 17 1981	Sydney	6-222*	Pakistan	4-223	Lost by 6 wkts
57	Dec 20 1981	Perth	9-188*	West Indies	2-190	Lost by 8 wkts
58	Jan 20 1982	Melbourne	193	Pakistan	6-218*	Lost by 25 runs
59	Jan 10 1982	Melbourne	146*	West Indies	5-147	Lost by 5 wkts
60	Jan 14 1982	Sydney	5-230*	Pakistan	9-154	Won by 76 runs
61	Jan 17 1982	Brisbane	9-185*	West Indies	5-186	Lost by 5 wkts
62	Jan 19 1982	Sydney	7-168	West Indies	189*	Won on run rate
63	Jan 23 1982	Melbourne	130	West Indies	8-216*	Lost by 86 runs
64	Jan 24 1982	Melbourne	107	West Indies	9-235*	Lost by 128 runs
65	Jan 26 1982	Sydney	8-214*	West Indies	168	Won by 46 runs
66	Jan 27 1982	Sydney	9-216	West Indies	6-234*	Lost by 18 runs
67	Feb 13 1982	Auckland	194	New Zealand	6-240*	Lost by 46 runs
68	Feb 17 1982	Dunedin	4-160	New Zealand	9-159*	Won by 6 wkts
69	Feb 9 1982	Wellington	2-75	New Zealand	74*	Won by 8 wkts
70	Sep 20 1982	Hyderabad	9-170	Pakistan	6-229*	Lost by 59 runs
71	Oct 8 1982	Lahore	4-206	Pakistan	3-234*	Lost by 28 runs
72	Oct 22 1982	Karachi	-	Pakistan	1-44*	No result
73	Jan 9 1983	Melbourne	2-182	New Zealand	181*	Won by 8 wkts
74	Jan 11 1983	Sydney	180*	England	149	Won by 31 runs
75	Jan 16 1983	Brisbane	3-184	England	182*	Won by 7 wkts
76	Jan 18 1983	Sydney	179	New Zealand	8-226*	Lost by 47 runs
77	Jan 22 1983	Melbourne	9-188	New Zealand	6-246*	Lost by 58 runs
78	Jan 23 1983	Melbourne	5-217	England	5-213*	Won by 5 wkts
79	Jan 26 1983	Sydney	109	England	207*	Won by 98 runs
80	Jan 30 1983	Adelaide	7-214	England	6-228*	Lost by 14 runs
81	Jan 31 1983	Adelaide	153	New Zealand	9-199*	Lost by 46 runs
82	Feb 6 1983	Perth	9-191*	New Zealand	164	Won by 27 runs
83	Feb 9 1983	Sydney	4-155	New Zealand	7-193*	Won by 6 wkts
84	Feb 13 1983	Melbourne	8-302*	New Zealand	153	Won by 149 runs
85	Mar 17 1983	Sydney	124	New Zealand	8-138*	Lost by 14 runs
86	Apr 13 1983	Colombo PSS	9-168*	Sri Lanka	8-169	Lost by 2 wkts
87	Apr 16 1983	Colombo PSS	5-207*	Sri Lanka	6-213	Lost by 4 wkts
88	Apr 20 1983	Colombo SSC	5-194*	Sri Lanka	-	No result
89	Apr 30 1983	Colombo SSC	3-124*	Sri Lanka	-	No result
90	Jun 9 1983	Nottingham	7-226	Zimbabwe	6-239*	Lost by 13 runs
91	Jun 11/12 83	Leeds	9-151	West Indies	9-252*	Lost by 101 runs
92	Jun 13 1983	Nottingham	9-320*	India	158	Won by 162 runs
93	Jun 16 1983	Southampton	7-272*	Zimbabwe	240	Won by 32 runs
94	Jun 18 1983	Lord's	6-273*	West Indies	3-276	Lost by 7 wkts
95	Jun 20 1983	Chelmsford	129	India	247*	Lost by 118 runs
96	Jan 8 1984	Melbourne	194	West Indies	7-221*	Lost by 27 runs
97	Jan 10 1984	Sydney	264*	Pakistan	9-230	Won by 34 runs
98	Jan 15 1984	Brisbane	0-15	Pakistan	6-184*	No result
99	Jan 17 1984	Sydney	9-195	West Indies	7-223*	Lost by 28 runs
100	Jan 21 1984	Melbourne	8-209*	Pakistan	166	Won by 45 runs
101	Jan 22 1984	Melbourne	226	West Indies	6-252*	Lost by 26 runs
102	Jan 25 1984	Sydney	8-244*	Pakistan	157	Won by 87 runs
103	Jan 29 1984	Adelaide	7-165*	West Indies	4-169	Lost by 6 wkt
104	Jan 30 1984	Adelaide	8-210*	Pakistan	140	Won by 70 runs
105	Feb 5 1984	Perth	8-211*	West Indies	197	Won by 14 runs
106	Feb 8 1984	Sydney	160*	West Indies	1-161	Lost by 9 wkts
107	Feb 11 1984	Melbourne	9-222	West Indies	5-222*	Tied
108	Feb 12 1984	Melbourne	8-212*	West Indies	4-213	Lost by 6 wkts
109	Feb 29 1984	Berbice	5-231*	West Indies	2-232	Lost by 8 wkts
110	Mar 14 1984	Port-of-Spain	6-194	West Indies	6-190*	Won by 4 wkts
111	Apr 19 1984	Castries	9-206*	West Indies	3-208	Lost by 7 wkts
112	Apr 26 1984	Kingston	7-209*	West Indies	1-211	Lost by 9 wkts

Game	Date	Venue	Australia	Opponent	Score	Result
113	Sep 28 1984	New Delhi	9-220*	India	172	Won by 48 runs
114	Oct 1 1984	Trivandrum	1-29	India	175*	No result
115	Oct 3 1984	Jamshedpur	-	India	2-21*	No result
116	Oct 5 1984	Ahmedabad	3-210	India	6-206*	Won by 7 wkts
117	Oct 6 1984	Indore	4-236	India	5-235*	Won by 6 wkts
118	Jan 6 1985	Melbourne	6-240*	West Indies	3-241	Lost by 7 wkts
119	Jan 8 1985	Sydney	4-240	Sri Lanka	7-239*	Won by 6 wkts
120	Jan 13 1985	Brisbane	191*	West Indies	5-195	Lost by 5 wkts
121	Jan 15 1985	Sydney	5-200*	West Indies	5-201	Lost by 5 wkts
122	Jan 19 1985	Melbourne	9-226*	Sri Lanka	6-230	Lost by 4 wkts
123	Jan 20 1985	Melbourne	9-206	West Indies	7-271*	Lost by 65 runs
124	Jan 23 1985	Sydney	7-242	Sri Lanka	6-240*	Won by 3 wkts
125	Jan 27 1985	Adelaide	9-200*	West Indies	4-201	Lost by 6 wkts
126	Jan 28 1985	Adelaide	2-323*	Sri Lanka	91	Won by 232 runs
127	Feb 3 1985	Perth	1-172	Sri Lanka	171*	Won by 9 wkts
128	Feb 6 1985	Sydney	6-247*	West Indies	221	Won by 26 runs
129	Feb 10 1985	Melbourne	3-271*	West Indies	6-273	Lost by 4 wkts
130	Feb 12 1985	Sydney	178*	West Indies	3-179	Lost by 7 wkts
131	Feb 17 1985	Melbourne	3-215	England	8-214*	Won by 7 wkts
132	Feb 24 1985	Melbourne	200	Pakistan	6-262*	Lost by 62 runs
133	Mar 3 1985	Melbourne	163*	India	2-165	Lost by 8 wkts
134	Mar 24 1985	Sharjah	8-178	England	8-177	Won by 2 wkts
135	Mar 29 1985	Sharjah	139*	India	7-140	Lost by 3 wkts
136	May 30 1985	Manchester	7-220	England	219*	Won by 3 wkts
137	Jun 1 1985	Birmingham	6-233	England	7-231*	Won by 4 wkts
138	Jun 3 1985	Lord's	5-254*	England	2-257	Lost by 8 wkts
139	Jan 9 1986	Melbourne	-	New Zealand	7-161*	No result
140	Jan 12 1986	Brisbane	6-164	India	161*	Won by 4 wkts
141	Jan 14 1986	Sydney	6-153	NewZealand	152*	Won by 4 wkts
142	Jan 16 1986	Melbourne	161*	India	2-162	Lost by 8 wkts
143	Jan 19 1986	Perth	6-161	New Zealand	6-159*	Won by 4 wkts
144	Jan 21 1986	Sydney	6-292*	India	4-192	Won by 100 runs
145	Jan 26 1986	Adelaide	8-262*	India	226	Won by 36 runs
146	Jan 27 1986	Adelaide	70	New Zealand	7-276*	Lost by 206 runs
147	Jan 29 1986	Sydney	7-239*	New Zealand	140	Won by 99 runs
148	Jan 31 1986	Melbourne	7-235*	India	4-238	Lost by 6 wkts
149	Feb 5 1986	Sydney	8-170*	India	159	Won by 11 runs
150	Feb 9 1986	Melbourne	3-188	India	187*	Won by 7 wkts
151	Mar 19 1986	Dunedin	156	New Zealand	6-186*	Lost by 30 runs
152	Mar 22 1986	Christchurch	205	New Zealand	7-258*	Lost by 53 runs
153	Mar 26 1986	Wellington	7-232	New Zealand	9-229*	Won by 3 wkts
154	Mar 29 1986	Auckland	231*	New Zealand	9-187	Won by 44 runs
155	Apr 11 1986	Sharjah	7-202*	Pakistan	2-206	Lost by 8 wkts
156	Sep 7 1986	Jaipur	3-250*	India	3-251	Lost by 7 wkts
157	Sep 9 1986	Srinagar	7-226	India	8-222*	Won by 3 wkts
158	Sep 24 1986	Hyderabad	6-242	India	1-41	No result
159	Oct 2 1986	New Delhi	6-238*	India	7-242	Lost by 3 wkts
160	Oct 5 1986	Ahmedabad	141	India	193*	Lost by 52 runs
161	Oct 7 1986	Rajkot	3-263	India	6-260*	Won by 7 wkts
162	Jan 1 1987	Perth	235	England	6-272*	Lost by 37 runs
163	Jan 2 1987	Perth	6-273*	Pakistan	9-274	Lost by 1 wkt
164	Jan 4 1987	Perth	91	West Indies	8-255*	Lost by164 runs
165	Jan 18 1987	Brisbane	4-261*	England	9-250	Won by 11 runs
166	Jan 20 1987	Melbourne	6-181*	West Indies	3-182	Lost by 7 wkts
167	Jan 22 1987	Sydney	8-233*	England	7-234	Lost by 3 wkts
168	Jan 25 1987	Adelaide	9-221	West Indies	5-237*	Lost by 16 runs
169	Jan 26 1987	Adelaide	6-225*	England	192	Won by 33 runs
170	Jan 28 1987	Sydney	194*	West Indies	158	Won by 36 runs
171	Feb 1 1987	Melbourne	5-248*	England	139	Won by 109 runs
172	Feb 6 1987	Sydney	8-195	West Indies	192*	Won by 2 wkts
173	Feb 8 1987	Melbourne	8-171*	England	4-172	Lost by 6 wkts
174	Feb 11 1987	Sydney	8-179	England	9-187*	Lost by 8 runs
175	Apr 3 1987	Sharjah	9-176*	Pakistan	4-180	Lost by 6 wkts
176	Apr 6 1987	Sharjah	6-176*	India	3-177	Lost by 7 wkts
177	Apr 9 1987	Sharjah	9-219	England	6-230*	Lost by 11 runs
178	Oct 9 1987	Madras	6-270*	India	269	Won by 1 run
179	Oct 13 1987	Madras	9-235*	Zimbabwe	139	Won by 96 runs

Game	Date	Venue	Australia	Opponent	Score	Result
180	Oct 19 1987	Indore	4-199*	New Zealand	9-196	Won by 3 runs
181	Oct 22 1987	New Delhi	233	India	6-289*	Lost by 56 runs
182	Oct 27 1987	Chandigarh	8-251*	New Zealand	234	Won by 17 runs
183	Oct 30 1987	Cuttack	5-266*	Zimbabwe	6-196	Won by 70 runs
184	Nov 4 1987	Lahore	8-267*	Pakistan	249	Won by 18 runs
185	Nov 8 1987	Calcutta	5-253*	England	8-246	Won by 7 runs
186	Jan 2 1988	Perth	7-249*	Sri Lanka	168	Won by 81 runs
187	Jan 3 1988	Perth	231	New Zealand	9-232*	Lost by 1 run
188	Jan 7 1988	Melbourne	216*	New Zealand	9-210	Won by 6 runs
189	Jan 10 1988	Adelaide	6-289*	Sri Lanka	8-208	Won by 81 runs
190	Jan 14 1988	Melbourne	8-243*	Sri Lanka	205	Won by 38 runs
191	Jan 17 1988	Brisbane	5-177	New Zealand	5-176*	Won by 5 wkts
192	Jan 19 1988	Sydney	7-189	Sri Lanka	9-188*	Won by 3 wkts
193	Jan 20 1988	Sydney	8-221*	New Zealand	143	Won by 78 runs
194	Jan 22 1988	Melbourne	2-180	New Zealand	177*	Won by 8 wkts
195	Jan 24 1988	Sydney	4-169	New Zealand	5-168*	Won by 6 wkts
196	Feb 4 1988	Melbourne	6-235*	England	8-213	Won by 22 runs
197	Oct 14 1988	Lahore	8-229*	Pakistan	7-229	Lost-less wkts
198	Dec 11 1988	Adelaide	1-178	Pakistan	177*	Won by 9 wkts
199	Dec 13 1988	Sydney	8-219	West Indies	220*	Lost by 1 run
200	Dec 15 1988	Melbourne	202	West Indies	236*	Lost by 34 runs
201	Jan 2 1989	Perth	178	Pakistan	7-216*	Lost by 38 runs
202	Jan 5 1989	Melbourne	226*	West Indies	8-218	Won by 8 runs
203	Jan 8 1989	Brisbane	5-204	Pakistan	9-203*	Won by 5 wkts
204	Jan 10 1989	Melbourne	4-258*	Pakistan	7-108	Won on run rate
205	Jan 12 1989	Sydney	5-215*	West Indies	8-154	Won by 61 runs
206	Jan 14 1989	Melbourne	9-204*	West Indies	9-202	Won by 2 runs
207	Jan 16 1989	Sydney	185	West Indies	9-277*	Lost by 92 runs
208	Jan 18 1989	Sydney	4-226*	West Indies	2-111	Lost on run rate
209	May 25 1989	Manchester	136	England	9-231*	Lost by 95 runs
210	May 27 1989	Nottingham	8-226	England	5-226*	Tied
211	May 29 1989	Lord's	4-279	England	7-278*	Won by 6 wkts
212	Oct 19 1989	Hyderabad	3-242*	England	3-243	Lost by 7 wkts
213	Oct 21 1989	Madras	6-241*	West Indies	142	Won by 99 runs
214	Oct 23 1989	Bombay	139	Pakistan	8-205*	Lost by 66 runs
215	Oct 25 1989	Goa	7-222*	Sri Lanka	194	Won by 28 runs
216	Oct 27 1989	Bangalore	8-247*	India	7-249	Lost by 3 wkts
217	Dec 26 1989	Melbourne	5-228*	Sri Lanka	198	Won by 30 runs
218	Dec 30 1989	Perth	1-204	Sri Lanka	9-203*	Won by 9 wkts
219	Jan 3 1990	Melbourne	3-162	Pakistan	161*	Won by 7 wkts
220	Jan 4 1990	Melbourne	7-202*	Sri Lanka	129	Won by 73 runs
221	Jan 11 1990	Brisbane	5-300*	Pakistan	233	Won by 67 runs
222	Feb 13 1990	Sydney	8-165*	Pakistan	5-167	Lost by 5 wkts
223	Feb 18 1990	Adelaide	3-159	Sri Lanka	158*	Won by 7 wkts
224	Feb 20 1990	Sydney	9-218	Pakistan	8-220*	Lost by 2 runs
225	Feb 23 1990	Melbourne	3-163	Pakistan	162*	Won by 7 wkts
226	Feb 25 1990	Sydney	6-255*	Pakistan	186	Won by 69 runs
227	Mar 3 1990	Christchurch	9-187*	India	169	Won by 18 runs
228	Mar 4 1990	Christchurch	8-244*	New Zealand	94	Won by 150 runs
229	Mar 8 1990	Hamilton	3-212	India	8-211*	Won by 7 wkts
230	Mar 10 1990	Auckland	6-239*	New Zealand	2-167	Won by run rate
231	Mar 11 1990	Auckland	2-164	New Zealand	162*	Won by 8 wkts
232	Apr 26 1990	Sharjah	5-258*	New Zealand	7-195	Won by 63 runs
233	Apr 30 1990	Sharjah	3-140	Bangladesh	8-134*	Won by 7 wkts
234	May 2 1990	Sharjah	3-332*	Sri Lanka	218	Won by 114 runs
235	May 4 1990	Sharjah	230	Pakistan	7-266*	Lost by 36 runs
236	Nov 29 1990	Sydney	9-236*	New Zealand	7-174	Won by 61 runs
237	Dec 2 1990	Adelaide	4-210	New Zealand	7-208*	Won by 6 wkts
238	Dec 9 1990	Perth	4-193	England	9-192*	Won by 6 wkts
239	Dec 11 1990	Melbourne	7-263*	New Zealand	8-224	Won by 39 runs
240	Dec 16 1990	Brisbane	5-283*	England	7-246	Won by 37 runs
241	Dec18 1990	Hobart	193	New Zealand	6-194*	Lost by 1 run
242	Jan 1 1991	Sydney	7-221*	England	153	Won by 68 runs
243	Jan 10 1991	Melbourne	6-222*	England	9-219	Won by 3 runs
244	Jan 13 1991	Sydney	4-202	New Zealand	7-199*	Won by 6 wkts
245	Jan 15 1991	Melbourne	3-209	New Zealand	6-208*	Won by 7 wkts
246	Feb 26 1991	Kingston	4-244*	West Indies	209	Won by 35 runs

Game	Date	Venue	Australia	Opponent	Score	Result
247	Mar 9 1991	Port-of-Spain	9-172*	West Indies	127	Won by 45 runs
248	Mar 10 1991	Port-of-Spain	7-245*	West Indies	3-181	Lost on run rate
249	Mar 13 1991	Bridgetown	6-283*	West Indies	246	Won by 46 runs
250	Mar 20 1991	Georgetown	4-252	West Indies	251*	Won by 6 wkts
251	Dec 8 1991	Perth	101	India	7-208*	Lost by 107 runs
252	Dec 10 1991	Hobart	2-176	India	8-175*	Won by 8 wkts
253	Dec 12 1991	Melbourne	9-173*	West Indies	164	Won by 9 runs
254	Dec 15 1991	Adelaide	4-158	India	157*	Won by 6 wkts
255	Dec 18 1991	Sydney	6-234*	West Indies	183	Won by 51 runs
256	Jan 9 1992	Melbourne	-	West Indies	7-160*	No Result
257	Jan 12 1992	Brisbane	203	West Indies	215*	Lost by 12 runs
258	Jan 14 1992	Sydney	1-177	India	175*	Won by 9 wkts
259	Jan 18 1992	Melbourne	5-233*	India	145	Won by 88 runs
260	Jan 20 1992	Sydney	9-208*	India	7-202	Won by 6 runs
261	Feb 22 1992	Auckland	211	New Zealand	6-248*	Lost by 37 runs
262	Feb 26 1992	Sydney	9-170*	South Africa	1-171	Lost by 9 wkts
263	Mar 1 1992	Brisbane	9-237*	India	234	Won by 1 run
264	Mar 5 1992	Sydney	171*	England	2-173	Lost by 8 wkts
265	Mar 7 1992	Adelaide	3-190	Sri Lanka	9-189*	Won by 7 wkts
266	Mar 11 1992	Perth	172	Pakistan	9-220*	Lost by 48 runs
267	Mar 14 1992	Hobart	6-265*	Zimbabwe	137	Won by 128 runs
268	Mar 18 1992	Melbourne	6-216*	West Indies	159	Won by 57 runs
269	Aug 15 1992	Colombo PSS	5-247*	Sri Lanka	6-251	Lost by 4 wkts
270	Sep 4 1992	Colombo Khett	7-216*	Sri Lanka	5-194	Lost on run rate
271	Sep 5 1992	Colombo Khett	5-208	Sri Lanka	6-207*	Won by 5 wkts
272	Dec 6 1992	Perth	7-160*	West Indies	1-164	Lost by 9 wkts
273	Dec 8 1992	Sydney	9-101*	West Indies	87	Won by 14 runs
274	Dec 10 1992	Hobart	7-228*	Pakistan	9-228	Tied
275	Dec 13 1992	Adelaide	2-196	Pakistan	6-195*	Won by 8 wkts
276	Dec 15 1992	Melbourne	8-198*	West Indies	194	Won by 4 runs
277	Jan 10 1993	Brisbane	190	West Indies	9-197*	Lost by 7 runs
278	Jan 12 1993	Melbourne	6-212*	Pakistan	7-180	Won by 32 runs
279	Jan 14 1993	Sydney	8-260*	Pakistan	6-237	Won by 23 runs
280	Jan 16 1993	Sydney	214	West Indies	8-239*	Lost by 25 runs
281	Jan 18 1993	Melbourne	147*	West Indies	6-148	Lost by 4 wkts
282	Mar 19 1993	Dunedin	4-258*	New Zealand	129	Won by 129 runs
283	Mar 21/22 '93	Christchurch	9-197	New Zealand	8-196*	Won by 1 wkt
284	Mar 24 1993	Wellington	126	New Zealand	214*	Lost by 88 runs
285	Mar 27 1993	Hamilton	7-247	New Zealand	7-250*	Lost by 3 wkts
286	Mar 28 1993	Auckland	8-232*	New Zealand	8-229	Won by 3 runs
287	May 19 1993	Manchester	9-258*	England	254	Won by 4 runs
288	May 21 1993	Birmingham	4-280	England	5-277*	Won by 6 wkts
289	May 23 1993	Lord's	5-230*	England	211	Won by 19 runs
290	Dec 9 1993	Melbourne	189*	South Africa	3-190	Lost by 7 wkts
291	Dec 12 1993	Adelaide	2-136	New Zealand	135*	Won by 8 wkts
292	Dec 14 1993	Sydney	9-172*	South Africa	69	Won by 103 runs
293	Dec 16 1993	Melbourne	5-202*	New Zealand	9-199	Won by 3 runs
294	Jan 8 1994	Brisbane	9-230*	South Africa	182	Won by 48 runs
295	Jan 11 1994	Sydney	185	New Zealand	9-198*	Lost by 13 runs
296	Jan 16 1994	Perth	126	South Africa	7-208*	Lost by 82 runs
297	Jan 19 1994	Melbourne	3-217*	New Zealand	166	Won by 51 runs
298	Jan 21 1994	Melbourne	202	South Africa	5-230*	Lost by 28 runs
299	Jan 23 1994	Sydney	6-247*	South Africa	178	Won by 69 runs
300	Jan 25 1994	Sydney	8-223*	South Africa	9-188	Won by 35 runs
301	Feb 19 1994	Johannesburg	5-227	South Africa	3-232*	Lost by 5 runs
302	Feb 20 1994	Pretoria	209	South Africa	5-265*	Lost by 56 runs
303	Feb 22 1994	Port Elizabeth	6-281*	South Africa	193	Won by 88 runs
304	Feb 24 1994	Durban	154*	South Africa	3-157	Lost by 7 wkts
305	Apr 2 1994	East London	3-159	South Africa	158*	Won by 7 wkts
306	Apr 4 1994	Port Elizabeth	201	South Africa	6-227*	Lost by 26 runs
307	Apr 6 1994	Cape Town	6-242*	South Africa	5-206	Won by 36 runs
308	Apr 8 1994	Bloemfontein	6-203*	South Africa	8-202	Won by 1 run
309	Apr 14 1994	Sharjah	1-158	Sri Lanka	154*	Won by 9 wkts
310	Apr 16 1994	Sharjah	3-208*	New Zealand	9-206	Won by 7 wkts
311	Apr 19 1994	Sharjah	9-244*	India	3-245	Lost by 7 wkts

Denotes batted first

Australia's Performances

Opponent	First match	Matches	Won	Lost	NR	Tie	Win %
England	1970-71	55	28	25	1	1	51.8
New Zealand	1973-74	60	41	17	2	-	70.6
Pakistan	1975	38	18	17	2	1	50
Sri Lanka	1975	25	18	5	2	-	78.2
West Indies	1975	69	26	41	1	1	38.2
Canada	1979	1	1	-	-	-	100
India	1980-81	41	24	14	3	-	63.1
Zimbabwe	1983	5	4	1	-	-	80
Bangladesh	1989-90	1	1	-	-	-	100
South Africa	1992	16	8	8	-	-	50
TOTALS		311	169	128	11	3	56.33

Note: NR indicates no result. Win % indicates win/result percentage.

On Australian Grounds

	First match	Matches	Won	Lost	NR	Tie	Win %
Melbourne	1970-71	66	35	28	2	1	54.6
Adelaide	1975-76	21	14	7	-	-	66.6
Sydney	1978-79	68	41	25	2	-	62.1
Brisbane	1979-80	14	9	4	1	-	69.2
Perth	1980-81	17	7	10	-	-	41.1
Hobart	1990-91	4	2	1	-	1	50
TOTALS		190	108	75	5	2	58.37

Overseas

Venue	First match	Matches	Won	Lost	NR	Tie	Win %
England	1972	34	16	17	-	1	48.4
New Zealand	1973-74	20	14	6	-	-	70
West Indies	1978	11	6	5	-	-	54.5
Pakistan	1982	5	1	3	1	-	25
Sri Lanka	1983	7	1	4	2	-	20
India	1984	23	13	7	3	-	65
Sharjah	1985	13	6	7	-	-	46.1
South Africa	1993-94	8	4	4	-	-	50
TOTALS		121	61	53	6	1	53.04

Most Wins in Succession

No.	Seasons	Opponents
10	1989-90 - 1990	New Zealand (4), Pakistan (2), India (2), Bangladesh, Sri Lanka.
9	1987-88	New Zealand (5), Sri Lanka (3), England.

Note: Between February 23, 1990, and March 9, 1991, Australia won 21 and lost two of 23 matches. One of these losses was by 1 run.

Most Losses in Succession

No.	Season	Opponents
5	1986-87	England (3), Pakistan, India

Note: In seven matches in 1982-83 and 1983, Australia's result sequence was: lost, lost, lost, no result, no result, lost, lost.

Margins of Victory - Largest Wins

Margin	Australia	Opponent	Score	Venue	Season
232 runs	2-323	Sri Lanka	91	Adelaide	1984-85
162 runs	9-320	India	158	Nottingham	1983
150 runs	8-244	New Zealand	94	Christchurch	1989-90

Note: Australia has won by nine wickets on seven occasions - against Sri Lanka (3), India (3) and Pakistan once.

Margins of Victory - Worst Losses

Margin	Australia	Opponent	Score	Venue	Season
206 runs	70	New Zealand	7-276	Adelaide	1985-86
164 runs	91	West Indies	8-255	Perth	1986-87

Note: Australia has lost by nine wickets on four occasions - against the West Indies (3) and South Africa once.

Margins of Victory - Closest Win

Margin	Australia	Opponent	Score	Venue	Season
1 run	6-270	India	269	Madras	1987
1 run	9-237	India*	234	Brisbane	1992
1 run	6-203	South Africa	8-202	Bloemfontein	1993-94
1 wicket	9-197	New Zealand	8-196	Christchurch	1992-93

* match rain affected

Margins of Victory - Closest Loss

Margin	Australia	Opponent	Score	Venue	Season
1 wicket	6-273	Pakistan	9-274	Perth	1986-87

Note: Australia has lost by 1 run on four occasions: v New Zealand (3), v West Indies.

Ties

Australia	Opponent	Score	Venue	Season
9-222	West Indies	5-222	Melbourne	1983-84
8-226	England	5-226	Nottingham	1989
7-228	Pakistan	9-228	Hobart	1992-93

Note: Pakistan (7-229) defeated Australia (8-229) by losing fewer wickets under the rules controlling the match at Lahore in 1988.

Highest Totals - For

Score		Opponent	Venue	Season
3-332		Sri Lanka	Sharjah	1989-90
5-328	(60 overs)	Sri Lanka	The Oval	1975
3-323		Sri Lanka	Adelaide	1984-85
9-320	(60 overs)	India	Nottingham	1983
8-302		New Zealand	Melbourne	1982-83
5-300		Pakistan	Brisbane	1989-90

Notes:
1. Australia's highest totals against other major countries:

v England	*5-283*	*Brisbane*	*1990-91*
v West Indies	*6-283*	*Bridgetown*	*1990-91*
v South Africa	*6-281*	*Port Elizabeth*	*1993-94*

2. Australia's highest totals batting second:

4-280	*(53.3 overs)*	*v England*	*Birmingham*	*1993*
4-279	*(54.3 overs)*	*v England*	*Lord's*	*1989*
274	*(58.4 overs)*	*v West Indies*	*Lord's*	*1975*
5-273	*(55 overs)*	*v England*	*Birmingham*	*1980*

(all innings of 50 six-ball overs duration unless otherwise stated.)

Highest Totals - Against

Score		By	Venue	Season
8-320	(55 overs)	England	Birmingham	1980
9-313	(50 overs)	West Indies	St John's	1978
8-291	(60 overs)	West Indies	Lord's	1975
6-289	(50 overs)	India	New Delhi	1987

Note: the highest score against Australia in Australia is:

9-277	*(50 overs) by West Indies*	*Sydney*	*1988-89*

Lowest Totals (completed innings) - For

Score		Opponent	Venue	Season
70	(25.2 overs)	England	Birmingham	1977
70	(26.3 overs)	New Zealand	Adelaide	1985-86
91	(35.4 overs)	West Indies	Perth	1986-87
101	(33.5 overs*)	England	Melbourne	1978-79
101	(37.5 overs)	India	Perth	1991-92

* indicates eight-ball overs
Notes:
1. In a rain-affected match reduced to 30 overs, Australia scored 9-101 and dismissed West Indies for 87 (29.3 overs) at Sydney 1992-93. This remains Australia's lowest score, batting first and winning.

2. Lowest totals against other major countries:

v Pakistan	*139*	*(43.2 overs)*	*Bombay*	*1989-90*
v South Africa	*126*	*(41 overs)*	*Perth*	*1993-94*
v Sri Lanka	*9-168*	*(45 overs)*	*Colombo PSS*	*1983*

Lowest Totals (completed innings) - Against

Score		By	Venue	Season
63	(25.5 overs)	India	Sydney	1980-81
69	(28 overs)	South Africa	Sydney	1993-94
74	(29 overs)	New Zealand	Wellington	1981-82

Highest Match Aggregates

Runs	Wickets	Overs	Opponent	Venue	Season
604	9	120	Sri Lanka	The Oval	1975
593	13	110	England	Birmingham	1980
565	18	118.4	West Indies	Lord's	1975
557	11	109.3	England	Lord's	1989
557	9	108.3	England	Birmingham	1993

Notes:
1. The highest match aggregate in Australia is:

533	*15*	*89.1*	*Pakistan*	*Brisbane*	*1989-90*

2. The highest aggregate in a match restricted to 50 overs per side involving Australia is:

550	*13*	*95.4*	*Sri Lanka*	*Sharjah*	*1989-90*

Lowest Match Aggregates (completed matches)

Runs	Wickets	Overs	Opponent	Venue	Season
127	11	46.5	India	Sydney	1980-81
149	12	49.3	New Zealand	Wellington	1981-82

2. AUSTRALIAN PLAYERS' CAREER AVERAGES

Batting and Fielding

Name	M	I	NO	Runs	HS	Avge	100	50	C	S
Alderman T.M.	65	18	6	32	9*	2.66	-	-	29	-
Beard G.R.	2	-	-	-	-	-	-	-	-	-
Bennett M.J.	8	4	1	9	6*	3.00	-	-	1	-
Bevan M.G.	3	2	1	64	39*	64.00	-	-	2	-
Bishop G.A.	2	2	-	13	7	6.50	-	-	1	-
Boon D.C.	162	158	11	5243	122	35.66	5	33	39	-
Border A.R.	273	252	39	6524	127*	30.62	3	39	127	-
Bright R.J.	11	8	4	66	19*	16.50	-	-	2	-
Callen I.W.	5	3	2	6	3*	6.00	-	-	2	-
Campbell G.D.	12	3	1	6	4*	3.00	-	-	4	-
Carlson P.H.	4	2	-	11	11	5.50	-	-	-	-
Chappell G.S.	74	72	14	2331	138*	40.18	3	14	23	-
Chappell I.M.	16	16	2	673	86	48.07	-	8	5	-
Chappell T.M.	20	13	-	229	110	17.61	1	-	8	-
Clark W.M.	2	-	-	-	-	-	-	-	-	-
Colley D.J.	1	-	-	-	-	-	-	-	-	-
Connolly A.N.	1	-	-	-	-	-	-	-	-	-
Cosier G.J.	9	7	2	154	84	30.80	-	1	4	-
Darling W.M.	18	18	1	363	74	21.35	-	1	6	-
Davis I.C.	3	3	1	12	11*	6.00	-	-	-	-
Davis S.P.	39	11	7	20	6	5.00	-	-	5	-
Dodemaide A.I.C.	24	16	7	124	30	13.77	-	-	7	-
Dyer G.C.	23	13	2	174	45*	15.81	-	-	24	4
Dymock G.	15	7	4	35	14*	11.66	-	-	1	-
Dyson J.	29	27	4	755	79	32.82	-	4	12	-
Edwards R.	9	8	1	255	80*	36.42	-	3	-	-
Edwards W.J.	1	1	-	2	2	2.00	-	-	-	-
Fleming D.W.	6	2	1	4	2*	4.00	-	-	1	-
Gilbert D.R.	14	8	3	39	8	7.80	-	-	3	-
Gilmour G.J.	5	2	1	42	28*	42.00	-	-	2	-
Graf S.F.	11	6	-	24	8	4.00	-	-	1	-
Hammond J.R.	1	1	1	15	15*	-	-	-	-	-
Hayden M.L.	13	12	1	286	67	26.00	-	2	4	-
Healy I.A.	109	73	24	989	50*	20.18	-	1	127	19
Hilditch A.M.J.	8	8	-	226	72	28.25	-	1	1	-
Hogan T.G.	16	12	4	72	27	9.00	-	-	10	-
Hogg R.M.	71	35	20	137	22	9.13	-	-	8	-
Holland R.G.	2	-	-	-	-	-	-	-	-	-
Hookes D.W.	39	36	2	826	76	24.29	-	5	11	-

Name	M	I	NO	Runs	HS	Avge	100	50	C	S
Hughes K.J.	97	88	6	1968	98	24.00	-	17	27	-
Hughes M.G.	20	9	4	37	13	7.40	-	-	4	-
Hurst A.G.	8	4	4	7	3*	-	-	-	1	-
Jenner T.J.	1	1	-	12	12	12.00	-	-	-	-
Jones D.M.	164	161	25	6068	145	44.61	7	46	54	-
Julian B.P.	1	-	-	-	-	-	-	-	-	-
Kent M.F.	5	5	1	78	33	19.50	-	-	4	-
Kerr R.B.	4	4	1	97	87*	32.33	-	1	1	-
Laird B.M.	23	23	3	594	117*	29.70	1	2	5	-
Langer J.L.	3	2	1	56	36	56.00	-	-	1	1
Laughlin T.J.	6	5	1	105	74	26.25	-	1	-	-
Lawry W.M.	1	1	-	27	27	27.00	-	-	1	-
Lawson G.F.	79	52	18	378	33*	11.11	-	-	18	-
Lillee D.K.	63	34	8	240	42*	9.23	-	-	10	-
Maclean J.A.	2	1	-	11	11	11.00	-	-	-	-
MacLeay K.H.	16	13	2	139	41	12.63	-	-	2	-
Maguire J.N.	23	11	5	42	14*	7.00	-	-	2	-
Mallett A.A.	9	3	1	14	8	7.00	-	-	4	-
Malone M.F.	10	7	3	36	15*	9.00	-	-	1	-
Marsh G.R.	117	115	6	4357	126*	39.97	9	22	31	-
Marsh R.W.	92	76	15	1225	66	20.08	-	4	120	4
Martyn D.R.	11	10	1	166	51*	18.44	-	1	6	-
Massie R.A.L.	3	1	1	16	16*	-	-	-	1	-
Matthews G.R.J.	59	50	13	620	54	16.75	-	1	23	-
May T.B.A.	34	10	6	35	15	8.75	-	-	1	-
McCosker R.B.	14	14	-	320	95	22.85	-	2	3	-
McCurdy R.J.	11	6	2	33	13*	8.25	-	-	1	-
McDermott C.J.	116	72	15	415	37	7.28	-	-	25	-
McGrath G.D.	18	8	4	13	5*	3.25	-	-	1	-
McKenzie G.D.	1	-	-	-	-	-	-	-	1	-
Moody T.M.	34	32	3	751	89	25.89	-	7	10	-
Moss J.K.	1	1	-	7	7	7.00	-	-	2	-
O'Donnell S.P.	87	64	15	1242	74*	25.34	-	9	22	-
O'Keeffe K.J.	2	2	1	16	16*	16.00	-	-	-	-
Pascoe L.S.	29	11	7	39	15*	9.75	-	-	6	-
Phillips W.B.	48	41	6	852	75*	24.34	-	6	41	7
Porter G.D.	2	1	-	3	3	3.00	-	-	1	-
Rackemann C.G.	52	18	6	34	9*	2.83	-	-	6	-
Redpath I.R.	5	5	-	46	24	9.20	-	-	2	-
Reid B.A.	61	21	8	49	10	3.76	-	-	6	-
Reiffel P.R.	40	25	13	237	58	19.75	-	1	14	-
Ritchie G.M.	44	42	7	959	84	27.40	-	6	9	-
Rixon S.J.	6	6	3	40	20*	13.33	-	-	9	2
Robinson R.D.	2	2	-	82	70	41.00	-	1	3	1
Serjeant C.S.	3	3	-	73	46	24.33	-	-	1	-
Sheahan A.P.	3	3	-	75	50	25.00	-	1	-	-
Siddons J.D.	1	1	-	32	32	32.00	-	-	-	-
Simpson R.B.	2	2	-	36	23	18.00	-	-	4	-
Slater M.J.	9	9	-	188	73	20.88	-	1	-	-
Smith S.B.	28	24	2	861	117	39.13	2	8	8	-
Stackpole K.R.	6	6	-	224	61	37.33	-	3	1	-
Taylor M.A.	57	55	1	1740	94	32.22	-	16	28	-
Taylor P.L.	83	47	25	437	54*	19.86	-	1	34	-
Thomson A.L.	1	-	-	-	-	-	-	-	-	-
Thomson J.R.	50	30	6	181	21	7.54	-	-	9	-
Toohey P.M.	5	4	2	105	54*	52.50	-	1	-	-
Trimble G.S.	2	2	1	4	4	4.00	-	-	-	-
Turner A.	6	6	-	247	101	41.16	1	-	3	-
Veletta M.R.J.	20	19	4	484	68*	32.26	-	2	8	-
Walker M.H.N.	17	11	3	79	20	9.87	-	-	6	-
Walters K.D.	28	24	6	513	59	28.50	-	2	10	-
Warne S.K.	22	11	1	108	55	10.80	-	1	8	-
Watson G.D.	2	2	1	11	11*	11.00	-	-	-	-
Waugh M.E.	75	71	5	2169	113	32.86	3	16	36	-
Waugh S.R.	167	147	36	3421	86	30.81	-	16	57	-
Wellham D.M.	17	17	2	379	97	25.26	-	1	8	-

Name	M	I	NO	Runs	HS	Avge	100	50	C	S
Wessels K.C.	54	51	3	1740	107	36.25	1	14	19	-
Whatmore D.F.	1	1	-	2	2	2.00	-	-	-	-
Whitney M.R.	38	13	7	40	9*	6.66	-	-	11	-
Wiener J.M.	7	7	-	140	50	20.00	-	1	2	-
Wood G.M.	83	77	11	2219	114*	33.62	3	11	17	-
Woodcock A.J.	1	1	-	53	53	53.00	-	1	-	-
Woolley R.D.	4	3	2	31	16	31.00	-	-	1	1
Wright K.J.	5	2	-	29	23	14.50	-	-	8	-
Yallop G.N.	30	27	6	823	66*	39.19	-	7	5	-
Yardley B.	7	4	-	58	28	14.50	-	-	1	-
Zesers A.K.	2	2	2	10	8*	-	-	-	1	-
Zoehrer T.J.	22	15	3	130	50	10.83	-	1	21	2

Bowling

Name	Balls	Mdns	Runs	Wkts	Avge	4wk	Best	RPO
Alderman T.M.	3371	75	2056	88	23.36	3	5-17	3.65
Beard G.R.	112	3	70	4	17.50	-	2-20	3.75
Bennett M.J.	408	6	275	4	68.75	-	2-27	4.04
Boon D.C.	28	-	41	-	-	-	0-5	8.78
Border A.R.	2661	11	2071	73	28.36	-	3-20	4.66
Bright R.J.	462	3	350	3	116.66	-	1-28	4.54
Callen I.W.	180	2	148	5	29.60	-	3-24	4.93
Campbell G.D.	613	9	404	18	22.44	-	3-17	3.95
Carlson P.H.	168	3	70	2	35.00	-	1-21	2.50
Chappell G.S.	3108	41	2096	72	29.11	2	5-15	4.04
Chappell I.M.	42	1	23	2	11.50	-	2-14	3.28
Chappell T.M.	736	4	538	19	2931	-	3-31	4.38
Clark W.M.	100	3	61	3	20.33	-	2-39	3.66
Colley D.J.	66	1	72	-	-	-	0-72	6.54
Connolly A.N.	64	-	62	-	-	-	0-62	5.81
Cosier G.J.	409	9	248	14	17.71	1	5-18	3.63
Davis S.P.	2016	46	1135	44	25.79	-	3-10	3.37
Dodemaide A.I.C.	1327	30	753	36	20.91	2	5-21	3.29
Dymock G.	806	16	412	15	27.46	-	2-21	3.06
Edwards W.J.	1	-	-	-	-	-	0-0	0.00
Fleming D.W.	331	5	215	7	30.71	1	4-39	3.89
Gilbert D.R.	684	3	552	18	30.66	1	5-46	4.84
Gilmour G.J.	320	9	165	16	10.31	2	6-14	3.09
Graf S.F.	522	4	345	8	43.12	-	2-23	3.96
Hammond J.R.	54	1	41	1	41.00	-	1-41	4.55
Hogan T.G.	917	12	574	23	24.95	1	4-33	3.75
Hogg R.M.	3677	56	2418	85	28.44	5	4-29	3.94
Holland R.G.	126	2	99	2	49.50	-	2-49	4.71
Hookes D.W.	29	-	28	1	28.00	-	1-2	5.79
Hughes K.J.	1	-	4	-	-	-	0-4	24.00
Hughes M.G.	1639	22	1115	38	29.34	1	4-44	4.08
Hurst A.G.	402	11	203	12	16.91	1	5-21	3.02
Jenner T.J.	64	1	28	-	-	-	0-28	2.62
Jones D.M.	106	-	81	3	27.00	-	2-34	4.58
Julian B.P.	66	1	50	3	16.67	-	3-50	4.55
Laughlin T.J.	308	3	224	8	28.00	-	3-54	4.36
Lawson G.F.	4259	94	2592	88	29.45	1	4-26	3.65
Lillee D.K.	3593	80	2145	103	20.82	6	5-34	3.58
MacLeay K.H.	857	8	626	15	41.73	1	6-39	4.38
Maguire J.N.	1009	12	769	19	40.47	-	3-61	4.57
Mallett A.A.	502	7	341	11	31.00	-	3-34	4.07
Malone M.F.	612	16	315	11	28.63	-	2-9	3.08
Marsh G.R.	6	-	4	-	-	-	0-4	4.00
Massie R.A.L.	183	5	129	3	43.00	-	2-25	4.22
Matthews G.R.J.	2808	21	2004	57	35.15	-	3-27	4.27
May T.B.A.	1820	6	1272	25	50.88	-	3-51	4.19
McCurdy R.J.	515	8	375	12	31.25	-	3-19	4.36
McDermott C.J.	6300	38	4258	171	24.90	5	5-44	4.05
McGrath G.D.	977	19	605	22	27.50	2	4-24	3.71
McKenzie G.D.	60	-	22	2	11.00	-	2-22	2.20
Moody T.M.	894	4	651	16	40.68	-	3-56	4.76

	Balls	Mdns	Runs	Wkts	Avge	4wk	Best	RPO
O'Donnell S.P.	4350	49	3102	108	28.72	5	5-13	4.30
O'Keeffe K.J.	132	3	79	2	39.50	-	1-36	3.59
Pascoe L.S.	1568	21	1066	53	20.11	5	5-30	4.07
Porter G.D.	108	5	33	3	11.00	-	2-13	1.83
Rackemann C.G.	2791	51	1833	82	22.35	4	5-16	3.90
Reid B.A.	3250	53	2203	63	34.96	1	5-53	4.27
Reiffel P.R.	2117	38	1282	48	26.70	1	4-13	3.63
Simpson R.B.	102	-	95	2	47.50	-	2-30	5.58
Smith S.B.	7	-	5	-	-	-	0-1	4.28
Stackpole K.R.	77	-	54	3	18.00	-	3-40	4.20
Taylor P.L.	3937	32	2740	97	28.24	1	4-38	4.27
Thomson A.L.	64	2	22	1	22.00	-	1-22	2.06
Thomson J.R.	2696	37	1942	55	35.30	1	4-67	4.32
Trimble G.S.	24	-	32	-	-	-	0-32	8.00
Walker M.H.N.	1006	24	546	20	27.30	1	4-19	3.25
Walters K.D.	314	3	273	4	68.25	-	2-24	5.21
Warne S.K.	1188	9	738	44	16.77	4	4-19	3.72
Watson G.D.	48	1	28	2	14.00	-	2-28	3.50
Waugh M.E.	1302	3	1048	40	26.20	1	5-24	4.82
Waugh S.R.	6831	44	5066	152	33.32	2	4-33	4.44
Wessels K.C.	737	2	655	18	36.38	-	2-16	5.33
Whitney M.R.	2106	42	1249	46	27.15	1	4-34	4.31
Wiener J.M.	24	-	34	-	-	-	0-16	8.50
Yallop G.N.	138	-	119	3	39.66	-	3-28	5.17
Yardley B.	198	5	130	7	18.57	-	3-28	3.93
Zesers A.K.	90	1	74	1	74.00	-	1-37	4.93

Notes:
1. RPO indicates Runs Per Over, and is calculated on six-ball overs.
2. In total, 117 cricketers have appeared for Australia in one-day international cricket.

3. BATTING

Most Runs

Runs		M	Inn	No	HS	100	50	Avge
6524	A.R. Border	273	252	39	127*	3	39	30.62
6068	D.M. Jones	164	161	25	145	7	46	44.61
5243	D.C. Boon	162	158	11	122	5	33	35.66
4357	G.R. Marsh	117	115	6	126*	9	2	39.97
3421	S.R. Waugh	167	147	36	86	-	16	30.81
2331	G.S. Chappell	74	72	14	138*	3	14	40.18
2219	G.M. Wood	83	77	11	114*	3	11	33.62
2169	M.E. Waugh	75	71	5	113	3	16	32.86
1968	K.J. Hughes	97	88	6	98	-	17	24
1740	K.C. Wessels	54	51	3	107	1	14	36.25
1740	M.A. Taylor	57	55	1	94	-	16	32.22
1242	S.P. O'Donnell	87	64	15	74*	-	9	25.34
1225	R.W. Marsh	92	76	15	66	-	4	20.08
989	I.A. Healy	109	73	24	50*	-	1	20.18
959	G.M. Ritchie	44	42	7	84	-	6	27.4
861	S.B. Smith	28	24	2	117	2	8	39.13
852	W.B. Phillips	48	41	6	75*	-	6	24.34
826	D.W. Hookes	39	36	2	76	-	5	24.29
823	G.N. Yallop	30	27	6	66*	-	7	39.19

Note: Wessels' figures for South Africa:

1387			42	41	3	90	-	10	36.5

Hundreds (39):

No.	Batsman	Score	Opponent	Venue	Season
9	G.R. Marsh	125	India	Sydney	1985-86
		104	India	Jaipur	1986-87
		110	India	Madras	1987
		126*	New Zealand	Chandigarh	1987
		101	New Zealand	Sydney	1987-88
		125*	Pakistan	Melbourne	1988-89
		111*	England	Lord's	1989

No.	Batsman	Score	Opponent	Venue	Season
		113	West Indies	Bridgetown	1990-91+
		106*	West Indies	Georgetown	1990-91+
7	D.M. Jones	104	England	Perth	1986-87+
		121	Pakistan	Perth	1986-87+
		101	England	Brisbane	1986-87
		107	New Zealand	Christchurch	1989-90
		102*	New Zealand	Auckland	1989-90
		117*	Sri Lanka	Sharjah	1989-90
		145	England	Brisbane	1990-91
5	D.C. Boon	111	India	Jaipur	1986-87
		122	Sri Lanka	Adelaide	1987-88
		102*	India	Hobart	1991-92
		100	New Zealand	Auckland	1992
		100	West Indies	Melbourne	1992
3	G.S. Chappell	125	England	The Oval	1977
		138	New Zealand	Sydney	1980-81
		108	New Zealand	Auckland	1981-82
3	A.R. Border	105*	India	Sydney	1980-81
		118*	Sri Lanka	Adelaide	1984-85+
		127*	West Indies	Sydney	1984-85+
3	G.M. Wood	108	England	Leeds	1981
		104*	West Indies	Adelaide	1984-85
		114*	England	Lord's	1985
3	M.E. Waugh	108	New Zealand	Hamilton	1992-93
		113	England	Birmingham	1993
		107	South Africa	Sydney	1993-94
2	S.B. Smith	117	New Zealand	Melbourne	1982-83
		106	Pakistan	Sydney	1983-84
1	A. Turner	101	Sri Lanka	The Oval	1975
1	B.M. Laird	107*	West Indies	Sydney	1981-82
1	T.M. Chappell	110	India	Nottingham	1983
1	K.C. Wessels	107	India	New Delhi	1984

+ indicates successive innings.

Analysis of Hundreds:

By Opponent

	in Australia	Overseas	Total
v New Zealand	3	6	9
v India	3	5	8
v England	3	5	8
v West Indies	4	2	6
v Sri Lanka	2	2	4
v Pakistan	3	-	3
v South Africa	1	-	1
TOTALS	19	20	39

By Batting Position

Position	100s
No. 1	14
No. 2	11
No. 3	10
No. 4	4

By Venue

in Australia (19)	Sydney 8, Melbourne 3, Adelaide 3, Perth 2, Brisbane 2, Hobart 1.
in England (7)	Lord's 2, The Oval 2, Leeds 1, Nottingham 1, Birmingham 1.
in India (5)	Jaipur 2, Madras 1, New Delhi 1, Chandigarh 1.
in New Zealand (5)	Auckland 3, Christchurch 1, Hamilton 1.
in West Indies (2)	Bridgetown 1, Georgetown 1.
in Sharjah (1)	Sharjah 1.

Most Scores Over 50 (including hundreds)

No.	Batsman	No.	Batsman
53	D.M. Jones	17	K.J. Hughes
42	D.C. Boon	17	G.S. Chappell
38	A.R. Border	16	S.R. Waugh
31	G.R. Marsh	16	K.C. Wessels
19	M.E. Waugh	16	M.A. Taylor

Most Successive Scores Over 50 (4)

Batsman	Seasons	Opponents	Scores			
I.M. Chappell	1975 - 1979-80	West Indies, England	62	63	63*	60*
D.C. Boon	1987-88	Zimbabwe, Pakistan, England, Sri Lanka	93	65	78	56
D.M. Jones	1989-90	Pakistan, Sri Lanka, India	58	85	53	85*
D.C. Boon	1991-92	West Indies, India	61	77	79*	78
M.E. Waugh	1992-93 - 1993	New Zealand, England	108	83	56	113

Highest Score for each Batting Position

Position	Score	Batsman	Opponent	Venue	Season
No. 1	126*	G.R. Marsh	New Zealand	Chandigarh	1987
2	122	D.C. Boon	Sri Lanka	Adelaide	1987-88
3	145	D.M. Jones	England	Brisbane	1990-91
4	127*	A.R. Border	West Indies	Sydney	1984-85
5	86	S.R. Waugh	South Africa	Pretoria	1993-94
6	80*	R. Edwards	Pakistan	Leeds	1975
7	74*	S.P. O'Donnell	Pakistan	Melbourne	1984-85
8	74	T.J. Laughlin	England	Sydney	1979-80
9	55	S.K. Warne	South Africa	Port Elizabeth	1993-94
10	21	J.R. Thomson	West Indies	Lord's	1975
11	16*	D.K. Lillee	West Indies	Lord's	1975

Highest Score against each Opponent

Opponent	Score	Batsman	Venue	Season
England	145	D.M. Jones	Brisbane	1990-91
New Zealand	138*	G.S. Chappell	Sydney	1980-81
Pakistan	125*	G.R. Marsh	Melbourne	1988-89
Sri Lanka	122	D.M. Jones	Adelaide	1987-88
West Indies	127*	A.R. Border	Sydney	1984-85
Canada	27*	K.J. Hughes	Birmingham	1979
India	125	G.R. Marsh	Sydney	1985-86
Zimbabwe	93	D.C. Boon	Cuttack	1987
Bangladesh	54*	P.L. Taylor	Sharjah	1989-90
South Africa	107	M.E. Waugh	Sydney	1993-94

Highest Score on each Ground

Venue	Score	Batsman	Opponent	Season
Melbourne	125*	G.R. Marsh	Pakistan	1988-89
Adelaide	122	D.M. Jones	Sri Lanka	1987-88
Sydney	138*	G.S. Chappell	New Zealand	1980-81
Brisbane	145	D.M. Jones	England	1990-91
Perth	121	D.M. Jones	Pakistan	1986-87
Hobart	102*	D.C. Boon	India	1991-92
Manchester	79	M.A. Taylor	England	1993
Lord's	114*	G.M. Wood	England	1985
Birmingham	113	M.E. Waugh	England	1993
Leeds	108	G.M. Wood	England	1981
The Oval	125*	G.S. Chappell	England	1977
Nottingham	110	T.M. Chappell	India	1983
Southampton	73	G.M. Wood	Zimbabwe	1983
Chelmsford	36	A.R. Border	India	1983
Dunedin	83	I.M. Chappell	New Zealand	1973-74
Christchurch	107	D.M. Jones	New Zealand	1989-90
Auckland	108	G.S. Chappell	New Zealand	1981-82
Wellington	71	S.R. Waugh	New Zealand	1985-86
Hamilton	108	M.E. Waugh	New Zealand	1992-93
St. John's	84	G.J. Cosier	West Indies	1977-78
Castries	90	A.R. Border	West Indies	1983-84
Berbice	60	S.B. Smith	West Indies	1983-84
Port-of-Spain	81	G.R. Marsh	West Indies	1990-91
Kingston	88*	D.M. Jones	West Indies	1990-91
Bridgetown	113	G.R. Marsh	West Indies	1990-91

Venue	Score	Batsman	Opponent	Season
Georgetown	106*	G.R. Marsh	West Indies	1990-91
Hyderabad (Pak)	52	G.M. Wood	Pakistan	1982
Lahore	91*	B.M. Laird	Pakistan	1982
Colombo PSS	94	M.A. Taylor	Sri Lanka	1992
Colombo SSC	60*	G.N. Yallop	Sri Lanka	1983
Colombo Khett	69*	D.C. Boon	Sri Lanka	1992
New Delhi	107	K.C. Wessels	India	1984
Trivandrum	12	K.C. Wessels	India	1984
Ahmedabad	62*	A.R. Border	India	1984
Indore	87	D.C. Boon	New Zealand	1987
Jaipur	111	D.C. Boon	India	1986
Srinagar	90*	A.R. Border	India	1986
Hyderabad (Ind)	84*	A.R. Border	England	1989
Rajkot	91*	A.R. Border	India	1986
Madras	110	G.R. Marsh	India	1987
Chandigarh	126*	G.R. Marsh	New Zealand	1987
Cuttack	93	D.C. Boon	Zimbabwe	1987
Calcutta	75	D.C. Boon	England	1987
Bombay	58	D.M. Jones	Pakistan	1989
Goa	85	D.M. Jones	Sri Lanka	1989
Bangalore	53	D.M. Jones	India	1989
Sharjah	117*	D.M. Jones	Sri Lanka	1989-90
Johannesburg	58	D.C. Boon	South Africa	1993-94
Pretoria	86	S.R. Waugh	South Africa	1993-94
Port Elizabeth	76	D.C. Boon	South Africa	1993-94
Durban	69*	A.R. Border	South Africa	1993-94
East London	67*	S.R. Waugh	South Africa	1993-94
Cape Town	71	M.E. Waugh	South Africa	1993-94
Bloemfontein	45	D.C. Boon	South Africa	1993-94

Highest Score on Debut

Score	Batsman	Opponent	Venue	Season
79	K.C. Wessels	New Zealand	Melbourne	1982-83
73	M.J. Slater	South Africa	Melbourne	1993-94

Carrying Bat Through Completed Innings

Batsman	Score	Total	Overs	Opponent	Venue	Season
B.M. Laird	91*	4-206	40	Pakistan	Lahore	1982
G.M. Wood	104*	9-200	50	West Indies	Adelaide	1984-85
G.M. Wood	114*	5-254	55	England	Lord's	1985
G.R. Marsh	126*	8-251	50	New Zealand	Chandigarh	1987
G.R. Marsh	125*	4-258	43	Pakistan	Melbourne	1988-89

Highest Score by Opponents

Score	Batsman	For	Venue	Season
167*	R.A. Smith	England	Birmingham	1993
153*	I.V.A. Richards	West Indies	Melbourne	1979-80
148	D.L. Haynes	West Indies	St. John's	1978

Highest Partnerships

Wkt	Runs	Batsmen	Opponent	Venue	Season
3rd	224*	D.M. Jones 99* / A.R. Border 118*	Sri Lanka	Adelaide	1984-85
1st	212	D.C. Boon 111 / G.R. Marsh 104	India	Jaipur	1986-87
2nd	185	G.R. Marsh 82 / D.M. Jones 145	England	Brisbane	1990-91
1st	182	R.B. McCosker 73 / A. Turner 101	Sri Lanka	The Oval	1975
2nd	178	G.R. Marsh 93 / D.M. Jones 101	England	Brisbane	1986-87
3rd	175	D.M. Jones 79 / M.E. Waugh 107	South Africa	Sydney	1993-94
4th	173	D.M. Jones 121 / S.R. Waugh 82	Pakistan	Perth	1986-87
4th	168	M.E. Waugh 113 / A.R. Border 86*	England	Birmingham	1993
2nd	167*	D.C. Boon 79* / T.M. Moody 87*	India	Sydney	1991-92
4th	164	A.R. Border 91* / S.R. Waugh 83*	England	Adelaide	1986-87

(* indicates undefeated partnerships)

THE PEOPLE'S GAME

Record partnerships for each wicket

Wkt	*Runs*	*Batsmen*	*Opponent*	*Venue*	*Season*
1st	212+	D.C. Boon 111 / G.R. Marsh 104	India	Jaipur	1986-87
2nd	185	G.R. Marsh 82 / D.M. Jones 145	England	Brisbane	1990-91
3rd	224*+	D.M. Jones 99* / A.R. Border 118*	Sri Lanka	Adelaide	1984-85
4th	173+	D.M. Jones 121 / S.R. Waugh 82	Pakistan	Perth	1986-87
5th	115*	B.M. Laird 71* / A.R. Border 53*	New Zealand	Dunedin	1981-82
6th	112	M.E. Waugh 62 / S.P. O'Donnell 71*	England	Sydney	1990-91
7th	102*	S.R. Waugh 57 / G.C. Dyer 45*	India	New Delhi	1986-87
8th	109+	P.R. Reiffel 58 / S.K. Warne 55	South Africa	Port Elizabeth	1993-94
9th	52	S.P. O'Donnell 69 / G.M. Wood 36	West Indies	Sydney	1984-85
10th	45	T.J. Laughlin 74 / M.H.N. Walker 9*	England	Sydney	1979-80

(indicates undefeated partnerships)*
(+ indicates world-record partnership for that wicket)

Batsmen sharing in most century partnerships

		Wicket									
No.	*Batsman*	*1st*	*2nd*	*3rd*	*4th*	*5th*	*6th*	*7th*	*8th*	*9th*	*10th*
28	D.M. Jones	-	17	6	4	-	1	-	-	-	-
25	G.R. Marsh	10	10	5	-	-	-	-	-	-	-
24	D.C. Boon	9	9	4	2	-	-	-	-	-	-
23	A.R. Border	-	3	11	6	3	-	-	-	-	-
12	M.A. Taylor	5	5	2	-	-	-	-	-	-	-
11	K.J. Hughes	-	3	4	4	-	-	-	-	-	-
10	M.E. Waugh	-	3	3	2	1	1	-	-	-	-
7	K.C. Wessels	2	2	2	1	-	-	-	-	-	-
6	G.S. Chappell	-	4	-	2	-	-	-	-	-	-

Most Hundred Partnerships by a Pair of Batsmen

		Wicket									
No.	*Batsmen*	*1st*	*2nd*	*3rd*	*4th*	*5th*	*6th*	*7th*	*8th*	*9th*	*10th*
8	D.C. Boon/G.R. Marsh	7	1	-	-	-	-	-	-	-	-
7	G.R. Marsh/D.M. Jones	-	7	-	-	-	-	-	-	-	-
7	G.R. Marsh/A.R. Border	-	3	4	-	-	-	-	-	-	-
6	D.C. Boon/D.M. Jones	-	6	-	-	-	-	-	-	-	-
4	D.M. Jones/A.R. Border	-	-	3	1	-	-	-	-	-	-

4. BOWLING

Most Wickets

Wkts	*Bowler*	*Mat*	*Balls*	*Runs*	*Best*	*5w*	*Avge*	*RPO*	*Rate*
171	C.J. McDermott	116	6300	4258	5-44	1	24.90	4.05	36.84
152	S.R. Waugh	167	6831	5066	4-33	-	33.32	4.44	44.94
108	S.P. O'Donnell	87	4350	3102	5-13	1	28.72	4.27	40.27
103	D.K. Lillee	63	3593	2145	5-34	1	20.82	3.58	34.88
97	P.L. Taylor	83	3937	2740	4-38	-	28.24	4.17	40.58
88	G.F. Lawson	79	4259		4-26	-	29.45	3.65	48.39
88	T.M. Alderman	65	3371	2056	5-17	2	23.36	3.65	38.30
85	R.M. Hogg	71	3677	2418	4-29	-	28.44	3.94	43.25
82	C.G. Rackemann	52	2791	1833	5-16	1	22.35	3.94	34.03
73	A.R. Border	273	2661	2071	3-20	-	28.36	4.66	36.45
72	G.S. Chappell	74	3108	2096	5-15	2	29.11	4.04	43.16
63	B.A. Reid	61	3250	2203	5-53	1	34.96	4.06	51.58
57	G.R.J. Matthews	59	2808	2004	3-27	-	35.15	4.28	49.26
55	J.R. Thomson	50	2696	1942	4-67	-	35.31	4.32	49.08
53	L.S. Pascoe	29	1568	1066	5-30	1	20.11	4.07	29.58
48	P.R. Reiffel	40	2117	1282	4-13	-	26.70	3.63	44.10
46	M.R. Whitney	38	2106	1249	4-34	-	27.15	3.55	45.78
44	S.P. Davis	39	2016	1135	3-10	-	25.79	3.37	45.81
44	S.K. Warne	22	1188	738	4-19	-	16.77	3.72	27
40	M.E. Waugh	75	1302	1048	5-24	1	26.2	4.82	32.55

RPO = *runs per (six-ball) over*
Rate = *strike rate, i.e. balls per wicket*

Most Wickets in an Innings

Total	Bowler	Opponent	Venue	Season
6-14	G.J. Gilmour	England	Leeds	1975
6-39	K.H. MacLeay	India	Nottingham	1983
5-13	S.P. O'Donnell	New Zealand	Christchurch	1989-90
5-15	G.S. Chappell	India	Sydney	1980-81
5-16	C.G. Rackemann	Pakistan	Adelaide	1983-84
5-17	T.M. Alderman	New Zealand	Wellington	1981-82
5-18	G.J. Cosier	England	Birmingham	1977
5-20	G.S. Chappell	England	Birmingham	1977
5-21	A.G. Hurst	Canada	Birmingham	1979
5-21	A.I.C. Dodemaide	Sri Lanka	Perth	1987-88
5-24	M.E. Waugh	West Indies	Melbourne	1992-93
5-30	L.S. Pascoe	New Zealand	Sydney	1980-81
5-32	T.M. Alderman	India	Christchurch	1981-82
5-34	D.K. Lillee	Pakistan	Leeds	1975
5-44	C.J. McDermott	Pakistan	Lahore	1987
5-46	D.R. Gilbert	New Zealand	Sydney	1985-86
5-48	G.J. Gilmour	West Indies	Lord's	1975
5-53	B.A. Reid	India	Adelaide	1985-86

Note: Best bowling against other opponents:

v Zimbabwe	4-39	S.P. O'Donnell	Madras	1987
v Bangladesh	2-22	S.R. Waugh	Sharjah	1990
		P.L. Taylor	Sharjah	1990
v South Africa	4-13	P.R. Reiffel	Sydney	1993-94

Best Bowling on Debut

Total	Bowler	Opponent	Venue	Season
5-21	A.I.C. Dodemaide	Sri Lanka	Perth	1987-88
4-39	C.G. Rackemann	New Zealand	Melbourne	1982-83

Note: Rackemann took 10 wickets in his first three innings: 4-39, 3-28, 3-28, all in 1982-83.

Best Bowling on each Ground

Venue	Total	Bowler	Opponent	Season
Melbourne	5-24	M.E. Waugh	West Indies	1992-93
Adelaide	5-16	C.G. Rackemann	Pakistan	1983-84
Sydney	5-15	G.S. Chappell	India	1980-81
Perth	5-21	A.I.C. Dodemaide	Sri Lanka	1987-88
Brisbane	4-24	G.D. McGrath	South Africa	1993-94
Hobart	4-42	C.J. McDermott	Pakistan	1992-93
Manchester	4-26	G.F. Lawson	England	1989
Lord's	5-48	G.J. Gilmour	West Indies	1975
Birmingham	5-18	G.J. Cosier	England	1977
Leeds	6-14	G.J. Gilmour	England	1975
The Oval	4-35	D.K. Lillee	England	1980
Nottingham	6-39	K.H. MacLeay	India	1983
Southampton	3-40	R.M. Hogg	Zimbabwe	1983
Chelmsford	3-40	R.M. Hogg	India	1983
Dunedin	4-20	A.I.C. Dodemaide	New Zealand	1992-93
Christchurch	5-13	S.P. O'Donnell	New Zealand	1989-90
Auckland	3-22	C.G. Rackemann	New Zealand	1989-90
Wellington	5-17	T.M. Alderman	New Zealand	1981-82
Hamilton	3-31	P.L. Taylor	India	1989-90
St John's	4-67	J.R. Thomson	West Indies	1978
Castries	3-24	I.W. Callen	West Indies	1978
Berbice	1-54	C.G. Rackemann	West Indies	1984
Port-of-Spain	3-29	C.J. McDermott	West Indies	1991
Kingston	4-34	C.J. McDermott	West Indies	1991
Bridgetown	3-34	M.E. Waugh	West Indies	1991
Georgetown	3-29	C.J. McDermott	West Indies	1991
Hyderabad (Pak)	2-63	T.M. Alderman	Pakistan	1982
Lahore	5-44	C.J. McDermott	Pakistan	1987
Karachi	1-22	T.M. Alderman	Pakistan	1982
Colombo PSS	3-27	T.G. Hogan	Sri Lanka	1983
Colombo Khett	2-33	G.R.J. Matthews	Sri Lanka	1992
New Delhi	4-41	C.G. Rackemann	India	1984

Venue	Total	Bowler	Opponent	Season
Trivandrum	4-33	T.G. Hogan	India	1984
Jamshedpur	2-3	C.G. Rackemann	India	1984
Ahmedabad	3-25	G.F. Lawson	India	1984
Indore	3-61	J.N. Maguire	India	1984
Jaipur	1-27	B.A. Reid	India	1986
Srinagar	2-37	B.A. Reid	India	1986
Hyderabad (Ind)	1-20	B.A. Reid	India	1986
Rajkot	2-50	S.R. Waugh	India	1986
Madras	4-39	S.P. O'Donnell	Zimbabwe	1987
Chandigarh	2-27	A.R. Border	New Zealand	1987
Cuttack	2-30	T.B. A.May	Zimbabwe	1987
Calcutta	2-37	S.R. Waugh	England	1987
Bombay	4-22	T.M. Alderman	Pakistan	1989
Goa	3-48	S.P. O'Donnell	Sri Lanka	1989
Bangalore	3-56	G.R.J. Matthews	India	1989
Sharjah	4-39	D.W. Fleming	Sri Lanka	1990
Johannesburg	1-29	G.D. McGrath	South Africa	1993-94
Pretoria	2-42	G.D. McGrath	South Africa	1993-94
Port Elizabeth	4-36	S.K. Warne	South Africa	1993-94
Durban	2-31	P.R. Reiffel	South Africa	1993-94
East London	3-27	A.R. Border	South Africa	1993-94
Capetown	3-31	S.K. Warne	South Africa	1993-94
Bloemfontein	2-34	P.R. Reiffel	South Africa	1993-94

Hat-trick

Bowler	Opponent	Batsmen	Venue	Season
B.A.Reid	New Zealand	B.R. Blair, E.B. McSweeney, S.R. Gillespie	Sydney	1985-86

Most Economical Bowling

O	M	R	W	Bowler	Opponent	Venue	Season
8	4	7	3	C.G. Rackemann	India	Trivandrum	1984
10	5	9	2	M.F. Malone	West Indies	Melbourne	1981-82

Note: the following analyses were the best recorded by bowlers taking at least four wickets:

O	M	R	W	Bowler	Opponent	Venue	Season
12	6	14	6	G.J. Gilmour	England	Leeds	1975
10	6	12	4	D.K. Lillee	England	Sydney	1979-80

Most Economical Bowling in a Career (qualification: 50 six-ball overs)

RPO	Bowler	Mat	Balls	Runs	Wkts	Best	5w	Avge
3.02	A.G. Hurst	8	402	203	12	5-21	1	16.91
3.06	G. Dymock	15	806	412	15	2-21	-	27.46
3.08	M.F. Malone	10	612	315	11	2-9	-	28.63
3.09	G.J. Gilmour	5	320	165	16	6-14	2	10.31
3.25	M.H.N. Walker	17	1006	546	20	4-19	-	27.3
3.37	S.P. Davis	39	2016	1135	44	3-10	-	25.79
3.40	A.I.C. Dodemaide	24	1327	753	36	5-21	1	20.91
3.55	M.R. Whitney	38	2106	1249	46	4-34	-	27.15

Most Runs Conceded in an Innings

Runs	Bowler	Overs	Wkts	Opponent	Venue	Season
75	C.J. McDermott	10	-	India	Jaipur	1986
72	A.A. Mallett	12	1	Sri Lanka	The Oval	1975
71	M.H.N. Walker	12	-	West Indies	Lord's	1975
70	C.J. McDermott	10	2	New Zealand	Adelaide	1985-86
70	S.R. Waugh	11	-	England	Lord's	1989
70	P.R. Reiffel	11	1	England	Birmingham	1993

(all overs are of six balls)

Most Expensive Bowling in a Career (qualification: 50 six-ball overs)

RPO	Bowler	Mat	Balls	Runs	Wkts	Best	5w	Avge
5.33	K.C. Wessels	54	737	655	18	2-16	-	36.38
5.21	K.D. Walters	28	314	273	4	2-24	-	68.25
4.84	D.R. Gilbert	14	684	552	18	5-46	1	30.66
4.82	M.E. Waugh	75	1302	1048	40	5-24	1	26.20
4.66	A.R. Border	273	2661	2071	73	3-20	-	28.36

Best Bowling by Opponents

Total	Bowler	For	Venue	Season
7-51	W.W. Davis	West Indies	Leeds	1983
6-50	A.H. Gray	West Indies	Port-of-Spain	1991

4. WICKET-KEEPING

Most Dismissals in an Innings

No.	Keeper	Opponent	Venue	Season
5 (all caught)	R.W. Marsh	England	Leeds	1981

Most Stumpings in an Innings

No.	Keeper	Opponent	Venue	Season
3	I.A. Healy	South Africa	East London	1993-94

Most Dismissals

Dismissals	Keeper	Mat	Ct	St
146	I.A. Healy	109	127	19
124	R.W. Marsh	92	120	4
48	W.B. Phillips	48	41	7
28	G.C. Dyer	23	24	4
23	T.J. Zoehrer	22	21	2

6. FIELDING

Most Catches in an Innings

No.	Fieldsman	Opponent	Venue	Season
4	M.A. Taylor	West Indies	Sydney	1992-93

Most Catches in Career

Catches	Fieldsman	Mat	Catches	Fieldsman	Mat
127	A.R. Border	273	34	P.L. Taylor	83
57	S.R. Waugh	167	31	G.R. Marsh	117
54	D.M. Jones	164	29	T.M. Alderman	65
39	D.C. Boon	162	28	M.A. Taylor	57
36	M.E. Waugh	75	27	K.J. Hughes	97

7. ALL-ROUND PERFORMANCES

50 and 4 Wickets

Runs	Wkts	Player	Opponent	Venue	Season
82	4-48	S.R. Waugh	Pakistan	Perth	1986-87
57*	4-36	S.P. O'Donnell	Sri Lanka	Melbourne	1989-90
57	5-24	M.E. Waugh	West Indies	Melbourne	1992-93

50 and 4 Dismissals

Runs	Dism	Player	Opponent	Venue	Season
70	3c, 1s	R.D. Robinson	England	The Oval	1977
75*	3c, 1s	W.B. Phillips	Sri Lanka	Perth	1984-85

500 runs and 25 wickets in a career

Player	Mat	Runs	Wkts
A.R. Border	273	6524	73
G.S. Chappell	74	2331	72
G.R.J. Matthews	59	619	57
S.P. O'Donnell	87	1242	108
M.E. Waugh	75	2169	40
S.R. Waugh	167	3421	152

500 Runs and 25 Dismissals in a Career

Player	Mat	Runs	Dism
I.A. Healy	109	989	146
R.W. Marsh	92	1225	124
W.B. Phillips	48	852	48

8. APPEARANCES

Most Appearances

App.	Player	Season		
273	A.R. Border	1978-79	-	1993-94
167	S.R. Waugh	1985-86	-	1994
164	D.M. Jones	1983-84	-	1993-94
162	D.C. Boon	1983-84	-	1994
117	G.R. Marsh	1985-86	-	1992
116	C.J. McDermott	1984-85	-	1993-94
109	I.A. Healy	1988	-	1993-94
97	K.J. Hughes	1977	-	1984-85
92	R.W. Marsh	1970-71	-	1983-84
87	S.P. O'Donnell	1984-85	-	1991-92
83	G.M. Wood	1978	-	1988-89
83	P.L. Taylor	1986-87	-	1991-92

Most Appearances in Succession

App.	Player	From	(match no.)		To	(match no.)
87	S.R. Waugh	1985-86	(139)	-	1989-90	(225)
83	A.R. Border	1980	(34)	-	1984	(116)
80	G.R. Marsh	1985-86	(141)	-	1989-90	(220)
60	R.W. Marsh	1979-80	(26)	-	1982-83	(85)
53	A.R. Border	1987	(177)	-	1989-90	(229)
51	I.A. Healy	1989-90	(212)	-	1992	(262)

Longest Career

Yrs	Days	Player	First match (no.)	Last match (no.)
15	74	A.R. Border	v Eng 24 Jan 79 (20)	v SAf 8 Apr 94 (308)
13	38	R.W. Marsh	v Eng 5 Jan 71 (1)	v WI 12 Feb 84 (108)
12	115	G.S. Chappell	v Eng 5 Jan 71 (1)	v SriL 30 Apr 83 (89)
12	12	R.J. Bright	v NZ 30 Mar 74 (5)	v Pak 11 Apr 86 (155)
10	324	G.M. Wood	v WI 22 Feb 78 (17)	v WI 14 Jan 89 (206)
10	299	D.K. Lillee	v Eng 24 Aug 72 (2)	v WI 18 Jun 83 (94)
10	153	J.R. Thomson	v Eng 1 Jan 75 (7)	v Eng 3 Jun 85 (138)
10	68	D.M. Jones	v Pak 30 Jan 84 (104)	v SAf 8 Apr 94 (308)
10	66	D.C. Boon	v WI 12 Feb 84 (108)	v Ind 19 Apr 94 (311)
10	29	K.D. Walters	v Eng 5 Jan 71 (1)	v NZ 3 Feb 81 (49)
9	299	M.R. Whitney	v NZ 17 Mar 83 (85)	v WI 10 Jan 93 (277)
9	213	T.M. Alderman	v Eng 6 Jun 81 (51)	v NZ 15 Jan 91 (245)

Youngest Players

Yrs	Days	Player	Opponent	Venue	Season	(match no.)
19	260	R.J. Bright	New Zealand	Dunedin	1974	(5)
19	267	C.J. McDermott	West Indies	Melbourne	1984-85	(118)
20	221	S.R. Waugh	New Zealand	Melbourne	1985-86	(139)
20	278	I.C. Davis	New Zealand	Dunedin	1974	(5)

Oldest Players

Yrs	Days	Player	Opponent	Venue	Season	(match no.)
42	68	R.B. Simpson	West Indies	Castries	1978	(18)
38	255	A.R. Border	South Africa	Bloemfontein	1993-94	(308)
38	223	R.G. Holland	England	Manchester	1985	(136)
36	110	I.M. Chappell	England	Sydney	1979-80	(32)

Same Team Most Matches in Succession

No.	Season	Opponents	Team
5	1982-83	New Zealand and England (match no's 73 to 77)	K.C. Wessels, J. Dyson, G.S. Chappell, K.J. Hughes, D.W. Hookes, A.R. Border, R.W. Marsh, G.F. Lawson, J.R. Thomson, R.M. Hogg, C.G. Rackemann.

9. CAPTAINCY

Captain	Seasons	Mat	Won	Lost	NR	Tie	Win %
W.M. Lawry	1970-71	1	1	-	-	-	100
I.M. Chappell	1972 - 1975	11	6	5	-	-	54.5
G.S. Chappell	1975-76 - 1983	49	21	25	3	-	45.6
R.B. Simpson	1978	2	1	1	-	-	50
G.N. Yallop	1978-79	4	2	1	1	-	66.6
K.J. Hughes	1979 - 1984	49	21	23	4	1	46.6
D.W. Hookes	1983	1	-	1	-	-	0
A.R. Border	1984-85 - 1993-94	178	107	67	3	1	61.1
R.J. Bright	1986	1	-	1	-	-	0
G.R. Marsh	1987 - 1990-91	4	3	1	-	-	75
M.A. Taylor	1992-93 - 1994	11	7	3	-	1	63.6

Notes: The most successive matches as captain is 53, by A.R. Border 1987 - 1989-90.

Highest Scores by a Captain

Total	Captain	Opponent	Venue	Season
138*	G.S. Chappell	New Zealand	Sydney	1980-81
127*	A.R. Border	West Indies	Sydney	1984-85
125*	G.S. Chappell	England	The Oval	1975
118*	A.R. Border	Sri Lanka	Adelaide	1984-85
108	G.S. Chappell	New Zealand	Auckland	1981-82

Best Bowling by a Captain

Total	Captain	Opponent	Venue	Season
5-15	G.S. Chappell	India	Sydney	1980-81
5-20	G.S. Chappell	England	Birmingham	1977

10. ATTENDANCES

Highest Crowds in Australia

Crowd	Opponent	Venue	Season
86,133	West Indies	Melbourne	1983-84
84,360	England	Melbourne	1982-83
82,494	England	Melbourne	1984-85
78,142	West Indies	Melbourne	1981-82

Note: The World Cup Final at Melbourne in 1992, between Pakistan and England, was attended by 87,182.

Highest Crowds at other Grounds

Venue	Crowd	Opponent	Season
Adelaide	34,897	England	1982-83
Sydney	52,053	West Indies	1981-82
Brisbane	29,810	Pakistan	1989-90
Perth	27,385	Pakistan	1988-89
Hobart	11,086	New Zealand	1990-91

11. THE WORLD CUP

Finals

Year	Result	Venue
1975	West Indies beat Australia by 17 runs	Lord's
1979	West Indies beat England by 92 runs	Lord's
1983	India beat West Indies by 43 runs	Lord's
1987	Australia beat England by 7 runs	Calcutta
1992	Pakistan beat England by 22 runs	Melbourne

Australia's performances

Year	Mat	Won	Lost	Venue	Year	Mat	Won	Lost	Venue
1975	5	3	2	England	1987	8	7	1	India & Pakistan
1979	3	1	2	England	1992	8	4	4	Aust & NZ
1983	6	2	4	England	Total	30	17	13	

Highest Innings Totals by Australia

Score		Opponent	Venue	Year
5-328	(60 overs)	Sri Lanka	The Oval	1975
9-320	(60 overs)	India	Nottingham	1983
7-278	(54.3 overs)	Pakistan	Leeds	1975
274	(58.4 overs.)	West Indies	Lord's	1975
6-273	(60 overs)	West Indies	Lord's	1983
6-270	(50 overs.)	India	Madras	1987
8-267	(50 overs.)	Pakistan	Lahore	1987

Note: The highest innings totals against Australia in the World Cup are:

8-291	*(60 overs)*	*West Indies*	*Lord's*	*1975*
6-289	*(50 overs)*	*India*	*New Delhi*	*1987*
7-286	*(60 overs)*	*Pakistan*	*Nottingham*	*1979*

Lowest Innings Total (completed innings) by Australia

Score		Opponent	Venue	Year
129	(38.2 overs)	India	Chelmsford	1983

Note: The lowest innings total (completed innings) against Australia in the World Cup is:

93	*(36.2 overs.)*	*England*	*Leeds*	*1975*

Hundreds (6)

Batsman	Score	Opponent	Venue	Year
A. Turner	101	Sri Lanka	The Oval	1975
T.M. Chappell	110	India	Nottingham	1983
G.R. Marsh	110	India	Madras	1987
G.R. Marsh	126*	New Zealand	Chandigarh	1987
D.C. Boon	100	New Zealand	Auckland	1992
D.C. Boon	100	West Indies	Melbourne	1992

Note: The highest individual score against Australia in the World Cup is:

C.H.Lloyd	*102*	*West Indies*	*Lord's*	*1975*

Most Runs

Runs		Mat	Inn	No.	HS	100	50	Avge
815	D.C. Boon	16	16	1	100	2	5	54.33
590	D.M. Jones	16	16	2	90	-	5	42.14
579	G.R. Marsh	13	13	1	126*	2	2	48.25
452	A.R. Border	25	24	-	67	-	1	18.83
354	S.R. Waugh	16	15	5	55	-	1	35.40

Best Bowling (5 wickets in an innings)

Bowler	Total	Opponent	Venue	Year
D.K. Lillee	5-34	Pakistan	Leeds	1975
G.J. Gilmour	6-14	England	Leeds	1975
G.J. Gilmour	5-48	West Indies	Lord's	1975
A.G. Hurst	5-21	Canada	Birmingham	1979
K.H. MacLeay	6-39	India	Nottingham	1983
Bowler	Total	Opponent	Venue	Year
C.J.Mc Dermott	5-44	Pakistan	Lahore	1987

Note: The best bowling against Australian in the World Cup is:

W.W. Davis	*7-51*	*West Indies*	*Leeds*	*1983*

Most Wickets

Wkts	Bowler	M	Balls	Runs	Best	4w	Avge
26	C.J. McDermott	16	876	587	5-44	2	22.57
19	S.R. Waugh	16	745	565	3-36	-	29.73
12	D.K. Lillee	9	588	400	5-34	1	33.33
11	G.J. Gilmour	2	144	62	6-14	2	5.63

Most Dismissals

Dism	Bowler	Mat	Ct	St
18	R.W. Marsh	11	17	1
11	G.C. Dyer	8	9	2

Most Appearances

App.	Player	Years
25	A.R. Border	1979 - 1983 - 1987 - 1992
16	D.C. Boon	1987 - 1992
16	D.M. Jones	1987 - 1992
16	C.J. McDermott	1987 - 1992
16	S.R. Waugh	1987 - 1992
14	B.A. Reid	1987 - 1992
13	G.R. Marsh	1987 - 1992
11	R.W. Marsh	1975 - 1983
11	T.M. Moody	1987 - 1992

Notes:
1. Border is the only Australian to play in more than two World Cup tournaments.
2. K.C. Wessels has played 12 World Cup matches: three for Australia in 1983 and nine for South Africa in 1992.

Player-of-the-Match Awards (16)

D.C. Boon 4, G.R. Marsh 2, S.R. Waugh 2, D.K. Lillee, A. Turner, G.J. Gilmour, A.G. Hurst, T.M. Chappell, C.J. McDermott, D.M. Jones, T.M. Moody.

12. WORLD SERIES

Season	Prelim. matches	Finals	Winner	Runner-up	Other team
1979-80	11	2	West Indies 2-0	England	Australia
1980-81	15	4	Australia 3-1	New Zealand	India
1981-82	15	4	West Indies 3-1	Australia	Pakistan
1982-83	15	2	Australia 2-0	New Zealand	England
1983-84	15	3	West Indies 2-0*	Australia	Pakistan
1984-85	15	3	West Indies 2-1	Australia	Sri Lanka
1985-86	15	2	Australia 2-0	India	New Zealand
1986-87	12	2	England 2-0	Australia	West Indies
1987-88	12	2	Australia 2-0	New Zealand	Sri Lanka
1988-89	12	3	West Indies 2-1	Australia	Pakistan
1989-90	12	2	Australia 2-0	Pakistan	Sri Lanka
1990-91	12	2	Australia 2-0	New Zealand	England
1991-92	12	2	Australia 2-0	India	West Indies
1992-93	12	2	West Indies 2-0	Australia	Pakistan
1993-94	11	3	Australia 2-1	South Africa	New Zealand

Notes:
*1. * indicates one final was tied.*
2. Matches abandoned without a ball bowled are excluded from the above.

Outstanding Players

Season	Player of the series	Player of the final
1979-80	I.V.A. Richards (WI)	C.G. Greenidge (WI)
1980-81	G.S. Chappell (A)	G.S. Chappell (A)
1981-82	Imran Khan (P)	I.V.A. Richards (WI)
1982-83	D.I. Gower (E)	K.J. Hughes (A)
1983-84	K.C. Wessels (A)	J. Garner (WI)
1984-85	I.V.A. Richards (WI)	A.R. Border (A) and M.A. Holding (WI)
1985-86	Kapil Dev (I)	G.R.J. Matthews (A)
1986-87	I.V.A. Richards (WI)	I.T. Botham (E)
1987-88	S.R. Waugh (A)	D.M. Jones (A)
1988-89	D.L. Haynes (WI)	A.R. Border (A) and D.L. Haynes (WI)
1989-90	D.M. Jones (A)	D.M.J ones (A)
1990-91	D.M. Jones (A)	M.A. Taylor (A)
1991-92	D.C. Boon (A) and G.R. Marsh (A)	D.M. Jones (A)
1992-93	P.V. Simmons (WI)	C.E.L. Ambrose (WI)
1993-94	S.K. Warne (A)	M.E. Waugh (A)

Australia's Performances

Matches	Won	Lost	No result	Tie
168	98	64	4	2

Australia's Performances against each Country

Opponent	Seasons	Matches	Won	Lost	Tie	NR	Win %
West Indies	8	50	17	31	1	1	34.6
England	4	19	10	9	-	-	52.6
New Zealand	6	37	25	10	-	2	71.4
India	3	18	14	4	-	-	77.7
Pakistan	5	24	16	6	1	1	69.5
Sri Lanka	3	13	12	1	-	-	92.3
South Africa	1	7	4	3	-	-	57.1
TOTAL	15	168	98	64	2	4	59.7

Australia's Performances on each Ground

Venue	Matches	Won	Lost	Tie	NR	Win %
Sydney	64	41	22	-	1	65.1
Melbourne	56	29	24	1	2	53.7
Adelaide	19	12	7	-	-	63.1
Perth	13	7	6	-	-	53.8
Brisbane	13	8	4	-	1	75
Hobart	3	1	1	1	-	33.3

Highest Innings Totals

Score		Opponent	Venue	Season
3-323	(50 overs)	Sri Lanka	Adelaide	1984-85
8-302	(50 overs)	New Zealand	Melbourne	1982-83
5-300	(50 overs)	Pakistan	Brisbane	1989-90

Note: The highest innings total against Australia is:

9-277	*(50 overs)*	*West Indies*	*Sydney*	*1988-89*

Lowest Innings Total (completed innings)

Score		Opponent	Venue	Season
70	(26.3 overs)	New Zealand	Adelaide	1985-86

Note: the lowest innings total against Australia is:

63	*(25.5 overs)*	*India*	*Sydney*	*1980-81*

Highest Individual Scores

Score	Batsman	Opponent	Venue	Season
145	D.M. Jones	England	Brisbane	1990-91
138*	G.S. Chappell	New Zealand	Sydney	1980-81
127*	A.R. Border	West Indies	Sydney	1984-85

Note: The highest score against Australia is:

*153**	*I.V.A. Richards*	*West Indies*	*Melbourne*	*1979-80*

Hundreds (16)

A.R. Border 3, G.R. Marsh 3, S.B. Smith 2, D.M. Jones 2, D.C. Boon 2, G.S. Chappell 1, B.M. Laird 1, G.M. Wood 1, M.E. Waugh 1.

Most Runs

Runs	Batsman	Mat	Inn	NO	HS	100	50	Avge
3899	A.R. Border	160	148	22	127*	3	23	30.94
3456	D.M. Jones	93	90	16	145	2	28	46.70
2632	D.C. Boon	86	83	6	122	2	17	34.18
2197	G.R. Marsh	65	64	3	125*	3	12	36.01
1659	S.R. Waugh	90	80	23	83*	-	6	29.10
1441	G.S. Chappell	48	48	7	138*	1	10	35.15

Note: The most runs in a season is 686 (average 68.6) by G.S. Chappell in 14 innings in 1980-81.

Highest Partnerships

Wkt	Total	Batsmen	Opponent	Venue	Season
3rd	224*	D.M. Jones 99* / A.R. Border 118*	Sri Lanka	Adelaide	1984-85
2nd	185	G.R. Marsh 82 / D.M. Jones 145	England	Brisbane	1990-91
2nd	178	G.R. Marsh 93 / D.M. Jones 101	England	Brisbane	1986-87

Best Bowling

Total	Bowler	Opponent	Venue	Season
5-15	G.S. Chappell	India	Sydney	1980-81
5-16	C.G. Rackemann	Pakistan	Adelaide	1983-84
5-21	A.I.C. Dodemaide	Sri Lanka	Perth	1987-88
5-24	M.E. Waugh	West Indies	Melbourne	1992-93
5-30	L.S. Pascoe	New Zealand	Sydney	1980-81
5-46	D.R. Gilbert	New Zealand	Sydney	1985-86
5-53	B.A. Reid	India	Adelaide	1985-86

Note: The best bowling against Australia is:

5-15	*R.J. Shastri*	*India*	*Perth*	*1991-92*

Most Wickets

Wkts	Bowler	Mat	Balls	Runs	Best	4w	Avge
89	C.J. McDermott	68	3584	2341	4-38	2	26.30
85	S.R. Waugh	90	3726	2626	4-33	1	30.89
71	P.L. Taylor	54	2783	1878	4-38	1	26.45
69	S.P. O'Donnell	52	2592	1826	4-19	4	26.46
68	D.K. Lillee	40	2150	1248	4-12	4	18.35
66	R.M. Hogg	49	2672	1785	4-33	4	27.05

Note: The most wickets in a season is 25 (average 14.64) by D.K. Lillee in 14 matches in 1980-81.

Four Dismissals in an Innings (5)

Keeper	Dism	Opponent	Venue	Season
R.W. Marsh (3)	4c	India	Sydney	1980-81
	4c	New Zealand	Perth	1982-83
	3c, 1s	Pakistan	Sydney	1983-84
W.B. Phillips (2)	3c, 1s	Sri Lanka	Perth	1984-85
	3c, 1s	New Zealand	Sydney	1985-86

Most Dismissals

Dism	Keeper	Mat	Ct	St
83	I.A. Healy	61	74	9
79	R.W. Marsh	59	78	1
29	W.B. Phillips	28	26	3

Note: The most dismissals in a season is 22 (all caught) by R.W. Marsh in 12 matches in 1982-83

Most Appearances

App.	Player	Season
160	A.R. Border	1979-80 - 1993-94
93	D.M. Jones	1983-84 - 1993-94
90	S.R. Waugh	1985-86 - 1993-94
86	D.C. Boon	1983-84 - 1993-94
68	C.J. McDermott	1984-85 - 1993-94
65	G.R. Marsh	1985-86 - 1991-92
61	I.A. Healy	1988-89 - 1993-94

Player-of-the-Match Awards

Of Australia's 168 matches in the 15 seasons of the World Series, 36 have been finals. Of the 132 preliminary matches, player-of-the-match awards have been given in 127 and 81 have been to Australians, as follows:

No.	Player
10	A.R. Border
9	S.R. Waugh
8	D.M. Jones
6	G.R. Marsh
5	G.S. Chappell
4	K.C. Wessels, S.P. O'Donnell
3	D.C. Boon, P.L. Taylor
2.	D.W. Hookes, S.B. Smith, M.A. Taylor, S.K. Warne
1.	R.B. McCosker, I.M. Chappell, D.K. Lillee, G.M. Wood, B.M. Laird, K.J. Hughes, J. Dyson, C.G. Rackemann, R.W. Marsh, G.R.J. Matthews, D.R. Gilbert, B.M. Reid, T.J. Zoehrer, M.R.J. Veletta, M.G. Hughes, T.M. Alderman, T.M. Moody, I.A. Healy, C.J. McDermott, M.E. Waugh, P.R. Reiffel.

13. WORLD SERIES CRICKET
(1977-78 and 1978-79. None of the records which follow are included in earlier statistics.)

Australian XI in World Series Cricket

1977-78 in Australia (all matches for the International Cup)

Date	Venue	Aust. XI	(overs)	Opponent		(overs)	Result
10 Dec	Adelaide	155	(34.2)	World XI	9-204	(40)*	lost by 49 runs
11 Dec	Adelaide	8-203	(40)*	West Indies XI	4-204	(33.5)	lost by 6 wkts
14 Dec	Melbourne	4-210	(34.3)	World XI	207	(40)*	won by 6 wkts
27 Dec	Melbourne	1-12	(3.1)*	West Indies XI		-	no result
7 Jan	Perth	121	(28)*	West Indies XI	4-123	(24.1)	lost by 6 wkts
8 Jan	Perth	7-146	(27.1)	World XI	9-145	(30)*	won by 3 wkts
21 Jan	Sydney	8-224	(40)*	West Indies XI	5-225	(34.2)	lost by 5 wkts
23 Jan	Melbourne	9-193	(38)*	World XI	9-138	(29.1)	won on run-rate
24 Jan	Melbourne	9-212	(38)*	West Indies XI	9-214	(37.7)	lost by 1 wkt
4 Feb	Sydney	4-129	(28.6)	World XI	128	(29)*	won by 6 wkts
5 Feb	Sydney	99	(18.7)	West Indies XI	124	(26.5)*	lost by 25 runs

1978 in New Zealand (all matches v World XI)

Date	Venue	Aust. XI	(overs)	World XI	(overs)	Result
7 Nov	Auckland	136	(49.1)*	106	(30.2)	won by 30 runs
9 Nov	Tauranga	94	(37.3)	178	(46.3)*	lost by 84 runs
13 Nov	Wanganui	124	(28.1)	7-149	(30)*	lost by 25 runs
14 Nov	Wanganui	178	(49.5)*	75	(31.2)	won by 103 runs
15 Nov	New Plymouth	68	(37.2)	156	(42.5)*	lost by 88 runs
16 Nov	Lower Hutt	8-171	(40)*	164	(37.2)	won by 7 runs
18 Nov	Hastings	107	(32)	3-147	(37)*	lost by 40 runs
19 Nov	Auckland	118	(40.4)*	9-122	(39.3)	lost by 1 wkt

1978-79 in Australia (all matches, except those marked +, for the International Cup.)

Date	Venue	Aust. XI	(overs)	Opponent	Score	(overs)	Result
23 Nov+	Perth	7-212	(46)*	World XI	138	(41.2)	won by 74 runs
25 Nov+	Perth	174	(47.5)*	West Indies XI	5-175	(42.1)	lost by 5 wkts
26 Nov+	Perth	123	(44.4)*	West Indies XI	9-125	(48)	lost by 1 wkt
28 Nov	Sydney	5-129	(37)	West Indies XI	128	(47.3)*	won by 5 wkts
29 Nov	Sydney	6-223	(50)*	World XI	4-99	(30.3)	won on run-rate
3 Dec+	Canberra	1-69	(24.4)	World XI	9-220	(50)*	lost on run-rate
4 Dec	Sydney	100	(43.2)	World XI	163	(48.1)*	lost by 63 runs
13 Dec	Sydney	217	(50)*	World XI	179	(45.5)	won by 38 runs
18 Dec	Melbourne	6-239	(50)*	World XI	167	(42.3)	won by 72 runs
19 Dec	Melbourne	6-216	(50)*	West Indies XI	5-217	(48.1)	lost by 5 wkts
27 Dec	Sydney	4-69	(18.3)	West Indies XI	66	(33.4)*	won by 6 wkts
31 Dec	Brisbane	165	(48.3)*	West Indies XI	126	(37.3)	won by 39 runs
1 Jan	Brisbane	54	(28.1)*	World XI	2-55	(12.3)	lost by 8 wkts
6 Jan	Adelaide	7-196	(50)*	West Indies XI	8-198	(49.1)	lost by 2 wkts
9 Jan	Melbourne	174	(49.3)*	West Indies XI	103	(39.5)	won by 71 runs
17 Jan	Sydney	9-149	(50)*	West Indies XI	4-65	(12)	lost on run-rate
27 Jan	Melbourne	5-208	(50)*	West Indies XI	9-169	(50)	won by 39 runs
28 Jan	Melbourne	8-189	(50)*	West Indies XI	6-192	(48.5)	lost 4 wkts
29 Jan	Melbourne	6-200	(49)*	West Indies XI	3-202	(46)	lost by 7 wkts
30 Jan	Melbourne	240	(50)*	West Indies XI	8-228	(46)	lost on run-rate

1979 in West Indies (all matches v West Indies XI)

Date	Venue	Aust. XI	(overs)	West Indies XI	(overs)	Result
20 Feb	Kingston	8-138	(40)	8-174	(40)*	lost by 36 runs
21 Feb	Kingston	9-133	(38.3)	132	(36.3)*	won by 1 wkt
3 Mar	St Lucia	184	(43.1)	189	(42.1)*	lost by 5 runs
6 Mar	Bridgetown	4-201	(45)*	159	(39.2)	won by 42 runs
7 Mar	Bridgetown	7-233	(45)	8-240	(45)*	lost by 7 runs
29 Mar	Georgetown	7-209	(45)*	4-212	(44.2)	lost by 6 wkts
31 Mar	Port-of-Spain	6-18	(15)	7-206	(45)*	lost on run-rate

Date	Venue	Aust. XI	(overs)	West Indies XI	(overs)	Result
1 Apr	Port-of-Spain	153	(36.5)	7-207	(45)*	lost by 54 runs
2 Apr	Port-of-Spain	9-206	(45)*	4-176	(26.5)	lost on run-rate
4 Apr	Dominica	9-137	(45)*	2-139	(37.1)	lost by 8 wkts

Notes:
1. * indicates batted first
2. eight-ball overs were bowled in 1977-78; six-ball overs were bowled in 1978, 1978-79 and 1979.
3. the following four matches were abandoned without a ball bowled and are otherwise excluded from these statistics:

1977-78	(1)	26 Dec	Melbourne	v World XI
1978-79	(1)	28 Dec	Sydney	v World XI
1979	(2)	4 Mar	St Lucia	v West Indies XI
		13 Apr	St Kitts	v West Indies XI

Australian XI Performances

		All matches				v World XI			v West Indies XI			
Season	Venue	M	W	L	NR	M	W	L	M	W	L	NR
1977-78	A	11	4	6	1	5	4	1	6	-	5	1
1978	NZ	8	3	5	-	8	3	5	-	-	-	-
1978-79	A	20	9	11	-	7	4	3	13	5	8	-
1979	WI	10	2	8	-	-	-	-	10	2	8	-
Totals		49	18	30	1	20	11	9	29	7	21	1

Highest Innings Totals

Score	Opponent	Venue	Season
240	West Indies XI	Melbourne	1978-79
6-239	World XI	Melbourne	1978-79
7-233	West Indies XI	Bridgetown	1979

Note: the highest innings total against Australian XI was:

8-240	West Indies XI	Bridgetown	1979

Lowest Innings Totals (completed innings)

Score	Opponent	Venue	Season
54	World XI	Brisbane	1978-79
68	World XI	New Plymouth	1978
94	World XI	Tauranga	1978
99	West Indies XI	Sydney	1977-78

Note: the lowest innings total against Australian XI was:

66	West Indies XI	Sydney	1978-79

Highest Individual Innings

Score	Batsman	Opponent	Venue	Season
136	K.C. Wessels	West Indies XI	Melbourne	1978-79
109	M.F. Kent	West Indies XI	Bridgetown	1979
89	R.B. McCosker	West Indies XI	Georgetown	1979
87	G.S. Chappell	World XI	Perth	1977-78
87	I.M. Chappell	West Indies XI	Perth	1978-79

Note: the highest individual innings against Australian XI was:

99*	I.V.A.Richards	West Indies XI	Perth	1978-79

Most Scores Over 50

No.	Batsman
7	I.M. Chappell, G.S. Chappell
4	K.C. Wessels, D.W. Hookes
3	I.C. Davis, B.M. Laird, M.F. Kent

Note: there were 33 scores over 50, recorded by nine batsmen.

Most runs

Runs	Batsman	Mat	Inn	NO	HS	50	Avge
1166	G.S. Chappell	44	43	3	87	7	29.15
968	I.M. Chappell	41	41	3	87	7	25.47
718	D.W. Hookes	39	38	4	68	4	21.12
606	R.W. Marsh	47	41	7	46	-	17.82

Runs	Batsman	Mat	Inn	NO	HS	50	Avge
582	B.M. Laird	30	30		83	3	19.4
549	I.C. Davis	30	30	1	69	3	18.93

Note: the highest batting averages were:

Avge	Runs		Mat	Inn	NO	HS	100	50
36.00	504	K.C. Wessels	15	15	1	136	1	3
30.38	486	M.F. Kent	21	20	4	109	1	2

Five Wickets in an Innings

Total	Bowler	Opponent	Venue	Season
5-19	G.S. Chappell	West Indies XI	Sydney	1978-79
5-23	M.H.N. Walker	West Indies XI	Melbourne	1978-79
5-26	M.H.N. Walker	World XI	Auckland	1978
5-30	L.S. Pascoe	World XI	Melbourne	1978-79
5-31	J.R. Thomson	West Indies XI	Kingston	1979

Note: The best bowling against Australian XI was:

5-6	G.S. le Roux	World XI	Brisbane	1978-79

Most Wickets

Wkts	Bowler	Mat	Balls	Runs	Best	4w	Avge
69	M.H.N. Walker	38	1882	1193	5-23	4	17.29
54	D.K. Lillee	36	1504	762	4-13	3	14.11
48	G.S. Chappell	44	1398	899	5-19	3	18.73
48	G.J. Gilmour	40	1907	1248	4-24	1	26.00
35	M.F. Malone	38	1883	913	4-9	1	26.09
33	L.S. Pascoe	21	1084	690	5-30	1	20.91

Note: the best bowling averages were by Lillee and Walker, as above.

Most Economical Bowling (in an innings)

O	M	R	W	Bowler	Opponent	Venue	Season
10	6	9	4	M.F. Malone	World XI	Wanganui	1978
7	2	7	0	L.S. Pascoe	West Indies XI	Sydney	1978-79
5	4	5	2	D.K. Lillee	West Indies XI	Sydney	1978-79

Note: The figures recorded by Pascoe and Lillee, above, were in the same innings. The West Indies XI were eventually dismissed for 66 in 33.4 overs. G.S.Chappell took 4-15 off 9 and G.J.Gilmour 3-9 off 5.4.

Most Runs Conceded (in an innings)

O	M	R	W	Bowler	Opponent	Venue	Season
9	1	74	2	M.H.N. Walker	West Indies XI	Bridgetown	1979
9	1	65	3	G.J. Gilmour	West Indies XI	Port-of-Spain	1979
8	0	62	1	G.D. McKenzie	West Indies XI	Adelaide	1977-78
8	0	62	1	R.J. Bright	World XI	Adelaide	1977-78

Runs Per Over   (calculated at six-ball overs; qualification 20 six-ball overs)

Least:	Bowler	Mat	Balls	Runs	Wkts
2.90	M.F. Malone	36	1883	913	35
3.03	D.K. Lillee	34	1504	762	54
3.63	K.D. Walters	18	147	89	10

Appearances

25 players represented Australian XI in the 49 matches. The most appearances were as follows:

No.	Player	No.	Player
47	R.W. Marsh	39	D.W. Hookes
44	G.S. Chappell	38	M.H.N. Walker
41	I.M. Chappell	36	M.F.Malone
40	G.J. Gilmour	34	D.K.Lillee

Notes:

1. W.Prior (8 matches) and R.S.Langer (4 matches) never represented Australia in a one-day international;

2. B.M.Laird (30 matches), M.F.Kent (21 matches), K.C.Wessels (15 matches) and T.M.Chappell (10 matches) represented WSC Australian XI before representing Australia in a one-day international.

3. The following players represented WSC Australian XI after playing their last one-day international for Australia: I.C.Davis, R.Edwards, G.J.Gilmour, G.D.McKenzie, K.J.O'Keeffe, R.D.Robinson, I.R.Redpath.

BIBLIOGRAPHY

The references used in the writing of *The People's Game* included the following:

Books

John Arlott, *The Ashes 1972*, London: Pelham Books, 1972
Eric Beecher, *The Cricket Revolution*, Melbourne: Newspress, 1978
Richie Benaud, *Benaud On Reflection*, Sydney: Collins, 1984
Richie Benaud (editor), *Lights, Camera, Action!: An illustrated history of the World Series*,
    Melbourne: Hamlyn Australia, 1990
Henry Blofeld, *The Packer Affair*, London: Collins, 1978
Allan Border, *Beyond Ten Thousand: My Life Story*, Nedlands WA: Swan Publishing, 1993
Mike Brearley and Dudley Doust, *The Ashes Retained*, London: Hodder & Stoughton, 1979
Dick Brittenden and Don Cameron, *Test Series '82: The Australian Cricket tour of New Zealand*,
    Wellington: AH & AW Reed Ltd, 1982
Andrew Caro, *With A Straight Bat*, Hong Kong: The Sales Machine, 1979
Richard Cashman, *Ave a Go Yer Mug: Australian Cricket Crowds from Larrikin to Ocker*,
    Sydney: Collins, 1984
Greg Chappell and David Frith, *the Ashes '77*, Brighton, UK: Angus & Robertson, 1977
Ian Chappell, *Tigers Among The Lions*, Coromandel Valley, SA: Lynton Publications, 1972
Ian Chappell, *Chappelli*, Melbourne: Hutchinson, 1976
Mike Coward, *Cricket Beyond the Bazaar: Australia on the Indian subcontinent*,
    North Sydney: Allen & Unwin, 1990
Patrick Eagar and Alan Ross, *Tour of Tours: Border's victorious Australians of 1989*,
    London: Hodder and Stoughton, 1989
Christopher Forsyth, *The Great Cricket Hijack*, Camberwell, Victoria: Widescope Publishers, 1978
Bill Frindall and Victor H Isaacs, *The Wisden Book of One-Day International Cricket 1971-1985*,
    London: John Wisden & Co, 1985
Gideon Haigh, *The Cricket War: The inside story of Kerry Packer's World Series Cricket*,
    East Melbourne: The Text Publishing Company, 1993
Derek Hodgson (editor), *Cricket World Cup '83*, London: Unwin Paperbacks, 1983
Martin Johnson and Henry Blofeld, *World Cup Cricket '87*, London: The Kingswood Press, 1987
Dean Jones, *One-Day Magic*, Newlands WA: Swan Publishing, 1992
Geoff Lawson, *Henry: The Geoff Lawson Story*, Sydney: Ironbark Press, 1993
Alan Lee, *A Pitch In Both Camps: England and World Series Cricket in Australia 1978-79*,
    London: Stanley Paul, 1979
Tony Lewis, *A Summer of Cricket*, London: Pelham Books, 1976
Dennis Lillee, *Over And Out*, Sydney: Metheun Australia, 1984
Craig McDermott, *Strike Bowler*, Sydney: ABC Books, 1992
Peter McFarline, *A Game Divided*, Melbourne: Marlin Books, 1978
Peter McFarline, *A Testing Time*, Melbourne: Hutchinson, 1979
Adrian McGregor, *Greg Chappell*, Sydney: Williams Collins, 1985
Rod Marsh, *The Gloves of Irony*, Sydney: Lansdowne, 1982
Rod Marsh, *The Inside Edge*, Sydney: Lansdowne, 1983
Rod Marsh, *Gloves, Sweat and Tears*, Ringwood, Victoria: Penguin, 1984
Christopher Martin-Jenkins, *Cricket Contest 1979-80: The Post-Packer Tests*, London: Queen Anne
    Press, 1980
Christopher Martin-Jenkins, *Twenty Years On: Cricket's Years of Change 1963 to 1983*, London:
    Collins Willow, 1984
Peter Roebuck, *Ashes to Ashes*, London: The Kingswood Press, 1987
NKP Salve, *The Story of the Reliance Cup*, New Delhi: Vikas Publishing House, 1987
Bob Simpson, *Simmo*, Sydney: Hutchinson, 1979
EW Swanton (General editor), *Barclays World of Cricket*, London: Collins, 1980
Andrew Thomas and Norman Harris, *Great Moments in Cricket*, London: Queen Anne Press, 1976
Steve Waugh, *Steve Waugh's Ashes Diary*, Sydney: Ironbark, 1993
RS Whitington, *Captains Outrageous: Cricket in the Seventies*, Richmond, Victoria:
    Hutchinson, 1972
Mike Whitney, *Quick Whit: The Mike Whitney Story*, Sydney: Ironbark, 1994
Peter Wynne-Thomas and Peter Arnold, *Cricket in Conflict: The story of major crises that have
    rocked the game*, London: Newnes Books, 1984

Magazines, Almanacs and Yearbooks

ABC Australian Cricket Almanac 1990 to 1993
Australian Cricket
Australian Cricket Annual 1979
Australian Cricket Yearbook 1970 to 1978
Australian Women's Weekly
Cricketer (Australia)
Cricketer (Australia) World Cup Special 1975
Cricketer (Australia) Yearbooks 1974 to 1982
Inside Edge
The Bulletin
The Cricketer (UK)
The Cricketer (UK) International Quarterly Facts and Figures 1978 to 1994
Wide World of Sports Cricket Yearbook 1985-1993
Wisden Cricket Monthly
Wisden Cricketers' Almanac 1972 to 1994
World of Cricket
World Series Cricket Magazine 1978-79

Publications of the Associations of Cricket Statisticians

One-Day International Cricket Records (1990)
International Cricket Yearbook 1988 to 1994
The Cricket Statistician (quarterly journal)

Newspapers

Daily Mirror (Sydney)
Daily Telegraph (Sydney)
Daily Telegraph-Mirror (Sydney)
National Times (Sydney)
The Advertiser (Adelaide)
The Age (Melbourne)
The Australian (Sydney)
The Courier-Mail (Brisbane)
The Herald (Melbourne)
The Independent (London)
The Sun (Sydney)
The Sun-Herald (Sydney)
The Sunday Times (London)
The Sydney Morning Herald
The Times (London)